THE TAO OF THE SPECIES

THE
TAO
OF THE
SPECIES

Investigations into the Psycho-History of the White Man and the Recovery of Eutopia

A Contribution to Critical Feminist and Race Theory

Jan Diepersloot

QiWorks
Walnut Creek, CA

The Tao of the Species: Investigations into the Psycho-History of the White Man and the Recovery of Eutopia
Copyright © 2023 by Jan Diepersloot

Published by QiWorks
P O Box 369
Walnut Creek, CA 94597
www.taoofthespecies.com

Library of Congress Control Number: 2023907011

Printed in the United States of America

Book design: Clarity Designworks

ISBN 978-0-9649976-5-3 (paperback)
ISBN 978-0-9649976-6-0 (ebook)

Contents

Introduction

University of California, San Diego Campus in La Jolla. One day in the Spring of 1968. Among the small group of progressive anti-war political activists on campus, the word spread fast: a meeting to discuss stunning new developments was going to be held that night at the professor's house. The professor was Dr. Herbert Marcuse, the famous left-wing philosopher and author, synthesizer of Marx and Freud, who was just finishing up his second year of teaching in the Philosophy Department at UCSD. The political activists were mostly his own graduate students—many of whom, like Angela Davis, had come from all over the U.S. to study with him—as well as a scattering of graduate students from other departments. The latter included yours truly who was a graduate student and Ph.D. candidate in the Linguistics Department.

The "stunning new developments" referred to the harassment and death threats Dr. Marcuse had received the days before. On July 12, 1968, Marcuse learned that a woman had called the telephone company, identified herself as Mrs. Marcuse, and had ordered his service shut off. On the same day, Marcuse had also received a scrawled letter. "Marcuse, You are a very dirty Communist dog. We give you seventy-two hours to live [sic] United States. Seventy-two hours more, Marcuse, and we kill you." The letter was signed "Ku Klux Klan."[1] These incidents were a culmination of sorts to a campaign of harassment and intimidation that the San Diego right-wing establishment had been waging against Marcuse. For example, such dignitaries as retired Marine Corps Admiral Charles Krulak, in a guest editorial in the *San Diego Union*, demanded the university regents fire Dr. Marcuse immediately.[2]

The purpose of the meeting was to determine, first, how seriously to take these right-wing provocations and threats and, second, how to respond to them. Naturally, among those present, there was much venting and heated discussion. Dr. Marcuse weighed in and told the group not to worry about him, since the semester was almost over and he was about to leave for the East Coast and Europe in a few weeks anyway. After much heated discussion, conclusions were reached and decisions were made. In the short-term, we stationed armed guards around Marcuse's home and patrolled the neighborhood with our cars. In the long term, we decided it was imperative to educate the public. And it seemed to us that the most effective way to counter the insidious right-wing campaign of disinformation and threatened violence would be to start publishing our own alternative radical newspaper to counter the Copley Press's *San Diego Union.*

A Fateful Choice

This last decision turned out to be a pivotal inflection point in my personal life, altering its course irrevocably. As the summer followed after the incident, most of the professor's active graduate students finished their courses of study with him and moved away from San Diego to their new teaching gigs at universities all across the country. This development left me to face a peculiar quandary and made a fork appear in the road I was traveling. Taking the secure path, I would write and finish my Ph.D. thesis, most likely leading to a job as an assistant professor of Linguistics at some college. Taking the uncertain path meant quitting graduate school and linguistics altogether and organizing the left-wing alternative newspaper to counter the monopoly of the right-wing Copley Press in San Diego. I followed my gut and heart rather than my brain and opted to engage the enemy. But why, you ask? Marcuse's situation had touched me to the core; his exposure to danger to life and limb at the hands of right-wing extremists resonated deeply within me. The event reawakened dormant childhood memories of my family's role in the Dutch Resistance during World War II to the violence the German

Nazis inflicted on the Dutch people in general and the persecution of the Jewish people in particular. And with the awakened memories rose the passionate fighting spirit of righteous indignation. I was gripped by the overpowering instinct of the organism readying itself for combat, saying, "No, this cannot be allowed to happen, not on my watch."

I was a war baby, born in occupied Holland in 1941 during World War II. Since I was so young, my own concrete memories of the war are few. I do remember the frightening spectacle of the German Army marching down our street. I remember when they came and arrested our neighbor and hauled him away, never to be heard from again. I remember the fright when an errant V1 rocket malfunctioned and fell in our backyard. Fortunately, it did not explode and obliterate us, but it sure made a big hole! Everybody in the crowd that gathered agreed on that: it was a really big hole. So both during and immediately after the war, anti-fascism was as much a staple of my diet as was my mother's milk, and the evils and violence of the Nazis and their collaborators were imprinted constantly on the structures of my perception and thought. During the war, my father was an active partisan in the underground, and like so many others, our house was a temporary haven for Jews in transit from the hell they were fleeing to a new destination and a new life. And after the war, when he recounted his dangerous wartime exploits, the very close calls he survived, the unbearable cruelties he witnessed, the admiration I had for him as a young boy grew boundlessly. He was my freedom fighter hero, and as a boy, I decided that when I grew up, I would be a freedom fighter against fascism too. Considering the context of my childhood, my decision to drop out of graduate school to establish a progressive left-wing publication to counter extreme right-wing ideology and terrorism was, in effect, continuing in the family tradition started by my father, the anti-fascist freedom fighter. In fact, the violence of fascism I experienced as a child became the basis of a life-long concern with its dangers, even well into my ripe old age when I felt compelled to write this book.

San Diego Free Press, Street Journal, People's Commune

With the stroke of a signature, I became the publisher of the *San Diego Free Press*. I also embarked on an organizing campaign, talking to all my fellow radicals in the student movement, to get folks with the necessary skills and talents to sign up and pledge to contribute. We needed help on all levels—writing, editing, designing, graphics, composing, advertising expertise, distributor ideas, etc. The response was encouraging. A dedicated cadre was formed, and office space was obtained. We started modestly, working out of an office donated to the cause by our favorite theater group, Theatre 5, in Pacific Beach. In October 1969, we celebrated our first issue seeing the light of day. We immediately reached out to the Black and Latino communities, and they began to collaborate in the *San Diego Free Press* with news relevant to their own communities. But from day one, it was a struggle to make ends meet. Revenue from ads and individual sales was not sufficient to cover costs, and we had to depend on the largesse of supporters in the community to keep going.

In 1969, we saw the arrival of much needed reinforcements. Some of Marcuse's core graduate students who had left San Diego to teach elsewhere returned to join the struggle. So did some of the undergraduate comrades who had just graduated or had just dropped out. Altogether, it was a memorable influx of intellectual power and physical capabilities. Community angels stepped up to the plate, allowing us to acquire two adjacent houses downtown.

With the numbers and finances in place, we started the People's Commune with about 30-some people who decided to give it a go with the collective sharing of resources and planning and decision-making. We were quite ambitious, if nothing else. We took on such projects as organizing in the military with the creation of the Movement for a Democratic Military, a dry goods store run and operated by the commune's women, an anti-police outreach in the beach communities featuring free meals, and even an outpost in the backcountry that we intended to develop into a small farm. But our main aim and claim to fame was what we did with the newspaper. With the influx of so much man- and womanpower, many of them seasoned researchers, we began to engage in some serious sleuthing. To mark this new chapter in our growth, we decided to change the paper's name from the *San Diego Free Press* to *San Diego Street Journal*. Soon the *Street Journal's* expanded investigative reporting scoops started rattling City Hall and the powers that be. A series of continuing exposés of local establishment corruption involving police, the mayor, the city council, as well as the city's financial movers and shakers, contributed to the arrest and convictions of many officials and bigwigs.

The Empire Strikes Back

In 1971, the empire struck back decisively and on several fronts, including unceasing police harassment and violent right-wing terrorism. At one point, we tallied, over a six-month period, more than 50 arrests between our commune members and vendors of the *Street Journal*. Eventually, we just stopped counting. Most of arrests were on the flimsiest of charges like blocking the sidewalk while selling our newspaper. Yours truly was arrested many times, including once on a charge of "selling alcohol without a license" at the commune's residence when we were hosting a fundraising party for the San Diego liberal community. Annoying to be sure, but there was a silver lining. A number of San Diego's liberal elite, including many lawyers and judges, though they were sympathetic with our aims, often felt we were exaggerating our complaints about police brutality. Being hauled off to jail right in front of their very eyes was very educational for them and, in the short run, certainly facilitated our fundraising efforts.

As annoying and expensive as all these trumped up arrests and official harassments were, at least we did not perceive them as life-threatening. The same could not be said for the violent terrorist acts that were directed at us from the extreme right-wing fringe. First, we experienced the systematic destruction and theft of our vending machines. This was a major economic blow because much of the *Street Journal's* operating expenses were paid for by the income from the vending machines. Next, the journal's downtown offices were burgled, and the vandals destroyed our Linotype machine and other equipment by pouring paint all over them.

Our commune residences were also harassed and intimidated by constant and suspicious stakeouts, not just by the cops but also repeatedly by nonofficial civilian vehicles, which would speed away when we would try to follow them. It got so bad, we again had to resort to posting armed guards on our balconies at night. We don't know how many attacks we averted or deferred that way, but despite our efforts at prevention, one such attack succeeded. One night, there was a drive-by firebombing of one of our cars parked in front of the commune. The car caught on fire and was totaled as a result. In another separate incident, there was a drive-by shooting at one of the residences also associated with the *Street Journal,* wounding one of the staffers in the elbow. Years later, research brought to light that the culprits had been the Secret Army Organization, an offshoot of the Minutemen and John Birch Society.

And if all this external pressure was not enough to drive us communards to the verge of a nervous breakdown, the commune's internal divisions caused by the women's movement were quite sufficient to finish the job. After months of rancorous debate, many of the women decided they could not live with the men anymore, or at least that they preferred the exclusive company of women, and started a women's commune in a third house a few blocks away. That, really, was the beginning of the end of the People's Commune. Within the span of a year, most of the original members of the People's Commune and the *Street Journal* packed their bags and scattered to the wind. Some going to the East Coast, some going to the Midwest, the majority, though, headed north. Some to the San Francisco Bay Area, including Berkeley, yet others even further north to Eugene and Portland in Oregon and Seattle in Washington. Yours truly, having many ties in the Bay Area, wound up joining collectives, first in Guerneville for two years, in 1971 and 1972, then in Berkeley for four years, from 1972 to 1976.

The early '70s were, for me, the period of depressive low that inevitably follows a manic high, a time of processing the incredible events of the past few years, a time of introspection and reflection. It was a time of physical decline, emotional doubt, and loss of direction.

As a result of continuously operating beyond my limits for the past half dozen stressful years, I was experiencing a kind of battle fatigue. I lost my appetite for uncovering corruption for the sake of uncovering corruption and became more and more interested in understanding the psychology of power and corruption, the big Why of it all. Conveniently, Richard Nixon, the president of the United States, had just revealed himself a master of the art of corruption and had, for all the world to see, been exposed for the crook that he was in the Watergate scandal. I, then, did an in-depth psychological study of Nixon, concentrating on his character formation in childhood and his rise in right-wing politics in the service of big money, whatever the nature of the business, from bankers to mobsters and back.

But I was neither well nor happy. As a result of no exercise, compulsive cigarette smoking, and continual stress, my physical health was deteriorating, and I started suffering from frequent debilitating migraines. Emotionally, also, I was experiencing a quagmire of self-doubt and insecurity. The relationship between the genders becoming increasingly contentious and dysfunctional, I despaired at the likelihood of ever finding a compatible mate.

Taiji Reset

Then, in 1975, I experienced a vision that once again would lead to a new chapter in my life. A friend invited me to come with him to a demonstration and lecture on Taijiquan, the ancient Chinese health and martial art that was becoming popular in the Bay Area. As the teacher performed his slow-motion dance, the ineffable quality of his movements engendered a transcendent experience in me. With utmost clarity, I knew this was my destiny, to learn and master, and teach this art. In a vision, I saw my future, older self teaching my students in the park, just as it has come to pass to be the daily reality of my life. I immediately signed up and started the study of Taijiquan. The physical benefits I was experiencing soon aroused my intellectual curiosity. I began reading the Taoist classics and soon discovered the beauty and elegance of the Taoist yin-yang philosophy of balance as a basis for understanding reality.

And that's where I left it for the next 40 years. As my life and career in these ancient Chinese health and martial arts flourished and progressed, I was content living my life, happily sharing my art and contributing my little bit to the health and happiness of humanity. I was fortunate to be able to study with some of the great ones in the field to guide me toward achieving mastery. I became successful locally teaching the art in my hometown of Walnut Creek, California. I also wrote three books on the subject, the Warriors of Stillness trilogy, that were received well by the global martial arts community and led to my traveling to many countries, giving lectures and workshops.

And my radical politics and concerns for social justice, you ask? What has become of them? Did I just chuck all that to the wayside these decades while blithely pursuing my own bliss? Well, not really. What I left behind is only the brash impulsiveness of my youthful actions, which ultimately proved self-destructive. Philosophically and intellectually, my fundamental outlook and values have not changed since they were forged in the social upheaval of the 1960s. And throughout all those years, I continued to read and research the many fundamental questions about the nature and origin of the authoritarian impulse and its cancerous conquest of our world. That ultimately led to the book you are now reading, *The Tao of the Species*.

Two things happened that prompted me to get real about writing this book: Donald Trump was elected president, and the Covid pandemic struck. When Trump was elected, I watched in such great disbelief and distress. All I could do was moan with countless others who had experienced Watergate, "Oh no, not again!" Watching him "govern" the country as a mob-style "family business," it soon became obvious that Trump was Nixon on steroids. With the scope of Trump's corruption dwarfing Nixon's, it became painfully clear that he was far more dangerous to the future of this country's democratic institutions than Nixon ever had been. I realized then that what I could to do to contribute to Trump's demise and to further the progress of civilization would be to synthesize all the various strands of my diverse research into a coherent theory on the origins and future of authoritarianism, misogyny, and racism. But while Trump was the immediate precipitating cause of my decision to do something and act, ironically, it was the Covid pandemic that gave me the time and isolation to do the research and writing. By committing to the project, I followed the infallible advice of a poet I once read but do not now recall who noted that anyone aspiring be a successful writer must "apply the seat of the pants to the seat of the chair" until the project is finished.[3] Indeed, proof of the infallibility of the poet's advice is the very book you are now reading.

The Tao of the Species

Over the past century, scientific discoveries have revealed there is a female neural-hormonal axis and a male one at work in human biology and sociology. The existence of these two axes is symbolized in Taoism by the yin and yang energies. Over many centuries, our societies have evolved to reach a state of imbalance between these two poles, with overemphasis of the male-centric values of warfare, hierarchy, and self-interest. This imbalance is currently causing the descent of the human race into a state of global dystopia, meaning, simply, a really "bad place." This book argues that we are at a revolutionary inflection point in which humanity has the opportunity to institutionalize a paradigm change. In this revolution, the female-centric values of harmony, peace, and egalitarianism can be made the foundation of a new global civilization called "Eutopia," meaning simply, a really "good place."

In the title of this book, I use the phrase "White Man" both in a narrow sense and in a broad sense. In the narrow sense, I use it to describe the authoritarian male-centric white race of Western European Anglo-Saxon ancestry that has become the dominant culture in the world today, whose misogyny and racism in the past 500 years have shaped the world into what it is today. However, let me hasten to add that in my use of the term "White Man," I certainly don't mean to imply or convey that the White Man has a monopoly on misogyny and racism. These twinned authoritarian traits are fundamentally color blind and are characteristic of all male-centric cultures, no matter what their color, be it white, Black, yellow, brown, or purple. I also use the term "Eutopia" in the title, and we've already examined the meaning of that choice of words as a Greek term basically meaning "a good place to live." Suffice it to add that "Eutopia," in this book, also refers to the future in as much as an egalitarian female-centric society most properly describes the next stage of evolutionary development of the human species.

This book is a story, a story of our species and our civilization. In order to fully grasp it, savor it, and learn the necessary lessons from it, the story must be read sequentially, from beginning to end. There are five parts to the story, each covering one of its essential chapters and each with its various subsections filling in the details.

Evolution and the Theory of Balance

Part one describes the convergence of modern sciences, including physics and biology, neurology and endocrinology, archeology and anthropology, with the ancient Taoist yin-yang theory of balance. The conclusions of the scientists and the Taoists support the common-sense knowledge of ordinary people that in the biological drama of life, women are the primary actors and men play the supporting roles.

In mammals particularly, the role of the yin, or female function, is primary and maximal because she is the vessel receiving the sperm, gestating the fetus, birthing it, and nurturing the offspring into independence. It is also obvious and common knowledge that these female functions are best accomplished under external conditions of maximum harmony and minimal threat of interference with the process. Through the activation of the various female hormones like estrogen, progesterone, estradiol, and others acting in concert with the hormone oxytocin, female physiology creates the internal conditions of harmony necessary for the long reproductive process to occur and succeed.

Commonsense observation and science also concur that in mammals, the role of the yang, or male function, is secondary and minimal. His main contribution to the process—providing his half of the DNA by means of his sperm—is usually brief. Secondarily, the male may provide a layer of physical protection for the mother and offspring when life or limb are threatened. The fact that the male has had to compete fiercely with his fellow males in order to win mating opportunities, plus the male's potential role as protector, defines the realm of typical male mammalian behavior as the realm of crisis and violence.

One of the main tenets of Taoism as a theory of balance is its theory of interpenetration. It is represented in the symbol by the black dot in the white part, and the white dot in the black part. Modern psychology and neurology have confirmed that the infinite complexities of human personality derive from the fact that in the human dyad, each sex contains its opposite. We are all both male and female. Neurology has established beyond the shadow of a doubt that all males also have female hormones, and all females also have male hormones. In the realm of psychology, Jung described this interpenetration of male and female, of the yin in the yang and the yang in the yin, as the female's animus and the male's anima. We will conclude this part by looking into the manifestation of yin-yang polarities in the social structures of our primate ancestors, the bonobo and chimpanzee apes, as well as the early human hunter-gatherer cultures.

The Great Polarity Reversal in Antiquity

Once the hunting-gathering cultures stopped moving and settled down to become farmers and herders, conditions allowed the development of two things. Number one was the gradual evolution of male-centrism displacing female-centrism in social and economic organization. And number two was the capture and subjugation of individuals from what were considered more primitive tribes as slaves for labor. In other words, the advent of agricultural civilization was the origin of both misogyny and racism as the twin pillars of the male-centric social paradigm.

This slow and gradual process of the displacement of female-centrism by male-centrism that occurred in the economic and social sphere was then completed in the religious and political spheres by a sudden and total reversal of female-to-male centrism. This displacement of female-centrism by male-centrism happened during the climatic and geological catastrophes that wreaked havoc in the Mediterranean basin in the second millennium BCE. In Greece and elsewhere, female-centric culture and polytheism was replaced by male centric polytheism, while in Egypt and among the Hebrews, female-centric polytheism was replaced by male centric monotheism.

After the demise of the Greek civilization, in the period from around 300 BCE to 300 CE, the rise and fall of the Roman Empire took place. The Roman Empire was the great consolidation of the yang male-centric paradigm's power over the ancient female-centric paradigm that extended across the whole of the Mediterranean archipelago and far beyond into Asia and Europe. Christianity then arose as the expression of revolt by the tradition of the ancient female-centric paradigm against the new universal supremacy of this male-centric paradigm. Original Christianity was Gnostic Christianity, which arose in opposition to the authority structures of the empire and corrupt local Hebrew religious practices. In its beliefs and practices, the original Gnostic Christians were radically female-centric, anti-authoritarian, and egalitarian.

But as Christianity grew rapidly in numbers, it suffered an existential crisis when it became the target of vilification and persecution by the pagan Roman Republic and Empire. Then, in the vacuum of confused leadership, Gnostic egalitarianism was thrown out the window by the very force it was rebelling against: male-centric authority. Authoritarian hierarchy replaced democratic norms, and in the new orthodoxy, women were excluded from the priesthood and all positions of power and made subservient to the male in all ways. So successful was the Church in its effort that as the Roman Empire declined, the Roman Catholic Church gained power until, under Constantine, Christianity itself was made the state religion of the now "Holy" Roman Empire.

The Global Ascent of the White Man

After the disintegration of the Roman Empire, the Catholic Church was in control in Western Europe. The period from about 500 to

1500 CE saw the birth of Western White Man in medieval Europe. Encouraged and organized by the Church, the White Man's expansionary impulses were directed toward the east. The Crusades. Planned and carried out jointly by the clergy and the aristocrats, the Crusades proved a very effective way to mobilize the medieval masses for the enrichment of both church and state through plunder and occupation of the heathen "lands of the infidel," in the name of the liberation of the "holy land." The Crusades were also the cradle of the White Man's racist persecution of the Semitic race, both Jews and Arabs.

After Luther, Calvin, and the Reformation came a period when the White Man turned his violence against himself, as expressed both in religious civil wars and wars between nations caused by the Catholic-Protestant rift. Simultaneously, it must be noted, both Catholic and Protestant White Men doubled their misogynist efforts and intensified the persecution of women, going after the pagan "witches" and degrading their general position in society.

White Man's aggressive expansionary economic and religious campaigns extended to the New World. In less than half a millennium after he discovered that the world was round, the White Man had conquered it. America and, to a lesser extent, Australia, New Zealand, and South Africa had special appeal for the British colonial interests. Not only were these lands sources of valuable local resources that could be brought home as products for sale and consumption, but they also became destinations for Europe's oppressed denizens. Millions of Europeans persecuted for religious and/or political reasons decided to leave their birth countries altogether and go to America and other promised lands to start life afresh and create new societies where their people would be free of political and religious oppression.

America was a case of the White Man's offspring outperforming his colonial parent. By (1) stealing the lands and territories from indigenous peoples and (2) using slave labor forcibly imported from Africa, the White Man created a wholly new nation that took a mere two centuries to expand exponentially into one of the most powerful civilizations ever to exist on this earth. Wave after wave, they came. Millions of Europeans fleeing their home countries on account of religious and political discrimination, famine, epidemics, and wars. Looking at a future that seemed to hold nothing but persecution, starvation, and death for their own and their children's generations, they decided to make their way to the new continent, start over, and not perpetuate the mistakes and cruelties of their home countries.

Right from the start in the creation of these United States, the White Man became seriously imbalanced in his mental-emotional makeup. He was torn between his dreams and aspirations on the one hand, and the chains of the past on the other. Part of him wanted to extend these rights universally to all races and genders. And a part of him also, most emphatically, did not want to extend these rights to any other races and genders. This schizoid split in the White Man personality came to be reflected in the split of the body politic. From day one, the authoritarian, racist, and misogynistic movement driven by the White Man's quest for power clashed sharply with the egalitarian, democratic progressives spearheaded by the feminists and people of color. In short, this schizoid split caused and defined the ongoing conflict between the dystopians and Eutopians.

The White Man's Global Descent into Dystopia

The trajectory of the dystopian history in the 20th century is characterized by (1) the sinking of the people as a whole into dystopian conditions of physical, mental, and emotional health, and (2) by the descent of educational, political, and economic institutions into dystopia.

The American people as a whole are not healthy or happy. The people, in their pursuit of happiness, are increasingly finding much unhappiness in America today. This has led to a rude awakening of the public's awareness to the fact that their flesh and spirit are being squeezed dry in every possible way. Their labor, their money, their attention, everything is always being taken from them without their consent and without fair compensation. Mass unhappiness has its yin and yang flavors. On the yin side of the coin, the unhappiness is internalized and expressed in depression, addiction, and suicide. On the yang side of the coin, the unhappiness is externalized as crime, violence, and political terrorism. The figures for each are truly stunning and should give everyone pause to think and reconsider. The politics of grievance represented by Trump and other extreme right-wingers consciously and skillfully fuels the dystopian exploitation of people's unhappiness. Through propaganda and lies, they blame people of different colors for the white people's problems, thereby splitting the people as a whole politically along racial lines into competing factions, inevitably leading to an increase of violence between them. Moreover, the right-wing politics of the Big Lie also serve to divert the attention of its white base from the real global problems of climate catastrophe, economic collapse, and political corruption.

A half century ago, the 1972 MIT study "The Limits to Growth"[4] predicted that society will collapse sometime in the 21st century. Its author, Gaya Herrington, recently reanalyzed data from ten key variables, namely population, fertility rates, mortality rates, industrial output, food production, services, nonrenewable resources, persistent pollution, human welfare, and our ecological footprint.[5] Ms. Herrington's research, unfortunately but indisputably, shows that our species is right on schedule and that the current business-as-usual trajectory of global civilization is heading toward terminal societal collapse by around 2040. Each of the variables Ms. Herrington explores must be understood as a dynamic that is accelerating civilization's crisis time toward its dystopian resolution of implosion or explosion. All of these variables are systems that continuously increase global stress levels. A failure in any one of these systems is likely to cause failure in one or more of the other systems, and each system failure could act as the triggering event that could cause the collapse of global civilization. As these systems are all interacting and unfolding simultaneously, they are increasing the temperature inside our global pressure cooker. The White Man is still at the peak of his power, but he has not yet realized that after he reaches the top of the mountain, there is nowhere to go but down. The descent and comedown can be peaceful, or it can be catastrophic. If the dystopian bozos like Trump,

DeSantis, et al., are in control when the process unfolds, the results will truly be catastrophic. These dystopians will be so preoccupied with continuing their personal grifts that they will be unable to grasp the true nature of the crisis. They will be incapable of resolving the crisis successfully and, thereby, are condemned to exacerbate it. But if rational actors like Biden and the progressive democratic coalition are at the helm of government, we will have a chance to minimize the damage, to control and guide the process into the Eutopian transformation of society.

The Global Paradigm Shift to Eutopia

The anti-war and anti-violence, music- and peace-loving counter-culture of the 1960s was the 20th century reassertion of the ancient Eutopian female-centric paradigm's values of harmony and cooperation. At its core, the strength of the counterculture was the joining together of the struggles of racial minorities for justice and equality with the newly reawakened women's liberation movement to challenge the racism and misogyny of the White Man's authoritarian and dystopian paradigm. More than a half century later, the 1960s counterculture seems like but a preview of the momentous struggle between the dystopians and the Eutopians for the soul of the nation that is unfolding in the 21st century. At the core of the Eutopian coalition are still the racial minorities and women demanding an end to racism and misogyny in our society. The replacement of the male-centric paradigm with the female-centric paradigm will be accompanied by paradigm changes in many sectors of society. These changes will entail redefining the relationship of the individual to society, the economics of class structure and function, the practice of political democracy.

In this final section, we will explore how these paradigm changes can be tackled to reorient our society toward Eutopianism. In this part, we will propose the general adoption of a New Social Contract. We will also make the case for sortition democracy as a way to circumvent the corruptibility of elected government.

In conclusion, dear reader, what I hope to do in this book is to stimulate your imagination to entertain new answers to the old questions about human values and social organization: How did things come to be so bad for our species, and how can we make things better in the future?

Endnotes

1   Judith Moore, "Marxist Professor Herbert Marcuse's years as UCSD," San Diego Reader (September 11, 1986): https://www.sandiegoreader.com/news/1986/sep/11/angel-apocalypse/.

2   Ibid.

3   Many authors have been accredited for this quote, but based on Quote Investigator, Mary Heaton Vorse was the first: https://quoteinvestigator.com/2015/09/24/chair/

4   Donella H. Meadows, et al., The Limits to Growth: A Report for the Club of Rome's Project on the Predicament of Mankind, (New York: Universe Books, 1972).

5   Nafeez Ahmed, "MIT Predicted in 1972 That Society Will Collapse This Century. New Research Shows We're on Schedule," Vice, (July 14, 2021): https://www.vice.com/en/article/z3xw3x/new-research-vindicates-1972-mit-prediction-that-society-will-collapse-soon.

Part 1

Evolution and the Theory of Balance

Chapter 1
....

Evolution from Fish to Primates (360-300 Million Years Ago)

Of Fish and Mammals

We humans don't usually appreciate how much, on very basic levels, we have in common with fish. We may perhaps know that fish, like humans, have spinal cords, which biologically, defines us both as members of the chordate phylum. But we are not generally aware of the fact that our basic neuronal and hormonal processes are already present and functioning on much lower evolutionary levels where little zebra fish dwell. One inch small, the zebra fish typically lives in shallow, clear water of canals, ditches, ponds, lakes, and rice paddies in South Asia. Science teaches us that to understand the complex, it often pays to understand the small things first. For that reason, we begin our inquiry into human beings with some preliminary observations about the lowly zebra fish.

The zebra fish has at least two profound lessons for us as a species. The first pertains to the findings regarding the nature of the hormone oxytocin as the hormonal basis of social behavior, both in fish and in humans. And the second pertains to its remarkable regenerative capability. The zebra fish, by means of the hormone oxytocin, is able to regenerate its heart muscle upon catastrophic injury. In zebra fish, as in human beings, it is the hormone oxytocin that is responsible for readying the brain to respond to social situations.[1] And in both, moreover, this process has to occur in a certain manner during a critical time window of brain development in which the social traits are established.[2]

Dr. Ana Rita Nunes and her colleague Michael Gliksberg began by creating a system for exploring the effects of oxytocin on the developing brains of zebra fish larvae. They developed a method by which they could cause the oxytocin-producing neurons in zebra fish larvae to malfunction and die at any given point in their development. This ability allowed them to compare normal development by oxytocin-producing neurons and abnormal development caused by lack of oxytocin-producing neurons in various stages.

In normal fish larval development (when the oxytocin-producing cells were not interfered with), the scientists found that at about four weeks of age, the centimeter-long juvenile fish that have just emerged from the larval stage begin to socialize, exhibiting a strong tendency to swim as a group in a shoal. The shoaling behavior of zebra fish requires sophisticated processing of visual and social cues. In particular, the zebra fish must be able to identify other fish as belonging to their own, "friendly"—as opposed to different, or worse yet, predatory—species.

In abnormal zebra fish larval development, where the oxytocin-developing neurons had been disabled, the scientists found that the larvae whose brains lacked oxytocin in the first two weeks of life grew into adult fish with an impaired capacity for social interaction, namely swimming in a shoal. The researchers further discovered the mechanisms by which oxytocin primes the growing brain for socializing. They showed that oxytocin-producing neurons were critical to the birth of another type of neuron, one that releases the neurotransmitter dopamine, which regulates feelings of reward and motivation.

As a result, zebra fish whose brains had not been exposed to oxytocin during the first two weeks of life had reduced numbers of dopamine-making neurons as well as a reduced number of connections to these neurons in several distinct brain areas. One of these areas is a system of neuronal connections known as the social decision-making network—a group of brain areas that work together to process social information. In fish whose brains had developed without oxytocin, the synchronization patterns of neuronal activities among these centers were completely different from those of regular fish.

The implications of all these findings for humans are quite profound. For if the mature adult social behavior of the zebra fish is compromised and or prevented from developing through trauma and malfunction in infancy, it is reasonable to postulate the same might be true for humans. Humans, like zebra fish, have an incentive to seek company because the group provides them with advantages in searching for food, overcoming weather events, avoiding predators, and finding mates. As such, the mechanisms revealed in the study of zebra fish provide a new basis for research into the genetic programs governing social behavior in humans.

In particular, to understand and explain the asocial or antisocial authoritarian behaviors of some of society's members, we must look for oxytocin-mediated changes in the developing brain during the critical early periods, when social abilities are being established. Doing so will reveal that the inability to experience empathy and follow social rules other than one's own, which is the essence of the pathologies of narcissism, misogyny, racism, class structure, and authoritarian power relationships of all kinds, originate in the early childhood developmental stages when the individual failed to develop the hormonal/neuronal oxytocin-dopamine pathways necessary for effective cooperative social interaction.

Finally, besides the social importance of oxytocin revealed by the study of the zebra fish, the zebra fish has also provided us with evidence of oxytocin's remarkable healing properties. Experts at Michigan State University recently conducted a study on zebra fish that concluded that oxytocin has the ability to repair injured heart cells and regrow damaged heart tissue.[3] It is known that when the heart is damaged (during a heart attack, for example), the cardiomyocytes, which are the cells which allow the heart to contract, die off in vast quantities, and they are incapable of regenerating themselves. The Michigan researchers found that when the zebra fish heart is injured, there is a twentyfold increase in oxytocin that stimulates the stem cells in the epicardium, the heart's outer layer, to migrate to the myocardium, its middle layer, and turn into cardiomyocytes. In this way the zebra fish heals itself by essentially growing a new heart. And while the applicability of these findings to the human situation is still being researched, testing human cells in the lab has already indicated that the future looks promising.

The Primacy of the Female Function

The principal characteristic of life, as has often been pointed out, is that it reproduces. That is, it makes more of itself by one of two methods: asexual or sexual reproduction. Asexual reproduction is the oldest method, utilizing cell mitosis, or the division of a cell into two identical cells to create and "give birth" to more of itself. Time allowed the evolution of sexual dimorphism and reproduction as a more efficient way to reproduce. This method of sexual reproduction works by combining two different sets of DNA (female and male) to form a third, distinctly different individual.

The main benefit of sexual reproduction was that it allowed life to adapt to changing environments faster by providing the mechanism by which entirely new species could evolve. In the sexual method of reproduction, the female sex obviously is the continuation of the original asexual process of growing and "birthing" of the new individual. The main evolutionary function of the male sex is primarily to contribute a second set of DNA to combine with the set of maternal DNA to produce a new individual that combines the various traits of its parents.

Since life's primary driving force is reproduction, it is not surprising that when, for whatever reason, sexual reproduction is not possible, life will try and revert to the more ancient method of asexual or parthenogenetic reproduction. In such "virgin births," instead of being conceived through sex and receiving a set of genes from a mother and father, the offspring is produced solely from cells that came from the mother. This is not as rare as one would expect. Many invertebrates, including aphids, water fleas, and some bees and scorpions, reproduce this way, but the phenomenon also occurs in vertebrates, such as Komodo dragons, hammerhead sharks, and cobras.[4] Birds, including turkeys, chicken, and condors, are known to produce virgin births too.[5] Offspring produced by this method have no male DNA and are entirely homozygous, meaning that instead of having a mix of dominant and recessive genes, all of their alleles were exactly the same.

So there can little doubt that with sexual reproduction, the female has the lead role and is the primary actor, while the male has the supporting role and is the secondary actor. From the parthenogenetic point of view, the appendage that makes someone a male also makes him the appendage of the female function. It is the female that does all the work. Carrying the fetus, giving birth, and nurturing the young—first with her milk, then with food—are all time-intensive, consuming activities. For the female to succeed at this primary (biological) mission to procreate and reproduce requires time periods of relative peace and security. By contrast, the physical contribution of the male is minimal. A brief sexual encounter suffices. It is the male's fate and function to play the supporting role in the very short-term, primarily through the contribution of half the genes and secondarily, at the higher levels of evolution, by providing protective services in case of threat or crisis.

The female's primary biological function is procreation of the species, birthing, rearing, and nurturing. First, she has to carry the offspring internally to let it grow to term, then she has to go through the extremely strenuous and taxing birthing process. The female body, influenced by the preponderance of female hormones, is specifically adapted for giving birth. It has evolved greater lower body strength, muscularly and skeletally, to facilitate the effort of the birthing process. Secondly, the female mammal is tasked with nourishing and nurturing it physically and emotionally for years until it is ready to enter its productive phase as a full-fledged member of the culture.

Nowhere is the primary, fundamental operating principle of the universe more in evidence than in the polarity of the sexes and the biological process of species reproduction. As such, life itself is female-centric. The primary business of life is to make more of itself;

that is the female function. Activating the female function (by insemination) and, on occasion, protecting the female and her offspring, are secondary; those are the male functions.

The chromosomal polarity of X and Y chromosomes that determine male or female differentiation of the fetus also determine the hormonal differentiation between the male and the female of the species. In most animals, and especially in mammals, including the human species, the female-male polarity is expressed by and reflected in polarity of their endocrine systems. The female and male sex hormones are made in the female and male reproductive organs, respectively, in the ovaries and placenta and in the testes.

The female hormones (estrogen and progesterone) and the male hormones (testosterone and androgen) influence different propensities in the sexes. These differences pertain to the division of labor within the context of both individual and species survival and defines many of their physical and psychological characteristics. In the female, estrogen is the hormone responsible for development and regulation of the reproductive system and secondary sex characteristics. Progestogens, such as progesterone, function in maintaining pregnancy as well as in estrous and menstrual cycles. Additionally, in females, oxytocin is intimately involved in the birthing process as well as the bonding between mother and child that takes place in the period after the birth.

Oxytocin and the Female Neural-Hormonal Axis of Harmony

When mammals diverged from reptiles and birds in the Carboniferous era, between 300 and 360 million years ago, they embarked on a course of evolution that would, over time, vastly increase the range of their emotional and cognitive capabilities. The first great evolutionary advance was in the reproductive sphere, which lent its name to the biological class. In mammals, the females not only evolved to give birth to offspring but also to nurture that offspring with milk from their mammary glands after birth until the offspring was ready to fend for itself. As the story of the lioness mother and the leopard cub below will aptly illustrate, the radical innovation of mammalian evolutionary strategy was to make trust so important to species survival and reproduction that natural selection generated a hormonal basis for it.

But not only did the evolution of mammals represent a giant step forward in the richness of their emotional lives, it likewise represented a giant step forward in the growth of their cognitive abilities. Because, relative to birds and reptiles, another crucial distinguishing characteristic that mammals evolved, and which applied equally to both female and male, was a larger neocortex in the brain. Eventually, in primates in general, and in humans in particular, this would favor the development of the problem-solving capacity and use of tools, language, and consciousness.

Now oxytocin, the neuropeptide, is produced in both sexes by the hypothalamus and released by the pituitary. Additionally, oxytocin has major functionality in the reproductive life of the female and is also produced in copious amounts by the female reproductive system (ovaries, uterus, placenta), especially during pregnancy, childbirth, and the nurturing period that follows. It plays an essential role in all social bonding. In my opinion, therefore, oxytocin should be considered basically a female hormone that is shared to a lesser extent by the male sex, much like females have some of the male hormone testosterone, and males also have some of the other female hormones.

So powerful is the strength of the oxytocin caring hormone that occasionally, cross-species adoption by a competing species has been observed. It appears to happen exclusively among mammals, and the chances appear greatest among closely related species. In one rare case of cross-species adoption, a bottlenose dolphin was observed adopting a newborn pilot whale calf off the coast of New Zealand in 2011.[6] Bottlenose dolphins have, in fact, a reputation for this kind of thing. Usually they will adopt calves from common dolphins, who are of the same size or smaller. They've even been accused of "stealing" calves from other species, not out of malicious forethought but as a result of "misplaced maternal instinct" that is so strong they can't help themselves.[7]

Another case of cross-species adoption was reported in 2020 in Gir National Park, in India, when a lioness adopted a leopard cub, nursing, feeding, and caring for him as if he were one of her own two sons about the same age.[8] The *New York Times* reported "The 2-month-old cub—all fuzzy ears and blue eyes—was adorable, and the lioness spent weeks nursing, feeding and caring for him until he died. She treated him as if one of her own two sons, who were about the same age."[9] This behavior was all the more remarkable in that lions and leopards in that habitat compete for the same prey and will usually kill each other's young if given the opportunity.[10] Even more remarkable was the behavior of a lioness on the Kenyan plain that reportedly had adopted an antelope calf, its customary prey, and nurtured it with maternal affection.[11]

The behavior of the lioness also illustrates the incredibly powerful action of the hormone oxytocin on animal behavior. Oxytocin has been identified as the major agent in mammals responsible for the biosocial bonding of mother and their offspring and is often called the hormone of empathy, caring, and trust. The lioness was, as it were, drunk on the love and compassion the oxytocin generated in her toward her own offspring. She was able to extend that sphere of love and compassion and accept to the leopard cub as one of her own rather than one of her competitors. It is clear that females will be most successful in their biologically imposed tasks of bringing to age competent new members of the culture if their environment—physical, social, and cultural—is largely harmonious, balanced, and free from external threats. The conclusion is straightforward and self-evident: the female hormonal axis of estrogen and oxytocin is the hormonal foundation for harmony, nurture, and empathy.

Oxytocin may also provide the answer to the age-old question that has baffled humankind for so long: Why do dogs love humans so much? It seems that in the evolution of undomesticated wolf to domesticated dog, the species developed a genetic makeup that created the propensity for deep emotional bonding between dog and human. This is mediated by the same type of oxytocin positive-feedback loop as is seen between mothers and their infants. A Japanese study reported on by the magazine *Science* found that dog owners experienced a jaw-dropping 300% increase in oxytocin levels after spending a half hour with their dogs, including time gazing into their eyes.[12] That locked gaze is key, the scientists found. The longer you stare, the more oxytocin is released and the deeper is the bonding that occurs. In fact, the scientists found no oxytocin increase in the dogs and owners who had spent little time looking into each other's eyes.[13]

The Complementarity of the Male Function

As in many mammals, in addition to contributing his half of the chromosomes necessary for the species' perpetuation, the human male serves the human female in several ways. On account of the preponderance of male hormones androgen and testosterone, the male evolved a relatively bigger and more muscular body adapted for the greater physical efforts required by the male. As with most mammals, and primates especially, the human male body evolved great upper-body strength, muscularly and skeletally, primarily to engage in competition to get mating privileges, as passing on of greater virility and strength definitely serves the evolutionary advantage of the species.

The evolution of the male's greater body strength facilitated procurement of food, as in hunting, fishing, farming, for sustenance. Also on occasions of crisis and emergencies, such evolved male bodies would afford greater protection for females and their offspring. In the human male, the combination of crisis hormones with male hormones produces a state of ready aggression to meet any threat that may occur. The role of testosterone and the male hormones in aggression cannot be underestimated. On the one hand, removal of male hormones from the system, through castration for example, can turn the mightiest and fiercest male into a nonaggressive creature. On the other hand, the injection of male hormones can quickly turn cowering weaklings, whether male or female, into ferocious aggressors. Conclusion: the male hormonal axis of testosterone and the crisis hormone adrenalin is the hormonal foundation for aggression and enmity.

Biology determines that the role of all males is to contribute, through mating, half of the chromosomes necessary for reproduction.

For that reason, males are driven by their desire to mate and remove any obstacles in their way, especially the other males of his species. He will compete with them and attempt to gain dominance over them so he can mate and fulfill his biological destiny. This makes the life of the individual male animal inherently a life of crisis management that often involves fighting to resolve conflict and win the right to mate. In other words, the male hormone of testosterone is intimately tied to the function of adrenalin, the hormone of aggression and violence, as is required by their competition mating rights and protective function. Apart from mating, the male's predisposition to fight can, and often is, marshalled in a collective effort of repulsing rival groups in territorial disputes or when his own group faces an external threat.

The Amygdala and the Neural-Hormonal Axis of Crisis

The amygdala, an almond-shaped organ that lies deep in the brain of all vertebrates, can be thought of as the interface between the neurosensory and the neuromuscular components of the nervous system. As part of the limbic system, that most primitive and ancient part of our brain that connects us to our reptilian past, the amygdala processes all sensory stimuli for information, whether or not it constitutes a threat to the organism, and determines what action to take on the fight-or-flight spectrum. These actions will be different for the male and female sexes, in as much as they are expressions of developmental differences between their respective neurohormonal paradigms.

The amygdala is structurally divided into two hemispheres that are functionally antithetical, and each hemisphere has its own memory storage system. The left hemisphere of the amygdala specializes in processing pleasurable stimuli and plays a significant role in the brain's reward system. Its right hemisphere, on the other hand, exclusively processes negative stimuli, including anxiety and pain, and the emotions of fear and rage. Significant developmental differences occur in the maturity between the right and left hemispheres of the amygdala. In the initial stages of the organism's growth, the left amygdala develops more rapidly than the right. But when the left amygdala stops growing, the right amygdala continues and, in the end, winds up to be the larger hemisphere.

It seems likely that the initial fast growth of the amygdala's left hemisphere in mammals may occur when the newborn is bonding with the mother, receiving maternal food and nurture, and constantly experiencing the joy of being alive. The subsequent enormous growth of the amygdala's right hemisphere occurs as a result of the young offspring discovering the dangerous and unpleasant side of life. It is the function of the amygdala's right hemisphere to respond to fearful stimuli posed by dangerous situations and, in the basolateral complexes of the amygdala, create an inventory of such experiences that will decrease the organism response time to threats.

It has long been established that the amygdala response on the fight-or-flight spectrum has a strong correlation with the testosterone levels of the animal. The salient fact here is that the amygdala is rich in androgen receptors that bind to the male hormone testosterone. This is the reason why the higher the testosterone level in the system, the more aggressive the organism's response will be to a threat, and the lower the testosterone level, the more likely it is the animal will attempt to flee. Not surprisingly, then, due to their hormonal differences, the development of the amygdala turns out to be different for males and females. Because females start with way less testosterone than males, the female amygdala stops growing one to two years sooner than the male amygdala. In the presence of so much testosterone, the male amygdala, and especially its right hemisphere, continues to grow until it outgrows the female amygdala by a lot.[14]

The greater size of the amygdala and the higher levels of testosterone in the male will predispose him to be more aggressive than the female in response to threats. In turn, with less testosterone, the female will be predisposed to fear, rather than aggression, in her response to threats. As a consequence, the male normally has more connections in the larger right hemisphere of the amygdala, while the female has stronger connections in the smaller left hemisphere of the amygdala. Thus the polarity of the amygdala triggers the fight-or-flight reflex differently in females and males depending on the mix of their yin and yang hormonal paradigms.[15]

So profound is the biological polarity of the fight-or-flight reflex mediated by the amygdala that on the species level, it also evolved as a fundamental standard of biological reality in the predator-prey relationship between species. But it must be stressed that, even in the context of the predator-prey relationship, the amygdala's primary function is to process existential anxiety and fear, and only secondarily does it trigger anger and aggression. When an animal is confronted with a superior threat, whether natural, intraspecies, or same-species, even the highest apex predator knows fear and turns tail to get away. When a lion is confronted by an elephant or two, he or she knows from experience that no good can come of it, and the amygdala will activate the fight-or-flight reflex. But when that same lion spots a nice little antelope, he also knows from experience that lunch is served, and his amygdala will activate the aggression and violence of the capture-and-kill reflex.

Oxytocin as the Antidote for Social Stress and Anxiety

Africa has a lion problem. There is not enough space for all of them. This can create a issue when too many lions that are strangers to each other have to share the same space. This happens not infrequently with captive lions on wildlife reserves. While African lions are extraordinarily social with the members of their own pride, they are violently, even deadly, antisocial when it comes to outsiders. Trying to find new ways of making the big cat strangers a bit more tolerant of each other to facilitate closer proximity, biologist Jessica Burkhart and colleagues administered oxytocin to 23 captive lions on a wildlife reserve in Dinokeng, South Africa, during the summers of 2018 and 2019.[16]

Delivering a dose of oxytocin to all these 400-pound lions was tricky, as one might expect. Protected by a strong fence, scientists lured the big cats close by offering them chunks of raw meat. When the lions approached to feed, the researchers used an atomizer, which resembles an old-fashioned spray perfume bottle, to deliver a dose of oxytocin directly up the lions' nostrils—where it had a direct route to the brain via the olfactory nerve. By all accounts, the experiment was a success. The lions mellowed dramatically and tolerated each other at greatly reduced distances. Burkhart reported that upon administering the drug, "You can see their features soften immediately, they go from wrinkled and aggressive to this totally calm demeanor... They totally chill out. It's amazing."[17]

The intranasal method of delivering oxytocin directly to the brain has been found effective in human beings also. Researchers at São Paulo University designed an intranasal shot that allowed them to administer the hormone directly into the brains of performance artists. They then did a study on a group of professional singers to determine if the administration of oxytocin before a public performance would lower their performance anxiety and improve how they felt about their performance afterward.[18] Half of the participants received an intranasal dose of oxytocin, while the other half received a placebo treatment. Their findings corroborated the mellowing effect of intranasal oxytocin administration to the African lions, making the performers feel less anxious and more confidently relaxed about their performance and the audience's reception.

Another group of researchers in Japan also explored the intranasal method of oxytocin administration in their study of its effects on Alzheimer's patients, with promising results. These scientists began their study inducing Alzheimer's disease in mice, then studied the effect of both direct injection of oxytocin into the brain and the nasal delivery method. They found both methods were about equally effective in reversing the damage caused by the disease, though the nasal drip was far superior in ease of administration.[19]

The Yin-Yang Interplay of the Female and Male Neurohormonal Axes

We have demonstrated that the "love hormone" oxytocin is the antidote to the aggression borne of the male hormone testosterone. And it works the other way around too! In an interesting study, a Dutch research team devised some ingenious experiments that proved increasing the level of testosterone in an individual inhibits the secretion of oxytocin, while increasing the level of adrenalin and the resulting violence and aggression.[20] On the one hand, oxytocin and female hormones (progestogen and estrogen) mutually reinforce each other. On the other hand, oxytocin and male hormones (testosterone and adrenalin) inhibit one another.

On the female side, it is well-known that during the process of birthing and the activity of breast feeding and lactation, the female hormones stimulate the secretion of copious amounts of oxytocin to facilitate the physical contractions of the uterus in birth, lactation after birth, and the psychological processes of bonding through caring and empathy. Oxytocin is one of the few hormones to create a positive feedback loop. For example, uterine contractions stimulate the release of oxytocin from the posterior pituitary, which in turn, increases uterine contractions. This positive feedback loop continues throughout labor. The combined effects of the female hormones and oxytocin is to reduce amygdala activity, decrease the secretion of adrenalin, inhibit the violence of aggression, and increase social interaction. This is why we may call it the *female neural-hormonal axis*.

On the male side, it is generally accepted that adrenaline is the hormone associated with the emotion of fear and the act of flight. It is also known and accepted that adrenalin is involved in anger and aggression. But there is less consensus as to the hormonal difference between fear and anger, and fight and flight. The answer is both surprising and obvious: testosterone. It is well-known that during crisis and emergencies of all kinds, the male hormone of testosterone combines with the action of adrenalin to turn flight into fight. The truth of it is that adrenaline without testosterone powers fear and flight and adrenalin with testosterone powers anger and fight. The combined effect of the male hormones and adrenalin is to trigger amygdala activity, increasing the secretion of adrenalin, stimulating the violence of aggression, and decreasing social interaction. This is why we may call it the *male neural-hormonal axis*.

Endnotes

1 Ana Rita Nunes, et al., "Developmental Effects of Oxytocin Neurons on Social Affiliation and Processing of Social Information," The Journal of Neuroscience 41, no. 42 (2021): 8742-8760, 10.1523/JNEUROSCI.2939-20.2021.

2 Ibid.

3 Caitlin Tilley, "Love Really Can Mend a Broken Heart: 'Cuddle Hormone' Repairs Cells Damaged After a Heart Attack, Study Finds," Daily Mail, September 30, 2022, https://www.dailymail.co.uk/health/article-11262301/Intimacy-hormone-repairs -cells-heart-attack-Michigan-researchers.html.

4 Tom Hale, "Baby Shark Born in Female-Only Tank May Be Species' First Virgin Birth." IFL Science, August 30, 2021, https://www.iflscience.com/baby-shark-born -in-femaleonly-tank-may-be-species-first-virgin-birth-60797.

5 Sara Harrison, "California Condors Are Capable of Asexual Reproduction" Wired, October 28, 2021, https://www.wired.com/story/california-condors-are-capable -of-asexual-reproduction/.

6 Rachel Funnell, "Bottlenose Dolphin Spotted with Pilot Whale Calf in Rare Cross-Species "Adoption," ILF Science, May 26, 2021, https://www.iflscience.com/bottlenose -dolphin-spotted-with-pilot-whale-calf-in-rare-crossspecies-adoption-59830.

7 11 Ibid.

8 Cara Giaimo, "The Leopard Cub with the Lioness Mom," New York Times, February 27, 2020, https://www.nytimes.com/2020/02/27/science/leopard-lion-adoption.html.

9 Ibid.

10 Ibid.

11 de Waal, Frans, Our Inner Ape: The Best and Worst of Human Nature, (London: Granta Books, 2005), 75.

12 David Grimm, "How Dogs Stole Our Hearts," Science, April 16, 2015, https://www.science.org/content/article/how-dogs-stole-our-hearts.

13 Kara Murphy, "The Science Behind Our Love for Pets," Hill's, January 20, 2022, https://www.hillspet.com/pet-care/behavior-appearance/why-humans-love-pets.

14 Eva H. Telzer et al., "'The Cooties Effect': Amygdala Reactivity to Opposite- Versus Same-Sex Faces Declines from Childhood to Adolescence," Journal of Cognitive Neuroscience 27, no. 9 (2015): 1685–96, 10.1162/jocn_a_00813.

15 Dick F. Swaab, "Sexual Orientation and Its Basis in Brain Structure and Function," Proceedings of the National Academy of Sciences of the United States of America 105, no. 30 (2008): 10273–4, 10.1073/pnas.0805542105. Some research suggests that this pattern may also hold in the gay community, with gay men tending to exhibit more feminine patterns of the amygdala and more neurological connections in the left hemisphere, while gay women, having more neurological connections in the right hemisphere, tend to exhibit more masculine patterns of the amygdala.

16 Brian Handwerk, "Can Spraying Lions with the 'Love Hormone' Help Them Live To-gether?" Smithsonian, March 30, 2022, https://www.google.com/url?client=internal -element-cse&cx=a675a2097c482ed77&q=https://www.smithsonianmag.com /science-nature/can-spraying-lions-with-the-love-hormone-help-them-live-together -180979836/&sa=U&ved=2ahUKEwjk29fNr7n_AhUUF2IAHWo5Cq4QFno ECAAQAg&usg=AOvVaw2bmpWt6WQWcBNhqh_nkPFQ.

17 Rachael Funnell, "Scientists Squirted 'Love Hormone' Oxytocin Up Lions' Noses to See If It Made Them Friendlier," IFL Science, March 30, 2022, https://www.iflscience .com/scientists-squirted-love-hormone-oxytocin-up-lions-noses-to-see-if-it-made -them-friendlier-63131.

18 Ingrid Fadelli, "A Dose of Oxytocin Could Reduce the Social Stress of Professional Singers During Performances," Neuroscience News, September 19, 2022, https://medicalxpress.com/news/2022-09-dose-oxytocin-social-stress-professional .html.

19 John Ely, "Could the Love Hormone Beat Alzheimer's? Giving Diseased Mice Oxytocin Spray Can Reverse Cognitive Impairment, Study Finds," Daily Mail, October 24, 2022, https://www.dailymail.co.uk/health/article-11348319/Could -love-hormone-beat-Alzheimers.html.

20 Nicholas Wade, "She Doesn't Trust You? Blame the Testosterone," New York Times, June 7, 2010, https://www.nytimes.com/2010/06/08/health/08hormone.html.

Chapter 2

The Theory of Balance and Harmony

Understanding the Taiji Symbol

Chinese cosmology teaches us that on the most profound level, Wuji is the "mother" of and "gives birth to" Taiji. Furthermore, it emphasizes that the Tao is "the Way" of Taiji. Let us unpack these terms to get to their meaning. "Ji" means energy, "wu" means nothing or none, and "tai" means everything or all. "Wu" and "ji" combined into Wuji refers to the energy of the undifferentiated reality, i.e., the potential of the field of the void and emptiness that exists prior to any existence. It is symbolized by the empty circle (Fig. A). "Tai" and "ji" combined into Taiji refers to the energy of differentiated reality, of all and everything that exists after it comes into existence. In Western cosmology the process of differentiation was the Big Bang, after which everything came into existence. The moment when differentiation occurred was the beginning when Wuji precipitated into the primal opposites of yin and yang of the Tao (Fig. B) and gave birth to Taiji.

FIG. A: WUJI

FIG. B: TAIJI

The Unity of Opposites

Ancient Taoism and modern physics share two fundamental conclusions on the nature of reality that are expressed by the yin-yang symbol. First and foremost, for the Taoists, the symbol expresses that the fundamental operating principle of the universe is polarity. The S curve divides the yin-yang symbol in two equal but opposing parts, the polarity of the two opposites of the white and black areas, the "fishes," as they are called on account of their shape. In the 20th century, when Niels Bohr discovered that the fundamental structure of the atom consisted of the positively charged nucleus and negatively charged electrons surrounding it, modern physics came to share this conclusion that the fundamental operating principle governing the universe is the polarity principle. And Bohr publicly acknowledged his debt to the ancient sages by choosing the yin-yang symbol as his coat of arms when he was knighted for his contributions to physics.

BOHR'S COAT OF ARMS

Secondly, when the ancients designed the S-wave curve to delineate the yin-yang opposition of the polarity principle, they also uncannily anticipated another basic discovery of modern physics. That discovery was made in 1924 by Louis de Broglie, who proved that the electrons' steplike orbits in Bohr's atomic model are easily understood if electrons are pictured as consisting of standing waves surrounding the nucleus.[1] What made this conclusion revolutionary was that it did away with the classical, commonsense, everyday understanding that objects in the material world have substance and solidity. With this new insight, modern science found itself agreeing once again with the old Taoists that there is nothing but energy. And since energy comes in waves, literally everything—electrons, baseballs, human beings, and every moving material object in the universe—is a wave.

In essence, of course, the wave theory of reality is a consequence of the polarity principle, for a wave is nothing but the periodic oscillation between the two extremes that define its amplitude. After Bohr's work on the atom, discoveries about the structure of subatomic reality further corroborated that the polarity principle also governed subatomic reality. The energy units that populate this reality, gluons and quarks, are defined by their spin, which always occurs in one of two opposite directions—the spin is either up and down, or left and right, or in the metaphor of ordinary space, vertical or horizontal. The yin and yang "fishes" in the Taoist symbol that are defined by the wave are always rendered in opposing colors. In Bohr's coat of arms, they are black and red, while in the Korean flag they are red and blue, but in Chinese culture, most often, the yin and yang are represented by black and white, respectively.

The Proportion of Opposites

In summary, the yin-yang symbolizes Taiji and the Way of the Tao. Taiji and Tao both refer to the reality that everything in our universe exists by virtue of its opposite, i.e., being one of two poles in a polarity structure. In as much as Taoism is a theory of harmony, the balance between opposites, it is also a theory of crisis, the imbalance between opposites. In this context we can discern three aspects of the yin-yang symbol that express whether the relationship under discussion is balanced or imbalanced. These are (1) the proportions of the opposites, (2) the interpenetration of the opposites, and (3) the placement of the opposites.

The proportion of opposites, i.e., the size of the white and black "fishes" relative to each other, is the first and most obvious criteria. When they are equal (as in Fig. A), there is balance. If (as in Fig. B), one is bigger and one is smaller, there is imbalance. In this case, the preponderance of the yang and the diminution of the yin express the imbalance in the male-centric, authoritarian paradigm of the White Man.

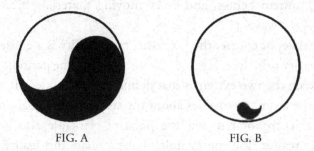

FIG. A   FIG. B

The Interpenetration of Opposites

The "interpenetration of opposites" refers to the Taoist teaching that there are no absolutes because each thing is always defined in terms of its opposite and, therefore, contains its opposite. In the Fig. C symbol, this interpenetration of opposites is expressed by the black dot within the white fish, and the white dot within the black fish.

FIG. C

Interpenetration is the second level of the balance-imbalance polarity that will lead us to a deeper understanding of the nature of phenomena in the various dimensions of existence—physical, biological, and psychological. A simple example would be the polarity of day and night. Night and day are not absolute but are based on the relative absence or presence of light. They do not transition from one to the other suddenly but gradually, as the light of the sun waxes and wanes with the Earth's rotation. Thus, except for the most extreme points in the cycle, most of the day will have some night in it, and most of the night will have some day in it.

The interpenetrating aspect of the yin-yang symbol further attest to the sophistication and depth of the Taoist worldview. The dots within the fishes also symbolize their conception of the universe as a mathematically binary recursive and infinitely branching, self-propagating algorithm. For example, the 64 hexagrams, or chapters, of the famous Taoist book of divination, the *I Ching*, are derived from the most fundamental property of the symbol, which is binary recursion; as each dot in the fishes divides into two additional yin and yang fishes with their own dots, and those dots again split into fishes with their own dots, and so forth. In five generations of splitting, you get the series of 2-4-8-16-32-64 to arrive at the number 64.

The rediscovery of the ancient Taoist understanding of the generative principle of binary mathematics by modern science opened up a whole new era of scientific investigations and understanding in the 20th century. Most obvious and far-reaching in its effects on human culture were the birth, growth, and development of computer science and its technological applications. In the human social sciences, moreover, significant progress was made in the understanding of human behavior through the application of binary mathematics in their explanatory analyses. In linguistics, for example, the universal generative grammar of Noam Chomsky is mathematically and functionally identical to that expressed by the yin-yang symbol. Likewise, in anthropology, Claude Lévi-Strauss used binary mathematics to lay bare the structure of kinship relationships. And in psychology, Piaget likewise used binary mathematics to define the stages of development in human infancy.

If Niels Bohr was the pioneer in physics who consciously recognized and built on the Taoist polarity principle, Carl Jung was the pioneer who did the same in the realm of psychology, the mysterious world of the human psyche, and the human interaction between the sexes. Carl Jung adopted the concept of the interpenetration of opposites to describe the biopsychological structure of the human dyad. Indeed, Jung made this Taoist doctrine into one of the cornerstones of his therapeutics. Recall, when Jung was alive and working, the prevailing conceptions of the sexes was that they had nothing in common and were rigidly defined by their biological and corresponding social functions. Jung's study of the structure of the human psyche was revolutionary and completely upended the traditional view of the sexes as diametrically opposed in all respects. He stressed that, "The psyche possesses its inner polarity, and nothing so promotes the growth of consciousness as this inner confrontation of opposites."[2] Thus Jung arrived at a very literal interpretation of these ancient Taoist concepts. He called the "yin in the yang," or the "female in the male," the anima and the "yang in the yin," or the "male in the female," the animus.

Jung demonstrated that the traditionally held view of gender relationships as simple binary opposites, represented by the symbol as the outer yin without the inner yang and the outer yang without the inner yin (Fig. D), was at the very root of pathologies of hyper-masculinity and hyper-femininity in the West. He concluded that recovering the biopsychological health of, and balance between, the male and female of the species will depend on their getting in touch with and accepting their inner opposites.

FIG. D

Science proved Jung right! As we already described in a previous section, biological science has proved beyond a shadow of doubt that each male and female has a mix of both female and male hormones corresponding to, and expressive of, the functional polarity of female and male that evolution has bequeathed on our species. Estrogen and other female hormones circulate in the blood of both males and females, though estrogen levels are, of course, considerably lower in males than in females. Androgens and testosterone increase in both male and female in puberty and function in both sexes to increase libido and sexual arousal, though females, of course, generally have way lower levels of androgens than males. The differences, then, between male and female are not absolute but relative.

The constitution of any one individual, male or female, is determined by the mix of female and male hormones, which in turn, is the result of both genetic endowments and cultural child-rearing practices. Each individual, female or male, is therefore a unique combination of different ratios of female and male hormones that seeks its complement to engage in the procreative dance of its species. This random distribution accounts for a fact readily observable in nature: in the vast majority of cases, the female must and will get together with a male in order for the process of propagation to successfully take place. But the vagaries of evolution are such that it produces in each sex a number of individuals that are attracted more to members of their own sex than the opposite sex.

History has also proved Jung right! The enormous global growth of the women's liberation and the LGBT movements in the decades that followed has been a testament to the truth that the traditional exclusionary male-centric paradigm of human sexuality is obsolete and needs to be replaced by the Taoist paradigm of balanced interpenetration. Today, it has also been established beyond any reasonable doubt that interpenetration of opposites goes well beyond the psychological reality described by Jung. Indeed, it manifests itself frequently in physical reality as well. Androgynous and hermaphroditic individuals who have both male and female sexual organs have been fully documented and proved to be much more common than previously known and admitted. Evolution also regularly produces some fascinating variations on the norm, as in the man who had a cyst removed that was found to contain embryonic female organs[3] and the woman who had two complete reproductive systems, including two vaginas, one each on the left and right sides of her body.[4]

The Placement of Opposites

We have looked at the two obvious ways in which the Taoist yin-yang symbol expresses the conditions of balance and harmony. The first was that the S curve must divide the circle into two equal parts, and the second was that the dots in the fishes must be of equal size. If the S curve divides the circle into unequal size fishes and/or if the dots in the fishes are not the same size, the situation represented is one of imbalance and crisis. Now we turn to examine the third, less obvious but no less essential criterion that must be met for the symbol to express balance and harmony and which, conversely, if not met, indicates a state of imbalance and crisis.

This third parameter pertains to the placement of the yin-yang opposites relative to each other. Here, there are only two possibilities. One possibility is the white fish, representing the yang, or the masculine principle, is positioned higher, on top of, or superior to, the black fish, which is inferior, lower, or underneath, the white fish, as in Fig. E. The second possibility is the opposite: the black fish, representing the yin, or feminine principle, is positioned higher, on top of, and superior to, the white fish, or the masculine principle, which is inferior, lower, or underneath the white fish, as in Fig. F.

FIG. E: A ROW OF VARIATIONS WITH YANG IN SUPERIOR POSITION

FIG. F: A ROW OF VARIATIONS WITH YIN IN SUPERIOR POSITION

Here is where our linguistic terminology reveals an unconscious bias. When we think, write, or talk about a particular polarity structure, the temporal nature of the activity forces us to consider one of the poles first and the other second. This makes the first one the primary or major one and the second one secondary or minor. For example, when we talk about the human species, we have to talk about the male-female polarity. In our male-centric culture, invariably the male is mentioned before the female, accurately reflecting the cultural bias that the male is considered the stronger and more dominant, active partner of the human dyad, while the female is considered the subdominant, more passive partner.

Translated into spatial positioning in the yin-yang symbol, this common male-centric conception will invariably position the yang masculine fish over, or on top of, the dark feminine fish, as in the row of Fig. E. But in as much as the Taoist conception of peace and harmony in society is female-centric, the ancient sages like Lao Tzu and Chuang Tzu were of the opposite opinion on that matter. Lao Tzu taught that to walk the path of righteousness, harmony, and balance, we must "know the yang but keep to the yin." And Huang Ti, the legendary Yellow Emperor, elaborated,

> Yin strives towards the interior;
> Yang reaches toward the outside…
> Yin creates peace and harmony;
> And the root of everything is peace and harmony
> The emanations of Yang have a dispersing and destructive effect.[5]

Taoism holds the female, yin, energy to be a sinking or gathering energy, while the male yang energy is said to be a rising and dispersing energy. Therefore, in designing their symbol, the Taoists placed the yin in the superior position. Both Chinese medical theory and Chinese martial arts theory are also of the view that human harmony and balance is the condition where the outward directedness of yang, male, energy is contained and restrained by the inward directedness of female, yin, energy.

In the symbol, this Taoist conviction that true equality, harmony, and balance between males and females in society can only exist when the female-centric social paradigm is dominant over its male-centric paradigm. In the symbol, this is expressed by the proper positioning of the black in the superior position over the white (Fig. F). Biologically, Fig. F expresses that all males also produce and have female hormones and feelings and that all females also produce and have male hormones and feelings. Psychologically and emotionally, then, the symbol expresses the possibility of empathy and understanding between the sexes.

The ancient Chinese sages, accordingly, would reject any representation of the yin-yang symbol with the white fish positioned on top of the black fish as unbalanced and liable to deterioration and collapse of the situation.

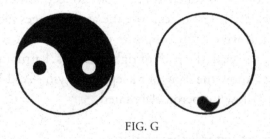

FIG. G

Fig. G represents the distortion and imbalance of the yin-yang symbol of the male-centric paradigm of human interaction. It expresses the disharmony created by the preponderance of yang in all three dimensions of proportion, interpenetration, and position. Proportion-wise, the disproportionate aggrandizement of the white (yang, male) and diminution of black areas (yin, female) reflects the male-centricity of Western man's paradigm. Interpenetration-wise, there is none. In the yin fish, the yang core has been suppressed, and in the yang fish, the yin core has been suppressed, aggravating the imbalances. Position-wise, the white yang (male) is in the superior position above the black yin (female), meaning the latter will be incapable of exerting a restraining influence on the former. Together, the three symbolize the imbalance of the White Man's culture where his hyper-masculinity has squeezed the female into hypo-femininity, where parity has been displaced by disparity, and equality by inequality.

Neurohormonal Yin-Yang of Harmony and Crisis

For all life, the primary yin-yang polarity is between harmony and crisis. At all times, the question for any living creature is whether its relationship to its environment is harmonic and conducive to growth or whether the relationship poses a threat to the creature's existence. Biologically, this is reflected in most, if not all, animals in the polarity of the nervous system, and the yin-yang of harmony and crisis is literally wired into our bodies. Our nervous system has the structure of polarity, being divided between the sympathetic and parasympathetic nervous systems to regulate the cycles of our biological activity and rest. The sympathetic nervous system is activated during all activity and effort but particularly when a crisis threatens existence; it regulates the use and expenditure of energy that causes the depletion of our reserves. The parasympathetic nervous system is activated and operates during periods of rest and inactivity, when conditions of harmony and balance prevail, to restore our energy levels and reserves.

Also wired into our bodies is the yin-yang of endocrine (hormonal) responses to crisis and emergency. When we are faced with an existential threat, our fight-or-flight system, which is regulated by the endocrine system, is activated. This enables us to either flee or fight for the purpose of restoring harmony and eliminating the threat. In the flight reaction, the animal will turn and run away to put sufficient distance between itself and the threat so that it no longer is a threat. Adrenaline is released by the hormonal system to mobilize and boost the animal's locomotive system to its maximum, especially the legs, for and during the flight.

When flight is not an option, even more adrenalin and related hormones, such as noradrenaline, are secreted by the adrenal medulla and pumped into the system to power the animal's fight response to physically eliminate or subdue the threat entirely. Whereas in the flight response, the energy was concentrated on the lower body and legs for running, in the fight response much of the energy and effort is redirected to the upper body, head, jaws, forelegs, arms, and paws for fighting purposes.

The larger and stronger body of the male adversely affects the equality and balance in the relationship between the sexes when there is conflict between them. Then the biological crisis polarity of fear and anger becomes embodied in and expressed by the sexes. The female is more generally ruled by fear of the male's greater physical strength, and the male more generally rules by anger and the violent use of his greater physical strength. Friedrich Engels already pointed out in the 19th century that "the first class structure of society in history was the subjugation of the female sex by the male."[6]

In the Beginning: The Yin-Yang of Our Creation Myth

To bring it all back home, the Judeo-Christian creation myth provides us with a concrete illustration of Taoist concepts. In Genesis 2, God first created Adam and placed him in the Garden of Eden. Then God saw that Adam was all by himself and lonely. To correct the problem, God fashioned Eve from Adam's rib while Adam was sleeping. Then, when Adam awoke, he recognized Eve as part of himself and accepted her as his companion.

But this creation story is actually the second of two creation stories contained in Genesis. The first and older version is presented in Genesis 1. Here, God fashions man and woman simultaneously. Genesis 1:27 reads, "So God created man in his own image, in the image of God created he him; male and female created he them."

In other words, Eve was not Adam's first wife but his second. The Christian Bible is silent on the name of the first wife and the circumstances that doomed their union. Fortunately, the Hebrew myths, legends, and lore as well as other Middle Eastern traditions have retained the essential information that can fill in the blanks and at least outline the bigger picture. Her name was Lilith, originally a goddess in Mesopotamian mythology. By means of cultural diffusion, Lilith was, in time, also incorporated into Jewish lore as Adam's first wife.

According to Jewish legend, as a couple, Adam and Lilith argued and fought all the time, mostly about sex. Adam always insisted to be on top in the dominant sexual position. Lilith argued that they should be able to take turns. When Adam would not consent to such an arrangement, Lilith decided to leave Adam.[7] Once outside the Garden of Eden, Lilith pursued her own pleasures and coupled with the archangel Samael. Happy with her new situation of not being subservient to Adam, Lilith refused all entreaties to come back to Adam in the Garden. That's why, according to Jewish lore, God had to go back to the drawing board and come up with an Eve to remedy the situation.

The first, earlier version, presented in Genesis 1, harkens back to an earlier time when human social organization was female-centric and egalitarian in its orientation. The legend of Lilith as Adam's first wife is a memory trace in the collective subconscious of the time when feminine power coexisted with masculine power in the original state of equality between the male and female components of the human dyad. Only in equality can there be harmony and balance between the sexes.

The second story of the creation of Eve from Adam's rib can be seen as the final expression of the displacement of the original female-centric cultural paradigm by a male-centric cultural paradigm. This second story, with Adam being the boss man and Eve created from his substance, subordinate to his authority, is strongly expressive of the male-centric nature of the Judeo-Christian tradition. Male authority will always perpetuate imbalance between the powerful men and the powerless women. And the fate of Lilith? In the ever-increasing male-centricity of the Hebrew paradigm, Lilith became the personification of feminine evil, demonized and portrayed in male-centric Jewish culture as an ally and instrument of Satan himself.

These two biblical creation stories confirm the wisdom of the Chinese sages. The ancient Taoists recognized that only within a female-centric social paradigm can social harmony and balance be achieved based on the inherent equality of the sexes and, therefore, will be inherently egalitarian. Conversely, they also had the insight that any male-centric culture will be based on the inequality of the sexes, on the dominance of the male and the subordination of the female, and therefore, will be inherently authoritarian.

Endnotes

1   Marcelo Gleiser, "Not Just Light: Everything Is a Wave, Including You," Freethink, January 06, 2023, https://www.freethink.com/science/wave-particle-duality-matter.

2   Carl G. Jung, Memories, Dreams, Reflections, (Vintage Books, 1962), 345.

3   ABC News, "Man with Twin Living Inside Him—A Medical Mystery Classic," August 23, 2006, https://abcnews.go.com/Health/man-twin-living-inside-medical -mystery-classic/story?id=2346476

4   Rebecca Shepherd, "Woman with 'Two Vaginas' Says She Uses One for Work and One for Personal Sex," LADbible, January 17, 2020, https://www.ladbible.com /community/woman-with-two-vaginas-uses-one-for-work-and-one-for-personal -sex-20220117.

5   Ilza Veith, tr., The Yellow Emperor's Classic of Internal Medicine, (California: University of California Press, 1972), 129.

6   Friedrich Engels, The Origin of the Family, Private Property, and the State, (New World Paperbacks, 1884), 50–58.

7   Ariela Pelaia, "The Legend of Lilith: Adam's First Wife," Learn Religions, April 16, 2019, https://www.learnreligions.com/legend-of-lilith-origins-2076660.

Chapter 3

Primates and Their Social Organization (70 Million Years Ago)

The Plasticity of Female and Male Function

The precise evolutionary mix of male-female functions and divisions of labor regarding parenting appears to a large extent to be determined by the environment. In some cases, the more severe and challenging the environment is vis-à-vis species propagation, the more cooperation and engagement is required by the male and female in the effort. In the bitter cold of the Antarctic, for example, the plight of the penguins is such that the eggs cannot be left alone lest they freeze and kill the young. Hence the penguins typically share parenting responsibilities, equally alternating so that one sits on the egg to keep incubating it while the other is out in the ocean fishing for the food the family needs.

This equal and cyclic alternating division of labor between male and female penguins is most likely an indication that both the male and female penguins have very high underlying production of the hormone oxytocin. This would inhibit testosterone production in the male and, thereby, create a species' greater tolerance for same-sex couples.

This has been confirmed by observation of same-sex pairings of penguin couples around the world. In all cases, the work of parenting stays the same regardless of whether the pairing is by heterosexual or gay couples.[1] In Spain earlier this year, the gentoo penguins Electra and Viola welcomed a chick at an aquarium after successfully adopting, incubating, and hatching the egg from another couple. Likewise, in Australia, two male gentoo penguins named Sphen and Magic became "inseparable" before the 2018 breeding season and began building their own nest. After practicing with a dummy egg, they were eventually given one from a couple that had two, and they successfully hatched a female.

At the Amersfoort Zoo in the Netherlands, things were taken even further. Two gay African penguins with a history of mischief carried out a brazen egg-napping. This was the second time the conspiratorial duo had stolen eggs from their neighbors. Previously, they had taken an egg from a straight couple in an "unguarded moment" and proceeded to incubate it. Unfortunately, that egg failed to produce a chick. Not in the least deterred, they tried again the following year and snatched a nest of eggs from another couple, unaware they were setting themselves up for failure again, as the couple was lesbian, which in all likelihood, meant the eggs were not fertilized and would not hatch. Oh well, perseverance furthers, and maybe they will discover that the third time is the charm!

Besides penguins, same-sex couplings have been observed in every class of the animal kingdom, including the Laysan albatross, the New Mexico whiptail lizard, Hermann's tortoise, Atlantic molly, dragonflies, orcas, giraffes, red foxes, koalas, and bonobos. Besides sheer numbers, the range of sexual behaviors among animals is diverse and fascinating. "Greenpeace UK reports that nearly 1,000 animals display homosexual behavior, and Canadian biologist Bruce Bagemihl detailed 450 examples in his book *Biological Exuberance: Animal Sexuality and Natural Diversity*."[2]

Bonobo and Chimpanzee Monkeys

When it comes to the evolution of mammalian social organization and how species adapt to changing environments, we also find that the yin-yang of the female-male hormonal axes have had a defining influence on human evolution. Indeed, the societal organization of cultures and civilizations can, and should be, assessed and described in terms of their relative male-centered and female-centered characteristics. As the closest living primate relatives to us humans, the chimpanzee and the bonobo monkeys have a lot to teach us. Bonobo and chimpanzee societies present us with the two extremes of primate social organization based on the yin-yang of mammalian hormonal axes.

On the one hand, bonobo society clearly exemplifies the female-centric social paradigm based on the progesterone/oxytocin hormonal axis. The social dynamics are democratic and rely on the dynamic of female cooperation for common purpose and mutual benefit. There is equality between the sexes, which creates harmony and tolerance. As the female's life and existence is concerned with making more life, this creates a climate of empathy, trust, love, and peace.

Chimpanzee society, on the other hand, is exemplary of the male-centric social paradigm based on testosterone/adrenalin axis and on the dynamic of male competition for power. Its social organization is authoritarian and perpetuates inequality between the sexes, i.e., male dominance and female subservience. As the male's life and existence is concerned with survival and avoiding death, the social structure is hierarchical and intolerant, creating a climate of enmity, distrust, hatred, and violence.

Primatologist Frans de Waal described the female-centric nature of bonobo society as a "gynecocracy," where at the top of the social hierarchy is a coalition of high-ranking females who dominate the majority of males and make the core of the group. While there is a clearly defined alpha male who leads the group, protects it from threats, and decides where they travel to and where they feed, he needs the loyalty of the resident females to retain this position. These alphas typically have a mutual, codominant relationship with the highest-ranking females. Only the alpha male can eat with the high-ranking females, while the other males wait at the periphery of the group. Females often have the final say on where the group travels.

Due to the promiscuous mating behavior of female bonobos, a male cannot be sure which offspring are his. As a result, the entirety of parental care in bonobos is assumed by the mothers and female bonobos enjoy greater sexual preferences—an advantage of female-female bonding—and actively seek out higher-ranking males. It is interesting to note in this respect that bonobos are the only nonhuman animal to engage in tongue kissing. Professor de Waal concludes that bonobos habitually exhibit altruism, compassion, empathy, kindness, patience, and sensitivity and include the practice of frequent sex as a proven means of conflict resolution and post-conflict reconciliation. The bonobos' female-centric paradigm promotes equality, tolerance, and egalitarianism to ensure long-term harmony.

In stark contrast to this female-centered bonobo society, their (and our) primate cousins the chimpanzees are organized on the male-centric paradigm of the testosterone-adrenalin hormonal axis, as exhibited by the following three widespread behaviors: (1) constant competition for alpha status among males within the group, (2) male dominance over females within the group, and (3) constant warlike interactions with other groups. Males remain in their natal communities, while females generally emigrate at adolescence. As such, males in a community are more likely to be related to one another than females are to each other.

The chimp's male-centric paradigm is built on male power and alpha-ness and the competition for mating. Having reached dominance through intimidation and force, the supreme leader alpha males remain aggressive even during dominance stability, always ready to reassert their dominance at the slightest challenge. While among the males there is a dominance hierarchy, the relation between the sexes is that basically all males are dominant over all females. In chimpanzee society, any male can coerce a female into mating with him, and a community's dominant male can restrict reproductive access to females. They have even been observed to practice infanticide to shorten the interbirth intervals in the females. In this regard, chimp society shows clearly that the fundamental class structure in primate society arises with the institutionalized dominance of male over female.

Chimpanzees live in communities that typically range from 20 to more than 150 members. During the day, they spend most of their time traveling and foraging in smaller, temporary groups consisting of a few individuals, which may consist of any combination of age and sex classes. In the interaction between different groups of chimpanzees, chimpanzees engage in wars, not to obtain mates but to control territory and the food that it contains. Smaller groups avoid contact with their larger neighbors because the large groups might take over the smaller group's territory, gaining access to more resources, food, and females. Patrol parties consisting mostly of males patrol the group's territory to probe the enemies' defenses for vulnerabilities and to protect their own group members and secure their food supply.

Chimpanzees prefer fruit above all other food items but also eat leaves and leaf buds, seeds, blossoms, stems, pith, bark, and resin. Females forage for themselves and their offspring, while males forage only for themselves. Chimpanzees are also known to hunt and to collect insects and other invertebrates. But such food actually makes up a very small portion of their diet, from as little as 2% yearly to as much as 65 grams of animal flesh per day for each adult chimpanzee in peak hunting seasons. Also, not surprisingly, male chimps hunt more and eat more meat than females.

Our Jungle Heritage and the Fate of the Species

Frans de Waal, the preeminent primatologist, described the human species as:

> One of the most internally conflicted animals ever to walk the earth. It is capable of unbelievable destruction of both its environment and its own kind, yet at the same time it possesses wells of empathy and love deeper than ever seen before. Since this animal has gained dominance over all others, it's all the more important that it takes an honest look into the mirror, so that it knows both the archenemy it faces and the ally that stands ready to help it build a better world.[3]

De Waal is talking about the necessity for the human species to take a serious look at itself, in view of what has been learned from our two closest relatives on the primate evolutionary line to save our species from senseless acts of global destruction and possibly self-extinction. As de Waal put it, "We can take the ape out of the jungle, but not the jungle out of the ape."[4] Both the worst and the best features of human nature can only be understood in light of our shared evolutionary heritage with our closest primate relatives, the chimpanzee and bonobo apes.

As I was reading de Waal's book *Our Inner Ape*, I felt he should have used the plural form and entitled it *Our Inner Apes*. In this book, de Waal clearly treats the chimpanzee-bonobo primates, our closest primate relatives from whom we humans diverged some 5.5 million years ago, as an evolutionary dynamic of yin and yang that still animates us today. He eloquently describes how, in the course of their evolution, the chimpanzee and bonobo came to embody the primate polarity of female-centric and male-centric social paradigms.

De Waal's great contribution to primate research has been to demonstrate conclusively that the gentle bonobo and their peaceful society are as much a product of evolution's fundamental mechanism as that which shaped the more aggressive and competitive chimps. That evolutionary mechanism is, of course, the natural elimination of unsuccessful genotypes, which led our two closest relatives, the male-centric chimps and the female-centric bonobos, to adopt diametrically opposite social strategies. As de Waal put it so succinctly, "Chimps resolve sexual issues with power," while the bonobo "resolves power issues with sex."[5]

The Way of the Chimpanzee

The way of the chimpanzee is the way of power and violence. Hierarchy permeates everything, and power is an all-or-nothing game, for rank determines who will have offspring and who will not.[6] Accordingly, they are built to fight. For one, the chimpanzee males are much larger than the females; they are gruff and buff looking. With their large heads, thick necks, and broad shoulders, male chimps look like they spent their lives in the gym, building upper body strength.

And their exterior matches their interior. They are ambitious and compete for power in the male-centric social-dominance hierarchy of their species. For chimpanzee males, the reward of power is sex, and a big part of an alpha's life is to safeguard his exclusive monopoly on sex with any female at any time, scaring off opponents and physically beating back all challengers. In other words, our fellow simians, the chimps, take the pursuit of power and sex just as seriously as we humans do.[7]

As a result of their male-centric hierarchical social structure, the chimpanzees have evolved collective and individual response patterns of great violence toward any challengers. Whether they come from within the group or from outside, any challenge will activate their testosterone-adrenalin axis, and they will employ physical force to assert their dominance and "settle" the dispute. Conflict resolution in male-centric chimpanzee culture, in other words, is always through power and violence.

And in as much as status is determined by who can beat whom, no male can rule by himself, at least for long, and therefore, in chimpanzee society, coalitions play an important role in the politics of male chimp power. With male dominance based on fighting abilities and support from friends, staying on top in chimpanzee society, like in human politics, is a balancing act between forcefully asserting dominance, keeping supporters happy, and avoiding mass revolt. A steady turnover is built into these dynamics of power because the impact of age on these male hierarchies inevitably weaken the strongest chimps. As a result, male alpha chimps rarely stay in power for more than four or five years, and top positions become vacant on a regular basis.[8]

Nowhere is the reign of violence by the male-centric chimp social order more evident, and more sickening, than in the practice of infanticide. Infanticide is, of course, well established in many mammalian species, such as the big cats, and includes the primate line of chimps, gorillas, and humans. Usually activated by a successful change of male leadership, a new supreme male may engage in an orgy of violence and kill all small offspring sired by his predecessor, which will ensure the females come back into estrus quickly to be inseminated by him.

Isolation is the female chimp's primary defense against infanticide. Indeed, female chimps stay away from large gatherings of their species for up to four years after giving birth. Female chimps spend a large part of their lives alone with their dependent offspring.[9] Isolation and moving away to another group serves the chimp female in yet another way besides preventing infanticide: it avoids inbreeding and the degradation any species suffers that practices it.

As their wild habitat resources are usually too dispersed for an entire chimp group to forage close together, individual chimpanzees live a spread-out existence, though often, they stay in touch by remaining within "shouting distance" of each other. Chimpanzee females with dependent offspring, especially, are often quite solitary, traveling alone and avoiding the central hub of political male interaction.[10]

In the chimpanzee universe, female individuals rise to the top over time; their status as emerging leaders is largely an issue of personality and the experience of age. And in closer quarters of zoos and reservations, it has been observed that in confinement, female chimps tend to band together to make alliances and control the males through unity, collectively disciplining any males that get too far out of line.

Chimpanzee and Human Violence

When we compare the violence of chimp and human behavior, it is obvious that all the fundamental elements of group identification, xenophobia, and lethal conflict that characterize the inhumane level of human violence in today's world are already present embryonically in these "primitive" chimps.[11]

Both species are strongly territorial, as both chimps and humans are capable of calculated, cold-blooded persecution and murder of their own kind.[12] With both humans and chimps, the gulf between the in-group and the out-group is so huge that aggression falls into two categories: one contained and ritualized within the group, the other all-out, gratuitous, and lethal violence between groups.

The in-group always finds reason to see itself as superior. An extreme example of this was Hitler's vilification of the Jews as an out-group, as less than human. In both humans and apes, the switches are controlled by the perception of shared versus competing interests. As long as individuals share a common purpose, like having a common enemy, negative feelings can be suppressed. But as soon as the common purpose is gone, tensions within the group can rise to the surface and cause internal strife.[13]

The evolutionary link between male-centric chimpanzee and human violent behavior is made clear by the fact that the only animals in which gangs of males deliberately set out to exterminate neighboring males happen to be humans and chimpanzees. "Lethal raiding," as it is called, is the human pattern most similar to that of the chimpanzees. Such raid activity consists of a group of males launching a surprise attack on another group when they feel they have the upper hand and that there's little chance they will suffer themselves. The chimp and human goal is to kill other males, abduct their women and girls, and expand their territory.

In the final analysis, from chimp to human, the adrenalin/testosterone pursuit of power defines the male-centric primate paradigm and culture of our species. In the human sphere, powered by geometric expansion, it has resulted in the global developmental, technological dilemmas, and catastrophes of such magnitude that the species is at the point of destroying the planet and committing suicide in the process.

The Way of the Bonobo

At first, the bonobo species was largely dismissed and relegated to secondary status by the scientific establishment. They were seen as a curious but minor variation of the chimpanzee. But thanks to the diligent work of Dr. de Waal and others, it soon became apparent that in truth, bonobo culture was the very antithesis of chimpanzee culture.

Unlike the physically impressive male chimpanzees, the bonobo males have slim upper bodies, narrow shoulders, and thin necks. A lot of their weight is in their legs, which are longer than a chimp's and, on the whole, present a less daunting and more cerebral appearance. Their social structure and cultural values, moreover, amount to a complete renunciation of the chimpanzee way.

Bonobos are egalitarian, free-spirited, peaceful by nature, empathetic, with a healthy sexual appetite, and their social structure is wholly female-centric. As the result of their egalitarian, female-centric social structure, the bonobos have evolved greater collective and individual nonviolent, empathic response patterns toward any challengers, whether they come from within the group or come at the group from the outside. In bonobo culture, as in other female-centric primate cultures, conflict resolution is through activation of the progesterone-oxytocin axis, through love and sex.

Bonobos demonstrate a rich sexuality with no prohibitions and few inhibitions in the absence of the cultural overlays that we humans put over our sex lives. Bonobos have sex in all conceivable positions and partner combinations. They disprove the notion that sex is intended solely for procreation, as three quarters of their sexual activity has nothing to do with procreation, being with the same sex or the opposite sex during non-fertile periods in the female.

And because bonobos have lots of sex, they, unlike chimps and humans, have no infanticide. By accepting the advances of many males, the female, in effect, buffers herself against infanticide because then the male could wind up killing his own cubs. These female-dominated, sexualized societies effectively put a halt to infanticide because males are in no position to know which is their offspring. This fact also allows bonobo females to rejoin their group right after having given birth, meaning they are ready to copulate again within months.

How did the bonobo manage to evolve into the extraordinarily sensitive, gentle creatures who don't engage in deadly warfare, do very little hunting, don't have male dominance, and enjoy enormous amounts of sex?[14] The secret to the bonobo way of peace, pleasure, and harmony points to the very essence of the evolutionary direction of mammals in general and primates in particular, which is the evolution of empathy that occurs in a female-centric paradigm and social culture.

It was first noted in the 1980s that the rich environment of their forest habitat allows bonobo groups to gather and operate in larger numbers than their chimp cousins. And while they take every opportunity to underline territorial boundaries, they keep the door open to friendly contact. The females especially intermingle peacefully with each other, leading to the trade of goods, sharing the river water, and even intermarriage between groups.

As the family structure of the bonobos is female-centric and egalitarian, the most stable bonds between female and male bonobos are not sexual but social. The deepest female-male bond pairing in bonobo society is not between the inseminator and the inseminated but between mother and son. Accordingly, the male hierarchy of the bonobos is a maternal affair and largely determined by female social rank.[15] And while, occasionally, individual male bonobos may supplant individual females, especially younger ones, females will always collectively dominate the males.[16]

By maintaining control of the food supply through female solidarity,[17] the female bonobos have done more than just erode the male supremacy so common among the chimps. They have actually turned the tables on the males and flipped the hierarchy upside down. As de Waal put it, among the bonobos, "instead of stirring from below, the weaker sex acts from above, making it the *de facto* stronger sex."[18] The lesson of the bonobos is that only female solidarity can control the excesses of male violence and maintain peace. Even among the chimpanzees, especially those in captivity, it has been observed that females occasionally employ female solidarity as a tool to control and subdue an out-of-control male. Among the bonobos, their long history of female bonding has taught them skills of working as a team to achieve their goals.

As they come into sexual maturity, bonobo females are not driven out by their community or abducted by neighboring males. They simply become vagabonds, hanging out increasingly at the group's periphery, breaking the tie with their mothers. They leave when they are about seven, at the time they develop their first genital swellings. They become floaters, visiting neighboring communities before settling down in one. Compared with chimpanzee society, social change in the female-ruled bonobo land is both less common and more gradual, for only when the top female weakens or dies will there be movement, and then, only near the top.

Bonobo and Human Kindness

We learned how zebra fish, if deprived from oxytocin, become developmentally impaired in their social interactions with other zebra fish in the life of the shoal. The oxytocin-deprived zebra fish fail to develop the proper responses to group stimuli and are unable to move in concert with their neighbors in the shoal. By their lack of proper behaviors within the group, they not only put the shoal in greater danger but they also mark themselves as targets and hasten their own demise.

In the evolution of mammals, timely exposure to oxytocin is also essential in producing socially successful offspring. The emotional process of bonding with our offspring resides in parts of the brain so ancient that we share them with mammals as diverse as rats, dog, elephants, and monkeys.[19]

Conceiving and bringing the young to term internally is another step to safeguard the longer developmental sequence of the young until they are capable of fending for themselves. Additionally, for all mammals, the dependency of the offspring on maternal care persists well after birth. During both phases of this process, the mammalian young are continually subjected to infusion with maternal oxytocin to ensure their proper hormonal and neurological imprinting in order to learn who or what is friend or foe.

In general, the purpose of evolution is to increase the chances of successful reproduction and the creation of the next generation in any given species. Bonobos teach us that "fellow-feeling" and empathy are as equally important parts of our mammalian and primate heritage as our chimp-like capacity and penchant for violence. Primatologists have documented numerous examples of bonobo kindness and empathy, both in the wild and in captivity, showing how apes can put themselves into another's shoes in emotionally meaningful moments.[20]

The evolution of the primates is further testament that the evolutionary roots of empathic thinking and action are likely to be found in mutuality and assistance of kin.[21] Looked at from this perspective, early human societies, much like the bonobos, must have been breeding grounds for the "survival of the kindest" aimed at fostering group coherence and reciprocation. In as much as evolution depends on the continued success of a trait over millions of years, parental care in mammals cannot be separated from lactation. During the 180 million years of mammalian evolution, females who responded to their offsprings' needs outreproduced those who were cold and distant.

It is no surprise, therefore, that in individual humans, development of empathy occurs even before the development of language and the distinction between self and others.[22] It's a well-known fact, for example, that babies will start to cry when they hear another baby crying before babies know how to comfort others. For the very same reason, we should not be surprised by gender differences in human empathy. They appear well before socialization: the first sign of empathy—crying when another baby cries—is already more typical in girl babies than in boy babies. And in later life, empathy remains more developed in females than in males.

Our close relatives, the bonobos, can teach us that compassion is not a recent weakness going against the grain of nature but a formidable power that is as much a part of who and what we are as the competitive tendencies it seeks to overcome.[23] It is not difficult to envision how, once this sensibility came into existence, its range could expand and sympathy for "the other" became a goal in itself as the centerpiece of human morality and a universal aspect of religion.

We urgently need kindness because the question facing a growing world population is not so much whether we can handle crowding but whether we will be fair and just in the distribution of resources. Will we go for all-out competition, or will we do the humane thing?

Oxytocin and the Revolution in Evolution

In primate evolution, survival of the individual and survival of the species involve the two basic ingredients of food and sex in a fundamentally asymmetric arrangement between the sexes. Among chimps, the situation is fairly straightforward. Everybody takes care of their own needs. Males forage for themselves, while females forage for themselves and their offspring. They stay away from the group's power dynamics, where the alpha male takes what he wants, either sex or food, from whatever female he wants.

Among the bonobos, it's a bit more complicated on account of the asymmetry. For female bonobos, food is most important, especially when they are pregnant or lactating, when they spend the majority of their time fulfilling their biological reproductive function—ovulating, being pregnant, birthing, nurturing, and educating the young. For the bonobo males, finding a mate is most important. Since the males are not "bringing up the kids," they have more free time to procure food and offer it to the females in exchange for sex. For the females it's a no-brainer; they are only too happy to seal the deal and engage in reciprocal intimacies.

Oxytocin, as we saw previously, is a critical hormone in reproduction and maternal care, which is why females have more of it than males. In female-centric societies such as the bonobos, where physical affection is common and sexual tolerance is high, it's likely the denizens have higher oxytocin levels. As the touchy-feely hormone, oxytocin secretion results in a peaceful and loving attitude. As de Waal put it, "Bonobos are probably brimming with the stuff."[24]

It has also been established that oxytocin is an active ingredient in the sexual experience of both sexes. The synthesis of this hormone spikes after sexual activity, producing post-coital symptoms of languor, contentment, and bliss. Given the unbelievable sexual promiscuity of all bonobos, female and male alike, there can be no doubt that the sex lives of the bonobos are entirely superior to those of the chimpanzees, and this difference further affects the health and lifespans of the respective species.

In the female-centric bonobo societies, the males are much less violence-oriented than their chimp cousins' male-centric societies. They lead longer and healthier lives than their chauvinistic chimp counterparts. Male chimps also do not stand much chance to enjoy the calming effects of oxytocin. The chimpanzees get way less of it than the bonobos! Under the influence of the testosterone-adrenaline axis, the fear-and-rage dialectics predominate in the chimp culture, both in social structure and individual chimp physiology.

Chimps in power do get a lot of sex, most if not all of it. But it cannot be said that they're exactly wallowing in bliss. Being in a position of power and having to constantly defend it is stressful, which is reflected in, and measurable by, the levels of the stress hormone cortisol in the blood.[25] Moreover, since stress compromises the immune system, it's not unusual for high-ranking chimps to develop the ulcers and heart attacks also common to corporate CEOs.

Compared to the bonobos, the sex life of chimps who are not in power is from minimal to none.[26] Sex is possible only when luring a willing female away from the old man's prying eyes for a secretive romp in the proverbial hay. Not only is the sex life of bonobos superior to that of the chimps, but the ratio of offspring survival also tells a significant tale. In the wild, the male-female ratio of bonobos is almost one to one, whereas the male-female ratio for the chimps is one male for every two females.[27] That means that the male chimp population suffers from an extraordinary rate of mortality, in which half of the male chimp babies do not survive, presumably killed by males newly risen to supremacy.

Evolution and the Bonobo-Chimpanzee Divergence

When we compare bonobo and chimpanzee societies, the interpenetration of their yin and yang, on both the individual and the species level, must always be kept in mind. On the individual level, each male and female has both male and female hormones so the percentages and ratios of empathy and caring, aggression and submission, differ to create an infinite number of unique individuals.

The interpenetration of the opposites also applies collectively on the species level. In the wild, as you would expect, bonobo males are half as aggressive as chimpanzees, while female bonobos are more aggressive than female chimpanzees. However, female bonobos also know aggression and fight, and male chimps can also display tenderness. Female dominance in chimpanzee society, likewise, is not unheard of, and neither is male assertiveness in bonobo society. And while chimpanzee social structure is often referred to as patriarchal, it is not unheard of for chimp females to forge coalitions against males, much as the bonobos do.

The lessons we can learn from a comparison of the bonobo and chimpanzee methods of social organization are many, but two jump out immediately. From the bonobos, we learn how the cooperation of women is capable of constraining the competitive drive of the males and creates an egalitarian society based on empathy and cooperation. From the chimpanzees society, we must learn the fundamental class structure in primate society arises with the entrenchment of short-term, male-centric crisis authority structures as permanent long-term power structures of institutionalized dominance of male over female.

Today, both species of primates live in similar environments of the tropical forests along the Zaire River—chimps north of the river, bonobos to the south. But about 2.5 million years ago, there was a severe and sustained drought in southern Zaire. One effect of the draught was to wipe out the preferred food plants of gorillas that shared the environment with the common ancestors of the chimps and gorillas, sending them fleeing north of the river. After the drought ended, the forests returned, but the gorillas stayed north and did not return south of the river.[28] This situation proved to be a boon for the chimps that had stayed south of the river. They now had the forests to themselves and could feast on the fiber foods that had previously been monopolized by the gorillas. With this additional food to tide them over between fruit trees, they could travel in larger, more stable parties, and form strong social bonds of female-centric society. They became bonobos.[29]

If the situation was a feast for the southern chimps, it meant famine and hardship for the northern chimps. Henceforth they had to compete for and share the territory and its resources with the gorillas. This meant that food resources became widely scattered. Having to continually compete for fruit, and occasionally meat, in order to find enough to eat, the female chimps dispersed daily, deep into the forest with their infants. In a cascade of cause and effect, this meant that the female chimps simply were unable spend enough time together to forge the strong, collective bonds necessary to control the male drive for dominance. And so, the changes in social behavior that occurred in response to this environmental reality led the chimps down the evolutionary path toward a more violent, male-centric society.

This evolutionary divergence between the chimpanzees and bonobos illustrates the basic thesis underlying this book, which we will develop further in subsequent chapters. This thesis is that societies faced with extreme challenges and that exist in a constant state of crisis tend to be more male-centric and authoritarian, whereas societies that have evolved to exist in relative ease and harmony tend to be more female-centric and egalitarian.

The knowledge of how and why the chimpanzee and bonobo societies evolved into such radically opposite types of primate can certainly help us humans make more informed decisions as to what kind of social structure we want for ourselves. Humanity's very awareness of the fact that such divergent and opposing paradigms of social structure can and do evolve gives our species the freedom to choose and make informed choices as to what type of social organization will maximize our health and happiness in our own society.

The Mellowing of the Old Fellas

One interesting phenomenon that seems to occur in all primate societies, regardless of their type of social organization, including bonobo, chimpanzee, and human, is the mellowing of the males with age. Drawing on many years of observations of chimps, researchers Dr. Rosati and Dr. Machanda, the director of long-term research at the Kibale Chimpanzee Project in Uganda, reported that male chimps, at least, display the very same inclinations as humans.[30] "As they got older, the chimps developed more mutual friendships and fewer one-sided friendships. They also exhibited a more positive approach to their whole community, continuing grooming of other chimps, including those that weren't close friends, at the same rate, but with a drop in aggression... Why chimps concentrate on fewer friends and behave less aggressively as they age are still unknowns..."[31]

Actually, I believe we do know why primate males mellow as they age, and the reason is to be found in the interaction between the female and male hormonal axes we discussed previously. There are two interrelated hormonal changes taking place as the primate male ages that account for the phenomenon. One is the natural decrease in the production of testosterone, the (mostly male) hormone involved in aggression, and the other is the natural increase in the production of oxytocin, the (mostly female) hormone associated with social bonding. The aging-related decrease of testosterone has been well-known and documented, but the aging-related increase in oxytocin has only recently been established. Paul J. Zak of Claremont Graduate University of California established in a study that people release more of the hormone as they get older. He concludes his study by saying that "oxytocin release increases with age and is associated with life satisfaction and prosocial behaviors."[32]

The greater sociability of aging primate males is quite understandable when we consider the inhibitory effect testosterone has on oxytocin. As primate males age and their production of testosterone decreases, the less inhibition there will be on the production of oxytocin, and consequently, the individual will tend to become more empathic, trusting, and social.

Endnotes

1   Josephine Harvey, "Egg-Napping Drama Unfolds in Dutch Queer Penguin Commu-
    nity", HuffPost, October 22, 2020, https://www.huffpost.com/entry/gay-penguins
    -egg-kidnapping-netherlands_n_5f920d86c5b66d4a0dbd72c6.

2   William Fischer, "Animal Species That Practice Same-Sex Coupling," Grunge,
    February 03, 2023, https://www.grunge.com/884335/animal-species-that-practice
    -same-sex-coupling/.

3   Frans de Waal, Our Inner Ape: The Best and Worst of Human Nature, (London:
    Granta Books, 2005), 237.

4   Ibid., 1.

5   Ibid., 18.

6   Ibid., 54.

7   Ibid., 1.

8   Ibid., 68.

9   Ibid., 104.

10 Ibid., 62.

11 Ibid., 129.

12 Ibid., 133.

13 Ibid., 136.

14 Ibid., 30.

15 Ibid., 65.

16 Ibid., 64.

17 Ibid., 11.

18 Ibid., 83.

19 Ibid., 178–9.

20 Ibid., 184.

21 Ibid., 172.

22 Ibid., 174.

23 Ibid., 168.

24 Ibid., 105.

25 Ibid., 46.

26 Ibid., 95.

27 Ibid., 65.

28 WGBH Educational Foundation, "Chimps and Bonobos," PBS, 2001,
    https://www.pbs.org/wgbh/evolution/library/07/3/l_073_03.html.

29 Ibid.

30 James Gorman, "No Grumpy Old Men in the World of Chimps," New York Times,
    October 22, 2020, https://www.nytimes.com/2020/10/22/science/aging-chimps
    -friendship.html.

31 Ibid.

32 Paul J. Zak, Ben Curry, Tyler Owen, and Jorge A. Barraza, "Oxytocin Release
    Increases with Age and Is Associated with Life Satisfaction and Prosocial Behaviors,"
    Frontiers in Behavioral Neuroscience 16 (2022), https://doi.org/10.3389/fnbeh
    .2022.846234.

Chapter 4

Hunter-Gatherer Societies (50,000–10,000 Years Ago)

The Domestication of Fire

Roughly 2.5 million years ago, our Australopithecus ancestors closely resembled modern primates, such as chimpanzees, who spend about eight hours a day foraging and eating. In between chewing and digesting all that raw pith, stalk, and root, gorillas and chimps sleep nine to 12 hours. Such a routine doesn't leave much daylight time for leisure activities more energy-intensive than lazy grooming.

Then fire changed everything. Learning how to use and control fire took place in several stages and occurred over a period of time of hundreds of thousands of years. Anthropologists don't know precisely how humans first began to marshal fire for their use, roughly 1 million years ago, but evidence of more complex fire management to change biomes can be found as far back as 200,000 to 100,000 years ago. Increasingly, the control of fire enabled important changes in human behavior, health, energy expenditure, and geographic expansion.

It most likely began through interaction with burned landscapes and foraging in the wake of wildfires, as observed in various wild animals. Even today, in the African savanna, chimpanzees are among the animals that preferentially forage in recently burned areas. The first step in the control of fire would have been to learn how to transport it, for transporting fire to another locale and setting that on fire would have provided advantages in food acquisition. Also, acquiring control over fire had the benefit of warding off predators and, thus, allowed our ancestors to climb down from their tree beds and sleep soundly on the ground in the open.

A second step in the control of fire would be the ability to maintain one. Maintaining a fire over an extended period, as for a season (such as the dry season), may have led to the development of base campsites. A next step would have been to build an enclosure such as a circle of stones or hearth around the fire which would have been conducive to establishing more permanent settlements. And if our ancestors needed to protect themselves from the weather, fire was also used to provide the more permanent and protected shelter of caves. Evidence suggests that fire was used first to clear out caves prior to occupation and second to keep warm while they were living in them. Fire was used increasingly as a tool in weapon making, in the creation of art, and in the carrying out of ceremonial and sacred activities.

Finally, the crowning achievement in the control of fire was acquiring the skill of starting one from scratch, generally with a friction device with hardwood rubbing against softwood, as in a bow drill.[1] The skill of creating fire allowed our ancestors to move into much colder regions that would have previously been uninhabitable after the loss of body hair.

By softening meat and vegetables, fire predigests our food, allowing us to eat and retain more calories in less time, allowing the evolutionary propensity of humans to grow huge, energy-greedy brains that gobble up about a fifth of our calories, a far greater proportion than other primates' brains consume.

As our forebear cousins on the web of evolution, both bonobo and chimps were well on their way to developing the primate intelligence seated in the brain's neocortex. They have been recorded using tools, modifying sticks, rocks, grass, and leaves and using them for hunting and acquiring honey, termites, ants, nuts, and water. The species has also been found creating sharpened sticks to spear small mammals. An evolutionary branching of the primate line continued for millennia and finally produced us, the Homo sapiens species, the hunter-gatherer societies that lived and flourished during the Upper Paleolithic era of 50,000 to 10,000 years ago.

The Traditional Consensus on Hunter-Gatherer Societies

The traditional scholarly consensus has been that early human hunter-gatherer societies were more male-centered and chimp-like than female-centered and bonobo-like, with alpha males running the show and the females largely subservient to the males. But research conducted more recently concluded that this view reflected the cultural bias of most researchers in our male-centric Western civilization and that, in reality, those early hunter-gatherer human societies were based on the more egalitarian female-centric bonobo paradigm.

It appears now that, like the bonobos, most human hunter-gatherer societies operated on enlightened egalitarian principles. Not only did men and women tend to have equal influence on where their group lived but also who they lived with. In hunter-gatherer societies, sexual promiscuity was encouraged among women and men alike. In other words, sexual equality is not a recent invention, but has been the norm for humans for most of our evolutionary history.[2]

Mark Dyble, an anthropologist at University College London, has argued that sexual equality is an important feature of human social organization that "hasn't really been highlighted before" though, as *The Guardian*'s Science Correspondent Hannah Devlin so aptly paraphrased, it has "played an important role in shaping human society and evolution."[3] One of these important features is that sexual equality resulted in uncertainty on the paternity of the offspring, which maximized the cooperative approach of all toward child-rearing.[4]

Recent excavations in South America have further confirmed Dyble's hypothesis of the equality of the sexes in the hunter-gatherer societies. The unearthing of new evidence has definitively disproven the generally accepted, culturally built-in male-centric assumption that prehistoric men hunted while women gathered and reared their young. The irrefutable evidence is that women in hunter-gatherer societies both gathered *and* hunted.

Randall Haas, the archaeologist from UC Davis who discovered this evidence, recalls the moment in 2018 when his team of researchers gathered around the excavated burial of an individual lain to rest in the Andes Mountains of Peru some 9,000 years ago. Along with the bones of what appeared to be a human adult was an impressive—and extensive—kit of stone tools an ancient hunter would need to take down big game, from engaging the hunt to preparing the hide. Haas supposes that "he must have been a really great hunter, a really important person in society."[5]

But they were in for a big surprise. Further analysis revealed that the remains found alongside the toolkit were from a biological female. What's more, this ancient female hunter proved not to be an anomaly. Spurred on by their discovery, Haas's team engaged in a review of previously studied burials throughout the Americas. They found that between 30 and 50% of big game hunters could have been biologically female.

The Human Innovation: The Nuclear Family

In view of our discussion of bonobo and chimpanzee society, the question arises as to which model of social organization our hunter-gatherer forebears adopted—the male centric one of the chimps or the female-centric one of the bonobos? Undoubtedly, in the primate evolution from apes to hunter-gatherer societies, climate would have been a factor too. In milder climates with abundance of food supply, the female-centric paradigm would likely emerge the dominant one, whereas in more severe climates with scarcity of resources, the male-centric paradigm would likely become dominant. Moreover, there is no reason to believe that this was an either/or choice rather than a both/and occurrence in the evolution of the primates. Undoubtedly, as the primates evolved, many experimental variations and combinations of the chimp-bonobo polarity were attempted. And eventually some mix occurred that led to the immediate predecessor of the present-day human species, the hunter-gatherer societies of the Paleolithic age.

These groups of humans led a nomadic lifestyle; they were always on the move and had few personal possessions. They were egalitarian, had no permanent or hereditary leaders, and made decisions on a rotation based on merit. Hunter-gatherer societies were structured as three-tiered networks. The fundamental unit was the household, most often consisting of five or six individuals, often parents and their children. The second, intermediate level consisted of a cluster of three to four closely related households who shared food frequently. The third and highest grouping is the wider camp generally consisting of some fifty to seventy people.

The early kinship grouping of the hunter-gatherers seemed to resemble more the "anything goes" attitudes of female-centric bonobo society than the authoritarian force-and-violence model practiced by the male-centric chimpanzees. Hunter-gatherer society kinship reckoning was matrilineal and, for the most part, matrilocal, with the husbands moving in with the wives. In this easygoing environment, one experiment that proved increasingly successful was one-to-one female-to-male pair bonding. This bond was based on an agreement, implicit if not explicit, to limit one's sexual activity to the partner and not engage in any "extramarital" sex. And though humans have by no means always been faithful to these restrictions, they did establish a universal human ideal.

The hunter-gatherer women realized that a man who was certain that he was indeed the father of his kids was much more motivated to care for them and bring home the bacon. This was especially important, of course, during the times when the female was primarily occupied with reproductive functions. Though normally cooperative and egalitarian, with both males and females hunting and gathering, during times of child-rearing, the female could not contribute as much energy to procuring food and could rely on "her" male to make up for the deficit. In the course of her reproductive life, the average Neolithic woman bore some 8 to 10 children, usually starting around age 19.

Thus, little by little, the nuclear family emerged as the next development in primate evolutionary process, and monogamy became the new gold standard of human behavior. As de Waal put it, ""Every human society has nuclear families, whereas apes have none…"[6] So what makes us unique as human primates is that our social organization is characterized by nuclear families. This process would lead to the entire restructuring of human society around the nuclear family units involving paternal care as well as maternal care for their offspring.

The nuclear family was evolutionary advancement because it promoted cohesion, bonding, and cooperation within the hunter-gatherer group. Whereas the bonobos had only male bonding, and the bonobos had only female bonding, the human nuclear family allows both female and male bonding within the larger group on the basis of female-centric or male-centric activities. Within the dyad, cooperation and the sharing of power between females and males was democratic and egalitarian. Neither female nor male was superior or inferior in social status, for they were equal. Between the household of a cluster, and between the clusters of a group, cooperation and egalitarianism likewise made for a largely peaceful and cooperative existence.

The cooperation and sharing of food was a particularly crucial adaptation to hunter-gatherer lifestyle, for no other apes share food like humans do, within the context of groups consisting of clusters of nuclear families. Food sharing was central to the resilience of hunter-gatherers and, therefore, proved central to the evolution of the human species. Thus, says de Waal, "our primate ancestors lived for millions of years in small groups of small-scale societies as true egalitarians. Hunter gatherers and horticulturalist, these societies, like the Navajo Indians, Hottentots, Mbuti pygmies, Kung San, Inuit, and so on, completely eliminated distinctions of wealth, power and status, except for differences between the sexes and the generations, and the emphasis was on equality and sharing."[7]

Daily Life Among the Hunter-Gatherers

Since hunter-gatherer societies are still living side by side with technological global culture, it is possible to observe and learn from them. Indeed, many anthropologists today are doing just that, visiting and spending time with the hunter-gatherer societies to observe and study firsthand the daily functioning of their female-centric culture. We can learn about their work-life balance, their parenting philosophy, and their religious conception of the world and their place in it.

Regarding work-life balance, the ancient and contemporary hunter-gatherers could teach modern humanity a thing or two. In his book, *Work: A Deep History, from the Stone Age to the Age of Robots*, James Suzman describes his decades of work with a typical hunter-gatherer tribe of Ju/'hoansi bushmen from Southern Africa.[8] The Ju/'hoansi continued to live and practice the ancient ways of their forebears, far away from and unpolluted by modern society, well into the 20th century. Suzman reported the Ju/'hoansi work less than 20 hours a week, which is less than half of the standard work week, not including domestic labor and child care, which left the Ju/'hoansi with considerably more downtime. Their work-life balance consisted of the fact that they liked to work but were not addicted to it. Their lifestyle was marked by an easy and productive rhythm of sleeping, eating, hunting and gathering, resting, lounging around, and spending time with the kids.[9]

In that downtime, the Ju/'hoansi remained strikingly free, over centuries, from the urge to cram it with activities that our modern culture would classify as "productive." By day, they did go on walks with children to teach them how to read the canvas of the desert for the footprints of animals. But they also lounged, gossiped, and flirted. During firelit evenings, they sang, danced, and told stories. All in all, Suzman described the Ju/'hoansi as "healthy and cheerful, perfectly content to work as little as possible and—not coincidentally—ingenious at designing customs that, by discouraging competition and status-seeking," maintain the essentially democratic nature of Ju/'hoansi society.[10]

For example, when a Ju/'hoan hunter returned with a big kill, one tribesman explained, "We always speak of his meat as worthless. This way we cool his heart and make him gentle," preventing the hunter from exhibiting excessive pride in his accomplishment. This practice became known among researchers as "insulting the hunter's meat." In a similar vein, the tribe also strongly discourages pride of ownership by insisting that "the actual owner of the meat, the individual charged with its distribution, was not the hunter, but the person who owned the arrow that killed the animal." Suzman explained that "by rewarding the semi-random contributor of the arrow, the Ju/'hoansi kept their most talented hunters in check, in order to defend the group's egalitarianism." A welcome result was that "the elderly, the short-sighted, the clubfooted and the lazy got a chance to be the center of attention once in a while."[11]

In their child-rearing methods, the hunter-gatherer culture also successfully utilizes the gentle way to raise balanced human beings who are eager and capable to participate in their society. Michaeleen Doucleff is one such anthropologist and parent who ventured forth into the field to study just this approach. In her book, *Hunt, Gather, Parent*, she relates "what ancient cultures can teach us about the lost art of raising happy, helpful little humans."[12] Ms. Doucleff took her daughter, Rosy, in tow and went to live and work in rural villages in Mexico, Canada, and Tanzania, to immerse herself and Rosy in the ancient local child-rearing techniques and try them out on her tempestuous daughter. Doucleff's main conclusion is that that hunter-gatherer parental strategy is a low-key approach that lets the kids learn from adult example and help out in the domestic chores without much of either corrective interventions or praise. This is how, in a gentle but effective method, kids acquire skills in childhood that will later enable them to pitch in naturally because they feel like part of the family enterprise.

This type of tolerant parenting also extends to the situations where the child is being disobedient or behaving antisocially. Hunter-gatherer parenting views kids as "illogical, newbie citizens trying to figure out the proper behavior," so their parents don't take misbehavior personally, and do not berate or shout at them; either they go silent and observe the child, or they walk away. Doucleff compares this to the Western ways in which parents often exclude their kids from their own activities and make them feel that they are not part of the team. She gives the example of parents who think they're saving time by plopping a child down in front of a screen while they cook dinner.[13]

Animating all these hunter-gatherer notions about work-life balance, child-rearing, male-female relations, friends and enemies, made up their religious beliefs and practices. Their life, spiritual and otherwise, centered around the inherent interconnectedness of all things, natural and human, as expressed in the belief system of what, today, is called "animism." Animism perceives that all objects, including rocks, rivers, weather systems, places, plants, critters, creatures, and humans possess a distinct energy, experienced as the spiritual essence, or soul, that animates their relative state of being and or aliveness. The egalitarian nature of hunter-gatherer societies predisposed them to imbue their gods and spirits with only limited powers to interfere in human affairs. As a consequence, the worship of ancestor spirits or high gods who are active in human affairs was absent in these early humans; certainly they were not considered omniscient or omnipotent, in any way. On the contrary, they were actually thought of as impersonal forces that were pretty much uncaring for human well-being and morality.[14]

Violence and War Among the Hunter-Gatherers

In the previous chapter, we described the bonobo-chimpanzee polarity as representing the yin-yang of primate nature. Extending this idea, we consider that the yin-yang of human nature can accordingly be best described in terms of our "inner apes," namely the bonobo and chimpanzee aspects of human nature. We then also described hunter-gatherer culture as essentially bonobo-like in its female-centric, cooperative, and peaceful nature and, accordingly, consciously sought to avoid conflict with other human groups.

Accepting this, the question arises, how did the yang component of the hunter-gatherer, the male-centric, neurohormonal, testosterone-adrenalin axis that produces violence in any primate, express itself in hunter-gatherer culture? Under what conditions in hunter-gatherer society did humanity's inner chimp have the opportunity to come out and express itself in violence? In answer to this question, it appears at least two types of conditions were conducive to creating outbreaks of hunter-gatherer violence. One such precipitating condition was found to be climate change, and the other was the perceived need to augment the numbers of females in their group and, thereby, assure the group's future through increased numerical strength.

One example of war between hunter-gatherer groups as the result of climatic catastrophe dates back some 13,000 years. With the increasing disappearance of the ice sheets covering much of the northern hemisphere during this period, major climatic and environmental changes occurred. In Africa, the Nile Valley was hit particularly hard and, during this time, became a refuge for different groups of humans that had once lived peacefully over a wide area,[15] but the crisis put them into conflict with each other, with disastrous results. As the increasingly arid climate drove rival groups toward the river, where it would have been easier to find animals to hunt and fish, they wound up competing with each other for food and resources.

Grisly evidence of this war was found in 1961, when the earliest known mass cemetery of killings was unearthed at Jebel Sahaba in the Nile Valley in present-day Sudan.[16] Sixty-one human skeletons were found at the site and all skeletons show injuries sustained as a result of brutal and intense violence. Radiocarbon analysis determined the bones to be over 13,000 years old, making them the earliest evidence of organized warfare between human groups. Everybody in what would have been a community of hunters, fishers, and gatherers had been the target of violence, with men, women, and children affected in an indiscriminate manner. That the injuries were mainly puncture wounds from weapons such as spears and arrows and that many of the victims had both healed and unhealed injuries strongly suggests that the dead were not the result of one violent engagement but of a string of recurring violent clashes that took place over several years.[17]

As mentioned, the other condition that would cause hunter-gatherers to go on the war path was the perceived need within the group to augment their numbers to secure their continued growth and expansion of the group. Frans de Waal writes, "The majority of hunter-gatherer societies follow a pattern of occasional 'lethal raidings,' i.e., waging limited war every couple of years for the purpose of killing the males and abducting the females."[18] In this respect, it is well to remind ourselves that unlike the bonobos, where male and female are close to the same size, the human male's chimp heritage is reflected in the size differences between the sexes.

Now the human males, mostly through cooperative hunting of larger game, were also learning to curb their individual aggressiveness and cooperate in teamwork with other males in a hierarchical structure. It prepared them to act collectively, both in defense of their wealth if attacked and offensively in acquiring more wealth through aggression and war. Thus, by pointing out that "only chimps and humans engage in these 'lethal raidings,'" de Waal stresses that to fully realize our humanity, we must come to terms with our inner chimp as well as our inner bonobo, and we will have to confront the reality of the human male's penchant for violence.[19]

The Transition from Hunter-Gatherer to Herder-Farmer

After the domestication of fire, the next leap forward in the evolution of the human species was the domestication of plants and animals and the transformation from the nomadic existence of the hunter-gatherer groups into the settled life of herders and farmers.

It is hard to underestimate the extreme influence that the change from nomadic existence to settled life had on the nuclear family and the role of the male in it. There was a marked change from an egalitarian partnership of caring to the male-centric paradigm becoming more dominant over the female-paradigm, especially in the economic sphere. The nomadic life of the hunter-gatherers did not favor the accumulation of material things. With settling down as farmers and herders came a natural accumulation of things, such as property and wealth, both collective and individual.

The cattle that were kept and herded, the grains, vegetables, and fruits that were grown and harvested represented collective and individual wealth and power, and these realms of influence were increasingly claimed by the male sex, as the female sex, over time, was relegated to, sub-ordinated to, and made dependent upon the male sex as the final decision maker and prime power in the nuclear family. When our ancestors settled down from a nomadic existence and began to accumulate material goods, the motivation for male control only increased. In addition to passing on genes to the next generation, the males were now also passing on their material wealth to their progeny.

This new male-centric nuclear family must really be thought of as an unintended but exceedingly consequential outgrowth of male assistance with the rearing of offspring. More than anything else, the nuclear family has been key to the rapid demographic evolution of humankind, allowing human expansion to cover the world and create a truly global civilization in only a few thousand years.

The first agricultural civilizations were made possible by the evolution of the nuclear family as a way to collectivize the competitive male spirit into a hierarchically unified, many-tiered effort. In this process, the simplistic authoritarian chimp model of social structure in which the superior strength of the alpha male enforced his sexual dominance in the group exclusive of all other males was modified into and replaced by what biologists call "cooperative breeding" among sexual competitors. With the evolution of the male-centric nuclear family, every male shared in the social hierarchy and power structure because he was the master of his own little domestic unit.

In other words, the secret of the long-term benefit of the nuclear family in the evolution of the human species stemmed from the fact that it allowed multiple individuals working together in a hierarchy on tasks that benefit the whole, allowing the community to accomplish more than each individual could ever hope to accomplish on his own. Moreover, by having a family to bring the spoils home to, each male was strongly motivated because he had a personal stake in the successful outcome of the cooperative effort.

The Neolithic Revolution and Agricultural Civilization

Some 11,000 years ago, an explosive change took place in the evolution of the human species that completely altered the course of its development. Human neural development and integration, which had slowly accumulated over millennia of evolution, reached another threshold and broke through to a new, higher level of intelligence and consciousness. If the leap from primate to hunter-gatherer society was made possible by the taming and control of fire, the next leap of human evolution into agricultural civilization was made possible through the taming and control of water.

It was called the Neolithic Revolution, and as it unfolded, the human species transitioned from the highly mobile social organization of hunter-gatherer societies to highly settled and stationary societies based on the organized, domesticated cultivation of plants and animals in agricultural and pastoral operations. Because the availability of water was a precondition for such societies to arise and flourish, many of them originated in valleys of major continental rivers or coastal areas of seas and oceans, such as the Mediterranean. Such locations came to be called "cradles of civilization" and occurred almost simultaneously all over the world, in the Tigris and Euphrates river valleys in Mesopotamia, the Nile in Egypt, the Indus river in India, the Yangtze and Yellow rivers in China, and on the Greek islands and mainland for the Minoans and Greeks.

The roots of all organized religion today can be traced back to this Neolithic Revolution that began 11,000 years ago in the Near East. The characteristics of early hunter-gatherer religion evolved in the proto-Neolithic and Neolithic periods. During this time, this hunter-gatherer belief system changed with the development of shamanism, the belief in an afterlife, and the worship of ancestors and high gods who are active in human affairs.[20] Shamanism developed by viewing animals as the essences of higher beings. Birds of prey, especially eagles, falcons, and ravens, as well as bears, wolves, and other predators became highly significant in shamanism and often assumed the proportions of a true animal cult. Hoofed animals, especially sheep and oxen, also played an increasingly important part as sacrifices, and bulls particularly assumed a leading role, as they were considered part of the masculine sphere.[21]

The enormous socio-economic changes occurring at that time were reflected in the evolution of religious beliefs and practices. The invention of agriculture powered a population explosion, accelerated the pace of technological development, and transformed human society from a hunter-gatherer lifestyle to a sedentary, agricultural lifestyle. As a result of the transition from foraging bands to states and empires, more specialized and developed forms of religion reflected the new social and political environment.

New kinds of economic and social organization, including the large-scale exploitation of human energy, the formation of ruling classes, hierarchical organization, and the administrative division of labor, were the decisive factors that brought about these early civilizations. This developing social order was mirrored in the evolving religious conception. Under such conditions, polytheism, which had undoubtedly been nascent before, could develop fully. The result was a divine hierarchy of gods based on the division of labor in the hierarchically structured city and state. Moreover, the concentration of power and people in one place, in contrast with the wandering of earlier nomadic cultures, enabled fixed central shrines to become influential.

In the religious aspect, and in addition to an agricultural connection with the earlier feminine aspects, the masculine aspect makes its appearance in the form of portrayals of sexual union. In various secular and sacred settings, both in portrayals of couples and families, "divine weddings" or "sacred couplings" of the divinities, female and male reproductive functions were portrayed as the sine qua non of human existence. This dualism of the masculine and feminine aspects was frequently depicted in terms of father sky or the sun and mother earth or the universe, who in their union as a couple, became the parents of all the creatures and humans of the world.

During this period of growth and evolution, humanity engaged in a collective exercise in anthropomorphism. By projecting human qualities onto natural phenomena, both terrestrial and celestial, humans created their gods and goddesses, and the simple template of female-male equality of the hunter-gatherer society could evolve into a polytheistic pantheon of agricultural civilization inhabited by a vast number of gods and goddesses.

The profound changes in human culture and existence brought about during the Neolithic Revolution had both tremendously positive and tremendously negative aspects, some of which we haven't come to terms with, even to this day. On the plus side of the equation, the Neolithic Revolution allowed vast increases of settled populations and provided secure food supplies to maintain socio-economic stability while offering opportunities for growth. Also on the plus side, the Neolithic Revolution saw a vast expansion of human knowledge in writing, mathematics, record-keeping, and metallurgy, allowing first bronze and, later, iron tools to help in the maintenance and growth of the first human civilizations.

On the negative side of the equation, economically, human society that operated on a barter economy and didn't know private property, slavery, or money was transformed into one based on class structure and private property, including slavery, and a money-exchange economy. The development of metallurgy allowed the creation not just of tools but tools of war and domination as well as the invention of coinage as the tool of economic exchange and control. All these developments were accompanied by an increase of male-centric power in the economic and political spheres of the society at large. Indeed, as Professor Dyble concluded, "It was only with the emergence of agriculture, when people could start to accumulate resources, that inequality [between the sexes] emerged."[22]

Endnotes

1   Wikipedia, "Control of Fire by Early Humans," May 28, 2023, https://en.wikipedia
    .org/wiki/Control_of_fire_by_early_humans.

2   Hannah Devlin, "Early Men and Women Were Equal, Say Scientists," The Guardian,
    May 14, 2015, https://www.theguardian.com/science/2015/may/14/early-men
    -women-equal-scientists.

3   Ibid.

4   Wikipedia, "Sexual Division of Labour," May 9, 2023, https://en.wikipedia.org/wiki
    /Sexual_division_of_labour.

5   Maya Wei-Haas, "Prehistoric Female Hunter Discovery Upends Gender Role
    Assumptions," National Geographic, November 4, 2020, https://www.national
    geographic.com/science/article/prehistoric-female-hunter-discovery-upends
    -gender-role-assumptions.

6   Frans De Waal, "Our Inner Ape: The Best and Worst of Human Nature," (London:
    Granta Books, 2005), p. 90.

7   Ibid., 74.

8   Derek Thompson, "How Civilization Broke Our Brains: What Can Hunter
    -Gatherer Societies Teach Us About Work, Time, and Happiness?" The Atlantic,
    Jan./Feb. 2021, https://www.theatlantic.com/magazine/archive/2021/01/james
    -suzman-work/617266/.

9   Ibid.

10 Ibid.

11 Ibid.

12 Michaeleen Doucleff, Hunt, Gather, Parent: What Ancient Cultures Can Teach Us
    About the Lost Art of Raising Happy, Helpful Little Humans, (New York: Simon &
    Schuster, 2021).

13 Ibid.

14 Hervey C. Peoples, Pavel Duda, and Frank W. Marlowe, "Hunter-Gatherers and the
    Origins of Religion." Human Nature 27, (2016): 261–282, https://doi.org/10.1007
    /s12110-016-9260-0.

15 Ibid.

16 Katie Hunt, "Earliest Known War Driven by Climate Change, Researchers Say,"
    CNN, May 27, 2021, https://www.cnn.com/2021/05/27/africa/violence-war-climate
    -jebel-sahaba-scn/index.html.

17 Ibid.

18 Frans De Waal, "Our Inner Ape: The Best and Worst of Human Nature," (London:
    Granta Books, 2005), 137.

19 Ibid.

20 Hervey C. Peoples, Pavel Duda, and Frank W. Marlowe, "Hunter-Gatherers and the
    Origins of Religion." Human Nature 27, (2016): 261–282, https://doi.org/10.1007
    /s12110-016-9260-0.

21 Karl J. Narr, "Stone Age Cultures," Britannica, n.d., https://www.britannica.com
    /topic/prehistoric-religion/Stone-Age-cultures.

22 Hannah Devlin, "Early Men and Women Were Equal, Say Scientists," The Guardian,
    May 14, 2015, https://www.theguardian.com/science/2015/may/14/early-men
    -women-equal-scientists.

Chapter 5
....

Bronze Age Civilizations (4000–1628 BCE)

Sumer: The First Civilization

The first great agrarian civilization was Sumer in Mesopotamia, between 6000 and 5000 BC. Here the rivers and canals enabled the trade that fueled the rise of city-states with populations of over 10,000. The city of Uruk has the distinction of being one of the earliest and the most urbanized cities in the world, with a population of over 50,000. At least during the period of formative growth, life appears to have been good and peaceful with the citizenry growing in number and enjoying the securities of civilized life. Towns were generally unwalled, and there is little evidence of any organized warfare between the cities.

Uruk and other Sumerian city-states were theocratic in their organization, headed by priest-kings, and assisted by a council of elders that included both men and women and operated a highly centralized administration of the employed and regulated specialized workers, including slaves. As early as the Uruk period, slavery was widely practiced in Sumer. Sumerian cities obtained slaves by organizing military-type raids into surrounding hill countries to capture and enslave their residents.

Even in the earliest texts have ample evidence of captured slaves as workers. In the Code of Ur-Nammu, for example, the oldest such codification yet discovered, Sumerian law codified its societal class structure. Beneath the lu-gal ("great man" or king), all members of society belonged to one of two basic strata: the free persons, or citizens, and the slaves that served them. The Code of Hammurabi also "refers to slavery as a common practice throughout the region which had been in place for thousands of years at the time it was written."[1]

The first lesson of the first human civilization is that the comforts and securities of a large citizenry have always been secured through the exploitation of labor of the less fortunate. From Sumerian times on, whenever ancient agricultural civilizations arose, they adopted the practice of slavery—in Ancient Egypt, Ancient China, Akkadian, Assyria, Babylonia, Persia, Ancient Greece, the Roman Empire, the Arab caliphates and sultanates, Nubia, as well as the pre-Columbian civilizations in the Americas.

Concomitantly, not only did Sumer and later agricultural civilizations establish an economic class structure between masters and slaves, but also simultaneously cleaved society in another class structure based on gender that upended the equality of the sexes characteristic of hunter-gatherer society. There was an increase in male social, economic, and political status and power, and a corresponding decrease in female social, economic, political status and power. This development was the result of the differing effects the rise of agricultural civilization had on the gender-determined roles and functions of securing the food supply, with the male as the main hunter and the female as the main gatherer in Paleolithic society.

Enhanced status for the males derived from the expansion of traditional, mostly male function of hunting. From hunting game for food to hunting humans to grow your food proved not much of a stretch. Then, managing and overseeing their slave labor gave the male population a vastly increased purpose, responsibility, and power. On the other hand, the traditional female "gathering" role and function as the main "breadwinner" (i.e., calorie contributor) of family and society was essentially wiped out by the advent of civilization and its agricultural monoculture. Diminishing their economic contribution to the welfare of society, the role of women became more and more restricted to just having children and raising them. One Sumerian proverb describes the ideal, happy marriage through the mouth of a husband who boasts that his wife has borne him eight sons and is still eager to have sex.[2]

In the earliest times, the Sumerians had maintained the very relaxed attitudes toward sex of the female-centric hunter-gatherer cultures. Their sexual mores were determined not by whether a sexual act was deemed immoral but rather by whether or not it made a person ritually unclean. The Sumerians widely believed that masturbation enhanced sexual potency, both for men and for women, and they frequently engaged in it, both alone and with their partners. The Sumerians did not regard anal sex as taboo either. Priestesses, for example, were forbidden from producing offspring and frequently engaged in anal sex as a method of birth control.[3]

But as Sumerian civilization developed and became more stratified, this sexual freedom and equality were replaced through the institutionalization of male dominance over female in marriage. It was recorded, for example, that King Urukagina of Lagash (circa 2300 BC) abolished the former custom of polyandry in his country, prescribing that a woman who took multiple husbands be stoned with rocks upon which her crime had been written.[4]

Still, the female-centric paradigm survived and continued to rule the religious sphere. Earliest cosmogenic myths of Sumerian religion saw creation as the result of a series of sacred marriages involving the reconciliation of opposites and was thought of as a coming together of the divine male and female beings who were the gods to create and nurture the universe, the earth, and all its creatures, including humans.[5]

Sumer's religion was basically anthropomorphic polytheism. People believed in many gods in human form who had created human beings from clay for the purpose of serving them. Indeed, the temples organized the mass labor projects needed for irrigation agriculture. Citizens had a labor duty to the temple, though they could avoid it by a payment of silver.[6]

Moreover, this polytheistic universe was female-centric, both in their religious beliefs and social structures. The worship of the Great Mother, the Sky Goddess, was central in religion and mirrored the function, role, and status of women in the family, priesthood, and society. The queen was always considered the incarnation or embodiment of the Great Mother Goddess, while the king merely represented her cosmic consort.

Under this female-centric formula, many male gods and female goddesses coexisted in a relative state of harmony and equality. There were Nammu and Anu, Tiamat and Abzu/Kingu, Kishar and Anshar, Shala and Adad, Inanna and Dumuzi, Ki and Anu, Enlil and Ninlil, Enki and Ningikuga, all anthropomorphic deity couples regulating some aspect of Sumerian existence, from the sky and the heavenly bodies to the earth and its lands and oceans, weather, seasons, directions… These deities formed a core pantheon; there were hundreds of minor additional ones. Sumerian gods could thus have associations with different cities, and their religious importance often waxed and waned with those cities' political power.

Egyptian Civilization

Around the same time as the beginnings of Sumerian civilization, around 6000 to 5000 BCE, the first settlements began to appear in Egypt along the length of the Nile River. In the Early Dynastic period (3050–2686 BCE), many "kings" competed for territory and power. The Old Egyptian Kingdom formally started with the unification of Upper and Lower Egypt circa 3100 BC, and lasted until 2181 BCE when the central unifying authority collapsed on account of adverse climatic conditions and population pressures. Balkanization occurred, and competing power centers in the north and south arose to fill the void. The following period, from 2181 to 1991 BCE, in which there was no central authority is usually called the First Intermediate Period or "dark age." The first dark age ended when, around 2055 BCE, the southern Theban ruler of the 12th dynasty conquered the north and reunified the country with a central authority. This was the beginning of the Middle Kingdom, which spanned the period from 2055 to 1650 BC and was also followed by a dark age.

Like Sumer, Ancient Egyptian society developed a highly stratified theocratic feudal state to manage the agricultural economy that was the foundation of its civilization. At the very top of society was the strong institution of theocratic kingship. The pharaoh and his consort were considered semidivine and were the absolute rulers of the country and, at least in theory, wielded complete control of the land and its resources. The pharaoh and his staff organized economic activity and religious life. The various functions of both were dominated by extended noble families whose members made up the upper class of scribes, officials, and priests. This upper class owned and managed the lands that produced the foods that fed everyone. They also organized religious activities to feed the spiritual needs of the people. Because the upper class prominently displayed their social status in art and literature, they were known as the "white kilt class" in reference to the bleached linen garments that served as a mark of their rank.

Below the upper-class nobility was a middle class consisting of physicians, engineers, craftsmen, and artists who had specialized knowledge and training in their fields. The middle class was also under strict state and religious control, working in the shops attached to the temples and paid directly from the state treasury. The lowest social class in Ancient Egypt, the bulk of its population, was made up of the farmers. Though the farmers did the actual work of producing the food that fed everyone, the food that they produced was owned directly by the state, temple, or noble family that owned the land. Farmers were also subject to a labor tax and were required to work on irrigation or construction projects.

In Egypt, as in Sumer and Minoan civilizations, even as the economic organization of society became more hierarchical and male-dominated in nature and women were increasingly discriminated against in the decision-making process, the female-centric paradigm of the original hunter-gatherer tribes remained the underpinning of religious and civil life. Accordingly, women in Ancient Egypt had

some special rights other women did not have in other comparable societies. Compared with their counterparts in Ancient Greece,
Rome, and even more modern places around the world, Ancient
Egyptian women had a greater range of personal choices, legal
rights, and opportunities for achievement. There were even women
pharaohs.

Significantly, the Ancient Egyptians viewed men and women,
including people from all social classes, as essentially equal under the
law.[7] Both men and women had the right to own and sell property,
make contracts, marry and divorce, receive inheritance, and pursue
legal disputes in court. Married couples could own property jointly
and protect themselves from divorce by agreeing to marriage contracts, which stipulated the financial obligations of the husband to
his wife and children should the marriage end.

Even in our modern culture, we still have remnants of the
Ancient Egyptian female-centric balance. Today, the concept of Justice is still represented by a blind female goddess who holds the
scales of justice in her left hand, which goes back to the Roman
goddess, Lady Justitia. The Romans got the idea from the Greeks,
whose name for Lady Justitia was Diki. Diki was the daughter of
the Greek goddess Themis, the embodiment of divine order, law,
and custom. The Greeks, in turn, inherited the concept from the
Egyptians goddesses Isis and Maat.

Since time immemorial, humanity has been largely right-handed,
and correspondingly, the right side of the body has been considered
the strong, masculine side. Conversely, the left side has always been
considered the weak, feminine side. The right side of the body is
masculine, and the right hand is the hand that wields power. This
makes the right, masculine side fundamentally amoral since "right
makes might, might makes right." Of course, then the question
arises: What can put the brakes on masculine power, when necessary?
The answer is: only morality and justice can counter power and balance it. Therefore, since the mists of prehistory, morality, justice, and
honor have been represented by a female goddess carrying the scales
of justice in her left hand. This, most likely, is also the reason why

Johann Bachofen dedicated his monumental study "The Mothers" with the Latin phrase "Major Honos Laevrum Partium," meaning "The Greater Honor of the Left."

Lastly, also note that the history of Ancient Egyptian civilization clearly shows a yin-yang polarity in religious life that reflects the social conditions of the prevailing harmony or chaos. In the peaceful and prosperous times of the Old Kingdom, the female-centric religion of Isis-Osiris, of fertility and moon worship, was dominant. Indeed, worship of the sky goddess Nut, the mother of Isis and Osiris, was already ancient in the First Dynasty. On the other hand, the sun god Ra's male-centric religion did not establish itself until the Fifth Dynasty and grew to the apex of its power only when the Old Kingdom collapsed in the Sixth Dynasty, and chaos reigned in a dark age that lasted centuries.

The Paradox of Early Human Progress

Sumerian, Minoan, Mycenean, Egyptian, all these ancient civilizations were fundamentally agrarian; their existence was intimately and ultimately dependent on the regularity and the predictability of natural rhythms and cycles. All functions of agrarian society, such as seeding, growing, sowing, reaping, and harvesting, being fundamentally female, the Bronze Age religions, the priesthoods, and life in general, evolved in a fundamentally female-centric way. Balance and timing being critical to success in all these agricultural stages, the function of religion and its priests in these agrarian cultures was to maintain the balance between man and nature by staying in the good graces of the gods, or even improve relations with them in order to grow and flourish.

When these civilizations were young and expanding and providing for the necessities of life, such as food and shelter, for the growing population, there was satisfaction in the people's hearts and minds that things were right between the people and the gods. The people had been observant in the rites and service to the gods as they had been instructed, and the gods had reciprocated with bountiful harvests and an increased standard of living. For this reason, the ancient female-centric religions that had developed during hunter-gatherer times could remain functional and productive in the development of the increasingly male-centric economic and political sectors of civilization.

Because agricultural cultivation supported vast increases in general population, it also required intensive sustained, coordinated labor. This presented a golden opportunity to the human male to get more in touch with the chimpanzee side of his ancestral legacy, as opposed to the bonobo side dominant in hunter-gatherer society. The human male resumed and even "improved" on the raiding parties that the chimps and early hunter-gatherer males used to engage in for the purpose of killing the men and obtaining the women. As there was an obvious need for the labor they could provide in a fast-developing agricultural civilization, killing the men was no longer necessary. So now the builders of agricultural civilization could hunt and capture other tribes, not only to capture the women for pleasure and procreation but also to capture the men and thereby obtain the necessary slave labor to fuel their civilization's growth and expansion.

The effect of slave labor force was to lessen the demands on women to be economically productive, pushing them to concentrate solely on the procreative function, bear as many offspring as possible, and manage the nurturing of the extended family. By and large, women appear to have accepted this change in status because this new way meant an easier life for them individually and collectively and allowed for the apparently infinite growth and sustenance of large families and great tribes.

But sadly this "improvement" of women's economic lot actually amounted to the impoverishment of their life as a whole, as they were pushed out of participating and decision-making in the sphere of economic production. Thus, not having to engage as much in productive labor of hunting and gathering constituted the economic basis of misogyny, as it served to cement the subservient ties of women to their husbands and the increasingly male-centric dominance in the sphere of economic production. This overthrow was not sudden but gradual and all the more pernicious because, superficially, it seemed to elevate the women while their subordination was occurring at a deeper level.

In the 19th century, Engels wrote that the "overthrow of mother right" was "the world-historic defeat of the female sex," an observation generally agreed upon by progressives. He also wrote that "the oppression of women by men in the patriarchal nuclear family constituted the first class structure in human society."[8] This statement seems more debatable now, as the evidence has mounted that the male-centric nuclear family and the rise of misogyny occurred simultaneously with the institutionalization of slavery. Ever since the flowering of agricultural civilization, the power-oriented, male-centric paradigm became increasingly obsessed with the commodification of all aspects of human existence. As the lands, the herds that roam on it, and the grains that grow on it were acquired, whether by cultivation, war, or other methods, they became property to be owned by the males.

It was but a short step to extend this attitude to cover human beings from other races and different in gender. And thus it was that racism and the ownership of other human beings as slaves and the misogyny and the subjugation of women that became the twin foundations of the male-centric society and state. Thus the great paradox of early human progress was that the change from hunter-gatherer society to agricultural civilization, with all the great many benefits that accrued from it, also gave birth to the historical origin of class society, of racism and slavery, of misogyny and the subjugation of women to men.

But while the agricultural revolution put the women in an inferior position relative to the male, this was not the case in the religious, spiritual dimension. In the religious sphere, women maintained their central role in the institutional and symbolic functions of the religious power structure. After all, at least in the beginning and early stages of the blossoming of agricultural civilization, it was the adherence to the laws of the female-centric universe that had empowered and enabled the material progress of civilization they were enjoying in untold numbers.

But what if conditions changed and the very existence of civilization and all its progress was threatened? What if, one day, the divine gods and goddesses stopped smiling on the sea of humanity and civilization was assaulted and reduced to ruins by undreamed of calamities? What would be the effect on the prevailing religious belief systems of that civilization? How would humanity respond? Would it try to appease the wrath of the gods by finding a culprit and making more offerings, dead or living? Or would the people turn on the gods that had turned on them, decide this was the wrong bunch to worship, and accept a different set of gods as their idols?

Endnotes

1   Restavek Freedom, "The History of Slavery," n.d., https://restavekfreedom.org
     /2018/09/11/the-history-of-slavery/.

2   Nemet-Nejat, Karen Rhea, Daily Life in Ancient Mesopotamia, (Connecticut:
     Greenwood, 1998), 132, ISBN 978-0-313-29497-6.

3   Ibid.

4   Ibid.

5   Samuel Noah Kramer, The Sumerians: Their History, Culture, and Character.
     (Chicago: The University of Chicago Press, 1963), ISBN 978-0-226-45238-8.

6   Ibid.

7   Janet H. Johnson, "Women's Legal Rights in Ancient Egypt," Fathom Archive,
     University of Chicago, 2002, https://fathom.lib.uchicago.edu/1/777777190170/.

8   Friedrich Engels, The Origin of the Family, Private Property, and the State, (New
     World Paperbacks, 1884), 50–58.

Part 2

The Great Polarity Reversal in Antiquity

The Age of Catastrophe, the Destruction of the Mediterranean World, and the Origin of Monotheism (1628 BCE)

The Yin-Yang of Evolution

Gradual and Punctuated Evolution

The theory of biological evolution, as developed and described by Charles Darwin, emphasized the gradual nature of the evolutionary process. "Gradualism," as this theory came to be called, considers evolution as generally smooth and continuous process that occurs uniformly by the steady and gradual transformation of whole lineages, as voluminously documented by the fossil record.

Still, the gradualist theory of evolution was unsatisfactory in that it failed to explain adequately the numerous occurrences in the fossil record where evolutionary change happened dramatically and very suddenly. To address these concerns, modern biologists, such as Ernst Mayr, Israel Michael Lerner, Niles Eldredge, and Stephen Jay Gould, developed a competing theory of "punctuated equilibria," which basically stated that evolutionary biological change could and does happen in very rapid bursts.[1]

The discussions and debates between the two camps were often quite passionate and contentious, the gradualist school deriding the punctuationists' work as "evolution by jerks"[2] and the latter retaliating and denigrating the effort of the gradualists as "evolution by creeps."[3] A third, middle way that emerged then combined these two opposites by understanding that they are not binary and exclusive of each other but complimentary. In other words, (1) the very slow and the very fast constitute the two extreme poles of a spectrum of the possible rate of evolutionary change, and (2) depending, by a large extent, on the nature of geological and climatic conditions, big changes can occur very fast while small changes can occur over a long period of time.

The history of our human species has shown these concepts of evolutionary change in biology are also applicable to our species' social, economic, and political institutions, as well the cognitive structures of our minds. Both the human way of organizing itself socially as well as their ways of thinking and their religious belief systems can evolve and change in either gradual or sudden ways depending on the environmental geological events and climatic conditions involved.

This chapter will detail the sudden and devasting effects the prehistoric age of cataclysms and catastrophe had on the evolution of Bronze Age humanity and agricultural civilizations in and around the Mediterranean basin. The event transformed a basically peaceful humanity into a state of perpetual war for resources and was responsible for supplanting the female-centric worldview and religion of equality and balance with the male-centric paradigm based on power and conquest.

The Great Catastrophe

In 1628 BCE, the Thera volcano on the Mediterranean island of Santorini exploded with such fury that it altered the Mediterranean world into unrecognizable shape. Its ferocious power is attributable to the fact that Thera is a subduction volcano, where the African plate is subducting beneath the Eurasian plate. This process is creating a system of enormous fissures and magma chambers in the earth. When the pressure in the magma chambers becomes greater than the surrounding rock on top of it, an eruption occurs. The Thera eruption was so powerful that it became a key marker for the end of Bronze Age Mediterranean world.

The 1628 BCE Thera eruption was the second largest explosive volcanic eruption in the past four millennia. In modern times, only the 1815 eruption of Tambora in Indonesia, which caused days of global darkness, was larger than the Thera event.[4] The Volcanic Explosivity Index (VEI) of the Thera explosion was calculated to be seven or more. As the name indicates, the VEI is assigned on the basis of how much material was ejected by the explosion, and the Thera cataclysm ejected the equivalent of 60 cubic kilometers of dense rock into the ocean and the atmosphere, with heights of 36 to 38 kilometers, well into the stratosphere. For comparison's sake, the Mount Saint Helen explosion in Washington in 1980 was only assigned a VEI of four.

For most of the 20th century, archaeologists, historians, and other social scientists placed the event at about 1500 BCE. But in recent decades, many geologists, tree-ring experts, and archaeologists have unearthed increasing evidence in the form of carbon dating and tree-ring dating that supports an earlier date, well over a century earlier, in 1628 BCE. This evidence has been meticulously collected and presented by Barbara J. Sivertsen, in her seminal book, *The Parting of the Sea: How Volcanoes, Earthquakes and Plagues Shaped the History of the Exodus*.[5]

When Thera blew its lid so to speak, volcanic tephra and ash shot up into the air with increasing violence and intensity, depositing up to seven meters of rose-colored, iron-rich pumice and ash on the islands of the Santorini archipelago. Next, erupting vents opened in the sea south of the first vent and allowed sea water to interact with the magma, causing violent explosions that pulverized the magma and exploded large blocks of it onto Thera.

As hot pyroclastic flows welled out of the caldera and down into the valleys, they combined with—and heated—the air above them, forming a buoyant column containing vast quantities of eruptive material. It was this column that produced most of the Theran tephra that deposited twelve more meters of ash and pumice, as attested to by cores recovered in the eastern Mediterranean Sea and from deposits to the northeast of Santorini, as far as the Black Sea. The explosive mixing of water and magma occurred several times. In the third phase, from a new vent to the west of the original one, 55 more meters of white pumice and ash, interbedded with larger rocky material, were deposited on Thera. Toward the end of this phase, the caldera, already subsiding, began its final collapse.[6] In prevailing wind patterns at the time were strong winds alternating from the northeasterly to the southeasterly direction. The airborne distribution of ash and pumice from the Thera explosion reached as far northeastward as Turkey and Anatolia, and as far southeastward as Egypt.

As these massive pyroclastic surges entered the sea, huge tsunamis were generated in all directions. This process culminated with the total collapse of the caldera that created a final powerful tsunami. Evidence from Palaikastro in northeast Crete, for example, shows that a massive tsunami or tsunamis from the Minoan eruption was directed to the southeast, directly toward Egypt.[7]

In short, the catastrophes of fire, air, and water unleashed by the Thera eruption scarred the entire geographical area, destroying all existing Mediterranean civilizations, including the Minoan, Egyptian, and early Greek cultures.

Centuries of Catastrophes

When we survey the post-catastrophic Mediterranean world in the period following the Thera eruptions, several things stand out. First, there was complete collapse of all central civil authority in the existing Minoan, Greek, and Egyptian civilizations. Their collective slide into a Second Intermediate Period or dark age with myriads of competing fiefdoms began in about 1674 and lasted until 1549 BCE.

Second, the eruption of Thera was no isolated event. It most likely was not the first, and it certainly was not the last, of a series of cataclysmic earthquakes that repeatedly struck the Mediterranean basin in the first and second millennia BCE, each followed by widespread destruction and collapse of civil society. Archaeological evidence indicates that at least one, possibly more, massive tsunamis generated by the Thera eruption devastated the coast of Crete and destroyed many Minoan, as well as non-Minoan, settlements as far away as the present-day coast of Turkey. Indeed, only recently, archeologists found the skeletons of two tsunami victims, a man and a dog, that were over taken and drowned by a tsunami generated by the Thera eruption.[8] Less than a century later, around, 1600 BC, Thera gave a repeat performance with another giant eruption that completely destroyed the palaces at Knossos, Phaistos, Malia, and Kato Zakros, wiping the Minoan civilization off the map completely, only leaving shards of pottery.

Third, in this period of accumulative chaos, the female-centric worldviews and religions based on balance were completely suppressed and replaced by male-centric worldviews and religions based on power as the cosmic operating principle. In Egypt, in Greece, and among the Hebrews, the male-centric cosmological sociopolitical revolution triumphed over the traditional female-centric socioreligious paradigm of sexual equality under religious polytheism. In the words of Sigmund Freud, "In those dark centuries which historical research is only beginning to explore, the countries around the Mediterranean were apparently the scene of frequent volcanic eruptions, which were bound to make the deepest impressions on the inhabitants... Everywhere in the Aegean world, the great Mother Goddess was then worshipped. There is hardly a doubt that in those obscure times, mother deities were replaced by male gods."[9]

The Destruction of Mediterranean Civilizations

Minoan Civilization and Its Destruction

The first and immediate "victim" of the beginning of the violent era of catastrophes, namely the Thera explosion of 1628 BCE, was the mysterious Minoan civilization on Crete, Santorini, and the myriad of islands in the Aegean Sea. At the time of the Thera explosion, the

Minoan civilization was a prosperous and advanced island civilization. It had a long life span that lasted for almost two millennia, from roughly 3000 to 1000 BCE, with three distinct phases or periods of growth and decline. The early Minoan period lasted from around 2700 to 2200 BCE; the middle Minoan period happened from around 2200 to 1600 BCE; and the late Minoan period lasted from 1600 to 1200 BCE. These periods of renaissance and resurgence were separated by dark ages of decline.

Because their language has yet to be deciphered, it is unknown what kind of government was practiced by the Minoans, though the palaces and throne rooms indicate a form of hierarchy, like in Sumer. But despite that limitation, Knossos, the ancient capital of Crete, has yielded the most continuous and varied evidence of the Neolithic age to the twilight of classical civilization. According to Arthur Evans, the famed explorer and anthropologist, indications were a "Minoan peace" existed, especially during the formative "early Minoan period. Few signs of warfare appear in Minoan art, and no evidence has been found of a Minoan army or the Minoan domination of peoples beyond Crete." Other archaeologists agreed that "the stark fact is that for the prehistoric Aegean, we have no direct evidence for war and warfare per se."[10]

The lack of linguistic knowledge has also proven to be a barrier to more fully understanding Minoan religion, as "the hierarchy and relationship of gods within the pantheon is difficult to decode from the images alone." But Minoan religion is considered to have been closely related to other Near Eastern prehistoric religions. It was focused on female deities, with women officiants and priestesses, and its central deity is generally agreed to have been a mother goddess. Often associated with this mother goddess was a younger male figure usually presented in contexts suggesting that he was either a consort, a son, or both. The goddess was also often associated with animals, especially the snake, but also with the bull, the lion, and the dove. Prominent Minoan sacred symbols include the bull and its horns of consecration, the labrys (double-headed ax), the serpent, and to some extent, the ankh.

The Evidence of the Maps

The extent of the devastation wreaked by these catastrophes is hard to imagine. Fortunately, there exists a record of it in the form of the ancient map drawn by Yehudi Ibn ben Zara of Alexandria that miraculously survived the ages. This map (Fig. A) was based on maps and information handed down, cartographer to cartographer, through the ages of the Aegean area as it looked before the great catastrophe.[11] When compared to a modern map of the area (Fig. B), the difference immediately jumps out: on the modern map, there are far, far fewer islands in the Aegean sea than there are on the Ibn ben Zara map. The tsunamis and rising sea levels caused by the volcanic catastrophes submerged or wiped out the majority of the Cycladic islands in the Aegean sea.[12]

As a final lesson, the demise of Minoan civilization shows the effects natural catastrophes can have on human society. Periods of sustained catastrophes cause cycles of the death and rebirth of cultures during which people become less peaceful and more predatory and warlike. For example, in its pre-catastrophic heyday, Minoan Crete had little internal armed conflict. But after the Thera catastrophe, its culture and institutions were severely crippled if not destroyed, meaning that Minoan society was vulnerable to attack from outside. Indeed, their distant relatives and trading and cultural partners, the Myceneans, who had been spared to a large extent by the immediate ravages of the Thera explosion, sensed an opportunity to be taken advantage of and invaded Crete. Mycenaean weaponry has been found in burials on Crete made soon after the eruption, attesting to the fact that the Mycenaeans "conquered" Crete and the Minoans during the late Minoan period, finally occupying the palace sites around 1420 to 1375 BCE.

After centuries of reconstruction following the collapse of late Minoan civilization between 1200 and 1150 BCE, Mother Nature spoke and acted again. Once more, a sudden and violent event ushered in a new dark age of famine and conflict in the entire Mediterranean and near Eastern regions, destroying every significant city in the

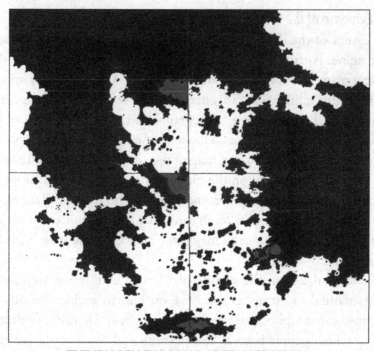

THE IBN BEN ZARA MAP, AEGEAN SECTION.

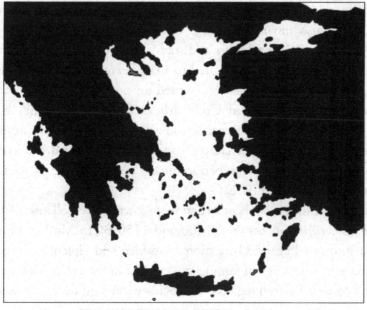

THE MODERN MAP OF THE AEGEAN.

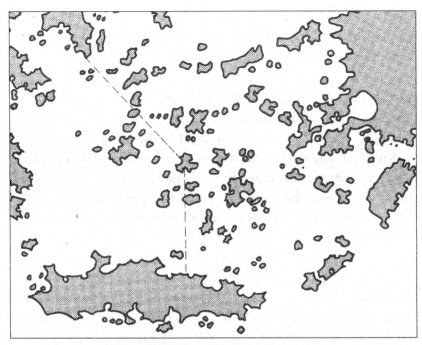

THERA ON THE IBN BEN ZARA MAP.

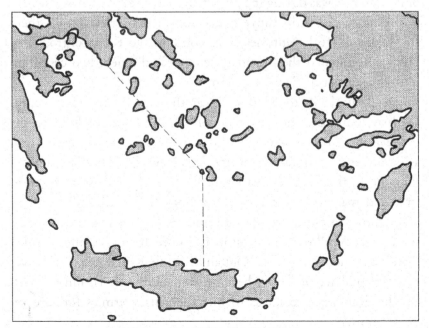

THERA ON THE MODERN MAP.

Eastern Mediterranean. After centuries of onslaught, many cultures, like the Minoan civilization, finally succumbed for good into the ashes of history, never to be rebuilt again.

Paradigm Change in Post-Catastrophic Egypt

Egypt was battered and shattered by the cataclysms but survived to rise again. The Thera explosion resulted in the collapse of the Middle Kingdom and marked the beginning of the Second Intermediate Period or dark age that lasted from about 1674 to 1549 BCE. This period was marked by disintegration of the central authority of the Egyptian state into a number of competing centers of influence in the North and in the South. In the power vacuum of this dark age Egypt, the Semitic Hyksos people who had been residing in Tell el-Dab'a area in the delta since the Eleventh Dynasty rose up to seize control of Egypt.

The Hyksos began their climb to power in the Thirteenth Dynasty and first gained control of Avaris and the Delta in the north before heading south in their campaign to conquer lower Egypt. The heyday of Hyksos rule was during the period of the Fifteenth Dynasty, which according to the Turin Papyrus, had six rulers over 108 years, then the 17th and 16th centuries BCE consolidated their control. The Hyksos dominated the Egyptian people for the next two centuries until the start of the New Kingdom.

In about 1550 to 1570 BCE, at the end of the Seventeenth Dynasty, Ahmose, the first pharaoh of the Eighteenth Dynasty, expelled the Hyksos and reunited Upper and Lower Egypt once again under central state authority. This New Kingdom, lasted from the 16th to the 11th century BCE. It was Egypt's most prosperous time and marked the peak of Egypt's power. For that reason, it is also referred to as the Egyptian Empire. Ahmose was a truly expansionistic and militaristic dictator, far more aggressive and warlike than his predecessors of the Old and Middle Kingdoms. Under his rule, the practice of slavery became more and more commonplace, and he even went so far as to hire mercenary armies for foreign expeditions.

Ahmose's authoritarianism and aggression was fueled by a new male-centric religion of domination and warfare of the sun god Ra that he promulgated as a replacement for the ancient, female-centric Isis-Osiris religion of peace, harmony, and equality between the sexes. The powerful pharaohs of this dynasty, in particular Ahmose's son Seti I and his grandson Ramesses II, would bring Egypt to new heights of imperial power. Seti I fought a series of wars in Western Asia, Libya, and Nubia, and when his time came, Ramses II sought to recover territories in the Levant that had been lost in earlier times.

For the next two centuries, successive rulers nurtured and fostered growth in the solar Ra religion, a process that led to increasing megalomania in the ruling pharaohs in the later New Kingdom, i.e., the Nineteenth and Twentieth Dynasties (1292–1069 BC).[13] Ramesses II built on a monumental scale to ensure that his legacy would survive the ravages of time. He used art as a means of propaganda for his victories over foreigners, which are depicted on numerous temple reliefs. Ramesses II erected more colossal statues of himself than any other pharaoh and also usurped many existing statues by inscribing his own cartouche on them.

During the Eighteenth Dynasty, the solar Ra religion reached its apex of power during Akhenaton's reign (1353–1336 BCE). Akhenaton's megalomaniacal solar monotheism rejected the polytheism of the old traditions. He considered himself to be the one god, the very incarnation of the solar disk, Aten. Speaking to the royal court, scribes, or the people, Amenhotep IV (Akhenaton) said that the old gods were ineffective and had ceased their movements and that their temples had collapsed. The pharaoh contrasted this with the only remaining god, the sun disc, Aten, who continued to move and exist forever.[14] His rule was radically ruthless. He abandoned Thebes, the city of the great moon god, Amen, erased all mention of him in temple inscriptions, and built himself a new city devoted to the sun, Amarna. Adherents of all other religions were by definition treasonous, and their proponents, therefore, candidates for erasure and eradication.

It was not to be. With Akhenaten's death, the Aten cult he had founded fell out of public favor. At first gradually, then with decisive finality, Akhenaten's successors attempted to erase Akhenaten and his family from the historical record, destroying the temples dedicated to Aten and reusing the building blocks in new construction projects, including temples for the newly restored god Amun. Less than 25 years after Akhenaten's death, his capital city at Amarna lay in ruins, wrecked by social upheaval.

The immediate successors of Ramesses II continued the military campaigns, though an increasingly troubled court complicated matters. As the heavy cost of this warfare slowly drained Egypt's treasury and contributed to its gradual decline, the Egyptian Empire was increasingly beset by difficulties of all kinds. There were invasions by the Sea Peoples from sea and land; there was below-normal flooding of the Nile that brought droughts and famines; there was corruption of public servants and officials and civil unrest as Egyptian the civilization and society once again slid backward into balkanization caused by a lack of central authority, and the darkness of the Third Intermediate Period lasted four centuries, from 1069 to 653 BCE.

The Hebrews and the Catastrophe: Moses and Monotheism Revisited

The Parting of the Sea

Sometime in the 19th century BCE, during the late Twelfth Dynasty, the pre-Mosaic Hebrews came to Egypt to escape famine. The patriarch Jacob led the Hebrew tribes from the Canaan-Syria area to Egypt, where they settled in the Nile delta in the land of Goshen, locally known as the Wadi Tumilat.

In her book *The Parting of the Sea*,[15] Barbara Sivertsen makes the case that the narrative of Hebrew exodus from Goshen and Egypt as we know it is the result of the oral transmission of at least two separate volcanic events, the aftereffects of which were amalgamated into Israelite oral history shortly after they happened. The first was the Minoan eruption of the Thera, or Santorini, volcano in 1628 BCE.

The second was an eruption of a shield volcano in the Midian area in northern Arabia at nearly the same time.

Geologically, Midian is on the border of two tectonic plates, the African and the Arabian. The Arabian volcanoes, including Sinai, the mountain of God where Moses heard His words, are different from subduction volcanoes like Santorini. Their magma is less explosive. It tends to flow out on the earth's surface in a continuous manner, producing different patterns of destruction.

What is important to us here is not so much the specific details of these conflagrations but their cumulative effect on (1) the human psyche and its impressions on their belief and value systems and (2) the expressions thereof in the interactions among themselves and with other human groups. From the point of view of world history, the person whose actions most symbolized and embodied the change of polarity from female-centric to male-centric cosmic operating principle in social structures and religious beliefs was the man Moses.

Moses and his articulation of male-centric monotheism was a total and complete repudiation of female-centric polytheism with its foundational values of balance, cooperation, and equality overthrown by values of power, competition, and inequality. As Freud put it so succinctly in *Moses and Monotheism*, "Jewish records and history show us emphatically that the idea of an only God was given to the people by Moses... It was one man, the man Moses, who created the Jews... Moses was not only the political leader... He was also their law giver and educator and the man who forced them to adopt a new religion."[16]

The biblical account describes vast geological upheavals and frightening atmospheric phenomena that combined to dislocate the entire ecosystem of the Mideast and caused the collapse of the entire Egyptian Middle Kingdom. Rivers were observed as turning into blood. Plagues of many kinds appeared—frogs, lice, killer flies, pestilence in cattle, boils and blisters on people, locusts, darkness, and mass death. People tried to climb the roofs of houses, and the houses fell down. They tried to climb the trees, and the trees cast them far away, and when they tried to escape in caves and caverns, these were suddenly closed.[17]

The relationship between the sexes was uprooted particularly violently. Males became crazed warriors, looting, killing, and raping in cathartic rage. The lament was heard the world over, "Oh, that there might be an end of men, no birth and no conception."[18] "None were able to speak or hear, nor could anyone venture to take food, but they lay themselves down their outward senses in a trance, overwhelmed by the affliction."[19]

In the ancient world, it was the task of the religious leadership to prescribe appropriate counteracting rituals and ceremonies, but the severity of the cataclysm rendered all traditional concepts and remedies obsolete. Egypt's Anat-Apis priesthood was powerless to restore social order. In the profound confusion of chaos, a vacuum of answers to theological questions was combined with an urgent need for action to meet the needs of the catastrophic moment.

Moses and the Hebrews

The Hebrew tribes turned out to be a convenient scapegoat for the Egyptians to lay the blame on for the catastrophes that were befalling Egypt. Their persecution left the Jews degraded, bitter, and frustrated at being unable to better their lot. When the adult Moses first appears in the biblical narrative, he is clearly in a hyper-agitated state of mind. Trained as a priest in the Anat-Isis-Osiris religion by the Egyptians, he was frustrated by the inability of the priesthood to influence the gods and stop the catastrophes, and at the persecution of his people. Witnessing such a persecution once, Moses lost his cool, unleashed his rage, and "slew the Egyptian."[20]

Adding insult to injury, instead of admiring his courage, his own people informed on him and sent the very group who had educated him, the priests, after him to catch him and bring him to justice. So Moses fled and crossed the desert into Midian. There, he married Zipporah, daughter of Jethro, a priest of the Midianite volcano god Yahweh, another local variation of the primordial Osiris. In true metronymic fashion, Moses moved into the house of his bride's father, in effect becoming his servant. He was put in charge of tending Jethro's flocks in the wilderness and pondering his fate.

Socially as well as theologically, the structure of belief and habitual actions of the Hebrews at the time of the exodus paralleled those of their Egyptian hosts. The goddess Anat (Nut, Neith) was the chief divinity of all the Semites, including the Jews, in the female-centric state of organization. As the Mother of All Living, she was the analogue of the human matriarch, free in her love, the fruitful mother of the clan, and its leader in peace and war"[21] As among all other Semites, the original form of social organization of the Hebrew clans was matrilocal and metronymic.

For the Jews as for the Egyptians, the worship of the sky goddess was closely intertwined with the worship of the moon, and the moon represented to them the supreme cosmic power, as it did to the whole Semitic race. Hebrew moon worship centered on the ancient worship of the bull god, Apis, regarded as the very embodiment of the life force, sexual virility and fecundity, the very "ka" or soul of the moon god Osiris.[22]

Tending his father in law's flocks, Moses spent a great deal of his time in the wilderness, wandering and wondering. He was obsessed with his need to find his own calling and chart his way in response to the needs of his people in the face of nature's chaos and violence. His experience with the burning bush was pivotal in this quest, resulting in an acute schizophrenic episode. His overtaxed nervous system suffered a psychotic break, complete with both visual and auditory hallucinations. In it, Moses experienced a white light of the burning bush that didn't burn and heard the divine voice of the Supreme God Yahweh identify himself and give him his marching orders.

The Mosaic Experience of Enlightenment

To set the stage, what Moses heard God tell him must be interpreted within the context of phallic worship in the female-centric religious practices of Ancient Egypt. The worship of the phallus in general, and the phallus of Osiris in particular, was widespread in ancient female-centric Egypt. All the temples of Isis in Upper and

Lower Egypt were adorned with wood and stone phalluses. In this female-centric setting, the worship of the phallus symbolized the supportive and subordinate masculine function of fertilization in the primary feminine process of procreation. In Egyptian mythology, the subordination of the phallus to female needs and pleasures was fully developed in the myth of Osiris. For the Hebrews, Apis, their golden calf and bull god, was also regarded as the very "ka," or soul, of Osiris. And Moses, as a religiously educated person, was well aware of this.

Hallucinating in front of the burning bush, Moses heard the voice from the bush assert, "I am Yahweh." "Yahweh" means "ultimate ground" or "generative principle" of the universe. Hearing the god of his father-in-law address him so directly, Moses knew then with utmost certainty that he was facing his master. But that was not all Moses heard. Moses also heard Yahweh further clarify to him that "Ahiy Ashir Ahiy." Now the meaning of "Ahiy" is "I am," and Ashir means "the ever erect one."[23] Given the prominence of phallic worship in those times, the new, true meaning of these words was crystal clear to Moses. His enlightenment consisted of the knowledge that from now on, the phallus, as the male instrument of power, would no longer be subordinate to the female principle but would henceforth be its master.

Thus Moses identified himself with the violence manifested in nature all around him and projected that power onto the Midianite God Yahweh, as an original member of the female-centric pantheon of deities of the area. A God of creative harmony was transformed into the one and only (male) God of the Universe, who rules only through total violence. Thus also, the female-centric value of "the greater honor of the left" was replaced by the male-centric value that since the right is might, "might makes right." Moses signed up to be Yahweh's conduit, channeler, interpreter, and enforcer. Psychologically identifying his own rage as part of the power that initiated, controlled, and directed the catastrophic cosmic violence, Moses now felt he had cosmic authority to wield power as he saw fit to reshape the social and political and religious structure of the Hebrew tribes in a strict, male-centric, authoritarian fashion, based on the twin pillars of racism and misogyny.

Moses's experience with the burning bush must also be understood as the occasion in which he experienced his own personal religious conversion. For what happens in the experience of religious conversions is that the extreme stress imposed on the neural-hormonal system reverses the value polarities of opposing psychological paradigms. In the moment of conversion, what was a previously uncritically accepted religious belief is rejected, becomes negatively charged, and is replaced by previously unacceptable beliefs that now become positively charged and accepted as unassailably true beyond the shadow of a doubt. For Moses, it was the previously held female-centric paradigm of the Isis-Osiris religious system, complete with its pantheon of deities, that was rejected. In its stead, Moses embraced as his new paradigm of interpretation its radical opposite, namely a conception of Yahweh as the sole male-centric monotheistic cosmic authority, who rules nature and the human species through the wielding of the raw power of violence.

It was the fate of Moses to become the personification, or embodiment, of the sudden evolutionary event that triggered the polarity switch of the human religious paradigm from female-centric to male-centric value system and paradigm. As the scholar R. Pettazone realized, "monotheism is always the accomplishment of a strong personality who, in a time of violent chaos, is driven to deny existing polytheistic beliefs and adopt the worship of the violence itself".[24] In the spectacle of Moses's experience with the burning bush, we witness (symbolically at any rate) the birth of a prototype: the first Western man, actively propagating the doctrine of racism and conquest, of misogyny and female oppression, all ordered by divine edict and providing cosmic justification for the use of any violence in the maintenance or expansion of the system.

Radical Social Restructuring
On the tribal level, the violence mobilized and directed externally to fight perceived enemies is the basis for all racism. Moses's monotheism

sets up the irreconcilable opposition between the believers and the nonbelievers, between the chosen people and those who are not. Monotheism provides cosmic justification to the believer to commit acts of aggression against the nonbeliever. Secure (though probably deluded) in the belief that the one God had chosen him and his people to prevail mightily over all who would contest and resist them. Moses sang his song of victory: "The Lord is a man of war... Thy right hand, Oh Lord is become glorious in power... Thy right hand, Oh Lord, has dashed in pieces the enemy... Thou stretches out thy right hand, the earth swallowed them."[25]

Moses now felt empowered, weaponized even, to proceed with his mission. First, he would lead the rebellion of the Hebrew tribes against Egypt and guide them to retake the old ancestral lands in Canaan. Second, once there, he was going to establish a nation ruled wholly on the superiority of the masculine principle of power in opposition to all surrounding female-centered kingdoms. As Yahweh commanded, "After the doing of the land of Egypt, wherein ye dwelt, shall ye not do, and after the doings of the land of Canaan, whither I bring you shall ye not do: neither shall you walk in their ordinances."[26]

To win over the Hebrews to his agenda, Moses employed the classic carrot-and-stick approach. The carrot was that as the "chosen people," they would enjoy the spoils of war in a "land of milk and honey." The stick was that all opponents of his plans would be put to death on the spot. And in fact, many did not agree with his plans and ideas. Time and time again, as the journey grew difficult, the people rebelled against Moses and sought refuge in their old gods and their ways. "Is this not the word that we did tell thee in Egypt saying, let us alone that we may serve the Egyptians? For it had been better for us to serve the Egyptians than die in the wilderness. Let us make a captain, and let us return to Egypt."[27]

On the family level, Moses expertly mobilized and directed the violence internally to physically dominate the perceived weaker female sex. The ten commandments represented his cosmic instrument for the legalization and institutionalization of the change from a female-centric to a male-centric social structure. They asserted the primacy of the male and the sanctity of his property, particularly women. Addressed only to the male sex, the commandments spelled out the new rules. "Keep all his statues and his commands... I command thee, and thy son, and thy son's son all the days of thy life."[28] Moses repurposed the religious and military organization with a male-centric emphasis. All firstborn sons were to be consecrated to the service of Yahweh: "Sacrifice to the Lord all that openeth the matrix, being males."[29] Jewish men were taught to pray, "Oh God, let not my offspring be a girl, for wretched is the life of women... Blessed be thou, Oh Lord our God, for not making me a woman."

Moses also reorganized the tribal living arrangements along male military lines of authority. "Everyman of the children of Israel shall pitch by his own standard, with the ensign of their father's house."[30] "From twenty years old and upward, all that are able to war in Israel, thou and Aron shall number them by their armies... Take ye the sum of all the congregation of the children of Israel, after their families, by the house of their father, with the number of their names, every male by their polls."[31]

Moses replaced the metronymic reckoning of descent and matri-locality of marriage with patriarchal order. Also, in the new Mosaic order, sexual freedom and honesty was replaced by sexual repression. This was necessary to guarantee the male line of descent. Only if a man knows that his wife is not sleeping with another man can he be sure that his son really is his son. Thus the abolition of sexual permissiveness went hand in hand with the subordination of women to men. Yahweh-Moses told the Hebrew tribes that, "I will put an end to your lewdness and harlotry brought from the land of Egypt."[32]

Despite the draconian measures Moses instituted to guarantee the success of his male-centric revolution, the Hebrew internally remained bitterly divided for many centuries. Dominance oscillated between the old female-centric ways and the new male-centric order of Yahwism. For example, as Moses was receiving his instructions on the mountain, the people once more reverted to their old ways and forced Aron to make a golden statue of the bull-calf Apis, the "ka" of Osiris, saying "These be thy gods oh, Israel, which brought thee out of the land of Egypt."[33] This really teed Moses off: "His anger waxed hot and he cast the tablets out of his hands, and broke them beneath the mount." He then gathered the sons of Levi and organized a wholesale slaughter as punishment, instructing the Levites to "put everyman a sword to his side, and go in and out from gate to gate throughout the camp, and slay everyman his brother, and everyman his companion, and everyman his neighbor."[34]

Historical Consequences

Even after the arrival of the Hebrew in Canaan, the Jews mainly worshipped Asherah, a local variation of Isis, for about six centuries. Only intermittently, and with gradually increasing intensity and frequency did the demand for the worship of Yahweh as the one and only god make itself heard and was heeded by the people and their leaders. So, for many centuries, Yahweh had to share center stage with Anat, Asherah, and other manifestations of the great goddess. For example, discoveries on the island of Elephantine, close to the first cataract of the Nile, have yielded information that an ancient Jewish colony there, whose chief was Jahu, worshipped female deities as well, and one of them was called Anat Jahu.

Just as the early Yahweh religion was unable to suppress worship of the Great Goddess, it was likewise unable to immediately suppress the ancient practices of social decision-making through sortition democracy. Even Moses, when faced with the need to decide how the spoils of the promised land were to be divided up, decided on the lottery. But when it matured, Judaism became a strong opponent of the practice of ancient sortition democracy. In Deuteronomy 8:10–11, Moses exhorts the Jews that "when you come into the land which Yahweh your God is giving you, do not learn to imitate the abominable customs of those other nations who listen to soothsayers and augurs, but Yahweh your God does not permit you to do this."[35]

Later variants of monotheism of the Islamic and Christian varieties joined Judaic monotheism in united opposition against the use of divinatory practices of oracles and lotteries. Islamic monotheism, through the Koran and its prophet Mohammed, strictly forbade divinatory practices, including lottery, on the grounds that all differences and disputes were to be referred to Allah through his prophet, and his hierarchical church structure, for resolution and judgment; this, of course, assured the totalization of his power.[36]

In other words, if there is only one chief cosmic decider, there is also only one human custodian and promulgator of the Word of God, the chief honcho of the Church. Fundamentally, sortition democracy challenges the authority of the hierarchies as desirable social decision-making mechanisms. The social hierarchy imposed by the monotheistic idea and power hierarchy is incompatible with inherently democratic nature of social and political selection through the sortition process.

Revisiting the story of Moses and monotheism is an example of the new, emerging field of geomythology that blends insights from geology and mythology to shed light on many ancient fables and stories to discern the historical truths they contain.[37] We've made the case that the Thera eruption of 1650 BCE was a contributing causal factor in the displacement of the female-centric social and religious values and systems of the ancient Mediterranean civilizations with male-centered social and religious values and systems in Egypt, Minoan Crete, and the Middle East desert kingdoms. Moreover, in his book *Geomythology: How Common Stories Reflect Earth Events*, Timothy J. Burbery also links the Thera eruption to the Ancient Greek mythological battle of the Titanomachy, the primordial battle in which the original pantheon of gods, named the Titans and headed by Uranus, was displaced by their own offspring, known as the Olympians, led by Zeus.[38]

Endnotes

1   Niles Eldredge and Stephen Jay Gould, Punctuated Equilibria: An Alternative to
     Phyletic Gradualism, (San Francisco: Freeman Cooper, 1972), 82–115.

2   John Turner, "Why we need evolution by jerks," New Scientist 101 (1984): 34–35.

3   Stephen Jay Gould and Steven Rose, ed., The Richness of Life: The Essential Stephen
     Jay Gould, (New York: W. W. Norton & Co., 2007), 6.

4   Christopher G. Newhall and Stephen Self, "The Volcanic Explosivity Index (VEI): An
     Estimate of Explosive Magnitude for Historical Volcanism," Journal of Geophysical
     Research 87, no. C2 (1982): 1231–1238, DOI:10.1029/JC087iC02p01231.

5   Barbara J. Sivertsen, The Parting of the Sea: How Volcanoes, Earthquakes and Plagues
     Shaped the History of the Exodus, (Princeton and Oxford: Princeton University Press,
     2009).

6   Ibid., 26.

7   Ibid.

8   Isaac Schultz, "Archaeologists Find Ancient Tsunami Victim on the Turkish Coast"
     Gizmodo, December 31, 2021, https://gizmodo.com/archaeologists-find-ancient
     -tsunami-victim-on-the-turki-1848288434.

9   Sigmund Freud, Moses and Monotheism, Vintage Books (New York: Random House,
     1996), 55, 145.

10   Olga Krzyszkowska, "So Where's the Loot? The Spoils of War and the Archaeological
     Record," In Robert Laffineur (ed.), Polemos: Le Contexte Guerrier en Egee a L'Age
     du Bronze. Actes de la 7e Rencontre egeenne internationale Universite de Liège, 1998.
     (Université de Liège, Histoire de l'art d'archeologie de la Grece antique, 1999),
     489–498.

11   Charles H. Hapgood, Maps of the Ancient Sea Kings, (New York: E.P. Dutton, 1979),
     144–150.

12   Ibid.

13   Cyril Aldred, Akhenaten, King of Egypt, (London: Thames and Hudson, 1988).

14   Ibid.

15   Barbara J. Sivertsen, The Parting of the Sea: How Volcanoes, Earthquakes and Plagues
     Shaped the History of the Exodus, (Princeton and Oxford: Princeton University Press,
     2009).

16   Sigmund Freud, Moses and Monotheism, Vintage Books (New York: Random House,
     1996), 18.

17   Immanuel Velikovsky, Worlds in Collision, (New York: Macmillan, 1950), 52.

18   Ibid.

19   Ibid., 58.

20   Exodus 2:13.

21   J. Hastings quoted by Merlin Stone in When God was a Woman, (Massachusetts:
     Houghton Mufflin Harcourt, 1978), 165.

22   Robert Briffault, The Mothers, (New York: MacMillan 1927), V.3, 192.

23   Allen Edwardes, Erotica Judaica: A Sexual History of the Jews, (New York, The Julian
     Press, 1967), 6.

24   R. Pettazone, "The Formation of Monotheism", in Less & Voight, eds., "Readers in
     Comparative Religion, Row and Peterson, 40.

25   Exodus 15:12.

26 Leviticus 18:3-5.

27 Numbers 14:3-4.

28 Deuteronomy 6:2.

29 Exodus 13:15.

30 Numbers 2:2.

31 Numbers 1:2-3.

32 Ezekiel 23:27.

33 Exodus 32:19.

34 Exodus 32:27.

35 M. Loewe and C. Blacker, "Oracles and Divination," Shambala, 218.

36 130 Ibid.

37 Timothy J. Burbery, Geomythology: How Common Stories Reflect Earth Events, (New York and London: Routledge, Taylor and Francis Group, 2021).

38 Ibid.

Chapter 7
....

From Archaic to Classical Greece (1200–400 BC)

The Yin-Yang of Ancient Greek Mythology

Greece and the Catastrophe

This chapter describes how the catastrophe that ended the Bronze Age in and around the Mediterranean basin was an instrumental factor in the paradigm shift from female-centric mythology and culture to male-centric culture, not only in Egypt and among the Hebrews, but also in Greece.

In the timeline of the Greek myths we see reflected the timeline of its history. In the beginning, the myths tell, the universe was female-centric. The Great Mother, Gaia, reproduced parthenogenetically until she decided to create a male partner, Uranus, to make a family with him. But soon Uranus grew greedy and engaged in a coup against his wife to seize power. Though unsuccessful, the idea of seizing power found fertile soil to grow in the minds of their offspring, especially the male gods. This led, ultimately, to the great War of the Titans, when the younger generations of gods revolted against their parents' generation and successfully dethroned them, taking their place as cosmic rulers.

The effect of the great catastrophes that started with the Thera explosion on the Greek culture and society was, well, catastrophic. Though not completely destroyed like the Minoan civilization, it was nearly obliterated and reduced basically to a chronic state of warfare between competing regions of city-states, much like Egypt. In these city-states, society was restructuring itself with male-centric institutions replacing female-centric institutions.

But this change from female-centric to male-centric was neither smooth nor homogenous. Different female-centric values survived in different nation-states and surrounding provinces, depending on political and economic needs. Athenian Democracy retained the female-centric value that all citizens are equal and must participate equally as well as the female-centric way of choosing representation through democratic sortition, where representation and membership on governing bodies was decided by a lottery system rather than an electoral process. And yet, Athenian democracy was highly misogynistic, as women were expressly excluded from being citizens and did not have the right to participate as equals in the democratic process. In contrast, Sparta, though an aggressive and militaristic regime, gave women full equal rights because the economics of their warfare made it expedient.

Primordial, Female-Centric Origin Myth

According to Hesiod in his *Theogony*, for the Greeks, Gaia represented the parthenogenic primordial ancestral mother of all life. She was even the mother of her own husband, for she alone and by herself conceived and birthed Uranus. She intended Uranus to become her equal and share power with him and, to that end, bequeathed to him the sky as the realm of his power. Gaia then took Uranus as her husband.

Not only did Gaia bring forth her husband, an intended equal, the sky, parthenogenically, she likewise created the Ourea (mountains) and Pontus (sea), and everything else on the world "without the sweet union of love,"[1] i.e., without father.

So Gaia, fecund Mother Earth, and Uranus, virile Father Sky, had twelve children: six boys and six girls. The boys were Oceanus, Coeus, Crius, Hyperion, Iapetus, and Cronus. The girls were Theia, Rhea, Themis, Mnemosyne, Phoebe, and Tethys. Gaia also gave birth to the Hecatonchires and the Cyclopses.

It is worth noting here that in the first three generations of male-centric Greek mythology, the myths still reflect the more ancient model of pre-catastrophic female-centric agricultural civilization in which mother-son and brother-sister marriages were prevalent. Siblings Cronus and Rhea would marry and produce offspring. And likewise, in the third generation, brother and sister Zeus and Hera would marry and produce offspring.

Life Among the Greek Gods: Misogyny, Incest, and Murder

After the honeymoon period, a discord grew between Gaia and Uranus, as (male) human passions disrupted their divine harmony. Uranus had gotten addicted to his power and developed the fear his children might challenge his rule and get rid of him. To prevent this from happening, imposing his will on his wife and offspring, Uranus imprisoned all of Gaia's children in Tartarus, the hellish underground.

The result? Universal misery, unhappiness, pain, and suffering. The misogyny of Uranus toward Gaia, his extreme violence against her, is the first recorded instance of the subordinate male-centric power supplanting the superior female-centric principle. The event fits into the process of post-catastrophic, male-centric polytheism replacing and supplanting pre-catastrophic female-centric polytheism.

As a showcase of male-centered polytheism, in which violence, war, and power struggles predominate, post-traumatic Greek mythology was populated by a testosterone-adrenalin suffused culture that reflected the Greek social reality of discord and war between tribes and nations, among conditions of geological and climatic chaos.

It also, as we shall see shortly, sets up the pattern of conflict and generational war by igniting the power struggle of the younger generation to supplant the older generation, their parents, both in the heavens and on earth, for immortals and mortals alike, as gods and rulers.

Gaia planned her revenge carefully. With her magical powers and skill, she created a great sickle and urged her children to use it and punish Uranus by castrating him. All her children refused, except Cronus, who agreed to do it. He hid in ambush when Gaia and Uranus met, then sprang forth and cut off his father's genitals and threw them into the sea. In retaliation, Uranus promptly prophesied that Cronus's own children would rebel against his rule and dethrone him.

Cronus then took his father's throne and, astonishingly, proceeded to repeat the very behavioral pattern that he had emasculated his father for. Like his father, Uranus, Cronus began consolidating power by imprisoning his siblings as well as the Hecatonchires and the Cyclopses, in Tartarus.

Cronus then mated with his older sister Rhea. Together they parented the second generation of gods. They had six offspring, the six Olympian gods, three male (Zeus, Hades, and Poseidon) and three female (Hestia, Demeter, and Hera).

Becoming more and more power mad like his horrible father, Cronus also killed all the children his wife Rhea bore him by swallowing them. Fortunately, Rhea managed to hide her youngest child, Zeus, by tricking Cronus into swallowing a rock in a blanket. Rhea bided her time and plotted her revenge.

War of the Titans

Rhea's revenge was not long coming. Zeus was brought up secretly by Amalthea in a cave in Crete, and when he became the proper age, he was insinuated into the court of Cronus as his cupbearer. The goddess Metis then provided Zeus a mixture of wine and mustard to give to Cronus to drink. Doing so caused Cronus to vomit out all his swallowed children, conveniently all grown up. Zeus then led his brothers and sisters in a renewed rite of misogynous and patricidal rebellion in the second male power grab by the Olympians, as they called themselves, after their divine retreat on Mount Olympus.

In this mythological War of the Titans, as it came to be called, the top couple, Cronus and Rhea, and their cohorts, were rebelled against and overthrown by their own offspring. Led by Zeus himself, the god of war, these first Olympians (including Poseidon, Hera, Demeter, and Hestia), along with the principal offspring of Zeus (Athena, Apollo, Artemis, Ares, Aphrodite, Hephaestus, Hermes, and Dionysus), overthrew and banished their own parents.

First, Zeus released the Hecatonchires and the Cyclopses from Tartarus, and they were very helpful in the struggle. The Hecatonchires hurled stones, and the Cyclopses fashioned for Zeus his iconic thunder and lightning. It took ten years, but eventually, the offspring beat their parents and became the supreme gods, imprisoning their parents in the lower depths of Tartarus.

As if to underscore the victory of the male-centric principle in this battle, Zeus proceeded to rape Tyche, the goddess of fate and fortune. Tyche, in turn, had her own revenge: she gave birth to a daughter who invented all the gambling games so that she could watch with "malicious delight" the quarrelsome chaos they sowed among men.

Archaic Greece (1200–1100 BCE)

The Trojan War

The war in the heavens between the Titans and the Olympians was mirrored on Earth in the Trojan War. The very same petty but deadly male-centric concerns with power and domination that motivated the war between the gods motivated the war between the humans. The Trojan War pitted the Achaeans (Greeks), united under Agamemnon, against the city of Troy and its royal house, King Priam and his sons (Paris among them). The ostensible reason for the war was revenge by the Greeks for Paris of Troy stealing Helen from her husband, King Menelaus of Sparta.

Homer's epics were likely a fusion of various tales, sieges, and expeditions by the Mycenean Greeks during the Bronze Age around the 12th or 11th century BCE. Amplified by Homer's fertile mind with a great number of supernatural feats and the interference and participation of the divine immortals gods in the war, the Trojan War was an inflection point, where Greece's mythology and history coincided, where gods interfered in the lives of men, and men dared question their claim to authority over them.

But Homer did not write the tale celebrating the Trojan War (the *Iliad* and the *Odyssey*) until some four or five centuries after it had occurred, in the late eighth or early seventh century BCE. For that reason, the events depicted there were, at first, relegated to myth by Western archeological science. But since time immemorial, the Greeks themselves always maintained that the Trojan War was history and that Troy was located somewhere near the Dardanelles.

This claim proved to be true when it was validated by the German archeologist Heinrich Schliemann in 1868. His excavations proved that ancient Troy was at the site of the current city of Hisarlik in Turkey.[2] The archeological evidence found there pointed conclusively to a catastrophic burning of Troy. Today, it is generally accepted that the Trojan War took place over ten years between 1194 and 1184 BCE, as claimed by Eratosthenes.

The Late Bronze Age Collapse

The Trojan War took place during a period in prehistory that is known as the Late Bronze Age collapse. So not only did the Trojans perish at the hands of the Greeks, but the Greeks themselves, as well as their gods and their religion, also perished in the chaos of the Bronze Age collapse. This collapse was the result of the latest wave in a series of natural conflagrations the Mediterranean had been enduring for the last 500 years, beginning with the eruption of Thera.

The Late Bronze Age collapse was, therefore, a "dark age" and transition period for the vast geographical area comprised of the Near East, North Africa, the Balkans, the Aegean, Anatolia, and the Caucasus. The nature of the transition was violent, sudden, and culturally disruptive and involved widespread societal and civilizational collapse.

The Greek Dark Ages lasted from the twelfth to the ninth centuries BCE.[3] During this period, significant shifts occurred. The palace economy of the Aegean region (including Mycenaean Greece and Anatolia) that characterized the Late Bronze Age disintegrated, and vastly more decentralized forms of socio-economic organization, in the form of small, isolated village cultures, took its place. In the eighth century BCE, these centers began to re-coalesce into the urban poleis of Archaic Greece.

The religion of a culture always expresses the conditions of its environment. If conditions are harmonious, the religious rituals will reflect and express a female-centric worldview. If the conditions are crisis-like, the religion will be male-centric and reflect the violence of the conflict. Zeus and his Olympians were the generation of gods that intermingled and interfered with the mortals at the time of the Trojan War.

With the repeated disintegration of the Mediterranean civilizations during the ages of chaos and the general victory of the male-centric paradigm over the female-centered paradigm, the latter, for the most part, disappeared with only fragments being retained in the sociopolitical structures of the various city-states that re-emerged from the chaos.

Athena's Birth and Its Meaning

Still today, the influence of Ancient Greece can be seen in our own values and behaviors. The quandaries, contradictions, and imbalances that threaten the very survival of our own civilization today were already present then. No part of the Greek experience has been more influential as a source of inspiration and enlightenment to Western civilization than the history and meaning of Athens. As the fountainhead of the ideals of our own democratic society, Athens and Greek democracy occupy a special place in our hearts. Athens was named after Athena, Zeus's daughter, the goddess of wisdom, war, and justice and was Athens's patron goddess. So, to understand Athens and the ideals it was founded upon, we must first appreciate the basic facts about Athena, her mythic birth, and how the city came to be named after her.

After Uranus, his grandfather, and Cronus, his father, Zeus was the third generation of the male-centric tradition who accomplished the violent overthrow of the existing power structure of the Greek gods by dethroning their parents, especially Cronus, his dad. Zeus, being the god of gods, had no rival, and he intended to keep it that way. He conquered his throne through fierce fighting with no intention of sharing it, even less of conceding it. So when Metis was about to give birth, Zeus, who was never short of a trick, sent his wife a challenge to see just how great a metamorphosis she was capable of. Metis, far from imagining what was really going on, entered into the game. She went through a series of incredible transformations until, urged by Zeus, she turned herself into a drop of water. Zeus congratulated, applauded, and swallowed her. Delighted with the trick he had played, the king of the gods went about his business. A short time later, Zeus was overcome with atrocious headaches. So sharp was the pain that he called upon all the divinities of Olympus for help. To ease Zeus, his son Hephaestus, god of the blacksmiths, struck him a terrible blow on the head with his sledgehammer. Immediately— wonder of wonders!—a young girl, armed and helmeted, sprang out of the crack. She gave a deafening war cry that echoed around Olympus. The gods were struck with fear. The rivers and the seas swelled with roaring waves, and the sun reined in his fire horses. Athena had just been born.

The meaning of the myth of Athena's birth must be interpreted within the context of the religious revolution in which the female-centric polytheistic universe was superseded by a male-centric pantheon of gods. In the words of Sigmund Freud, "In those dark centuries which historical research is only to beginning to explore, the countries around the Mediterranean were apparently the scene of frequent volcanic eruptions, which were bound to make the deepest impressions on the inhabitants... There is hardly a doubt that in those obscure times mother deities were replaced by male gods."[4]

In this revolution, the male-centric power victors had one small origin problem, that of explaining where they themselves came from. Could the gods be more powerful than that which brought them forth? Faced with the female parthenogenic principle of the universe, these all-powerful male gods still had to explain somehow why and how the male principle of power gives birth to the female principle of procreation.

As described above, Zeus attempted to solve the problem by tricking his wife Metis, and "giving birth" to Athena himself, an act of ultimate diminishment of the female principle by the male principle. As Freud noted, by this act, Zeus reduced the Great Mother Goddess to a daughter, robbed Athena of her mother, and was condemned by her father to remain an eternal virgin who would never have children herself.[5]

Athena and Athens

During the ceremonies that marked the process by which the Olympian gods had decided to each adopt and associate themselves with one particular city, a conflict arose between Poseidon, Zeus's brother, and Athena, Zeus's daughter. The tension in the meeting mounted as both Poseidon and Athena claimed possession of Attica. Seeing his brother and his daughter arguing more and more violently, Zeus decided that the king of Attica, the wise Cecrops, would be the arbitrator in this conflict.

As "the first king of Athens," Cecrops was the exemplary sovereign. He forbade human sacrifices. He made his region of Attica the most civilized country in the world. He established monogamy, marriage, and created the first laws and courts. And something unheard of, not only did he give men the right to vote, but he also gave it to women. Cecrops did as Zeus wished and retired to his palace. A few hours later, he reappeared and declared that the patron of the town would be the god who gave man the most useful gift.

Poseidon was convinced he would win. The god of the oceans aimed his trident at the ground and made a magnificent water spring appear. The salt water flowed across the arid plains. He offered the inhabitants of Attica a sumptuous lake, a sort of gigantic swimming pool in which men were able to take their leisure and practice the water sports which they loved so much. Then he topped off his gift by offering Cecrops himself a splendid black stallion, a magic, reputedly invincible warhorse, which sprang from the spray.

Athena considered carefully. Then, with a wave of her hand, she made a tree grow out of the earth, an immense tree with silver branches and a knotted trunk, an olive tree. An olive tree whose leaves she proclaimed would never fall, not even when winter came. "This tree," she declared, "will bear fruit that you will press when it is fully ripe. I will feed you, your children, and your children's children. This tree will be a symbol of the peace and fertility that I grant you."

To the inhabitants of Attica the choice was simple and straightforward: Poseidon offered them entertainment and war. Athena offered them peace and agriculture. Under the watchful eye of Themis, the goddess of justice, the inhabitants of Attica began to vote. And it was the women's vote that tipped the divine balance in favor of Athena.

Poseidon flew into an uncontrollable rage. In revenge for this humiliation, he determined to submerge Attica beneath the waves. But Zeus, who had attentively followed the battle, forbade him to do it. So, the lord of the oceans left Olympus, full of bitterness and hatred toward Zeus's daughter. He plunged into the abyss and returned to his palace, where he hid away to consider some fresh revenge.

In homage to the goddess, the people of Attica decided that, henceforth, their city would be called Athens, and Athena's own son, Erichthonius, would be the first king to reign over the newly named city. Indeed, it was Athena who inspired mortals to be audacious and clearheaded, giving them a new form of bravery guided by reflection and cunning instead of disorganized, blind fury. Athena, the goddess of war, appeared to mortals as the opposite of her brother Ares, who was also god of war, but a god of carnage and blood. Athena, unlike Ares, put intelligence in the service of war in order to bring about peace, as opposed to the extermination of the enemy.

As the protectress of the city's heroes, Athena played a major part in the success of their exploits. Without her precious help, Perseus would never have managed to beat the horrible Medusa, whose scowling face then decorated Athena's shield—a gift from the heroic Perseus to his protectress. During the Trojan War, Athena gave the Greeks the strategic idea of hiding inside a giant horse. Later she helped Odysseus return to Ithaca. It is also she who, disguised as a wise mentor, guided the efforts of the young Telemachus to trace his father. Finally, Athena also allowed Prometheus to secretly enter Olympus so he could steal fire, which he took back to Earth to give to the mortals.

In time, Athena also became protectress of the state, a guarantor of the equity of laws and their correct application, but she quickly realized that without prosperity, laws alone were not enough. So, in order for men's well-being to develop, she gave them the plow and the yoke for their oxen. She also taught them numbers. She instructed the women in the culinary arts as well as weaving and spinning. She passed on the intricacies of shipbuilding—how to work wood, polish planks, and assemble the different elements of the structure. In this way, she supervised the construction of the *Argo*, in its time, the biggest ship ever built. Aboard it, Jason and his sailors would go to retrieve the famous Golden Fleece.

In conclusion, in the myths of Athena, we can see the persistence in Greek culture and history of the pre-catastrophic human conception of a female-centric cosmos. Through the male-centric revolution in Greece, the Great Mother was not eliminated, as with Moses and the Hebrews, but in Athena, she was demoted from her supreme position to a subordinate position as the offspring of, and therefore under the authority of, her father, Zeus, and his male-centric divine culture.

Classical Greece (600–400 BCE)

Solon in Athens

It took at least half a millennium after the Late Bronze Age collapse for Greek society to re-evolve and reinvent itself. In 600 BCE, Athens was still in the early stages of rebuilding the city after its destruction, still unassuming in its appearance and proportions. Neither the Parthenon, nor the Temple of Hephaestus (known as the Theseion or Theseum), nor other sumptuous feats of architecture had yet been built. However, the Agora Plaza was already the center of the athletic, artistic, business, social, spiritual, and political life of the new Athens being reborn.

The class structure of Athenian society at that time was dominated by the Eupatridae, the aristocrats who owned the best land and monopolized the government. Below them in the social pecking order were the intermediate classes of farmers, craftsmen, and merchants, who had little to no political power. As for the less fortunate and most destitute on the lowest rung of the ladder, they were easily and habitually driven into debt, mortgaging their land, and even themselves, and thus risking losing their freedom and being sold into slavery. For the vast majority of people, life was still a brutal struggle for survival.

And yet, it seems like the spirit of Athena still watched over her city, imbuing at least a few of the rulers with her spirit of wisdom, compassion, and justice to make changes to the social fabric to benefit the greater good of all. The sage Solon (c. 630 to c. 560 BCE) was one such man, a sage remembered particularly for his efforts to legislate against political, economic, and moral decline in Archaic Athens.

When Solon came into power, he introduced a revolutionary law, the Seisachtheia, which means "shaking off burdens." With this law, all outstanding debts were forgiven and all land mortgages disappeared. Whoever had become a slave because of his debts was liberated. He also instituted a census of annual income and divided the citizens into four income groups according to political privilege. All citizens were entitled to attend the General Assembly, which passed laws, elected officials, and heard appeals. Additionally, he created a Supreme Court, whose members were former chief rulers of Athens. All in all, Solon offered the Athenians a humane code of laws and a balanced constitution. He did not seek perfection in his legislation, believing that the lawmaker must tailor the law to the limits of human nature and not ask too much. So while his reforms may have failed in the short-term, on account of the class structure of Athenian society, he is often credited with having laid the foundation for democracy.[6] In the end, Solon's stellar reputation as a civic leader was cemented by his humility in relinquishing the extra-ordinary authority that had been bestowed upon him. After the completion of his economic, political and moral reforms, Solon left Athens for an extended period of time to allow the Athenians to absorb and codify his reforms themselves free from his influence.[7]

Class Structure in Classical Greece

One of the innovations that was made during this period was instrumental to enabling the Archaic Greek culture to evolve rapidly into the Classical Greek culture. It was the discovery and extensive use of iron that enabled civilization to be re-established more powerfully than ever before. It allowed the Greeks to embark on a renewed campaign of the colonization of the Mediterranean basin. On the Greek mainland in the fifth and fourth centuries BCE, this culminated in the establishment of Classical Greece, whose ideas and culture are still fundamental to our culture today.

The ancient world of Classical Greece, like the modern world up to this point, was based on the economics of scarcity and class structure as the prerequisite for civilization. Both Athens and Sparta, for example, being the most powerful city-states, had a male-centric class structure that, depending on how you counted them, consisted of the slave class, the lower class, the middle class, and the upper class (the 1%, so to speak).

People in the slave class were used as servants and laborers and had no legal rights. Both the city-states, such as Athens, and citizen families could own slaves. Slave women performed innumerable tasks depending on the type of household they belonged to, including spinning and weaving, cooking, cleaning, fetching water, etc. Or they might have been a child's nurse. Some were employed as waitresses, or as dancers or entertainers, even as prostitutes.

The lower class was made up of noncitizens, freedmen who, at one point, had been slaves. In numbers, the lower-class population vastly exceeded that of the upper class, who ruled over them. Lower-class men were not allowed to vote and were told what to do by upper-class men. Lower-class women had to work for a living, selling homemade cloth or foodstuffs.

The middle class consisted mostly of noncitizen professionals: merchants, contractors, manufacturers, managers, tradesmen, craftsmen, and artists. These were free men, and not slaves, but as noncitizens, they could never become citizens, could not vote, own land, or marry into the family of a citizen. Middle-class women had much work to do and fewer or no slaves to do it for them.

The ruling upper class, or 1%, was characterized by their freedom from having to contribute any actual social, collective human labor. That was relegated to the lower classes! Those of the upper class were not supposed to do any work but fully devote themselves to the pursuit of what was defined as noble and virtuous in their culture. So the Spartan 1% were wholly occupied by and devoted to the pursuit of war and military matters of strategy, tactics, conditioning, etc. The Athenian 1%, on the other hand, devoted all their time and passion to the civil and peaceful pursuit of politics and philosophy in their democratic society.

Athens and Sparta flourished in the fifth and fourth century BCE and came to represent a kind of yin-yang polarity among the Ancient Greek city-states. Each city-state, though clearly male-centric in their social organization, also remembered and incorporated in their social structure different elements of the ancient female-centric paradigm. In Athens, there developed a proud intellectual and political culture that featured democratic decision-making. In Sparta, a profoundly physical culture flourished in which equality of the sexes was an integral structural element of its social organization.

The Casting of Lots and Sortition Democracy

We have seen that the collective decision-making mechanisms of pre-cataclysmic, female-centric world order relied more on the principle of synchrony than diachrony. That is, the meaning of an event was determined more by the context of other events, or gestalts, that were happening simultaneously with it, rather than deriving the meaning from a cause and effect of sequential temporal unfolding. The ancient Taoist practice of the *I Ching* is the most profound and complete example of this. It is an oracular system that exemplifies this approach to divine meanings from the coincidence or simultaneity of events. By following certain procedures of "choosing" sticks from a pile, or simply through the throwing of coins, the *I Ching* provides the answer to the questions asked by petitioners.

An integral part of this approach consisted of settling the eternal questions about decision-making and decision makers through use of the justice of chance: the inherently democratic and egalitarian method of the lottery would decide who would do or get what among a set of equally qualified claimants.

No big surprise, therefore, when, at the end of the battle of the Titans, it came down to dividing the spoils, Zeus and his brothers, Poseidon and Hades, fell back on the most ancient and the most democratic method, drawing lots to determine who would get what, how the realms of power were to be divided, and especially, who among them should be the supreme ruler of the universe. That's how Zeus got the sky, Poseidon got the oceans, and Hades got the underworld and the world of the dead.

As it developed, Athenian democracy was a sincere and admirable attempt, though flawed and incomplete, to do away with hierarchical, autocratic decision-making and introduce the democracy of chance. Because it utilized the lottery in regulating the affairs of society and selecting its agents of responsibility, Athenian democracy was called "sortition democracy." The inspirational legacy of Athenian sortition democracy was to show the world how to utilize the power of fate and the justice of chance to promote the common good.

The Athenian 1% upper class was a leisure-loving class that lived in material abundance. Aristotle declared that the virtuous life was not one devoted to work: "In the most nobly constituted state... the citizens must not live a mechanic or a mercantile life, for such a life is ignoble and inimical to virtue... nor yet must those who are to be citizens in the best state be tillers of the soil."[8]

In other words, people who are too busy working don't have the time to perform their civic duty or develop sophisticated morals. This, of course, referred to the lower classes, the merchants and farmers, and especially to slaves, who, by definition, were excluded from equality and citizenship in the democracy.

Athenian democracy was also an echo of the egalitarianism of the ancient female-centric paradigm in the conditions of inequality of the male-centric class structure of society. For citizenship was hereditary only in the male line. As a male, you were born into the upper class, and inherited your citizenship from your father. Citizen males were forbidden to have jobs; slaves were there to do the work of tending to their land and fortunes. Only this arrangement could guarantee them the leisure for things like government, war, literature, and philosophy.

Aristotle and the Athenians defined their concept of democracy as follows: "It is accepted as democratic when public offices are allocated by lot; and as oligarchic when they are filled by election."[9] In a democratic society, government officials are selected directly by lottery from the pool of citizens to do the necessary work of the state.

For Aristotle and the Athenian democrats, equality, freedom, and duty were inextricably linked. Athenian upper-class democracy was based on the idea that citizens who are equal in any respect are equal absolutely. Likewise, all citizens who are free are, therefore, absolutely free.

But the freedom of equality enjoyed by the upper class also entailed a responsibility to society: since all citizens are equal, they all have the equal duty to participate in the nuts and bolts of running society.[10] Collectively, they are the pool of "eligibles" from which public office holders would be selected by lottery. This is called "sortition" democracy (from the Latin *sors*, meaning "lot"). The lottery selection process is the only process that can guarantee fair and democratic results.

According to the Ancient Greek definition of democracy, modern Western democracies are not political democracies at all, but political oligarchies. For in oligarchy, government officials are elected by their fellow citizens as their proxies to do the necessary work of the state. Our current democratic concepts of majority rule, one vote per person, and elected representation were not original features of Greek democracy but were characteristics of the oligarchic makeup of most Greek city-states as well as that of their successor, the Roman Republic.

Aristotle and the Athenians strongly opposed the oligarchic model of electing representative as guaranteeing the eventual corruption of the candidates running for office by the wealthy ruling class. They predicted that any oligarchical civilization chosen by electoral methods would be brought down from internal corruption and the ownership of the political class by the economic powerhouses. Roman civilization proved the point, and now, Western man's global civilization is proving it for the second time on an unimaginable scale.

Sparta: Oligarchy and Equality of the Sexes

On the banks of the Eurotas River in the Lakonian region of Greece, the city-state of Sparta rose to military dominance as a land power in the mid-seventh century BCE.[11] Sparta was an oligarchy. The state was ruled by two hereditary kings, the heads of two ancient families equal in authority. They controlled all aspects of religious, judicial, and military life, in other words, true autocrats with militaristic ambitions. Aristotle said of the Spartan kings that their role and function was that of "a kind of unlimited and perpetual generalship,"[12] since Sparta's socio-economic organization was optimized to carry out their militaristic aims and strategies.

The Spartans were a minority of the Lakonian population. To be a citizen, one had to be able to trace their ancestry to the original inhabitants of the city. The largest class of inhabitants were the helots, prisoners of war, whose status and function were more akin to those of serfs and slaves, to provide the labor force, since all Spartan citizens did not have time for work. Being soldiers and all, their only concern was war, battle, and the "spoils of war."

Spartan women of the citizenry class enjoyed a status, power, and respect that was unknown in the rest of the classical world. Unlike in Athens, Spartan girls were fed the same food as their brothers from the beginning. They were not confined to their father's house and prevented from exercising or getting fresh air as in Athens. Indeed, they exercised and even competed in sports. Most importantly, rather than being married off at the age of 12 or 13, Spartan law forbade the marriage of a girl until she was in her late teens or early 20s. Spartan women, better fed from childhood and fit from exercise, stood a far better chance of reaching old age than their sisters in other Greek cities, where the median age for death was 34.6 years or roughly 10 years below that of men.

The reason women were treated well in Sparta was their strategic role in the city-state's military goals, as defined by the oligarchs and kings. Women were encouraged to engage in polygamous or polyandrous behavior in order to bear as many strong-bodied children as they could. As the Spartan population was hard to maintain due to the constant absence and loss of the men in battle, and on account of the Spartan belief that breeding should be between the most physically fit parents, the practice of wife-sharing was common in Sparta. Many older men allowed younger, more fit men to impregnate their wives, and unmarried or childless men might even request another man's wife to bear his children if she had previously been a strong child bearer.

Certainly, the women in Sparta had a better lot than their counterparts in Athens, where women were completely subservient to men and expected to marry into their social status of citizen wife. As such, they could not own land or engage in politics, literature, philosophy, and war. Instead, they were expected to spend a lot of their time spinning and weaving, for producing the cloth used for family clothing and bedding was the most important task for upper-class females, who more likely than not, also had slaves to help them do their tasks.

In the end, the greatest shortcoming of Athenian sortition democracy was that it actually institutionalized the victory of the new, male-centric culture. Not only were foreigners and slaves forbidden to participate in the Athenian democratic process but also, specifically, women! Only males of the proper race and class were to be admitted to the democracy of fate and the justice of chance.

It's well-known, of course, that Athens and Sparta developed a fierce economic and cultural rivalry that culminated in military conflict—the Peloponnesian War, which lasted from 431 to 404 BCE. Though a protracted conflict, in the end, Sparta emerged the victor and defeated Athens. But as the saying goes, the more things change, the more they stay the same. Only 50 years later, circa 350

BCE, Philip II of Macedon conquered all of Greece except Sparta, and a few decades later, Philip's son Alexander finished the job and subjugated Sparta in 331 BCE.

After the Macedonians reduced the viability of both Athens and Sparta as city-states, in the 200 years from 323 to 146 BCE, Hellenistic civilization fueled an expansion that spread it from the Western Mediterranean to Central Asia. This Hellenistic expansion of Greek society came to an end in 146 BC when the Roman Republic, after having defeated the armies of Alexander the Great, annexed Greece.

Greek Male-Centric Polytheism and Hebrew Male-Centric Monotheism

Polytheism's essential psychological mechanism is the projection of human characteristics onto the forces of nature, whether terrestrial or celestial, imbuing them with immortality and magic powers, thus creating its myths and narrative. In other words, the human mind created the gods based on the human image. Comparing Hebrew and Greek religions, we saw a switch from female-centered religion to male-centered religion. Male hierarchical structure of the dominator and the dominated are expressed as misogyny and racism. Both being products of the testosterone-adrenalin axis that is at the root of their desire for power, men will seek to dominate women and other men they are in competition with for the women and, in the larger collective sense, will militarily assert the superiority of their own tribe in its relations with other groups and ethnicities.

In Greece, the male-centric principle of power displaced the female centeredness in such a way that female-centric polytheism changed into, and was superseded by, male-centric polytheism. The change from female-centric to the male-centric polytheism by the Greeks did not change this mechanism but only reversed the dominance of the polarity from yin to yang. In Hebrew religion, the change was even more radical, since female-centric polytheism was replaced, in one fell swoop, by male-centric monotheism, and the corresponding hierarchical social structures were imposed on the people by force and maintained by threat of death.

The psychological mechanisms involved in conceiving a mono-theistic, all-powerful, male deity were a powerful tour de force relying on perception, identification, and projection. First, Moses identified completely with the violence of the catastrophe that was punishing humanity. And then Moses projected his own violent character traits onto whom he knew to be heavenly instigator of the violence.

By projecting his own character onto the local god Yahweh, then elevating this local god's stature as the violent and rage-filled solitary master of the universe, Moses, in fact, created God in his own image, a violent god, a god of wrath. In other words, the Mosaic God was the product of the mind of a madman in conditions of extreme chaos and violence. In the final analysis, the Mosaic experience with the burning bush refutes the fundamental premise and creation stories of all three monotheistic religions: it tells us that man was not created by an act of God's imagination but that God was created by an act of man's imagination.

Thus a violent and rage-filled man became the perfect messenger and host for a violent and rage-filled God. And as the servant of Yahweh, Moses accepted his perceived mission to impose Yahweh's will on the Hebrews. The Book of Exodus clearly recounts Moses's ruthlessness in converting the Hebrew's female-centric religious and social institutions into male-centric ones. Using the carrot and the stick—the "promised land of milk and honey" if they obeyed and death if they didn't—Moses molded the Hebrews into the chosen people, and convinced them they were chosen specifically by God and his prophet to conquer and rule over other human beings.

In polytheism, the female procreative functions of fertility, fecun-dity, and birthing were habitually supreme and the basis of the equal-ity of the sexes in the social and economic organization of their society. The male-centric reinterpretation of this bedrock principle required some creative thinking, as the story to be told had to describe the male-centric power function as being the source of, or giving birth to, the female birthing function. Thus, in Greek mythology, Athena was born and sprang fully formed from the head of Zeus, and in Hebrew monotheism, Yahweh created Eve from one of Adam's ribs.

Since the depth of trauma experienced will influence the severity of the psychosocial reaction, perhaps the Hebrews experienced the catastrophes more intensely than the Greeks. The Hebrews in 1600 BC may have been more directly impacted, being closer to the center of the catastrophes. Some 500 years later, what the Archaic Greeks were experiencing in the Late Bronze Age collapse was somewhat less severe, coming in the form of aftershocks, since they were located on the periphery of the main events.

The Greeks, as expressed by Homer's hero Odysseus, concluded that, once man realizes the gods were created by the mind of man, he does not need them anymore and the gods will effectively die. The Hebrews, unfortunately, stayed caught in the religious trap Moses lured them into, and the triumph of their monotheism over polytheism represented the ultimate triumph of the male-centric paradigm over the female-centric one.

Endnotes

1   Hesiod, Theogony, line 104, http://www.perseus.tufts.edu/hopper/text?doc=urn:cts
    :greekLit:tlg0020.tlg001.perseus-eng1:104-138.

2   Trevor Bryce, The Trojans and Their Neighbours, (Oxford: Taylor & Francis,
    2005), 37, ISBN 978-0-415-34959-8.

3   Robert Drews, The End of the Bronze Age: Changes in Warfare and the
    Catastrophe ca. 1200 BCE, (Princeton: Princeton University Press, 1993), 22,
    ISBN 978-0691048116.

4   Sigmund Freud, Moses and Monotheism, Vintage Books (New York: Random House,
    1996), 55.

5   Ibid., 145.

6   Ibid.

7   Herodotus 1.29 (e.g. Campbell's translation 2707); see also, Plutarch, Solon 25.1.
    see also: Plutarch, Solon 25.1.

8   Aristotle, H. Rackham (trans.), Politics, (Cambridge: Harvard University Press;
    London: William Heinemann Ltd., 1944), 7.1328b, http://www.perseus.tufts.edu
    /hopper/text?doc=Perseus%3Atext%3A1999.01.0058%3Abook%3D7%3
    Asection%3D1328b.

9   Ibid., 4.1294be.

10 Ibid., 1301a28–35.

11 Paul Cartledge, Sparta and Lakonia: A Regional History 1300 to 362 BC (2nd ed.),
    (Oxford: Routledge, 2002), ISBN 0-415-26276-3.

12 Aristotle, H. Rackham (trans.), Politics, (Cambridge: Harvard University Press;
    London: William Heinemann Ltd., 1944), Pol. iii. 1285a.

Chapter 8

....

Roman Civilization and the Rise of Christianity (300 BCE–284 CE)

The Male-Centric Nature of Roman Civilization

Male-centric social structure and religion became dominant, not only in Jewish beliefs and society but in all the post-catastrophic cultures and civilizations to emerge in the Mediterranean area. First in Greece, but even more in the subsequent Roman civilization, we find aggressively expansionist and warlike behavior, "chosen people" ideology, and dominance of the male-centric principle that "might makes right."

The Roman Republic began in the sixth century BCE. After initial victories over the Etruscans and other leagues of Italian city-states, the Roman Republic ascended to unchallenged supremacy within the Italian peninsula in less than a century. Subsequently, they embarked on their outward expansion. The Romans went on to conquer and consolidate the fragmented and warring Greek city-states under its control in 146 BC. In the process, they basically copied and appropriated the Greek male-centric religion and myths as their own.

When the Roman Republic transitioned from an aristocratic government to a more oligarchic one, voting became more open, but running for office became more restricted, with more property requirements in addition to having served at least 10 years in the military. Then, as now, elections were often characterized by tension between the patricians (the ruling class, the 1%) and the plebeians (which represented over 90% of the people). These elections were dominated by the oligarchic elite (businessmen and politicians, about 5 to 10% of the people).

Then, as now, many candidates resorted to bribery to convince people to cast their votes for them. Pay-to-play, Roman-style bribery was seen as a normal part of the political process. Frequently, those already in power would preselect candidates for office, which along with the Roman system of patronage, effectively tied the votes of the lower classes to an elite.

Then, as now, with many voters increasingly seeing elections as irrelevant to their own lives, the corruption of the democratic electoral process caused a lack of faith in it. In Rome, this led, in part, to civil war, and eventually, the corruption of the electoral process led to the abolition of democratic elections altogether. First, civil war broke out in the first century BCE between Julius Caesar and Pompey and later between Octavian and Mark Antony (which Octavian won).

Octavian arose and promised to unify and "make Rome great again." He hastened the final decline of democratic elections in Rome and, eventually, eliminated elections entirely and had himself crowned as Caesar Augustus, the first Roman Emperor. By the time of Caesar, however, even though the frontiers of the Roman Empire continued to expand, its internal integrity had begun to wane. The transformation from Republic to Empire really just masked its weakening and disintegration.

The intertwined factors of this disintegration are many, but chief among them were a growing moral bankruptcy, the decline of indigenous religion, the demoralization of the armies, and a disastrous decline in agricultural productivity. The growth of an idle urban proletariat added to the discontent and anger of the oppressed and exploited peoples of the Mediterranean and beyond. And nowhere of course was this anger better demonstrated than in the volatility of the relationships between the Jews and their conquerors at the time of Christ, culminating not only in his crucifixion but in the deaths of some 30,000 Jews ten years later and, finally, in the destruction of Jerusalem itself in 70 CE.

Rise of Female-Centric Gnostic Christianity

As a result of the disintegration of the male-centric religious and social systems occurring behind the façade of imperial strength, the female-centric tendencies began to reassert themselves throughout the Mediterranean area. In Rome itself, beginning with the upper classes, women increasingly insisted on living their own lives, and the archaic Roman marriage laws were gradually replaced by new forms in which the man and the woman bound themselves to each other with voluntary and mutual vows.

In Greece and Asia Minor as well as in Egypt, women led the way in revivals of the ancient religions of the Mother Goddess, particularly the goddess Isis. Women everywhere took up education, the arts, and the professions. In particular, and not surprisingly in Egypt, the land of original female-centric civilization, women attained a relatively advanced state of emancipation, socially, politically, and legally.

The Christian doctrine and movement were also part and parcel of the universal upsurge of female-centrism. In particular, Christ, his disciples, and his followers were the expression of the poor, uneducated Jewish masses who were equally oppressed by their own male-centric monothetic hierarchy and the Roman Emperor cult. As Fromm wrote, "The people hated intensely the authorities that confronted them with fatherly power: the priests, scholars, aristocrats, in short all those who excluded them from the enjoyment of life."[1]

Fromm also pointed out that this hatred was not only directed at the earthly authorities but also at the heavenly father himself: "The people's hostility to the divine father figure found expression in the Christ phantasy, in which a man was elevated to the stature of God the Father as an equal. Through identification with this man, the people expressed their oedipal wishes: if a man could become God, the latter was deprived of his privileged father position."[2] Indeed, Christ's message went beyond mere rebellion against the authorities. He preached to the people that "gnosis" (Greek for knowledge) was the path to human reintegration, fulfillment, and ecstasy.

Christ and his followers violated the standards of male-centric authority by accepting women in their movement as equals. Because "in Christ there is neither male nor female," women acted as prophets, teachers, preachers, and evangelists. Their concept of the divine, likewise, restored female-centrism to its rightful status as the equal, if not the superior, part in the divine dyad. Considering the divine a dyad, a polarity of female and male forces, they prayed, "From Thee, Father, and through Thee, Mother, the two immortal names, parents of the Divine being."[3]

"Christ's teaching was to make the inside like the outside, and the outside like the inside, and the above like the below... When you make the female and the male one and the same, then you will enter the kingdom."[4] As Elaine Pagels points out, the early Christian concept of the divine as a "harmonious, dynamic relationship of opposites is a concept... akin to the eastern view of yin and yang, but remains alien to Judaism and Christianity."[5]

The early Gnostic Christians also stressed the feminine in the Divine because of its association with the generative capacity, in the tradition of Nut, Isis, and other manifestations of the Great Goddess:

> For I am the first and the last
> I am the honored one and the sacred one
> I am the whore and the holy one
> I am the wife and the virgin
> I am the barren one and many are her sons
> I am the silence that is incomprehensible
> I am the utterance of my name[6]

The superiority of the feminine and the hostility toward God the Father frequently found expression in the early Christian portrayal of Him as the ignorant son of the Great Mother who was castigated for his arrogance: "He was even ignorant of his own mother [and] it was because he was foolish and ignorant of his own mother that he said 'I am God, there is none beside me.'"[7] Above all, the Christians attributed wisdom to the Divine Mother, much like the Greeks worshipped their goddess Sophia (meaning "wisdom" in Greek). As the first universal creator, the Divine Mother was considered the source of all powers of thought, intelligence, and foresight, and her silence was the womb of all gnosis, knowledge, and enlightenment.

Contrary to Jewish and later Christian orthodoxy, original Gnostic Christianity believed that the root of human suffering was not sin but ignorance. Hence they considered that the key to ending human suffering was not salvation through a savior but through the ecstasy of self-knowledge. As Christ taught, "If you bring forth that which is within you, what you bring forth will save you. If you do not bring forth what is within you, what you do not bring forth will destroy you."[8] For the Gnostics, whosoever achieved gnosis (enlightenment) by means of meditative techniques and other spiritual disciplines would enter into the way of immortality by becoming "no longer a Christian, but a Christ."[9]

The early Gnostic Christians stood in opposition to the hierarchical structure of Judaic orthodoxy. Not only were their communities based on the inherent equality of the sexes, with women having equal access, equal participation, and equal claim to knowledge. They also sought to deinstitutionalize any exercise of functional authority. Meetings could be called by anyone, and distinctions of rank were made permanently impermanent. Determination as to who would be bishop, priest, and prophet for the meeting was made by lot.

The Gnostics thoroughly appreciated the democratic nature of lottery and saw in it a manifestation of divine justice and cosmic order. The Gnostics determined all questions as to who would lead the services, read scriptures for worship, offer sacraments, and give spontaneous spiritual instructions by lot. Thus the roles and functions of priest, bishop, and prophet were rotated democratically, with all initiates, men and women alike, participating equally in the drawing; this, of course, avoided the creation of permanent hierarchies in the congregation.[10]

The freedom of any constraint of authority except the self in its quest for gnosis allowed the Gnostics to freely attend pagan festivals, sacrifice to idols, and refuse to follow the rules of sexual abstinence and monogamy. Economically, they frequently pooled resources into collective ownership and management. Thus we see in early Christianity a close approximation of the ancient female-centric culture and way of life. In rebellion against the corrupt, authoritarian, male-centric Roman culture, the Gnostics were anti-misogyny and anti-racist. They preached and practiced male-female equality and racial-ethnic equality, socialistic sharing of resources, and sortition democracy.

Rise of Male-Centric Christian Orthodoxy

The tremendous growth of Christianity unleashed intense persecution by the threatened Roman authorities. The integration of these masses of new believers into an effective struggle for survival in the face of the persecution required a clear and simple framework of hierarchical organization. In fact, as Elaine Pagels noted, the three-rank hierarchy of bishops, priests, and deacons that the Christians adopted was modeled upon the very structure of Roman political and military systems that were inflicting the persecution.

Simultaneously, in order to become "Catholic and universal," the Christian orthodoxy developed clear and objective criteria for church membership. Doctrinal and ritual content, such as the confession of the creed, were formulated above all to reinforce the idea that obedience to the clergy was the way to salvation. These tendencies were wholly contrary to the original Gnostic orientation, in which the definition of Christianity and church membership were based on elusive, qualitative criteria, and the focus on the difficult process of self-illumination tended to limit membership.

Moreover, the orthodox hierarchy stood in fundamental opposition to the original Gnostic perspective and practice of anarchistic democracy. The Gnostic identification of the self with the divine provided ample theological justification for refusing to obey the authority of the bishops. The Gnostics steadily criticized the orthodoxy for wanting "to command one another in their empty ambition" and "for being inflated with a lust of power."[11]

The exigencies of hierarchy determined that the orthodox theological doctrine would re-embrace the masculine monotheism of Judaism and reject the dyadic and pluralistic notions of the divine propounded by the Gnostics. The orthodox who rallied around the slogan "one God, one bishop," were led by bishops such as Ignatius of Antioch and Clement of Rome, who theorized, to their own benefit, of course, that as God rules in heaven over a divine council, so does the bishop on Earth rule over a council of priests. And as the heavenly divine council stands above the apostles, so do the priests rule over the deacons. The deacons themselves rule over the laity, who are "to revere, honor and obey the bishop as if he were God."[12]

Concurrently, there also occurred a transition from early widespread use of oracles and lotteries as a way of divining God's will to the complete interdiction of such practices because of the challenge they represented to the power of the Church hierarchy. So as Christianity evolved, Gnostic egalitarianism lost out to the ever-growing orthodox hierarchy. Like orthodox Islam and orthodox Judaism, orthodox Christianity violently opposed the Gnostic Christians and their use of oracles and lotteries because their essentially democratic nature threatened the Church's command structure. Indeed, the very concept of lottery was an intolerable threat to the developing orthodoxy of the God-pope-bishop-priest-layman pyramid. It threatened the very justification of hierarchical power. For this reason, the orthodox church persecuted and wiped out their Gnostic brothers and sisters and established their hierarchy of fear and domination.

Emphasizing a return to the purely male-centric monotheism of Judaism, by 200 CE, all the feminine imagery representing God had disappeared from the orthodox Christian tradition. Women, moreover, were forbidden to take an active part in the life of the Church, whether as prophets, priest or in any other role. According to the orthodox "precepts of ecclesiastical discipline concerning women," "it is not permitted for a woman to speak in church, nor is it permitted for her to teach, nor to baptize, nor to offer [the Eucharist], nor to claim for herself a share in any masculine function—not to mention any priestly office."[13]

The differences held by the Gnostics and the orthodoxy regarding the resurrection of Christ expressed their differences on social structure and the political function of the Church. The orthodox dogma of bodily resurrection served the essential political function of legitimizing the authority of the Church hierarchy, whereas Gnostic beliefs were highly subversive. Because Peter and the apostles had been the only witnesses to Christ's bodily resurrection, they became the first leaders of the Church who were unquestionable in their authority and, thereby, earned the power to ordain future leaders as successors. Thus, from the second century on, the doctrine of bodily resurrection served to validate the apostolic succession of the bishops, beginning with Peter. This remains the basis for papal authority today.

To the Gnostics, this entire orthodox scheme was hogwash and considered "the faith of fools." Belief in it, as in the virgin birth, was a naïve misunderstanding of a deeper mystery the Gnostics held. In their accounts, Jesus never appeared in bodily form but always as a luminous presence speaking out of the light. To them, in other words, "the resurrection is a moment of enlightenment," something to be experienced in the present instead of the past or future. It consisted not of a literal seeing but a spiritual vision, in dream or trance states, accompanied by ecstatic experiences of awe and joy. Thus, Gnostic teachings were highly subversive to the developing church hierarchy, since they offered every initiate direct access to a god of whom the priests and bishops might be ignorant.

The differences between Gnostics and the orthodoxy toward persecution and suffering was perhaps what sealed the fate of the Gnostics and condemned them to oblivion. The Gnostics, who avoided persecution wherever they could, denied agony was the way to salvation from sin, and affirmed the ecstasy of gnosis was the way to freedom from illusion. Even the agony of physical suffering, they believed, could be transcended by the spirit into ecstasy.

The orthodox teachings, as espoused by Tertullian, were certainly more suited and expressive of the dark age reality civilization was sinking into. They believed that "you must take up your cross and bear it after your master" and that "the sole key to unlock paradise is your own life's blood."[14] In other words, agony cleanses and purifies the sinful soul. Martyrdom is the road to salvation because a Christian enduring persecution, and by extension all other human suffering, becomes one with the crucified Christ.

The Decline of the Roman Republic and the Rise of the Roman Catholic Church

In 64 CE, in Rome, in a neighborhood near the circus, a fire started in one of the shops that stored flammable goods. It was a stormy night, and the winds whipped the fire into a great conflagration that nearly destroyed the city, wiping out three of its 14 districts and reducing seven more to rubble. To redirect from the widespread rumors that Nero, the mad emperor, had himself ordered the fire to be set, Nero blamed the Christians. He therewith began the first official and organized campaign of persecution against the Christians by the Roman authorities that would last on and off for about two centuries.

Perhaps the worst of them was Diocletian (284–305 CE), who waged unrelenting war on the Christians and engaged in systematic persecution. Still, if we combine all the victims of all these persecutions in the 300 years from the crucifixion of Christ to the conversion of Emperor Constantine, it turns out that in these three centuries, the polytheistic Romans killed no more than a few thousand Christians.

As the patriarchal civilization that had formed the foundation of the empire cult began to crumble along with the empire itself, the Roman ruling class increasingly accepted Christianity as its own religion. Indeed, as the disintegration of Roman civilization accelerated, the universalization of orthodox Christianity gathered momentum. The combination of the supremacy of the masculine principle, the insistence on obedience to authority, and the identification with suffering as the way to salvation of the soul made Christianity compatible with the interests of the declining Roman ruling class.

As the interests of the Roman ruling class and orthodox Christianity merged, the fate of Gnostic Christianity was sealed. Already by 200 CE, the battle between the Gnostic and the Orthodox factions had become an irreconcilable schism, each claiming to be "the one true church" and accusing the other of hypocrisy and heresy. Not surprisingly, under these conditions of crisis, the orthodoxy, initiating the break, expelled the Gnostics. This they accomplished through rigorous enforcement of the orthodox definition of true Christianity and church membership, including acceptance of the canon of the New Testament, confession of the apostolic creed, and the affirmation of the Church hierarchy.

Catholic Christianity encouraged the masses of people to accept the misery resulting from their class oppression while also providing cosmic justification to the ruling class for continuing their exploitative practices. First, the lower classes, then the middle classes, and finally the higher classes, including the ruling aristocracy, adopted the orthodox religion. Over the next two centuries, suppression and oppression of the Gnostics increased in proportion to the extent that orthodoxy was adopted by the upper classes of society. Almost immediately after Constantine made Christianity the official state religion, the orthodoxy began to supervise systematic persecutions, seizing Gnostic books and burning them. This they did with ruthless efficiency and almost total success until the discovery of the Nag Hammadi library that unearthed the Gnostic gospels in 1945. It seemed that the Christian orthodoxy had taken the lessons of their persecution by the Roman emperors to heart and applied them with even greater zeal on their own brethren in Christ, the Gnostics.

During the third and fourth centuries CE, the Roman Empire was still able to ward off external challengers, such as the Sassanid rulers of Persia but increasingly at the price of its integrity. Its eastern client states were granted more autonomy, and a buffer zone was, in effect, created between Roman and Persian lands. In the long run, the disintegration of the empire was inevitable. Peoples who had been Roman subjects turned inward against their former rulers, aggravating the growing crisis in the head of the body politic—the Roman ruling class suffering from widespread corruption and vicious internal power struggles, declining agriculture, and a rebellious urban proletariat.

The development of armored cavalry was a revolutionary change in military tactics and techniques that finally enabled Rome's adversaries to crush her legions of infantry and light cavalry. The new conquerors, products of the heavy, well-watered souls beyond the Mediterranean fringe, had the abundant fodder for a vast expansion of its cavalry, while Roman agriculture, long neglected, could not support both the urban proletariat and the necessary cavalry.

The Western Roman empire shook under the Huns, and the Visigothic and Germanic invaders shattered it. The year 476, when Romulus Augustus was forced to abdicate to the Germanic warlord Odoacer, marked the literal and symbolic end of the Western Roman Empire and ushered in the beginning of the feudal dark ages that would be dominated by Catholic Christianity and transient petty states under Visigothic or Frankish chieftains. Centralized power survived in the Eastern Mediterranean for another millennium. Also known as the Byzantine Empire, the Eastern Roman Empire ended in 1453 with the death of Constantine XI and the fall of Constantinople to the Turks.

The Cruelty and Violence of Christianity

The evolution of Christianity from being an anti–Roman Empire upstart religion to becoming the state religion of the Roman Empire was marked by a profound shift in emphasis in religious doctrine and teachings. The early Christians were not much concerned with the afterlife because of their belief system. Heaven would come down on earth, and everybody would be saved. So the afterlife was, for them, a kind of moot and academic question.

In particular, later Christianity's opulent mythology of hell as "God's eternal torture chamber" is not a dominant feature of the scriptural texts. It's certainly not in St. Paul's writings. Neither is it found in the other New Testament epistles or in any documents from the earliest post-apostolic period.[15] On the other hand, many New Testament passages promise the eventual salvation of everyone here on Earth. For example, "Therefore, as one trespass led to condemnation for all men, so one act of righteousness leads to justification and life for all men"[16] or "For as in Adam all die, so also in Christ shall all be made alive."[17] Indeed, during the first half millennium of Christianity—especially in the Greek-speaking Hellenistic and Semitic East—believers in universal salvation apparently enjoyed a large ratio of the faithful.[18]

But once the Christian Church became part of the Roman Empire's political apparatus, spiritual terror became an ever more indispensable instrument of social stability.[19] Medieval Roman Catholicism fully embraced and utilized the carrot-and-stick approach of the afterlife. The medieval faithful were given the choice between eternal bliss in heaven or eternal suffering in hell. Believe and submit, you will get the carrot of heaven. Disbelieve and rebel, you will get the stick of hell.

Thomas Aquinas even believed and taught that the beatitude of the saved in heaven will be increased by their direct vision of the torments of the damned in hell. How can we be winners, after all, if there are no losers? What success can there be that isn't validated by another's failure? What heaven can there be for us without an eternity in which to relish the impotent envy of those outside its walls in the pits of hell?[20]

Thus the Christian Church and believers created the deep, emotional, psychological, spiritual, and social need for an eternal hell.[21] Even today nothing elicits a more indignant and hysterical reaction from many Christian believers than questioning the tenet of their faith that asserts the existence of everlasting hell, as if something unutterably precious was at stake for them.[22] For them the idea of hell is the treasury of their most secret, most cherished hopes—the hope of being proved right when so many were wrong, of being admired when so many are despised, of being envied when so many have been scorned.[23] That is the cruelty of the Christian belief in hell.

The story of what happened to Hypatia of Alexandria In 415 CE illustrates the particularly virulent hatred that the (exclusively masculine) Christian clergy had for the numerous (mostly women) practitioners and priestesses of the pagan religions it tried to supplant. Hypatia was born in the great cosmopolitan city of Alexandria sometime between 350 and 370 CE. Unique among her generation, she became a famous philosopher, expert astronomer, and unrivalled mathematician. She was a highly respected celebrity in her city and preeminent in its social and intellectual life.

Students from all over the empire, of all religious and philosophical stripes, came to study with her. Though she herself was a pagan and believed in the old polytheistic deities, she was tolerant of the Christian religion that was becoming ever more popular. She even had Christian students, though at that time, relations between Christians and non-Christians (pagans) were becoming more and more tense.[24]

The Christian congregation of Alexandria at that point consisted mostly of members of the roughly hewn, uneducated lower classes. They were led by a male clergy that distinguished itself by its religious zealotry and its hatred of the pagan gods and the women who worshiped them. First, Bishop Theophilus set the tone of confrontation with the pagans. His nephew, Cyril, followed in his footsteps, and within a few years of his coming to power, his violence had begun.

The Jews were among the first to suffer. The new generation of intolerant clerics preached that Jews were not a people with an ancient wisdom that could be learned from; they were, instead, like the pagans, the hated enemies of the Church. The preacher John Chrysostom, who would be quoted with admiration by the Nazis two thousand years later, called "the synagogue not only a brothel... it is also a den of robbers and a lodging of wild beasts... a dwelling of demons... a place of idolatry." Chrysostom promoted and orchestrated Christian violence against the Jews, killed scores of them, took possession of their synagogues, transformed them into churches, stripped the Jewish congregants of their possessions, and sent them out into the desert.[25]

The aristocratic governor of Alexandria, Orestes, a friend of Hypatia, was appalled. He wrote to the emperor to complain to little avail. In fact, the numbers of the bishop of Alexandria's militia increased to more than 500 monks. Unwashed, uneducated, and unwavering in their faith, they descended from their shacks and caves in the nearby hills, determined to fight for their bishop. One day, as Orestes rode in his chariot through the city, this mob stopped and accosted him, accusing him of being a pagan idolater. Orestes's head was gravely injured by a rock thrown by one of the assailants. His servants scattered, and he was left to his own devices. Luckily, some locals helped him get away. The intimidation did not work on Orestes but only made him more determined. He arrested and put to death the monk who had thrown the rock that had injured him. Many of the city's aristocrats and public figures, including Hypatia, supported Orestes in his actions against the violence of Cyril and his Christian mob.[26]

That is when the rumors began. It was Hypatia's fault, according to the Christians, that the governor was so stubborn. They called the astrolabe and other scientific instruments Hypatia used "instruments of the devil." She was not a philosopher but a creature from hell, who was turning the entire city against God with her trickery and spells. She had "beguiled Orestes through her magic." Then one day in March 415 CE, Hypatia, while on her daily ride through town, was stopped and assaulted by a Christian mob. Led by a church magistrate named Peter, who was "a perfect believer in all respects in Jesus Christ," the mob seized Hypatia and dragged her through the streets into a church. Once inside, they ripped the clothes from her body and, using broken pieces of pottery as blades, flayed her skin from her flesh. Some say that while she still gasped for breath, they gauged out her eyes. Once she was dead, they tore her body into pieces and threw what was left of the "luminous child of reason" onto a pyre and burned her.[27]

What can be learned about the inherent violence of Catholic Christianity from Hypatia's horrendous story? We can only draw the conclusion that the growth of Orthodox Catholic Christianity represented the further consolidation of the male-centric principle and its culture of violence in the new civilization that was rising in the west from the ashes of the Roman Empire.

Endnotes

1   Erich Fromm, The Dogma of Christ: And Other Essays on Religion, Psychology, and Culture, (New York: Anchor Books, 1966), 48.

2   Ibid.

3   Elaine Pagels, The Gnostic Gospels, (New York: Random House, 1979), 49.

4   James M. Robinson, ed., The Nag Hammadi Library, (California: Harper and Row, 1988), 121.

5   Elaine Pagels, The Gnostic Gospels, (New York: Random House, 1979), 51.

6   Ibid., xvii.

7   Ibid., 57–8.

8   Ibid., 126.

9   Ibid.

10 Elaine Pagels, The Gnostic Gospels, (New York: Random House, 1979).

11 Ibid., 141.

12 Ibid., 35.

13 Ibid., 160.

14 Ibid., 88.

15 David Bentley Hart, "Why Do People Believe in Hell?" New York Times, January 10, 2020, https://www.nytimes.com/2020/01/10/opinion/sunday/christianity-religion-hell-bible.html.

16 Romans 5:18

17 1 Corinthians 15:22

18 David Bentley Hart, "Why Do People Believe in Hell?" New York Times, January 10, 2020, https://www.nytimes.com/2020/01/10/opinion/sunday/christianity-religion-hell-bible.html.

19 Ibid.

20 Ibid.

21 Ibid.

22 Ibid.

23 Ibid.

24 Catherine Nixey, The Darkening Age: The Christian Destruction of the Classical World, (New York: First Mariner Books edition, 2017), 136–147.

25 Ibid.

26 Ibid.

27 Ibid.

Part 3

The Global Ascent of the White Man

Chapter 9
....

The Birth of the White Man in Medieval Europe (500–1500)

The Yin-Yang of Crisis

The yin-yang of life and existence are harmony and crisis, life promoting and life-threatening. The yin-yang of crisis are fear and rage, flight and fight, withdrawal and aggression.

The yin of civilization crisis refers to the dark ages that occur after the fall of one civilization and before the rise of the next one, such as the Egyptian dark ages, the Greek dark ages and the Western European dark ages. In the wake of the breakdown of civilization's established order of doing things, social and economic contractions deepen, and chaos prevails. A regression occurs into the primeval crisis dialectic between fear and submission, on the one hand, and rage and aggression, on the other. With gang and tribal warfare the order of the day, with plunder, rape, and murder a daily fare, the violence of the most powerful becomes the law of the land and the prevailing social emotions of the citizenry are deep-seated fear and loathing.

In the transformation of yin civilization of crisis into yang, the fear-and-submission complex, as physiological basis of collective life, is replaced by the anger-and-aggression complex. The late Egyptian New Kingdom, the Roman Empire, Western Europe, and the U.S. civilizations all exhibited this male-centric expansion fueled by the lethal mix of testosterone, adrenalin, and hyperstimulation of the sympathetic nervous system.

It is only when the female-centric paradigm is dominant and the male-centric is subdominant that the state of equality between male and female is possible. For when the male-centric paradigm is dominant in civilization, the crisis mode will be constant and class-structure frozen in the dialectic of fear and rage between the powerful and the powerless.

We, as a species, have an unconscious memory of the more harmonious state of affairs in human existence. We still have a little of the bonobo in us as well as the hunter-gatherer, and on some level, those trace memories fuel our hope for a more equitable existence in terms of the relationships between the sexes and genders, races and ethnicities.

Catastrophe and Recovery in the Early and High Middle Ages

The Middle Ages began with the fall of the Western Roman Empire in the fifth century and merged into the Renaissance and the age of discovery in the 15th century. The medieval period is generally subdivided into three periods: the Early Middle Ages (500–1000), the High Middle Ages (1000–1350), and the Late Middle Ages (1350–1500). The Early and Late periods both began with calamities, while the High Middle Ages, in between, showed improvement in living conditions and quality of life.

In Western Europe, it turns out that the term "dark ages," as synonym for the Middle Ages, is quite literally true and descriptively accurate. Modern researchers recently nominated 536 CE as "the worst year to be a human" on account of a massive volcanic eruption in Iceland. This eruption spewed an enormous cloud of ash that shrouded the northern hemisphere in darkness. The sustained darkness, in turn, caused a drop in temperatures that led to widespread crop failures, famines, and social upheaval.[1]

A few years later, in 542 CE, the first bubonic plague struck the Eastern Roman Empire, inflicting unimaginable suffering on the already hungry masses and causing the death of an estimated 24 to

50 million people.[2] The combined effects of these calamities was to turn human existence into an unimaginable horror.

What had begun in late antiquity continued in the Early Middle Ages: There was a precipitous decline in population; people were fleeing the cities in a counter urbanization movement; invasions on a small and large scale by marauding bands and tribes was an ever-present reality; and physical calamities set in motion mass movements of people.

It literally took some 400 to 500 years for society to regroup from these calamities and usher in the High Middle Ages in which there was a marked improvement in living conditions and quality of life. Several factors favored the tremendous increase in population during the High Middle Ages. Between 1000 and 1347, the population exploded from 35 to 80 million. The little ice age caused by the Icelandic volcano eruption was waning, and with the warming of the climate, the crop yields again became more plentiful. Slave holding declined, and technological and agricultural innovations allowed trade to flourish.

Christian Racism and the Crusades

Toward the end of the eleventh century, Turkish armies went on a westward spree of conquest, colonizing lands and threatening Emperor Alexis I of the Byzantine Empire. Pope Urban II saw his chance, heard the Lord's call, and heeded His command to carry the sword to nonbelievers. He saw the opportunity to vastly increase the power, territory, and influence of the Church as well as his own power and glory. The large increases in population provided ready-made armies of soldiers for Christ. So in 1095, Pope Urban issued the clarion call to all believers to unite in the First Crusade to reclaim the Holy Land and save it from Muslim nonbelievers. With this, he set a pattern: from 1095 to 1291 there were nine attempts to reclaim the Holy Land from Islam and the Turks. The enthusiastic support of Urban from all classes in Western Europe established a precedent for other Crusades. Volunteers became Crusaders by taking a public vow and receiving plenary indulgences from the Church. Some were hoping for a mass ascension to heaven in Jerusalem or God's forgiveness for all their sins. Other participated to satisfy feudal obligations, obtain glory and honor, or to seek economic and political gain. Crusaders often pillaged as they traveled, and their leaders generally retained control of captured territory instead of returning it to the Byzantines. As a result, during the First Crusade, four new Crusader states were established: the County of Edessa, the Principality of Antioch, the Kingdom of Jerusalem, and the County of Tripoli.

The Crusades proved to be the crucible during which the Western White Man first developed overt racism (in this case anti-Semitism) for political and religious purposes. Of course the anti-Semitism of that time was directed at both Arabs in general and Jews in particular. The Arabs in general were the enemy because they occupied and ruled the Holy Land, and the Jews in particular were the enemy because they had killed the Lord Jesus. These facts alone, in the eyes and minds of the Crusaders, justified pretty much anything the Arabs and Jews had coming to them. It was only later in history, when the Jewish people had integrated more fully in European society while Arab civilization was retreating that the term anti-Semitism became synonymous with anti-Jewishness.

During these centuries, a holy messianic sadism gripped the Christian Church, which would become the hallmark and defining characteristic of the religion and civilization the White Man crafted, first in Europe and later in America. Thomas Aquinas (1225–1274) articulated the defining principle behind this when he declared heresy (a spiritual crime) to be equivalent to, if not worse than, the civil and economic crimes that are punishable by death: "Wherefore if forgers of money and other evil doers are forthwith condemned to death by the secular authority, much more reason is there for heretics, as soon as they are convicted of heresy, to be not only excommunicated but even put to death."[3]

In the second half of the Crusade period, at least half a dozen other Crusades took place outside the Holy Land, directed toward pagan enemies of the Church on the fringes of the Catholic hegemony in Western Europe. For example, the Albigensian Crusade that was carried out between 1209 and 1229 in the Languedoc region of

France and Spain and the Northern Crusades that were carried out in the 12th and 13th centuries against the Balts, Fins, and West Slavic peoples. The Hussite Wars against Czech and Bohemian cultures took place from 1419 to 1434. The People's Crusade, in which thousands of Jews were murdered, is now called the Rhineland massacres.

Pope Nicholas V, in his papal bull of June 18, 1452, reiterated the opinion of Aquinas by granting the kings of Spain and Portugal "full and free permission to invade, search out, capture, and subjugate the Saracens and pagans and any other unbelievers and enemies of Christ wherever they may be, as well as their kingdoms, duchies, counties, principalities, and other property... and to reduce their persons into perpetual servitude."[4]

The human costs of the Crusades are pretty much incalculable, for their accumulation continued unabated for centuries. Estimates of direct deaths caused by Christianity in the Crusades alone range from one to nine million, with three million being a median estimate.[5] Counting all direct deaths caused by Christianity over time, the largest and most famous estimate is 56 million. A more conservative estimate gives 9 to 28 million.[6] If we count the deaths caused by Christian societies in general, the number would rise to 82 to 106 million.[7]

Renewed Calamities and Increasing Violence in the 14th Century

The beginning of the 14th century was marked by great famines as a result of the slow transition from the medieval warm period to the "little ice age." The years 1313 and 1314 and 1317 to 1321 were exceedingly rainy throughout Europe. Accompanied by severely declining annual temperatures, the result were widespread crop failures, a severe economic downturn, and the Great Famine of 1315 to 1317 significantly diminished Europe's population. Then, in 1347, a second bubonic plague pandemic struck and ravaged Western Europe. Again the scale of suffering and loss of human life was unimaginable. Between 1347 and 1350, the plague was responsible for killing a third of the population.

People felt they were experiencing the end of times when, as predicted in the book of Revelations, the four horsemen of the apocalypse (conquest, war, famine, and death) were ravaging the earth and humanity. As the mass mortality rate cheapened life, society became more violent with increasing warfare, crime, popular revolts, waves of flagellants, and persecution. The violent nature of European medieval society made life "brutish, nasty and short"[8] (in the words of Hobbes), a state of chaos, anarchy, and continual tribal conflict, a war of all against all.

From tribal into feudal times, society's economic resources consisted of (1) land, or territory, to grow and provide food and (2) the labor to work that land to grow the food and transform the energy of their subjects into wealth. The expansion of a tribe or nation's power was only possible through warfare. Conquest and the subjugation of conquered peoples created ever-larger units of exploitation that became constituent units of medieval feudalism. The hierarchy of violence started from highway robbers to thugs, to captains, to noblemen, to dukes, and finally, at the top of the hierarchy, the king. Once acquired by force, land then was passed down the generations through the laws of inheritance as blessed by the Church and enforced by the nobles' armed forces.

The economic cornerstone of medieval society was that both property and power were hereditary. There were only two classes: the haves and the have nots, the lords and the serfs. The 1% shared a symbiosis of secular and religious power. Indeed, there was a profound unity of Church and state, as members of the ruling families controlled both secular and religious institutions. The 1% controlled the majority on various levels, ranging from the spiritual, to the psychological, the emotional, and the physical realms. The medieval "Mother" Church and its clergy were assigned to train their subjects from spiritually and religiously to psychologically and emotionally to accept their earthly lot of subjugation and exploitation as a condition to entering heaven in the hereafter. If these measures proved inadequate to gain compliance, they could and would always fall back on the physical force at their disposal, which depending on their strength and numbers, were called gangs, militias, or armies.

In summary, in Western European feudal society, the ruling aristocracy was living under conditions of abundance, having appropriated through force the social wealth of society at the expense of their wretched subjects. For the majority, there was no freedom of thought, no religious freedom, no economic freedom, no political freedom; there was only indentured servitude and institutionalized dominance of male over female. The latter harbored secret desires to go back to the ancient pagan way of doing things. In between these two layers of the haves and the have-nots was the ultrathin layer of the "middle class" of craftsmen, artists, and merchants who lived in the towns.

The Life of Women in Medieval Times

With the degradation and failure of the male-centric Roman Empire in the early medieval period, there was an opening for the re-emergence of the female-centric paradigm in both secular and religious life. And indeed, the early Catholic Church of the feudal era incorporated many aspects of the ancient Great Mother religion. In the words of the sociologist and psychoanalyst Erich Fromm, "Under the guise of the fatherly god of the Jews, who in the struggle with near eastern motherly divinities had gained dominance, the divine figure of the Great Mother [became] the dominating figure of medieval Christianity… first in the role that the church, as such, [began] to play, and second, in the cult of Mary."[9] Thus there was indeed a relative improvement in the lot of women in the early medieval period due to the efforts of the Church, which offered them a haven of protection from the violence of the outside world. Education was made available to some women in the convents, and "those who wished to devote themselves to scholarship and arts gathered there, with or without taking religious vows."[10]

Economically also, women achieved greater power and freedom:

Countless noblewomen established and ruled religious houses. These abbesses had the rights and privileges of feudal barons. They usually were members of the royal family and acted as representatives of the king during their absences. They often administered vast lands; managed convents, abbeys, and double monasteries, provided their own troops in wartime, had the right of coinage, and were consulted in political and religious affairs: … the family emerged as the most stable force of the secular world, and women, who were central to the family, achieved greater freedom. They could own and administer property and, in their husband's absences, managed the estates, presided over courts, signed treaties, made laws, and, in some cases, commanded troops.[11]

It must be emphasized that these trends were limited to the ruling aristocracy and religious authorities. There was no corresponding improvement in the lot of women among the majority of the people who were serfs and who remained suffering, not only from hunger, malnutrition, and illness, but also from degradation of the personhood by the male sex—their husbands and their priests.

And alas, even despite this very limited improvement of the female condition, the rebirth of female-centricity culture was stillborn. It was again forcefully aborted by the male-centric paradigm that was resurgent during the Late Middle Ages, when it carried out the Crusades against the heathen unbelievers. In fact, the "Holy" Catholic Church became the essential purveyor of misogyny and the primary oppressor of women and their rights. The male-centric monotheistic paradigm once again reasserted its priorities of dominance as it conceived of and carried out its last Crusade: a misogynist war on women. Thomas Aquinas summarized the teachings of the Holy Mother Church that in marriage, "the woman is subject to man on account of the weakness of her nature… Man is the beginning of woman and her end, just as God is the beginning and end of every creature. Children ought to love their Father more than they love their mother."[12] Indeed, the law of the land in the dark ages was that all women were required to be subordinate to some male, whether father, husband, or other kinsman. Not to put too fine a point on it, in the Catholic "Mother" Church, for example, women were forbidden to be priestesses and serve the sacraments; their only option was to become nuns.

Being oppressed and denigrated made women the natural suspects to blame for the universal misfortunes of famine and plague in the 15th century. Aquinas also was of the opinion that most women were secretly, in their hearts of hearts, still pagan witches who deserved to be burned at the stake. The Catholic Church accordingly made it an article of faith. It was the women, especially those witches who had shown a desire to go back and worship the old pagan deities and engage in the rites of healing and divination, who were the cause of, and had to be held responsible for, the natural calamities that God had visited upon men. This conviction caused the Church to embark on yet another Crusade against its own women to rid itself of the many elements of the Great Goddess religion it had tolerated for centuries. The results were nothing less than genocidal. In the witch hunts instigated by the Catholic Church from the 13th to the 17th century, an estimated 69 million people were killed, approximately 85% of whom were women.

The Life of Children in Medieval Times

What about the children? What was their life like under the conditions of medieval, male-centric society? We've previously observed the essential differences between child-rearing practices in female-centric and male-centric societies.

In female-centric primate societies of bonobo and hunter-gatherer societies, we saw that close relationships between the females as a group and their babies were the norm. As the fathers of the children in these female-centric cultures are unknown, there was a marked absence of infanticide.[13] And the general attitude toward children is one of nurturance and empathy.[14] In male-centric medieval Europe, the prevailing methods of child-rearing closely resembled those of other male-centric primate societies, such as the chimps and agricultural and feudal civilizations. The most important feature these male-centric societies have in common is the practice of infanticide, where the dominant male may attempt to kill any babies he has not fathered,[15] which is further reflected in the general attitude toward children as one of cruelty and exploitation.[16]

In the pre-Christian male-centric civilizations of antiquity to the fourth century CE, the killing of children was already an accepted

social custom. "It is well-known that infanticide of both legitimate and illegitimate children was a regular practice of antiquity...
Indeed," in Grecian and Roman times, "scholars promoted the practice as a means for coping with abnormal or excessive children."[17]
"Illegitimate children were killed routinely, girls frequently, the third
or later boy invariably, and abnormal children always. Child sacrifice... drowning, starving or exposure of unwanted babies" was common in the period before and after Christ.[18]

Until the fourth century, neither Christian law nor public opinion found infanticide wrong. It was only after Christianity concluded,
in the fourth century, that children had souls and, therefore, it was
"unchristian" to kill them, that the killing of legitimate children
slowly decreased in Western male-centric Christian society, though
"illegitimate children continued to be killed up into the nineteenth
century."[19] In other words, life in the Middle Ages for most kids was,
well, hell. If they were not killed, their chances of survival were grim
indeed. In antiquity, around one-quarter of infants died "in their first
year of life" and "almost half of children died before the end of puberty."[20] In the Middle Ages, the distressingly high infant mortality rate
in the first year of life numbered around 300 to 350 per 1,000 live
births. Today, this figure is in the single digits for rich countries.[21]

As the practice of infanticide was no longer acceptable on religious grounds, it was replaced by a most peculiar form of child abandonment. From 400 until 1300 CE, it became standard practice for
Europeans to keep their children at home until the age of seven, or
nine at most. At that age, the parents would "put them [the kids] out,
both males and females, to hard service in the houses of other people,
binding them generally for another seven or nine years."[22] Condoned
by the medieval childcare paradigm, this practice guaranteed and
perpetuated a system of childcare and rearing in which children
under age 15 were habitually "killed, abandoned, beaten, [exploited
economically,] terrorized emotionally and abused sexually."[23]

So widespread was the custom that it was practiced in all strata
of society, from the lowly serfs to the high aristocracy, as "the unfortunate children were sent away regardless of their class, 'for everyone,

however rich he may be, sends away his children into the houses of others, whilst he, in return, receives those of strangers into his own.'"[24] The pious rationale was, of course, that this was "for the children's own good" and essential to their moral and physical development. The real reason was considerably darker and mercenary in nature: it was very convenient to have "other people's children in the household because [the host] could feed them less and work them harder,"[25] thus guaranteeing and perpetuating the cruel nature of medieval childhood.

"Anna Burr, in her 1909 review of 250 medieval autobiographies, noted that not one contained happy memories of childhood, whilst Valentine, reading letters covering a 600-year period, was unable to find a father who wasn't insensitive, moralistic and self-centered."[26] And as one boy complained in a letter after being put out, "For all that was to me a pleasure when I was a child, from three years old to 10… while I was under my father and mother's keeping, be turned now to torments and pain."[27]

Masochism and the Feudal-Catholic Character Structure

Erich Fromm[28] observed that, in feudal Catholic society, the character structure cultivated and perpetuated by the Church in "the people" was fundamentally masochistic. A fundamental fear and insecurity was instilled during the oral, yin, stage of childhood development by means of insufficient nurturance, both physical and psychological. This burdened the individual with lifelong subconscious longing for love, food, and security expressed in their adoration of Mary the Great Mother figure. It also predisposed them to the fear-and-submission response to authority, whether civil or religious.

To imbue this masochistic mentality in the masses of people, the Church used the carrot-and-the-stick approach. The carrot was: though your life is miserable on earth, if you believe and obey, you will gain heavenly peace and everlasting life after death. In fact, the Church nurtured the belief that the more you suffered on earth, the greater your heavenly reward would be, conditioning people to expect and accept continued misery and suffering as their lot on earth. The deal was further sweetened by the Mother Church offering earthly assistance and nurturance, symbolized, above all, by the baby Jesus suckling the ample bosom of Mother Mary. The suffering for love was transmuted into the love of suffering. The stick was the assurance of continued, eternal suffering after death in hell.

Fromm pointed out that in the degeneration of early Christianity into Roman Catholicism, "the decisive element was the change from the idea of man becoming God to that of God becoming man."[29] If the Gnostic Christians was intrinsically optimistic in the belief that humanity was capable of ascending to a higher plane of divinity and immortality, the feudal Catholic doctrine expressed itself in reactionary pessimism that required the divine to descend to the lower level of humanity to save them by suffering for them.

The character of Christ, accordingly, underwent a twofold transformation in the Catholic reinterpretation. First, the revolutionary superman of early Christianity became, in Catholic dogma, a reactionary suffering masochist. In the words of Fromm, the emphasis of medieval dogma was "no longer on the overthrow of the father, but on the self-annihilation of the son [...] in the phantasy of the crucified Jesus, pardon is obtained by a passive, self-castrating submission to the father."[30] Second, feudal Catholic dogma projected its fear complex onto the great ancient primordial religious theme of mother and son. In Mary and Jesus, it reduced the Isis and Horus myth from a symbol of continuity to one of uncertainty. The worship of Jesus as a suckling child at the breast of Mary expressed in archetypal form the insecurities dominating dark age mentality.

The phantasy of the great pardoning mother is the optimal gratification which Catholic Christianity had to offer. The more the masses suffered, the more their real situation resembled that of the suffering of Jesus, the more the figure of the happy, suckling babe could, and must, appear alongside the figure of the suffering Jesus. But this meant also that humanity had to regress to a passive and infantile attitude. Medieval society impressed upon the people the psychic attitude of a hierarchical structure that precluded active revolt and produced human beings who were dependent on rulers for their minimum sustenance and for whom hunger was proof of their sins.[31]

The essence of human existence during the feudal dark ages was that life was ruled by the complex of fear, insecurity and paralysis in all its aspects: physically, psychologically, socially, politically, economically, and religiously. However, beneath the surface of the medieval church-state hegemony partnership in oppression, turmoil was brewing. From the depths of despair arose a hope borne of fierce desire for a better life, a desire to taste the joy, freedom, happiness, and contentment missing in the current one. Quietly and privately at first, but ever more insistently and publicly as time went on, people began questioning the validity of the moral basis of the existing religious and secular authorities.

Slowly, the wheel of time began turning and set into motion a historical reversal of polarity. The yin stage of Western man, the feudal Catholic era and paradigm based on the masochism of fear and submission, was about to be replaced by the yang stage of Western man, the paradigm based on hope, independence, and initiative that would usher in the Protestant capitalist era.

The newly emerging anti-oppression and anti-authoritarian paradigm articulated the values of the new era based on the people's holistic quest for freedom of mind and the freedom of action. The demand for freedom of the mind included the religious desire for freedom of faith and intellectual yearning for freedom of knowledge and science. The demand for freedom of action covered economic and political freedom. Two keystone events came to symbolize the interrelatedness of these various quests. One was the discovery of America in 1492 by Columbus. The second was Martin Luther nailing his *Ninety-Five Theses* on the church doors in Wittenberg, Germany, in 1517.

Endnotes

1   Jack Guy, "The Worst Year to Be a Human Has Been Revealed by Researchers," CNN, November 21, 2018, https://www.cnn.com/2018/11/20/health/worst-year-536 -scli-intl/index.html.

2   Ishaan Tharoor, "Top 10 Terrible Epidemics," Time, October 26, 2010, https://content.time.com/time/specials/packages/article/0,28804,2027479 _2027486_2027546,00.html.

3   Thomas Aquinas, Summa Theologica, Vol. II–II, (Fathers of the English Dominican Province, 1920), Question 11, Article 3, https://www.newadvent.org/summa /3011.htm#article3.

4   Ziauddin Sardar and Merryl Wyn Davies, The No-Nonsense Guide to Islam, (New York: Verso, 2004), 94, ISBN 1-85984-454-5.

5   Tim Urban, "The Death Toll Comparison," Wait But Why, August 5, 2013, https://waitbutwhy.com/2013/08/the-death-toll-comparison-breakdown.html.

6   Andrew Holt, "Death Estimates for the Crusades," APHolt, January 30, 2019, https://apholt.com/2019/01/30/death-estimates-for-the-crusades/.

7   Juan Cole, "Did Christians Kill Thirty to Fifty Times as Many People in Political Violence as Muslims in the 20th Century?" Skeptics, June 17, 2020, https://skeptics .stackexchange.com/questions/34270/did-christians-kill-thirty-to-fifty-times-as -many-people-in-political-violence-a.

8   Thomas Hobbes, Leviathan, (Germany: Macmillan, 1963).

9   Erich Fromm, The Dogma of Christ: And Other Essays on Religion, Psychology, and Culture, (New York: Anchor Books, 1966), 12.

10   Judy Chicago, The Dinner Party: A Symbol of Our Heritage, (New York: Anchor-Doubleday Books, 1979).

11   Ibid.

12   Sarah Woodbury, "Child Rearing in the Middle Ages," Journey to Medieval Wales…, January 3, 2013, https://www.sarahwoodbury.com/child-rearing-in-the-middle-ages/.

13   WGBH Educational Foundation, "Chimps and Bonobos," PBS, 2001, https://www.pbs.org/wgbh/evolution/library/07/3/l_073_03.html.

14   University of Notre Dame, "Child rearing practices of distant ancestors foster morality, compassion in kids," ScienceDaily, September 22, 2010, https://www.sciencedaily.com/releases/2010/09/100921163709.htm.

15   WGBH Educational Foundation, "Chimps and Bonobos," PBS, 2001, https://www.pbs.org/wgbh/evolution/library/07/3/l_073_03.html.

16   Neil McKerrow, "Parents of Child-Rearing," NACCW, January 2003, https://cyc-net.org/cyc-online/cycol-0103-mckerrow.html.

17   Ibid.

18   Ibid.

19   Ibid.

20   Max Roser, "Mortality in the Past: Every Second Child Died," Our World Data, April 11, 2023, https://ourworldindata.org/child-mortality-in-the-past.

21   Gmatclub, "In the Middle Ages, the Distressingly High Infant Mortality Rate," January 15, 2020, https://gmatclub.com/forum/in-the-middle-ages-the-distressingly -high-infant-mortality-rate-314383.html.

22   William Kremer, "What Medieval Europe Did with Its Teenagers," BBC, March 23, 2014, https://www.bbc.com/news/magazine-26289459.

23 Neil McKerrow, "Parents of Child-Rearing," NACCW, January 2003, https://cyc-net.org/cyc-online/cycol-0103-mckerrow.html.

24 William Kremer, "What Medieval Europe Did with Its Teenagers," BBC, March 23, 2014, https://www.bbc.com/news/magazine-26289459.

25 Ibid.

26 Neil McKerrow, "Parents of Child-Rearing," NACCW, January 2003, https://cyc-net.org/cyc-online/cycol-0103-mckerrow.html.

27 William Kremer, "What Medieval Europe Did with Its Teenagers," BBC, March 23, 2014, https://www.bbc.com/news/magazine-26289459.

28 Erich Fromm, The Dogma of Christ: And Other Essays on Religion, Psychology, and Culture, (New York: Anchor Books, 1966). Most of this section is based on this book.

29 Ibid., 73.

30 Ibid.

31 Ibid., 73.

Chapter 10
....

The Manifest Destiny
of the White Man (1500–1900)

The White Man's Gathering Storm in Western Europe

The Quest for Religious and Political Freedom

The Reformation started out as a movement to reform the Catholic Church from within and cleanse it from its corruption. When Luther nailed his *Ninety-Five Theses* on the church doors in Wittenberg, Germany, in 1517, he could not foresee that the consequences would go far beyond his original intentions. It would create a deep schism in the Christian Church between the traditional Catholics and the reform-minded Protestants, which turned into a holy, and very bloody, civil war.

Luther's anti-authoritarian act of protest against the Catholic Church was deeply symbolic of the unhappiness of the people due to the corruption of the Church, and a societal desire for freedom of religion and belief. Besides Luther, many other preachers began speaking out about the corrupt excesses of the Church and proposed actions to remedy them. One of the most important ones was a young pastor in Geneva, Switzerland, by the name of John Calvin.

Calvin's idea was to take one city, his city of Geneva, and transform it into a model Kingdom of God where God would not only rule over the Church but also over politics and economics, art and music, and every other aspect of life. As we will see, Calvin's ideas inspired the Puritans who settled New England, the Presbyterians who dominated the middle colonies, and the Baptists who would dominate the American South. In the process, as we will elaborate later, they ran smack into opposition by the Founders who, as humanists and agnostics, if not atheists, wanted to keep religion out of politics and keep the state separate from the Church.

Religiously, people began to deeply resent being denied direct access to the divine. The Church taught that the only way a person had access to God was through acceptance of the Church and its hierarchy of power as the necessary intermediary between them and God. Practically, such acceptance allowed the Church hierarchy to control people's lives with their edicts and directives.

In one sense, then, the Reformation was a protest against the secular values of the Renaissance itself. The three Renaissance popes— Alexander VI, Julius II, and Leo X—matched the profligacy, the materialism, the intellectual hedonism, and the spiritual corruption of the despotic Italian kings. With their deep involvement in secular national and international politics, in secular events and humanistic interests, as patrons of renaissance art and architecture, these popes indeed exemplified church-state hegemony and its unbridled control over the lives of the millions of their subjects (believers and non-believers alike). The Protestants simply wanted a return to the purer, more direct form of Christianity that would not try to micromanage and control the form and content of their lives.

The response of the Roman Catholic Church to the Protestant Reformation was severe. It could not withstand the challenge to its authority, and reacted violently by launching the Counter-Reformation. The Inquisition engaged in a holy civil war with the Protestants, treating them as the new pagans that deserved to be tortured and eradicated from the face of the earth.

Renewed Persecution of Women

The Catholic effort against the Protestants coincided with the intensification of Catholic persecution of witches and pagans. Driven partly by the natural calamities of the era—the Black Death, the

Hundred Years War, and a gradual cooling of the climate that modern scientists call the Little Ice Age (between about the 15th and 19th centuries)—the Catholic prosecution of paganism and witchcraft generally became more prominent throughout the late medieval and Renaissance era and largely coincided with the age of the Reformation, the Catholic Counter-Reformation, and the Inquisition.

This certainly put the women of the age between a rock and a hard place, for the Protestants were not much of an improvement over the Catholics as far as their treatment of women is concerned. The Protestants were as misogynistic, if not more, than the Roman Catholic Church they were rebelling against. With the Reformation, the oppression and subjugation of the female to the male increased significantly. Women were barred from all universities, guilds, and professions. Women's property and inheritance rights were eliminated. A woman became the sole property of her husband; her only duty was obedience to him, and her education was restricted to reading and writing for the purpose of teaching the Bible to his children.

Protestantism became hyper-male-centric and replaced the female-centric aspects of the Catholic Church with an even more extreme version of the male-centric Old Testament God of Moses who led his chosen people to the Promised Land. Protestant doctrine and belief systems re-energized the twin pillars of Mosaic monotheism: racism and misogyny. The "chosen people" doctrine providing cosmic justification for outward aggression. Western European man began to turn back ever more strongly to the father God Yahweh for justification of his expanding sexual and economic oppression and exploitation.

Ultimately, the differences between Protestants **and** Catholics in the area that would become Germany led to the Thirty Years' War, from 1618 to 1648. Initially, Emperor Ferdinand II of the Holy Roman Empire decided to go after the Protestants who were challenging his secular and religious authority. As the process went on, it enlarged and drew in every country in Europe, pitting nations against nations in a continental spasm of realignment of political and religious boundaries.

In the end, France, Sweden, and their allies aligned on the winning side, and the losers were the Spanish-Austrian Habsburg dynasty, whose empire was chopped up and reduced. In the final agreement, the Peace of Westphalia, what emerged was the religious makeup of Europe as it is today. The Protestants wound up in charge of Western and Northern Europe, and the Catholics in greater control over central and Southern Europe. The price paid by the European Christians for their internal civil war was high indeed. Estimates of total military and civilian deaths range from 4.5 to 8 million, mostly from disease or starvation. In some areas of present-day Germany, up to 60% of the population died.[1]

Under the fundamental hegemonic unity of church and state under feudalism, the same few families controlled both the secular and the sacred aspects of life. When the Reform happened, this system had to give way to a new system suitable for a new era that was based on its very opposite: the separation of church and state. Politically, thinking folk began to question the doctrine of divine authority claimed by kings and the aristocracy as being above the human laws that apply to the lower classes. A collective awareness began to grow that the ability of each citizen to freely pursue his or her religious practice and political values without fear of being persecuted for them could only be realized under a democratic system that itself was secular and nonreligious.

Thus, democratic ideals began to percolate in Western European philosophy. Increasingly, democracy was seen as a more appropriate form of social organization to secure the basic freedoms for all people. Indeed, the very basic tenets of democracy (i.e., elected representatives, majority rule, one vote per person, the rule of law applying to rulers and ruled alike) would guarantee religious freedom, political freedom, economic freedom, freedom of thought, and freedom of movement. First on the European, and then on the American continent, the democratization of the pursuit of power, political as well as economic, became the essential driving force of Western European man's civilization. The idea of a better life, based on a level playing field where anyone and everybody had equal opportunity, economically and politically, grabbed a hold of the Western European imagination and powered a global expansion.

The Quest for Control of Space and Territory

The Western European countries of the 1500s had something in common with many of the ancient Mediterranean civilizations: they were seafaring, and trade was one of the prime generators of wealth that allowed for civilization to flourish. But while the ancient world was limited to the Mediterranean and immediate land areas surrounding it, the Western European nations existed on the shores of an infinite sea, the boundaries to which had never been found.

Like the imperialism of the Roman Empire, this new Western European imperialism was made possible by the growth of science and technology. Advances in naval technology and ship building let the maritime nations of Europe, such as Spain and Portugal, Britain and Holland, France and Belgium, explore further and further away from home, discovering new lands and territories in the process that were rich with potential for exploitation and profit.

Economically, only a few centuries after the earth was rediscovered to be round, first the Spanish and Portuguese, then the English, the Dutch, the French, and the Belgians, roamed the globe, ruthlessly conquering its peoples and exploiting their resources. Indeed, the globalization of exploration and the resulting colonization of foreign territories, the appropriation by force of gold, gems, and valuables, the exploitation of natural resources, and the slavery of local populations powered the rise of Western European man's civilization. The script was pretty much always the same. First came the explorers. Then came the merchants and the missionaries. Lastly, but inevitably, the armed occupation forces arrived to enforce the new status quo of service and exploitation.

In feudal Catholic society, the sources of wealth consisted of land and the labor to work it (the 99% peasants). Capitalism, as the anti-authoritarianism pursuit of economic freedom, provided the opportunities to make new fortunes outside of the straightjacket of feudal class structure. Powered by economic expansion of colonization and industry, the effect of the full-blown development of capitalism in Western Europe and its imposition of colonialism on the rest of the world was to add a third layer of wealth and power. This new layer of wealth and power demanded, fought for, and obtained, a reorganization of the political power structures of the European countries that reflected their newfound muscle.

The new wealth so accumulated through colonization abroad fueled a new expansionary period at home in the arts and sciences. It stimulated a new Renaissance of innovation in science and technology, in politics and economics, in religion and philosophy, in painting and sculpture, in architecture and literature.

The Quest for Control of Nature and Time

During the Middle Ages, humanity was visited by a constant and continuous barrage of natural disasters. Volcanic eruptions, mini-ice ages, famines, and waves of bubonic plague struck repeatedly, emphasizing humanity's powerlessness in the face of nature. At first mostly unconscious but more and more conscious as time went on, the urge to conquer nature was born in the traumas that nature inflicted on medieval humanity.

Parallel to the geographical exploration of earthly space, the Western European man also began to engage intensively and extensively in the intellectual exploration of nature for the purpose of conquering, i.e., appropriation and exploitation of the very structure of space-time to his benefit and profit.

In other words, Western man's thirst for scientific knowledge developed not in unity with nature but in opposition to her. His journey of scientific exploration and discovery was never about the wisdom of stewardship but always about power to exploit. As such, it became second nature to him to think that nature should exist as separate from man rather than that humanity should exist within and as part of nature. His interests were focused almost wholly on treating her energies and creatures in terms of their use value to him in his ever-expanding quest for power.

The invention of clocks was a development of critical importance in this effort. By giving us a concrete, objective expression of time as a linear sequence of equal units, clocks became the instrument of choice to control and bend nature to our will. Among the first to draw attention to this was the famous linguist Benjamin Whorf. According to Whorf, the Western mind is predisposed by its language itself to conceive of time as an object existing in space. In our Western languages, he wrote, "concepts of time are objectified, i.e., visualized as counted quantities, made up out of units, as length can be visibly marked off in inches. A 'length of time' is envisioned as a row of similar units, like a row of bottles."[2]

Whorf wrote that the first traces of this objectification of time as a line were to be found in the Hebrew language of the ancient Jews and that, by the time of the Roman civilization, it had flourished in Italy. In the Middle Ages, he continued, "the patterns... began to interweave with the increased mechanical inventions, industry, trade, and scholastic and scientific thought. The need for measurement in industry and trade, the stores and bulks of 'stuffs' in various containers, the type of bodies in which various goods were handled, standardization of measure and weights, units, inventions of clocks, and the measurement of 'time,' keeping records, accounts, chronicles, histories, the growth of mathematics and the partnership of mathematics and science, all cooperates to bring our thought and language form into its present form."[3]

Western man's monotheistic-religious and secular-scientific concepts of time show both a strange unity and a divergence into contradiction. Both are linear, but one is pessimistic and the other is optimistic. The Western monotheistic-religious notion of time is a linear progression of evil taking over the world, resulting in its final apocalyptic calamity, the end of the world and natural time, and the beginning of no-time, the eternity of heavenly existence. Western man's secular-scientific conception of linear time is, initially, more optimistic. He considers his historical time a straight line of progress that goes from the murky past through the present into the bright future. It sees humanity as an evolutionary product of life that arose out of the muck, over the eons, iterating itself over and over again until consciousness evolved into human form. In this, his concept of historical time epitomizes the aggressive optimism characteristic of the yang of emergency. This aggressive optimism seeks the infinite expansion of power, the appropriation of space and time economically, politically, militarily, scientifically, and technologically. His view of history was defined as the progressive conquest of the world and nature: locks to "own" space and control territory and clocks to tame time and control nature.

Sadism and the Formation of the Capitalist-Protestant Character Structure

The oppression, fear, and masochism complex of feudal existence engendered in people's hearts and minds a duality of emotion: hope for a better future and hatred of the oppressor. Unfortunately, when the opportunity arose to put this hope and optimism into action and create a better future, Western man's rebellion against authority to secure his freedom did not result in the re-establishment of equality, balance, and harmony of the female-centric social paradigm. On the contrary, his fight for freedom from oppression by authority was perverted into a quest to become the authority. He became what he was fighting against, only more so, succeeding only in switching the yin and yang of oppression of the male-centric paradigm of the pursuit of power and aggression. From being the oppressed, Western man became himself the oppressor of the working people of his own countries and the indigenous peoples in the rest of the world.

The cultural and technological developments that transformed European society of the late Middle Ages into the beginning of the early modern period accommodated and expressed the new mass longings for freedom and stirrings of passions of exploration, geographical and intellectual. It was in this period that the change of polarity occurred, in which the yin, fear-based crisis paradigm of feudalism was replaced by the yang, aggression-based crisis paradigm of capitalism. It was in this period, also, that the contradiction between Western man's conscious hope and optimism and his unconscious sadistic complex of racism and misogyny came to define his schizoid nature and split personality.

It is by means of the formative processes of early infant and child-rearing practices that cultures imprint on its people the character structure necessary to perpetuate themselves. With the advent of the new expansionist Protestant-capitalism-colonialism era, the feudal model of mass masochistic character structure was no longer suitable, as the emerging complex of expansionist conquest required far greater numbers of very aggressive personalities. The transformation of masochistic feudal Catholic character structure into sadistic capitalist Protestant character structure was accomplished by adopting radical changes in child-rearing practices in the second, male-centric stage of infantile development that resulted in a life-long pathological need to pursue wealth and power over people.

To instill the acquisitive-competitive character traits, it was discovered, you first withhold love in the first, yin stage of development, then you enforce a regimen of strict discipline (i.e., physical and psychological punishment) in the second, yang stage of development. That's how you produce a person with a lot of internal rage but with enough self-discipline to channel it into the pursuit and accumulation of wealth and power over others. Sigmund Freud, of course, was the first to draw attention to this dynamic. He analyzed and described how the quest for power stems from interference with the natural development of the excretory functions and oedipal conflicts. Freud found that premature and severe interference with the natural acquisition of voluntary control over the excretory functions invariably produces an adult individual with obsessive anal-retentive traits.

Freud found these traits are indicative of the anal character's larger complex of obsessional concern with issues of control and power: "They are especially orderly, parsimonious, and obstinate,"[4] traits that tend toward extreme cleanliness and punctuality, avarice and hoarding, and defiance and aggression, respectively. It is precisely these traits that define the capitalist's essentially sadistic character structure and drive him to the pursuit of wealth and power to the point of obsession. Fachinelli added that the common denominator of these apparently diverse traits found by Freud to constitute the anal character is a certain attitude toward time. "They all imply some way of employing, saving and producing time. The economic metaphor is no accident, for as the attitudes of parsimony, avarice, and obstinacy are displaced onto time, the anal character treats time like money."[5]

The yang-crisis structure of Western man's character, in the final analysis, is based on the equivalence of time and money. To have money is to have power and to have power is to control someone's life by controlling their time. With money as the medium of exchange of power for time, the capitalist tells the worker, "My money in exchange for your time." By embracing the worship of Mammon, the god of money, the Protestant capitalist did a complete 180 from the basic tenets of the very first Christians. The early Christians were antiestablishment rebels who saw "money as the root of all evil" and decried the worldly excesses of the secular Roman and religious Jewish power structures. In sharp contrast, the capitalist-Protestant faith in God embraced the pursuit of wealth and power, and that, as a matter of Divine Providence, "God helps those who help themselves."

When the power addict gets completely taken over by his addiction, the inevitable result is pathological narcissism, paranoia, and megalomania. Modeled on the emperors of the Roman Empire, the Western European White Man's kings, emperors, and dictators consider reality as their creation, which they have a right to impose on people, lest they be made to taste the bitter fruit of humiliation through domination. From Julius Caesar to Napoleon to Hitler, Stalin, Putin, Trump, and their thousands of lesser wannabes, the lure of ultimate power has proved irresistible. The saying that "power corrupts and absolute power corrupts absolutely" describes the addictive nature of power. Henry Kissinger once famously boasted that "power is the ultimate aphrodisiac,"[6] and as the individual matures and the need for power finds expression, the craving grows with each use. Creating an enemy, doing battle, and dominating is the power addict's way of shooting up and getting high. In this way, power acts like a drug, necessitating ever more of it to sustain the desired high, and the power addict engages in compulsion as surely as the drug user.

The Europeans Come to America and Conquer a Continent

Two Competing Protestant Visions for the Soul of America

One of the main criticisms of the Catholic Church by the European Protestants in the Middle Ages had been its increasing secularization. Over time, the focus of the Catholic Church had become less and less concerned with the spiritual development and health of their congregations, demanding only their unswerving obedience to the Church discipline. Simultaneously, it had become more and more focused on the obsessive pursuit of material wealth and political power.

The initial waves of Western Europeans that came and settled in North America were Protestants of many stripes and persuasions, primarily English and Dutch but also French and Scandinavian. Of course, these Protestant immigrants brought with them the various religious factions that had grown out of the Protestant Reformation. When the time came for the colonists to sever ties with the old countries and embark on the creation of an independent new nation, these differences between them took on new and greater significance insofar as it would shape the very nature of the social, economic, political, and religious institutions of the new Eutopian enterprise.

In the framing of the problem and the solutions put forward, two versions and visions emerged in Protestantism that would be fated to do battle with each other for centuries for control over the soul, or essence, not just of Protestantism but of America itself. The yin vision of Protestantism consisted of what we may call Humanist Protestants, characterized by their democratic approach to governing. Opposing them was the yang vision of Protestantism, consisting of what we may call the Theocratic Protestants, who favored a hierarchical approach to religious and civil organization.

The guiding vision of the more democratic and humanist faction of Protestantism was based on the total separation of church and state. They believed that religion should have no role whatsoever in the operation of the secular realms of politics and economics. Precisely in order to assure that everyone would be totally free to worship as they choose, they argued that there should be not more integration of the secular and the sacred realms but a complete separation between them.

By 1776, when the American nation was born, it was our good fortune that the majority of the founders rejected theocracy in favor of democracy. In their framing of the Declaration of Independence, the Constitution, and the Bill of Rights, they rejected the narrow, exclusive, theocratic vision of both Catholicism and theocratic Protestantism, and embraced the more inclusive democratic humanistic vision. That's why the First Amendment of the Constitution barred not just the Christian religion, but any religion, from exercising a favored status under the law.

Theocratic Protestantism

The guiding vision of the more theocratic faction of Protestantism was opposed to the vision put forth by the Founders. They envisioned the total and hierarchical integration of church and state. The most influential propagator of this doctrine was John Calvin, the preeminent Swiss theologian. Calvin had concluded that the only way to eliminate the religious and secular corruption of feudal Catholicism and to purify Christian religion and practice was by uniting the sacred and secular in a new kind of theocratic state governed by His Reformed Church. In Europe, Calvin had focused his efforts on a single city, Geneva, and sought to transform it into a model kingdom of God, a city where God's religious authority, through his representatives, of course, would rule not only over the Church but also over politics, art, music, and every other aspect of human life.

The Founders recognized that Calvin's theocratically hierarchical society was fundamentally antidemocratic. According to Calvin's theory of salvation, all men are not created equal because some have been "chosen" or "predestined" by God to be believers who will inherit both heaven and earth and the rest, while the others had been chosen by God to be condemned to sin and suffer, first on earth, then in hell. The Founders had a greater comprehension of the big picture: they had to provide freedom of worship to a multitude of faiths that were coming to the continent and calling it home. They understood that to sign on to a theocracy would be to do away with democracy. The founding documents of the United States were expressions of a vision of liberty and human equality grounded in "Nature and Nature's God," as Thomas Jefferson put it in the Declaration of Independence.

By providing cosmic justification for the continued existence of white male privilege and power, Calvinism was fated to play a wholly and deeply reactionary role in American history. Indeed, by 1776, Calvin's vision of a social order, ruled by his concept of the Christian

God, informed the majority of the faithful throughout most of the 13 colonies. His work inspired the Puritans, who settled New England, the Presbyterians, who dominated the middle colonies, and the Baptists, who would dominate the American South.

If the religious orientation of the Founders was more New Testament and oriented toward Christ's female-centric teachings, the theocratic Protestantism of John Calvin and his followers unabashedly re-embraced the aggression and violence demanded by the Old Testament, male-centric, Mosaic, monotheistic God.

As we have seen, the image and idea of this God began as (and still is today) the projection of an all-powerful "hegemonic masculinity" as top dog in the hierarchy of the cosmos. The ruling principle of monotheism is inherently antidemocratic and holds that all people are *not* created equal. The male gender is created more equal than the female; the white race is created more equal to all non-white races. In other words, Calvinism, as it has played out in the U.S., not only explicitly believes and promotes Christian dominance but also implicitly has promoted, for centuries, two other forms of cultural and political power—whiteness and patriarchy.

With this religious foundation of racism and misogyny, millions of Protestants continued to buy into the Calvinist doctrine of the "chosen people syndrome." Like the Israelites, they believed themselves to be the "the chosen people," preordained by God to subdue the world and all other peoples and critters on it, in His name and Glory (and for their profit). So deeply ingrained became these attitudes that by the 1950s, most Americans understood that the ideal of Christian America meant Protestant, white, male, and heterosexual dominance. There was little quarter given to anyone who seriously questioned these boundaries.

Humanistic Protestantism

The split between the theocrats and the democrats was dramatized by the public reaction to publication of Thomas Paine's book *The Age of Reason* in 1794. The criticisms he unleashed in this book against the teachings of Protestantism, Catholicism, Judaism, and other "revealed" religions were severe. They brought into stark relief the two opposing factions within the religious community: those free-thinking liberals who wanted church disestablishment from political life and the Christian conservatives who wanted Christianity to continue having a strong social influence.

Professing to be a follower of the deism then popular in England among progressive thinkers, Paine simply believed that "my own mind is my own church" and declared that "all national institutions of churches, whether Jewish, Christian or Turkish, appear to me no other than human inventions,... set up to terrify and enslave mankind, and monopolize power and profit."[7] Paine's critique of institutionalized religion and advocacy of rational thinking influenced many freethinkers in the 19th and 20th centuries, both in Europe and America. His vision unified Philadelphia merchants, British artisans, French peasants, Dutch reformers, and radical intellectuals from Boston to Berlin in one great movement.

Paine and other founding architects who articulated the new American ideals of democracy got their ideas from Western European Enlightenment and Renaissance philosophy and thinkers. The separation of church and state, religious freedom, political freedom, economic freedom, freedom of the press and thought, elected representatives, majority rule, one vote per person, all our modern ideas about democracy and capitalism originated in this fertile period.

Recall the true, original Christianity was a re-emergence of the quest for equality and harmony of the female-centric paradigm for world order. In as much as the American Dream was based on hope, it can be said that the Founders of the new American experiment in democracy walked in the footsteps of Jesus, giving voice to and creating opportunity for oppressed and marginalized people. Certainly, the documents our Founders produced expressed the same universal values of equality and prosperity that were championed by the early Christians.

I have chosen to use the phrase "Founders" rather than "Founding Fathers" because, while the latter phrase correctly expresses the deeply ingrained reality of their racist and misogynist prejudices, likewise the institutions the Founders created were far from perfect, incorporating those same profound racist and misogynist flaws and prejudices. But the Founders did not claim, as did the Calvinists, that these racist and sexist prejudices were divinely ordained rights and proof of their superiority as God's "chosen people." They understood that the history of the United States as a nation would be written as the ongoing struggle between the forces of progress and equality for all and the forces of reaction and inequality where the few have power over the many.

The Linking of Capitalism and Democracy

The Founders sought to establish on the new continent the kind of state that would empower the common European people to pursue their happiness. The institutionalization of this pursuit of happiness would be assured through the democratization of the pursuit of economic wealth and political power—in the economic realm through the adoption of the capitalism and the competitive principle, and in the political realm through the adoption of the competitive spirit in representative electoral democracy.

By democratizing the pursuit of power, the Founders sought to devise a system of political democracy and economic capitalism that would safeguard against any possible come-back victory of the oppressive features of feudalism, including its rigid class structure, the hereditary transmission of wealth and power, and the lack of separation of church and state. To prevent the accumulation of royal or otherwise dictatorial power by any one individual, they made it axiomatic that no one individual could be above the law or could claim to be the law. They accomplished this by developing the concept of the separation of powers into three coequal branches to achieve a balance of powers between the executive, legislative, and judicial branches of the government.

The Founders were convinced that the economics of capitalism would result in wider sharing and redistribution of the economic wealth and power for all people. Concomitantly, they believed the democratic electoral process should and would guarantee the people their voice and vote in political matters, as encapsulated in the phrase "government of the people, for the people, and by the people."

To a large extent, the Founders were successful and created a system of greater equality and opportunity. In the America of the 18th and 19th century, (1) vast wealth was created and anybody could go out and make a fortune in business, and (2) theoretically, if not practically, any citizen could run for election and rise to political power. Moreover, capitalist economics, with its concept of upward mobility, vastly improved conditions of the masses of people, compared to the stagnant class structures of feudal society. Beyond the two classes of feudalism—the aristocratic "haves" and the peasant "have-nots"—capitalist democracy allowed the development a third, middle class of "have-some-things."

Capitalism, Christianity, and the Price of Conquest

Protestant Christianity and Capitalism

In medieval Christianity, all that was required to be saved was to believe and submit in order to earn eternal life in heaven after death. In other words, if you're good, you'll get your reward, but you're going to have to wait till after death.

In the capitalist era, Protestantism sweetened the offer with a bigger carrot. It promised that you didn't have to wait till after death to reap the rewards of the faith. For in this earthly life, they believed "God would help those who helped themselves," that if you were a believer, one of your best bets was to become a capitalist and make lots of money, for your wealth would become the yardstick of salvation. You could be pretty sure that you were saved and merit eternal life after death. Having been given cosmic justification and even "ordered" by the Almighty to spread civilization (i.e., Christianity and capitalism), the operative principles of the European colonists who arrived on the continent's shore were "might makes right" and "to the victor go the spoils."

The first really great fortunes made by Christian capitalists in the U.S. were made in the South. By the eve of the Civil War

(1861–1865), the Mississippi Valley was home to more millionaires per capita than anywhere else in the United States, and New Orleans boasted a denser concentration of banking capital than New York City.[8] All of this thanks to the four interrelated industries of real estate, slavery, cotton, and banking.

In the early 19th century, as millions of European immigrants continued streaming into the country to try make their fortune, the U.S. needed to expand its territory to accommodate them. First to the south, then to the west, the process always followed the same script. The United States government solved its growing land shortage by expropriating millions of acres from Native Americans, often with military force. In this way, Georgia, Alabama, Tennessee, and Florida were acquired in the South. The government then proceeded to sell that land on the cheap—just $1.25 an acre in the early 1830s ($38 in 2023 dollars)—to white settlers. Naturally, the first to cash in were the land speculators. Companies operating in Mississippi flipped land, selling it soon after purchase, commonly for double the price.[9]

Now, on the land taken from the natives by force, the white European settler entrepreneurs put to work, by force, the slaves imported from Africa to farm, harvest, and process the miracle of cotton. Indeed, it was the fields of Georgia and Alabama, and their cotton houses and slave auction blocks, that were the birthplace of America's approach to capitalism, and that defined its characteristics. As slave labor camps spread throughout the South, production surged and fortunes grew. By 1831, the country was delivering nearly half the world's raw cotton crop, with 350 million pounds picked that year. Just four years later, it harvested 500 million pounds.[10] Cotton grown and picked by enslaved workers was the nation's most valuable export. The combined value of enslaved people exceeded that of all the railroads and factories in the nation and the Southern white elites grew very rich, indeed.

The fact that conquest and slavery were the foundations of U.S. capitalism left a lasting imprint on the American character. Today, only a few generations later, the cruelty with which the native peoples and the Black slaves were treated are still a deep part of our collective psyche that we have not yet come to terms with. Indeed, in the final analysis, what made the cotton economy boom in the United States, and not in all the other far-flung parts of the world with climates and soil suitable to the crop, was our nation's unflinching willingness to use violence on non-white people and to exert its will on seemingly endless supplies of land and labor. As the *New York Times* author, Matthew Desmond put it so succinctly, "given the choice between modernity and barbarism, prosperity and poverty, lawfulness and cruelty, democracy and totalitarianism, America chose all of the above."[11] Moreover, as the historian Bonnie Martin has written, "slave owners worked their slaves financially, as well as physically from colonial days until emancipation" by using them as collateral for loans in other business projects.[12] Thomas Jefferson mortgaged 150 of his slaves to build Monticello. People could be sold much more easily than land, and in multiple Southern states, more than eight in ten mortgage-secured loans used slaves as full or partial collateral.

In the financial realm, the boom of the slave trade became a truly international phenomenon. The huge profits to be made in and by the slave trade beckoned European financial markets who saw the opportunities and got in on the action at an early stage. When Thomas Jefferson mortgaged his slaves, it was a Dutch firm that put up the money. The Louisiana Purchase, which opened millions of acres to cotton production, was financed by Barings Bank, the well-heeled British commercial bank. A majority of credit powering the American slave economy came from the London money market.

Years after abolishing the African slave trade in 1807, Britain, and much of Europe along with it, was still bankrolling slavery in the United States. To raise capital, state-chartered banks pooled debt generated by slave mortgages and repackaged it as bonds promising investors annual interest. During slavery's boom, banks did swift business in bonds, finding buyers in Hamburg and Amsterdam, in Boston and Philadelphia.[13]

So looking back on the framing of our democratic society, it appears the Founders were working under an unintentionally limited awareness that was, in a historical sense, unavoidable.

Religious Persecution of the Native Peoples

The first limitation the Founders came up against pertains to the separation of church and state. While the goal was laudable, its implementation was incomplete and, therefore, not successful. Especially not in the hearts and minds of the new immigrants who arrived. Having fled the religious persecutions and economic deprivations of their home countries, the new immigrants immediately began imposing the very things they were fleeing and running away from, namely religious persecution and economic deprivation, on anyone who stood in the way of their continental expansion.

To justify their actions and behaviors on religious grounds, they espoused the doctrine of Manifest Destiny (based on Calvinist persuasions), which was basically the belief that their God had not only sanctioned but commanded the conquest of the American continent in His name and to his greater glory. Such was the poisonous legacy of the belief in Manifest Destiny, decreed by the white male image projected onto the universe as monotheistic God and cosmic authority. This doctrine was symbolic and expressive of both the "chosen gender" syndrome and "chosen people" syndrome, the misogyny of the white male authority over female, and the xenophobic racism of the white race over non-white races.

The miracle of wealth and progress on the American continent was won at the cost of stealing a continent from its native inhabitants, either killing or relocating them, while building their new society with slave labor imported from yet another continent. Then, by repeating and perpetuating many of the original sins of their fathers, capitalist democracy paid a moral price, and our pride in the success of the American experiment remains forever tainted by the curse and shame of the human toll extracted in the realization of the American Dream.

Genocide and Its Unintended Consequences

Between 1830 and 1850, the U.S. government engaged in a campaign of ethnic cleansing and enforced displacement of more than 60,000 native people.[14] Five Indian tribes (Cherokee, Muskogee, Seminole, Chickasaw, and Choctaw) were forcefully evicted from their native lands in the Southeast and were driven westward toward the Indian Territory in present-day Oklahoma. The effort amounted to a genocide as some 15,000 people perished on this Trail of Tears as the horrific episode came to be called.

The extent of the genocide perpetrated by the Europeans on the American continents, North, Central, and South, has been documented by recent research from University College, London. Geography Professor Mark Maslin and colleagues did the math and came to the stunning conclusion that in less than one century after Columbus discovered America, European settlers had killed 58 million indigenous people across the Americas.

This stunning historical fact had other, even more stunning, if unintended, historical consequences, one climatic and one economic. First, as a result of the genocide, humongous areas of farmland in the Americas were abandoned and reforested themselves as a result. Maslin and his colleagues estimated the total area so affected to equal the size of France. These new forests sucked up such a massive amount of carbon dioxide that it resulted in a massive decrease of carbon dioxide in the global atmosphere, sufficient to cool the entire globe and create the Little Ice Age in the 1600s.

Second, the death of indigenous Americans directly contributed to the success of the European economy. As natural resources and food were shipped from the New World back to the Old World, Europe's population could both expand and begin working in industries other than farming for sustenance and money. Thus, concluded Maslin and his colleagues, "the depopulation of the Americas may have inadvertently allowed the Europeans to dominate the world" and "allowed the industrial revolution."[15]

As a country and nation, we have not yet taken full responsibility for addressing and redressing theses injustices of our past, so that our future may fully realize the humanity of our nation's soul. Later chapters will address the question of whether the Democrats can and will step up to the plate.

The Big Business of Slavery, and the Struggle for Emancipation

Capital, Labor, and Race

As the large slave-labor camps of the 19th century grew increasingly efficient, enslaved Black people became America's first modern workers, their productivity increasing at an astonishing pace. During the 60 years leading up to the Civil War, the daily amount of cotton picked per enslaved worker increased 2.3% a year. That means that in 1862, the average enslaved fieldworker picked 400% as much cotton as his or her counterpart did in 1801.[16]

Plantation owners used a combination of incentives and punishments to squeeze as much as possible out of enslaved workers. Some beaten workers passed out from the pain and woke up vomiting. Some "danced" or "trembled" with every hit. An 1829 first-person account from Alabama recorded an overseer shoving the faces of women he thought had picked too slowly into their cotton baskets and opening up their backs. To the historian Edward Baptist, before the Civil War, Americans "lived in an economy whose bottom gear was torture."[17]

The imprint of slavery on the emerging American capitalist system and industry was profound and persists today. The Southern, slave-based cotton industry became the prototype for industry in the rest of the country. Cotton planters, millers, and consumers were fashioning a new economy, one that was global in scope and required the movement of capital, labor, and products across long distances. In other words, they were fashioning a capitalist economy. "The beating heart of this new system," Sven Beckert writes, "was slavery."[18]

The large-scale cultivation of cotton hastened the invention of the factory, an institution that propelled the Industrial Revolution and changed the course of history. In 1810, there were 87,000 cotton spindles in America. Fifty years later, there were five million. Slavery, wrote one of its defenders in *DeBow's Review*, a widely read agricultural magazine, was the "nursing mother of the prosperity of the North."[19] In the North, a new class of entrepreneurs, inspired by the success of the Southern cotton industry, erected textile mills to form, in the words of Massachusetts Senator Charles Sumner, an "unhallowed alliance between the lords of the lash and the lords of the loom."[20]

Even today, the core impulse behind the technology that has facilitated unremitting workplace supervision, particularly in the service sector, is that of the plantation, which sought innermost control over the bodies of their enslaved workforce.[21] Modern-day workers are subjected to a wide variety of surveillance strategies, from drug tests and closed-circuit video monitoring to tracking apps and even devices that sense heat and motion. *Today's modern technology* companies have developed software that records workers' keystrokes and mouse clicks, along with randomly capturing screenshots multiple times a day. A 2006 survey found that more than a third of companies with workforces of 1,000 or more had staff members who read through employees' outbound emails. So don't be fooled if the technology of workplace supervision can make it feel futuristic. What's driving it is still the denial of the humanity of the workforce and the deeply entrenched instinct to treat the workers fundamentally as slaves.

Abraham Lincoln, the Fight Against Slavery, and the Civil War (1861-1865)

Prior to the American Revolution, slavery, which had been around for thousands of years, was considered normal and was not a significant issue of public debate. The Revolution changed that and made it into an issue that had to be addressed. From day one, the issue of slavery divided the nation. During the framing of the Constitution, slavery was already a controversial issue that had been left unsettled. As a result, shortly after the Revolution, the Northern states quickly started outlawing slavery. Even in Southern states, laws were changed to limit slavery and facilitate manumission. The amount of indentured servitude (temporary slavery) dropped dramatically throughout the country.

Since most of the immigrants, north or south, were Protestants, they had religious arguments supporting the divine correctness of their position, whether pro- or anti-slavery. Whether one chose to oppose slavery or support it, in the end, turned out to be more a question of economics and morality rather than religion. Northern anti-slavery Protestants chose basic human values such as freedom over profit and power, while Southern pro-slavery Protestants did the opposite and placed profit and power over those same human values. In 1854, the Republican Party was founded on a rising tide of opposition to the expansion of slavery to additional states. One of its founders was a young attorney by the name of Abraham Lincoln (1809–1865), who rose to fame, and in 1860 became the first GOP president.

On the eve of the Civil War, in 1860, 4 million of the 32 million Americans were Black slaves. Lincoln made good on his sacred vow to end slavery when he issued the Emancipation Proclamation in 1863. It took 12 years, in what was known as the Reconstruction era, for the political reintegration of the nation to be accomplished. During that time, three new constitutional amendments were passed and signed into law for the purpose of granting the newly freed slaves with citizenship and full civil rights.

Lincoln and Marx

The anti-slavery movement in the U.S. was inextricably entwined with the larger labor movement in the 19th century that was springing up worldwide. Across the U.S., Western Europe, and Russia, mass movements were organizing themselves into political opposition to the ongoing and increasing exploitation of the working class by the capitalist merchant class. Indeed, in its beginning, the origin and development of the GOP was radically to the left of center. And nothing was more illustrative of this orientation than the close philosophical and political relationship between Abraham Lincoln and the very scourge of capitalism himself, Karl Marx.

When Lincoln served his sole term in Congress in the late 1840s, the young lawyer from Illinois became close friends with Horace Greeley, a fellow Whig who served briefly alongside him. Greeley was better known as the founder of the *New York Tribune*, the newspaper largely responsible for transmitting the ideals that formed the Republican Party in 1854.[22] And what were those ideals? They were anti-slavery, pro-worker, and sometimes overtly socialist, according to John Nichols, author of the book *The "S" Word: A Short History of an American Tradition...Socialism*. The *New York Tribune* championed the redistribution of land in the American West to the poor and the emancipation of slaves.

Marx was also friends with Charles A. Dana, an American socialist fluent in German who was the managing editor of the *New York Tribune*. In 1852, Dana hired Marx to be the newspaper's British correspondent. Over the next decade, Marx wrote nearly 500 articles for the paper. Many of his contributions became unsigned columns appearing on the front page as the publication's official position. Marx later "borrowed liberally" from his *New York Tribune* writings for his book *Capital*, according to Nichols.[23]

There can be no doubt that Abraham Lincoln and Karl Marx influenced each other. Like a lot of nascent Republicans, Lincoln was an avid reader of the *Tribune*. It's nearly guaranteed that, in the 1850s, Lincoln was regularly reading Marx. Many of Lincoln's pronouncements had a distinctly Marxist flavor, like when he said that "Capital is the fruit of labor, and could never have existed if labor had not first existed."[24] In January 1865, Marx wrote to Lincoln on behalf of the International Workingmen's Association, a group for socialists, communists, anarchists, and trade unions, to "congratulate the American people upon your reelection."[25] Marx wrote further "an oligarchy of 300,000 slaveholders" had defiled the republic and that "the workingmen of Europe feel sure that, as the American War of Independence initiated a new era of ascendancy for the middle class, so the American Antislavery War will do for the working class."[26]

A few weeks later, a reply came via Charles Francis Adams—son of former president John Quincy Adams, grandson of former president John Adams, and U.S. ambassador to Britain under Lincoln. Adams told Marx that Lincoln had received his message and it was "accepted by him with a sincere and anxious desire that he may be able to prove himself not unworthy of the confidence which has been recently extended to him by his fellow citizens and by so many of the friends of humanity and progress throughout the world."[27] Lincoln also gave perhaps a more eloquent rendering of Marx's famous rallying cry, "Workers of the World Unite!" when he said that "the strongest bond of human sympathy, outside of the family relation, should be one uniting all working people, of all nations, and tongues, and kindreds."[28]

When the socialist orator and frequent presidential candidate Eugene V. Debs made a campaign stop in Springfield, Illinois, in 1908, he told the crowd, "The Republican Party was once red. Lincoln was a revolutionary."[29] Years later, Martin Luther King echoed the same sentiment when he said, "It is worth noting that Abraham Lincoln warmly welcomed the support of Karl Marx during the Civil War and corresponded with him freely... Our irrational obsessive anti-communism has led us into too many quagmires to be retained as if it were a mode of scientific thinking."[30]

The gains of Reconstruction soon began to be systematically undermined in the South during what became known as the Jim Crow era. Southern states began passing all manner of laws and regulation to disenfranchise and remove political and economic progress made by Black people during the Reconstruction era.

The Goddess Returns and the Women Awaken to a New Century

The Statue of Liberty

Two women were critically important in keeping alive the flame of hope and justice for all by means of American Democracy: one of bronze and one of flesh. The first was the Statue of Liberty in New York harbor, and the second was Emma Lazarus, the poet who immortalized her appeal and mission. The Statue of Liberty, representing the Roman goddess Libertas or "Liberty" was a gift from the people of France to the people of the United States. Designed by the sculptor Frederic Auguste, and its inner metal framework built by Gustave Eiffel, it was dedicated October 28, 1886, as a monument to the ideals that linked the American and French revolutions. In her right hand, Libertas holds a torch above her head, and in her left hand, she carries a tablet inscribed with July 4, 1776, the date of the Declaration of Independence. A broken shackle and chain lie at her feet as she is walking forward, symbolic of her gaining her freedom.

In Roman times, Libertas was worshipped as early as 238 BC in a temple on the Aventine Hill. In the later Republic, she was featured on coins, often depicted as a standing figure holding out, but never wearing, a pileus, the soft cap that symbolized the granting of freedom to former slaves. She is also represented as carrying a rod, which formed part of the ceremony for the act of manumission, or granting a slave his or her freedom. Digging even deeper into her story, Lbertas was only the latest, Roman version of the Queen of Heaven who was worshipped universally in all the ancient cultures of the Near East. These included the civilizations and cultures of Sumer, Egypt, Minoan Crete, Mycenean Greece, and Hebrew tribes, where she was known variously as Astarte, Ishtar, Nut, Anat, and Ashtoreth, among others. Like them, Libertas embodied the unity of several opposites. She was the protectress of marriage and motherhood but also known as the mother of harlots in as much as prostitution was part of her religious practices. Like them, Libertas was also both a fertility goddess as well as a warrior and storm goddess and was worshipped both in her good as well as evil aspects.

Even the Hebrew tribes, before the rule of Yahweh as sole male God had been completely consolidated, worshipped a local version of Libertas, named Asherah. Indeed, as Raphael Patai first pointed out, in the Book of Kings, Asherah was considered the wife of Yahweh, and they were worshipped as a couple.[31] And even Christianity has maintained a connection to this very ancient idea of the Queen of Heaven, where Mary, the mother of Jesus, is assigned that role. The Catholic Church's teaching is that Mary, at the end of her earthly life, was bodily and spiritually assumed into heaven and that she is there honored as the Queen of Heaven.

The realization that the great Statue of Liberty in New York's harbor is, in fact, a giant representation of the ancient Queen of Heaven evoked deep feelings of awe and surprise in me. More than anything, I experienced a sense of giddiness, in that as the statue of the goddess, she was emanating a renewed sense of appropriateness and relevance for the modern age of our 21st century. For what is more appropriate than the Great Cosmic Mother welcoming the teeming masses of the earth who left their homelands because of threats to their very existence to come to this land and work to improve their lot? Isn't it the perfect symbol of hope and freedom? And as such, we may also interpret her presence in the New York harbor as a herald for the future and the female-centric Eutopian rebirth of our civilization.

One the other hand, I also experienced a feeling like glee, realizing that all this time, the Great Cosmic Mother dominated the very entrance to the heart of the kingdom of Christianity and capitalism. I mean, how did that whole project ever get by the Christian censors? One can only surmise, of course, but ignorance and a lack of historical knowledge and insight seems the most plausible answer. And of course, as the fact becomes more well-known, the Christian zealots in the GOP will probably start a campaign to tear down the goddess as an anti-Christian pagan threat. Seeing as the GOP has already transformed itself into the party opposing democracy and democratic values, it will have no qualms about seeking to destroy the female-centric symbolism of the goddess Libertas.

Emma Lazarus

Emma Lazarus (1849–1887) was the gifted Jewish poet and activist who wrote the words that would henceforth symbolize the mission of Libertas and her promise to those entering our shores in search of a better life. The celebrated lines of her sonnet "The New Colossus" in 1883 were inscribed on a bronze plaque on the pedestal of the Statue of Liberty in 1903.

The sculptor Frédéric Auguste Bartholdi who made the Statue of Liberty named it "La Liberté Eclairant le Monde," which translates as "Liberty Enlightening the World." Paul Auster properly proclaimed it to be "a symbol of hope to the outcasts and downtrodden of the world."[32] But it was Emma Lazarus whose words would touch and warm our souls by expressing the poetry of the sculpture and inject its altogether more radical and egalitarian message and mission in our hearts. Her poem, "The New Colossus," has entered the pantheon of American statements, NPR's "Credo of America," alongside the memorable words uttered by such historical progressive luminaries as Thomas Paine, Abraham Lincoln, and Martin Luther King. It was Thomas Paine who expressed the hope that this human experiment in America might "begin the world over again," Abraham Lincoln who asserted that "all men are created equal," and the Reverend Martin Luther King, Jr.'s call to bend the arc of history toward the realization of that promise with a civil rights revolution sufficient that all Americans might declare themselves to be "free at last."[33] And it was Emma Lazarus who gave Libertas the words:

> Give me your tired, your poor,
> Your huddled masses yearning to breathe free,
> The wretched refuse of your teeming shore.
> Send these, the homeless, tempest-tost to me,
> I lift my lamp beside the golden door!

The Women's Suffrage Movement

As the Western White Man was expanding and consolidating his global power and influence over the non-white races, the other side of his racist, authoritarian, male-centric complex subjected the other half of the population to exploitation through his misogyny. The white woman, though sharing in his wealth derived, began to wake up to the state of their essential subservience and exploitation.

Already in the 19th century, women's right activists like Elizabeth Cady Stanton and Lucretia Mott met at the World Anti-Slavery Convention in London in 1840 and protested vigorously when they were denied seats on account of their sex.[34] In 1868, Susan B. Anthony began to encourage working women from the printing and sewing trades in New York, who were excluded from men's trade unions, to form Working Women's Associations. As a delegate to the National Labor Congress in 1868, Anthony persuaded the committee on female labor to call for votes for women and equal pay for equal work.

Throughout the 19th century, individual states began to pass legislation that allowed women to vote in different types of elections. Some states only allowed women to vote in school or municipal elections. Others required that women own property if they wanted to vote. And while some territories extended full suffrage to women, once they became states, they rescinded those rights. Because the principle of gender equality needed to be established once and for all, this first wave of feminism in the late 19th and early 20th centuries focused on securing gender equality in voting rights and property rights on the highest, federal level.

But on a federal level, it would not be until the next century that women would be successful in getting the right to vote. The conditions created by World War I proved to be the fertile grounds that favored the re-emergence of the women's movement and stimulated the growth of women's consciousness. The women's contribution to the war effort had clearly disproven the notion of women's physical and mental inferiority, and made it more difficult to argue that women were, both by constitution and temperament, unfit to vote. In the short run, if women could work in munitions factories, it was a slap in the face to deny them a place in the voting booth.

And in the long run, the vote was much more than simply a reward for wartime work. The main effect of women's participation in the war was to help dispel the fears that surrounded women's entry into the public arena.[35] With the ratification of the Nineteenth Amendment in 1920, the women's movement was finally victorious in its campaign to have the U.S. officially extend the right to vote to all women. It was a victory of principle, though it was neither uniform nor universally applied. Black women, although legally entitled to vote, were effectively denied voting rights in numerous Southern states until 1965. Yet, it was a harbinger of further progressive developments to take place in the 20th century.

Endnotes

1 Outram, Quentin (2001). "The Socio-Economic Relations of Warfare and the Military Mortality Crises of the Thirty Years' War" (PDF). Medical History. 45 (2): 151–184. doi:10.1017/S0025727300067703. PMC 1044352. PMID 11373858. Archived (PDF) from the original on 25 June 2022. Retrieved 7 October 2020.

2 Benjamin Lee Whorf, Language, Thought, and Reality, (Massachusetts: MIT Press, 1964), 140.

3 Ibid., 153.

4 Sigmund Freud, Character and Culture, (London: Collier Books, 1972), 27.

5 E. Fachinelli, Anal Money Time, reprinted in The Psychology of Gambling, Peter Halliday and Jon Fuller, eds., (New York: Harper Colophon Books, 1975), 283.

6 Sentinel Staff, "The World Still Turns on Sex," Orlando Sentinel, December 5, 2001, https://www.orlandosentinel.com/2001/12/05/the-world-still-turns-on-sex-power/.

7 Thomas Paine, The Age of Reason, (London: D. I. Eaton, 1794).

8 Matthew Desmond, "American Capitalism Is Brutal," New York Times, August 14, 2019, https://www.nytimes.com/interactive/2019/08/14/magazine/slavery-capitalism.html?mtrref=www.google.com&gwh=260E221D8B1C37381A1EF681A1796368&gwt=regi&assetType=REGIWALL.

9 Ibid.

10 Ibid.

11 Ibid.

12 Ibid.

13 Ibid.

14 Patrick Minges, "Beneath the Underdog: Race, Religion, and the Trail of Tears," US Data Repository, 1998, http://www.us-data.org/us/minges/underdog.html.

15 Lauren Kent, "European Colonizers Killed So Many Native Americans That It Changed the Global Climate, Researchers Say," CNN, February 2, 2019, https://www.cnn.com/2019/02/01/world/european-colonization-climate-change-trnd/index.html.

16 Matthew Desmond, "American Capitalism Is Brutal," New York Times, August 14, 2019, https://www.nytimes.com/interactive/2019/08/14/magazine/slavery-capitalism.html?mtrref=www.google.com&gwh=260E221D8B1C37381A1EF681A1796368&gwt=regi&assetType=REGIWALL.

17 Ibid.

18 Ibid.

19 Ibid.

20 Ibid.

21 Ibid.

22 Gillian Brockell, "You Know Who Was into Karl Marx? No, Not AOC. Abraham Lincoln," Washington Post, July 27, 2019, https://www.washingtonpost.com/history/2019/07/27/you-know-who-was-into-karl-marx-no-not-aoc-abraham-lincoln/.

23 Ibid.

24 Ibid.

25 Ibid.

26 Ibid.

27 Ibid.

28 Ibid.

29 Ibid.

30 Ibid.

31 Jennifer Viegas, "Did God Have a Wife? Scholar Says That He Did," NBC News, March 18, 2011, https://www.nbcnews.com/id/wbna42154769.

32 John Nichols, The "S" Word: A Short History of an American Tradition…Socialism, (New York: Verso Books, Kindle Edition, 2011), 49.

33 Ibid.

34 The National Susan B. Anthony Museum and House, "Her Life," Retrieved September 2, 2021, Susanbanthonyhouse.org.

35 Leslie Hume, The National Union of Women's Suffrage Societies 1897–1914, (Routledge, 1982), 281, ISBN 978-1-317-21326-0.

Chapter 11

The American Century (1900-1975)

White Male Racism, Empire Building, and the Domestic Price of Greed (1900-1925)

The Global Anglosphere

With the turning of the wheel of time, at the beginning of the 20th century, the ethics of domination that had powered the conquest of the American continent now became determinative in shaping the foreign policy of the nation. More often than not, U.S. foreign policy was expressed in the humanistic terms of the spread of democratic values worldwide. But underneath the rhetoric about democratic values, there was also, more often than not, the reality of the ruthless exploitation of peoples and resources of the world that was necessary for the growth of American dominance, profit, and power.

Around the turn of the 20th century, unprecedented global migrations and racial mixing were occurring in the countries and colonies of Britain, the United States, Australia, South Africa, New Zealand, and Canada.[1] Because of their common Western European roots, these countries are often referred to collectively as the Anglosphere.[2] As the elites of the "higher races" struggled to contain mass disaffection generated by the traumatic change of globalization in the late 19th century—loss of jobs and livelihoods amidst rapid economic growth and intensified movements of capital, goods, and labor—sharpened what Teddy Roosevelt called the "race selfishness."[3] By forging an alliance between "capital and mob," as Hannah Arendt described it, the fearful ruling classes of rich and powerful whites channeled the economic anxiety of those rendered superfluous by industrial capitalism into social discrimination and political rage.[4]

Exclusion or degradation of non-white peoples proved the way for those marginalized by economic and technological shifts to maintain pride of their identity.[5] By the early 20th century, violence against indigenous peoples, immigrants, and African Americans reached a new ferocity, and nativist and racist demagogues entrenched a politics of dispossession, segregation, and disenfranchisement.[6] Anti-minority passions in the United States peaked with the 1924 immigration law (much admired by Hitler and, more recently, Jeff Sessions and Donald Trump), which impeded Jewish immigrants and barred Asians entirely.[7]

Two men were responsible for ushering in the 20th century and, through their actions, defining it as the American Century. Theodore Roosevelt and Woodrow Wilson, each in their own way, became the personification of the triumph of Manifest Destiny. Teddy Roosevelt did so by starting a war with Spain, to help liberate the Cubans from Spanish yoke and acquire a bunch of colonies at the same time. Wilson did so by imposing the peace at Versailles at the end of the Western European carnage of World War I. But in so doing, both men evidenced the unique combination of American racism, imperialism, and idealism that came to define the USA as the dominant world power of the 20th century.

Only 50 years after its creation, the GOP started shifting right after 1912, a long process that would be completed by Nixon's Southern Strategy in the 1970s and culminated in Trump's attempted coup in 2021.

Teddy Roosevelt and the Spanish-American War

Around the turn of the 20th century, a robust, urbanizing public had the time and education to read newspapers, to think about the world's problems, and to come to believe, through an alchemy of Christian moralism and American can-do-ism, that they could fix these problems. Particularly affecting to the American public was the plight of the Cuban people in their liberation struggle against colonial Spain. It was close by, they identified with the objectives of liberation and self-determination, and it was brutal. Over the three years from 1895 to 1898, hundreds of thousands of Cuban civilians died. Many of the deaths occurred in the Spanish concentration camps. The existence of these camps spurred hundreds of Americans to join illegal filibuster missions to aid the rebels.

In this case, the American government was not far behind the American public. It was Theodore "Teddy" Roosevelt who was fated to become the embodiment of the new American spirit of the age, a self-confidant can-do attitude of progress. The Spanish-American War captured the imagination of millions and changed how everyday citizens saw their place in the world. At the behest of President McKinley, Roosevelt quit the Department of the Navy in 1898, and took charge of one of the brigades that were to be sent to Cuba to help the Cubans in their war of liberation from the Spanish. Roosevelt and his "Rough Riders," as the brigade was soon called by the press, landed in Cuba on June 22, 1898. The war only lasted ten weeks. By August, Spain sued for peace after the United States captured Puerto Rico, Guam, and the Philippines.[8]

The situation provided Roosevelt with the perfect opportunity to establish himself as a dominant player in the world of global politics, ready and confident he could bend world history to the arc of his own belief system and values. Thus the Spanish-American War of 1898 heralded the global ascendency of American power and influence and announced loudly that the 20th century would be the American Century. At the core of Roosevelt's value system was a rock solid belief in the supremacy of the white race and its spiritual destiny to rule, if not own, the world. To Roosevelt, his "Big Stick" diplomacy was the White Man's spiritual. Sanctioned by God and faith, the White Man was destined to consolidate his control and rule the world.

In 1897, Roosevelt wrote admiringly, "democracy, with the clear instinct of race selfishness, saw the race foe, and kept out the dangerous alien."[9] In other words, to Roosevelt, the use of military force was

entirely acceptable if it furthered the White Man's expansionist goals
to establish global hegemony and dominion over the non-white races.
Roosevelt stressed the point that even after conquering the American
continent, its new white rulers could not afford to slack off and rest
on their laurels, in as much as "a rich nation which is slothful, timid
or unwieldy is an easy prey" to those who envy her and scheme to
obtain her wealth. No, the (white) people must remain ever vigilant
and ready to exercise "those most valuable of all qualities, the sol-
dierly virtues,"[10] in defense of her gains. The poet Rudyard Kipling
celebrated the White Man's toxic mix of colonialism and racism in
his famous poem "The White Man's Burden."

Woodrow Wilson's Peace Failure at Versailles

Woodrow Wilson, like Roosevelt, was a White Man and believed that
it was the White Man's divinely ordained destiny to rule the world.
Wilson also worked to preserve, as he put it, "white civilization and
its domination of the planet."[11] After the bombs stopped falling and
the soldiers stopped shooting, no one was better prepared to put the
shattered pieces of Europe back together after World War I than Wilson.[12] He was the undisputed and wildly popular leader of the most
powerful country on Earth. He had a compelling vision of a League
of Nations that would prevent war through the self-determination
of all peoples of all nations, including the colonies of the warring
European powers. Wilson was thoroughly prepared. A large staff had
meticulously researched the issues and had produced detailed reports
and gorgeous maps.

But Wilson, like Roosevelt, was a White Man, and believed that
it was the White Man's divinely ordained destiny to rule the world.
In the end Wilson was unable to resolve the inherent contradictions
between self-determination for the colonies and looking out for the
inherently racist interests of the White Man. This setback resulted in
the failure of his personal health as well as his political agenda. Not
only did Wilson suffer the precipitous decline of his physical, emotional, and mental health, but the failure of the Treaty of Versailles,

far from producing a lasting peace, set the stage for the even more unspeakable horrors of World War II.

This contradiction between Wilson's belief and value system of the White Man's racist supremacy doctrine doomed his efforts to eventual failure. For, when push came to shove, Wilson's white race allegiance consistently triumphed over his stated democratic beliefs. When the Japanese delegation proposed that racial equality should be a guiding principle of the new League of Nations, Wilson defeated it through a parliamentary procedure. From Europe to the Near East and the Far East, the discussions on all areas were highly contentious and volatile, and hope often turned to fury when the new proposed maps were unveiled. For example, after a disputed peninsula was cut off from China and given to Japan, the Chinese delegation refused to sign the treaty, and tumultuous riots soon engulfed Chinese cities. Other Asians tried and failed to build support for their causes. One was a young Vietnamese patriot, Nguyen Tat Thanh, who came to Paris to plead for his country but was unsuccessful and was met with derision. Decades later, as Ho Chi Minh, he would remember how undemocratic it had felt to be in Paris in 1919.

But nothing furthers like perseverance, even if it fathers nothing but perversions of the original intent of the event. Eventually, a document was produced for signature by the global participants. The signing ceremony took all of 37 minutes.[13] Exhilarated, Wilson took a train to the seaport of Brest and promptly sailed for America. Before leaving, all but messianic in the splendid isolation of his delusions of grandeur, Wilson declared that his "new order" had begun. Then, immediately after Wilson returned to the U.S., he found himself engaged in a political duel to the death with the Republican Senate. The Senate had become impatient with a president who had been gone for months, and they wanted to add their own modifications to the treaty. But Wilson, more imperious than ever, would have none of it. He refused to alter "a single period" and grew angry at the legislators; "The Senate must take its medicine," he said, as if talking to a five-year-old.[14] Instead, he tried to go over their heads, speaking in an increasingly erratic manner at public rallies far from Washington. The effort nearly killed him. After hundreds of speeches, he finally collapsed in Colorado, disabled for the rest of his presidency. In November, the Senate rejected the treaty. As a result, the United States never joined the League of Nations that it had done so much to create.[15]

Not only did Wilson fail personally, physically, emotionally, and mentally, but more importantly for the globe, he failed in his political mission of achieving a radical reorganization of the world on democratic principles. In a narrow European sense, the Treaty of Versailles was but another chapter in the history of Franco-German wars that amounted to a replay in reverse of the events of 1871, when the Germans had imposed a humiliating surrender upon the French. In the Treaty of Versailles in 1919, the French settled their score with the Germans, setting the stage for yet another global battle in the not-too-distant future. In the broader global sense, as the leader of the White Man's world, what Wilson presided over in Versailles was the convocation of all of Europe's ruling White Men as they were divvying up the spoils of global colonialism for the purpose of more permanent and sustained exploitation.

Bipolar Disorder and Herd Instincts

The American culture of capitalism is the "low road" variety of taking, using, and throwing away. It is a winner-take-all capitalism of stunning disparities not only permitting but rewarding financial rule-bending. It is a union-busting capitalism of poverty wages, gig jobs, and normalized insecurity, where so-called "unskilled workers" are typically incentivized through punishments, not promotions, and where wages are depressed as businesses compete over the price, not the quality, of goods. It is a racist capitalism that ignores the fact that slavery denied Black freedom while it built white fortunes and is responsible for the Black-white wealth gap that even today grows wider each year.[16] "It's a capitalism where inequality reigns and poverty spreads, where the richest 1 percent of Americans own 40 percent of the country's wealth, while a larger share of working-age people... live in poverty than in any other nation belonging to the Organization for Economic Cooperation and Development (OECD)."[17]

Capitalism is not a healthy, self-regulating system; it is, by nature, aggressive and needs to be restrained. It is a culture that reigns globally, unchecked and unconstrained, and is parasitic on the human species. It must be contained, lest it destroy us all. For by creating cycles of boom and bust, of bubble and crash, the price of greed is that it is ultimately self-destructive of the capitalist system itself. And the bigger the bubble when it bursts, the greater the damage the crash inflicts and the more the people suffer. "This culture of greed brought us the Panic of 1837, the stock-market crash of 1929, and the recession of 2008. It is the culture that has produced staggering inequality and undignified working conditions."[18] It is more like a cancer, consuming and destroying the body it feeds on until everyone dies, guests as well as host.

In its economic cycles of boom and bust, bubbles and crashes, capitalist culture resembles and mimics the psychological yang-yin switch in the bipolar disorder of an individual patient from manic, aggressive behavior into depressive and self-destructive behavior.

In the healthy individual, emotional balance is maintained and the highs and lows regulate themselves. But in individuals who suffer from bipolar disorder, either in prolonged states of mania or depression, or in the rapid mood swings between the two, medical intervention tries to artificially regulate and balance the swings from one extreme to the other through medication.

In capitalist society, the government acts like the medical doctors who diagnose the nature of the illness and its stage of development, prescribing the necessary meds to regulate and maintain the patient's swings from boom to bust and back into a more or less steady state of balance.

The initial diagnosis of the capitalist disease is that greed acts like an addiction in its pathology. Much like methamphetamine or cocaine, greed creates in the participants the experience of the manic high of the bipolar spectrum that makes them delusional and feel invulnerable, all-powerful, and all knowing. As with all addictions, the satisfaction of greed is always temporary and the need for more (profit) always intensifies, in the end overwhelming rational behavior and expressing itself as deeply self-destructive, irrational behavior. As the cycle progresses and the individual gets more desperate, he will tend to increasingly engage in more reckless behavior in an attempt to stop and reverse the process.

Any addiction is, of course, lamentable, but the addiction to greed is especially dangerous and pernicious because of its social implications. Due to the herd instinctual behavior, the greed addiction and recklessness of the individual is highly contagious and can trigger the same response on a mass scale almost instantaneously. Multiplied geometrically in the market participant population, mass greed addiction is the root cause of the periodic bubbles and crashes of the capitalist system.

The herd instinct, in its simplest formulation, is a biological programming that tells the individual to do what he observes his herd mates doing. This is the secret of the synchronized mass movement of flocks of birds and schools of fish, for example. If you are a fish or a bird and your neighbor turns right or left, goes up or down, you do the same. Such simple and primal movements are often part and parcel of a holistic emotional and physical organismic response to the environment. If a bird perceives danger and changes direction in fright, his fellow birds will also experience fright and change direction. Likewise, if the bird changes direction because she notices a tree full of ripe berries, her fellow birds will understand the emotion and follow suit. The motion and the emotion are inseparable.

Bubbles and Busts, Manias and Panics

In the human herd of economic interaction and the stock market, emotions, whether positive or negative, are highly communicable and infectious; optimism in one begets optimism in another; panic in one person causes panic in the next person, etc. In other words, the herd instinct is operative both in the creation of the economic bubbles, or boom cycles, as well as in the crashes, or bust cycles.

Economic bubbles are created and characterized by a prolonged period of rising prices for a particular product or commodity. Such "bull markets" create an excessive and infectious collective economic optimism in its participants. With price-earning ratios exceeding long-term averages and extensive use of margin debt and leveraging, market participants suspend disbelief, steadfastly ignore any emerging cautionary signs, and whip themselves up into a frenzy of reckless behavior.

Take, for example, the Tulip Mania in Holland in the 17th century. Tulips had been introduced to Western Europe in the middle of the 16th century and became a status symbol of successful merchants, especially in Holland. In the 17th century, the cultivation of many colorful tulip varieties promised a handsome return on the investment, as each plant would spawn a number of new bulbs in the next several years. As a result, the price of tulip bulbs rose steadily until the peak of Tulip Mania, in February 1637, when some single tulip bulbs sold for more than ten times the annual income of a skilled crafts worker.

Once a sudden drop in prices has occurred in an economic bubble, prices can fluctuate erratically and become impossible to predict from supply and demand alone. This is when the speculations and miscalculations of the businessmen combine with external economic events and crowd psychology to create a positive feedback loop driven by herd panic behavior that leads to the stock market's crash. As prices drop, for example, selling by some market participants drives more market participants to sell. That is the moment when greed, mania, and gambling turn into panic and despair, causing more and more participants to sell. In 17th-century Holland, there were fortunes to be made... and lost. Tulip growers and traders alike assumed that wealthy individuals would always purchase bulbs of the novel vivid varieties, regardless of the price. It turns out they assumed wrong! It became very clear very quickly that no one would actually pay such outrageous prices, and the market collapsed dramatically in February 1637. Many who had purchased expensive tulip bulb futures lost their shirts and their fortunes and were left holding the bag (containing the bulbs).

In the pre–Civil War Southern states, the slavery and cotton industries combined to "build a culture of speculation unique in its abandon,"[19] that has defined American capitalism ever since. Thanks to an abundance of cheap land, labor, and credit, the slavery and cotton industries created an immense bubble of prosperity and wealth. With more and more people wanting to invest to cash in later, so much cotton was produced that eventually "consumer demand couldn't keep up with supply, and prices fell. As early as 1834, the value of cotton started to drop before plunging like a bird winged in midflight, setting off the Panic of 1837."[20]

After the bubble burst, the economic downturn went beyond the South and affected the entire nation by setting off a destructive chain of events in the banking and financial services sector. Over 600 banks failed in this period. Speculation markets were adversely affected. In the South, the cotton market completely collapsed, and agriculture everywhere suffered crop failures of various kinds.

The Liberal Capitalist Era, World War II, and the Global Fight Against Fascism to Save Democracy and Capitalism (1925-1950)

The 1929 Crash and the Great Depression: How Booms Fuel Busts

Building on postwar optimism, rural Americans migrated to the cities in vast numbers throughout the 1920s with the hopes of finding a more prosperous life in the ever-growing expansion of America's industrial sector.

The roaring twenties was a decade-long orgy of wealth and excess. A speculative boom of "steel production, building construction, retail turnover, automobiles registered, and even railway receipts advanced from record to record. The combined net profits of 536 manufacturing and trading companies showed an increase—in the first six months of 1929—of 36.6% over 1928, itself a record half-year. Iron and steel led the way with doubled gains."[21]

"Such figures set up a crescendo of stock-exchange speculation that led hundreds of thousands of Americans to invest heavily in the stock market. A significant number of them were borrowing money to buy more stocks."[22] "By August 1929, brokers were routinely lending small investors more than two-thirds of the face value of the stocks they were buying. Over \$8.5 billion was out on loan, more than the entire amount of currency circulating in the U.S. at the time."[23]

The way the bubble was created was that rising share prices encouraged more people to invest in anticipation of more and greater returns. As a result, large numbers of people placed their savings and money into investments by means of 'margin buying', which meant that they stood to lose a lot of money if the market suffered a downturn.[24]

And boy, did the market suffer a downturn. "On October 29, 1929, 'Black Tuesday' hit Wall Street as investors traded some 16 million shares on the New York Stock Exchange in a single day. Around \$14 billion of stock value was lost, wiping out thousands of investors. The next day, the panic selling reached its peak with some stocks having no buyers at any price. [25] It is no exaggeration to say that together, the 1929 stock market crash and the Great Depression formed the largest financial crisis of the 20th century."

By his actions and inactions, President Herbert "Hoover favored policies in which government, business, and labor worked together to achieve economic prosperity, but he was much opposed to a direct role for the federal government in the economy... after he took office, Hoover tried to combat the ensuing Great Depression by reassuring public confidence and working with business leaders and local government... As the depression worsened in 1931 and 1932, Hoover reluctantly gave in to calls for direct federal intervention, establishing the Reconstruction Finance Corporation and signing a major public works bill. At the same time, he signed the Revenue Act of 1932, which sought to maintain a balanced budget by raising taxes."[26]

But it was too little, too late. "The catastrophic economic effects of Hoover's domestic policies" combined with "the outrage caused by the deaths of veterans in the Bonus Army incident in the summer of 1932" "reduced [Hoover's] chances of a second term from slim to none."[27] And indeed, as the economy did not recover, and with many Americans blaming him for the Great Depression, Hoover suffered an overwhelming defeat in the 1932 election.

To the Rescue: Roosevelt and the New Deal

On November 8, 1932, the people decided they'd had enough of the bumbling Hoover and elected Franklin D. Roosevelt president of the USA with 472 Electoral College votes (90%) to Hoover's 59 (10%), and 57.4% of the popular vote to Hoover's 39.6%. FDR is today remembered as a president who embraced Keynesian economics with programs like the Works Progress Administration and the Civilian Conservation Corps that helped lead America out of the Great Depression.

It is not generally known that when FDR began his 1932 campaign for the presidency, he was espousing orthodox fiscal beliefs very similar to his opponent. Like Mr. Hoover, FDR "believed that a balanced budget was important to instill confidence in consumers, business, and the markets, which would thus encourage investment and economic expansion."[28] The difference between them was that Hoover had proved rigid and inflexible, unable to adapt to the necessities of the moment, whereas Roosevelt proved extremely flexible and had great capacity to adapt to the changing conditions and do what was necessary. It could also be said that Hoover was a capitalist before he was a humanist, and FDR was a humanist before he was a capitalist. But as the severity of the Great Depression became clear, FDR recognized that emergency relief programs were critical no matter the cost. Speaking at a campaign rally in 1936, he declared that "to balance our budget in 1933 or 1934 or 1935 would have been a crime against the American people... When Americans suffered, we refused to pass by on the other side. Humanity came first."[29]

As the economy began to improve, FDR eventually reverted and caved in to the conventional wisdom of a "balanced budget" and tried to cut back on spending, triggering the so-called Roosevelt Recession of 1937.[30] Duly chastened by the painful effects of his attempt at balancing the budget, FDR was persuaded to more fully embrace the theories of John Maynard Keynes and called for more deficit spending beginning in 1938 and continuing throughout World War II. His change of heart culminated in his famous speech calling for an Economic Bill of Rights in 1944, in which he said, "We have come to a clear realization of the fact that true individual freedom cannot exist without economic security and independence. 'Necessitous men are not free men.' People who are hungry and out of a job are the stuff of which dictatorships are made."[31]

Keynes's main ideas that FDR learned to run with were to ignore and reject the two pillars of economic orthodoxy that (1) demanded a balanced federal budget and (2) that capitalism was a self-regulating system that brooked no government involvement. FDR discovered soon that conditions would not improve until he gave up on the idea of a balanced budget and fully embraced government intervention by engaging in enormous deficit spending. FDR realized that since the main problem was that there was no economic demand because people had no jobs, that to create demand he had to create jobs and better working conditions for the people.

During his 12-year tenure as president, FDR initiated a systemic recovery effort to prevent the complete disintegration of the capitalist system. Through the New Deal (1929–1934), the Second New Deal (1935–1936), and the Third New Deal (1937–1938), he implemented a dizzying array of programs, restructuring practically every aspect of a crumbling society. There were programs for economic stimulus and stabilization, bank stabilization and financial reform, relief and welfare, public works programs, arts and culture programs, rural and farm assistance, housing aid and mortgage reform, labor law, health and public safety, land and wildlife conservation, regulation of trade, transport and communications, Indian lands and U.S. territories. In the four decades between the 1930s and the 1970s, the domestic and foreign policies of the United States were largely conceived and executed by the progressive, left-leaning Democratic Party.

The Nature and Threat of Fascism
Fascism is the militarization, weaponization, of far-right populism and is manifested collectively in the politics of nationalism,

xenophobia, and racism. Fascism is always characterized by the following three conditions:

1. There are un- or undereducated, suffering masses.
2. There is an autocratic, charismatic leader.
3. There is the practice of "grievance politics."

In grievance politics, the blame for the suffering and misery of the populace is projected by the charismatic leader onto outsiders who then become the enemy that needs to be fought collectively before victory can give the people their just rewards.

The following general statement explained the origin of early 20th century right-wing populist movements in Europe prior to World War II, while it also eerily captures the essence of Trump's appeal to his base in the U.S. of the 2020s. For Trump, as for Hitler, "An economic crisis yields widespread economic suffering, feeding an appetite for a nationalistic and extremist leader. The leader rides to power promising a return to national greatness, deliverance from economic suffering and the defeat of enemies foreign and domestic."[32] These enemies always prominently include immigrants and foreigners, while paying lip service to casting big business as a threat. Yet in reality, of course, "the charismatic leader seeks alliances with the large enterprises and the great monopolies, so long as they obey him, for each has something the other wants: He gets their loyalty, and they avoid democratic accountability."[33]

Three countries constituted the fascist Axis responsible for World War II—Germany, Italy, and Japan. In Germany, a revanchist nationalism emerged after World War I on account of significant territorial, colonial, and financial losses imposed on Germany by the Treaty of Versailles. Germany lost 13% of its home territory and all its overseas colonies in the war, was prohibited by the treaty from annexing any territory, had reparations imposed and limits placed on the size of its armed forces.

Chafing against these restrictions, Hitler and his Nazis rose to power on the need for the expansion ("lebensraum") of German economic interests and territory. When the stock market crashed in the United States in 1929, the repercussions in Germany were dire. Millions were thrown out of work and several major banks collapsed. Hitler and the Nazi Party prepared to take advantage of the emergency to gain support for their party. They promised to repudiate the Versailles Treaty, strengthen the economy, and provide jobs. The austerity measures taken by the democratic government to combat the Great Depression's effect on Germany brought little economic improvement and were extremely unpopular. Hitler exploited this by targeting his political messages specifically at people who had been affected by the inflation of the 1920s and the Depression, such as farmers, war veterans, and the middle class.

And who did he blame? The Jews, of course. The fact was that during the difficult postwar period, many non-white Jewish people had managed to survive and even flourish in many traditional and upper-class trades and professions, especially in business and banking. So with whiteness as the criteria of purity, being portrayed as exploiters and money grubbers, the Jews were a logical target at which to direct the pent-up rage of the German masses. It is instructive to note here that when Hitler and the Nazis were doing research as to what legal system they wanted to emulate in their racist society, they chose the American model as most exemplary in how to treat non-whites.

After President Paul von Hindenburg and the Reichstag appointed him as the chancellor of Germany in 1933, Hitler abolished democracy, intensified his radical call for a racially based revision of the world order, and soon began a massive rearmament campaign. In 1935, Hitler repudiated the Treaty of Versailles, reintegrated the Saar region into Germany, introduced conscription, accelerated his rearmament program, and began plotting the annexation of Austria, the occupation of Poland, the Low Countries and France, and the war against Russia.

Italy, as an Entente ally, had made some postwar territorial gains; however, Italian nationalists were angered that the promises made by the United Kingdom and France to secure Italian entrance into the war were not fulfilled in the peace settlement. From 1922 to 1925, the fascist movement led by Benito Mussolini seized power in Italy with a nationalist, totalitarian, and class collaborationist agenda that abolished representative democracy, repressed socialist, left-wing, and liberal forces, and pursued an aggressive expansionist foreign policy aimed at making Italy a world power, promising the creation of a "New Roman Empire," and claiming Ethiopia as its colony.

In 1931, the increasingly militaristic Empire of Japan, which had long sought influence in China as the first step in what its government saw as the country's right to rule Asia, staged the Mukden incident as a pretext to invade Manchuria. In 1937, Japan first captured Peking then Shanghai. In response, the Nationalist Chinese Kuomintang and the Communist Chinese, who had been waging a civil war against each other, declared a mutual cease-fire to join in the common effort to fight their common enemy, Japan. In short, the unholy alliance of the Axis began the campaign for world domination by fascism in its local sphere of influence, as they instigated armed conflict across the globe in Europe, Africa, and Asia.

Herd Behavior and Fascism

Herd behavior is a coordinated, collective action in response to the activation of the fight-or-flight system, always involving fear and often violence. There is a beauty and power of herd behavior; there is an awesomeness to the flight of flocks of birds, the swirls and whirls of schools of fish, and there is fearsome power in stampeding herds of bison or other cattle.

The origin and basis of herd behavior in fish, birds, mammals, including humans, is quite simple: in a crisis, every individual of the species is genetically programmed to do what the individual next to them does. If your neighbor dives, you dive; if she goes up, you go up; if she goes right, you go right. Call it instinct, or whatever, but it is always the perception of a change in the environment that sets off an evasive maneuver on the part of one individual, which in turn sets off the chain reaction of collective behavior to flee from the danger.

When the environment changes to become threatening, human beings, too, have the impulse to flee to an environment free of threats and fears. The less time there is to prepare, the more chaotic and instinctual it will be, the more our behavior will resemble that of fish or birds, everyone doing the same thing as their neighbors, trying to get away, and nobody being aware of the what or why of it.

If there is more time, there can be more planning and rationality, and a collective strategy can be devised to deal with the threat. Oftentimes, a charismatic leader will emerge by articulating a vision and strategy that galvanizes the individuals' energy into a collective will and desire to solve the problems.

Though both Europe and America were in the throes of a prolonged socio-economic crisis in the 1930s, which was exacting an excruciating toll on their peoples, different conditions in the two continents combined to produce two different types of leadership that led their people into complete and opposite directions, both domestically and geopolitically.

The U.S. had the good fortune to have FDR, the unifier par excellence, emerge from obscurity. FDR's positive and enlightened, long-term vision regarding workers' rights, racial and ethnic rights, and women's rights helped stabilize the economic situation, ushering in a period of peace and justice, political and economic egalitarianism, and progress of prosperity for all.

Across the pond, Europe had the misfortune to have Hitler, the divider par excellence, emerge from obscurity. Hitler, whose negative and short-term vision celebrated darkness and power, preached the virtues of totalitarianism, authoritarianism, aggression, conquest, the supremacy of the male over the female, and that of the white race, and the inequality and the inferiority of all other races.

Fascism, with its twin components of misogyny and racism, is the ultimate expression of the male-centric pathology of power addiction. It is a type of human herd behavior that is based on ignorance and the inability to think rationally.

In fascism, the supreme leader, the charismatic personality, is able to channel the human herd instinct for irrational, collective action induced by fear and flight into the violence of rage in the persecution of minorities and/or in warfare against neighboring states. In fascism, therefore, the instigator is always the divider because his method is to aggravate and intensify social discord and tension between ethnic groups.

And what the fascist instigator peddles to his base and people is grievance politics. The "Great Leader" and his minions begin by blaming a minority for the woes of the majority, then goad the majority into violent action against that minority. Fascism thus preys upon the lack of education on the part of the people as a whole, prejudice, racial, or otherwise, and such scapegoating makes it easy for instinct and emotions to triumph over rational thought.

Fascism is always based on the Big Lie, which consists of winning people's hearts and minds by blaming the suffering of their majority as the fault of a minority.

Joining the Fight

In December 1941, Japan simultaneously attacked British and American forces in Southeast Asia and the Central Pacific, including the attack on Pearl Harbor. This was the straw that broke the proverbial camel's back. The attack on Pearl Harbor forced the hand of the United States to formally join the Allies in 1941. It had not been a sure thing. Even though the democratic and communist nations of Europe had been conquered by the German war machine, many Americans were isolationist and against joining any one side. And in fact, the racism of Hitler's fascist Nazi movement had many open and secret sympathizers in the U.S. in high positions of political and economic power. Fortunately, they lost the argument, and the good guys won the day for democracy and capitalism.

But once fully committed, the military might of the U.S. was developed and marshalled successfully against the worldwide Nazi juggernaut. It was the effort of the United States that won the war and made the world safe for our ideas of progress through democracy and capitalism. Serendipitously, domestically, the unparalleled economic effort to ramp up for and conduct the war pretty much did away with the chronic unemployment that had haunted the Great Depression of the 1930s. As many men were in the armed forces fighting, many jobs became available for everybody, including women, and this had the effect of lifting the spirits and raising the standard of living of the American people.

Two opposing military alliances, the Allies and the Axis powers, engaged in a global conflict that involved more than 100 million personnel from over 30 countries, throwing their entire economic, industrial, and scientific capabilities behind the war effort, blurring the distinction between civilian and military resources. It was the deadliest conflict in history, resulting in 70 to 85 million fatalities, most of them civilians. Tens of millions of people died in genocides, including the Holocaust, starvation; massacres; and disease by the time the war ended in 1945.

The Concentration of Wealth and Fascism

The rise of fascism in Germany taught us that the concentration of wealth and power is the critical, if not the main, ingredient in the rise of fascism and, therefore, poses an existential threat to liberal, constitutional democracy.[34]

In the post–World War I era, the economic structure of Germany was dominated in a few short years by monopolies and cartels. This proved essential in Hitler's consolidation of power. Germany had built up a great series of industrial monopolies in steel, rubber, coal, and other materials. After the monopolies consolidated their power in Germany, they backed and promoted Hitler's rise to power and allowed him to instigate a new world war because it was "good for the economy," i.e., their bank accounts and pocketbooks. After they defeated Germany in that war, the Allies broke up the major Nazi monopolies specifically so that they could not, in the words of the law passed to compel it, be "used by Germany as instruments of political or economic aggression."[35]

The U.S. realized it had to institute similar measures at home to ensure they would never be able to follow the German example. In 1950, Congress passed the Anti-Merger Act of 1950 to curb politically and economically dangerous concentrations. It tasked the Justice Department and Federal Trade Commission to block or undo mergers when the effect was "substantially to lessen competition or to tend to create a monopoly."[36]

In recent years, the anti-monopolistic measures the U.S. undertook post–World War II to avoid the kind of concentration of wealth that allowed fascism to triumph in Germany have been eliminated or diluted. The result, not surprisingly, has been not just to fail to stop the increasing concentration of wealth in the U.S. but to actually encourage it, creating a parallel situation between 1930s Germany and today's USA insofar as creating the opportunity for fascism to arise.

In the healthcare field, we have allowed the unhealthy consolidation of hospitals and the pharmaceutical industry. In the tech industry, we have failed to prevent firms like Facebook from buying up their competitors. We have allowed an extraordinarily concentrated banking industry to develop despite its repeated malfeasance. AT&T, after a well-deserved breakup in the 1980s, has been allowed to reconsolidate. Over the last two decades, more than 75% of U.S. industries have experienced an increase in concentration, while U.S. public markets have lost almost 50% of their publicly traded firms.

The link between concentration of wealth and power and the distortion the of democratic process can be very direct. For example, concentrated industries, like the pharmaceutical industry, find it easy to organize to take from the public for their own benefit. Take the law that prevents Medicare from negotiating for lower drug prices. Though that particular lobbying project cost the industry more than $100 million, the payoff was well worth it. As a direct result, the pharmaceutical industry receives some $15 billion a year in higher payments for its products.

Domestic Anxiety, International Tension, and the Re-Emergence of the Female-Centric Paradigm in the Counterculture (1950-1975)

The Global Fight Against Communism to Save Democracy and Capitalism

The domestic, economic, and sociological psychological issues that were generating widespread angst in the psyches of post–World War II Americans were exacerbated by international political and military developments. Immediately upon winning one hot global war, the U.S. entered into a new global Cold War with the international communist movement, spearheaded by our erstwhile ally in the fight against Hitler and fascism, Soviet Russia.

The development and acquisition of large stockpiles of nuclear bombs and the missiles to deliver them by both sides resulted in a balance of terror and gave rise to the most imminent of dangers. The threat of nuclear war with the Soviet Union was the prime foreign cause contributing to the general level of anxiety of the American people.

The global polarization between the democratic and capitalist West and the communist East was about world domination. The unique characteristic of this conflict was that for the first time in history, the contending parties had the power to wipe each other off the map by means of atomic warfare. Each country had sufficient nukes to retaliate overwhelmingly if the other tried anything. With the threat of total annihilation, it was truly a balance of terror.

There is no doubt that the real possibility of such a conflict was a significant ingredient in the mix of things contributing to the growing post–World War II malaise. Who can forget the digging of the atomic shelters by people in their backyards? And who can forget the school drills of hiding under our desks as practice for an atomic attack?

So, with military victory not possible, the prize at stake was economic and political influence over the present and former colonies of the Western European powers in Asia, Latin America, Africa, and the Near East that one by one, were throwing off the shackles of colonialism and becoming independent nations.

The U.S. was in a position of global dominance, military, economic, and political, undisputed leader of the Free World, dedicated to spreading its gospels of democracy and capitalism. It had profound interest in seeing the establishment of pro-democracy, capitalist-oriented regimes with a Western bias.

For their part, Russia and the communists, preaching the doctrines of economic justice, wanted to do much the same and pull those countries into Soviet orbit, and to that purpose had been promoting, supporting, and financing rebel movements worldwide.

Having suffered severe exploitation for centuries and having fought for freedom and self-determination against their colonial masters, the new, aspiring movements and nations of the developing world were only too happy to accept Soviet help. So, while the arena of the conflict between West and East would take place between proxies in the developing world, the danger was that any local conflict could escalate into a worldwide atomic conflagration, as almost happened with Cuba.

Fulgencio Batista held power in Cuba twice. The first time was from 1933 to 1944 as elected president. The second time was from 1952 to 1959 as its right-wing military dictator backed by the U.S. government. During that time, Batista was also in partnership with U.S. organized crime, including such luminaries as Meyer Lansky and Lucky Luciano, in running the lucrative gambling and tourist industry.

In 1959, Fidel Castro and his cadres mounted a successful revolution, ousted Batista and organized crime, and established an outpost communist state right in America's backyard. As the U.S. instituted a total trade embargo, Cuba had no choice but become a client state of Russia, dependent on Russia for almost everything.

In 1962, in a provocative move, possibly motivated by fear of U.S. retaliation, Cuba agreed to allow Russia to come and install Russian missiles in Cuba as a deterrent to U.S. reprisals. The rockets had the range to attack the U.S. They were on their way to Cuba from Russia on Russian ships. This, the U.S. could not tolerate, and atomic war was a real prospect. Fortunately, cooler heads in the Kremlin prevailed, and the ships turned around and went back home with their missiles. This event came to be known as the Cuban Missile Crisis that came close to igniting an atomic tit for tat between Russia and the U.S.

Another hot spot appeared on the other side of the globe in Asia. Here, the French were being forced to let go of their colonies in Southeast Asia, particularly Vietnam. Many of those colonies aspired to become communist nations. The origin of the Vietnam War must be traced back to the fear in Washington that the fall of French

Indochina to communists could create a domino effect in Southeast Asia. In response, JFK, already in 1961, sent the first unofficial troops to Vietnam.

That action did nothing to improve either the situation there or the fear in Washington. That fear was intensifying into a chorus call for action to send a lot of troops to Vietnam for an intervention to fight back communism and safeguard democracy. And lo, a convenient crisis occurred to marshal public opinion and support. A naval incident occurred in the Gulf of Tonkin, a military scarp between the U.S. and North Vietnam. At first, the U.S. blamed North Vietnam, and President Johnson used it as an excuse to enter the war more openly. Later, that was shown to be a lie, and the truth was the U.S. had engineered the crisis and fired the first shots.

With the 1964 Gulf of Tonkin incident and the Congressional Authorization Resolution, the U.S. entered the war officially and openly. The Gulf of Tonkin incident was the lie that started the process of thousands of U.S. soldiers going to war and dying for a lie. With that pretext, Johnson launched a three-year bombing campaign and ordered the increasing deployment of U.S. troops till, at its peak in 1967, the U.S had half a million troops in Vietnam.

But still, the war dragged on and only got worse. Increasingly the American people expressed that they'd had enough of the whole sorry mess. In 1967, huge protests erupted throughout the country, in Washington, New York, San Francisco, and an untold number of other cities in the U.S. and worldwide. In response, Johnson basically admitted defeat, halted the bombing, and announced he would not run for president again in 1968. It was left to Nixon, who won the 1968 election, to sign the papers at the Paris Peace Accord in 1973, making it official that the U.S. had lost the war.

But anti-communism was also a war fought at home, in the U.S., with the development of the extreme right-wing populist phenomenon of McCarthyism, named after Senator Joseph McCarthy from Wisconsin, who was its instigator, promulgator, cheerleader, and front man. McCarthy's political strategy was to equate the traditional American liberal values and policies then being implemented by the

Democratic Party in control of the government as being in cahoots with, and a part of, the international communist conspiracy.

The specific focus of McCarthy's efforts was to conduct an ongoing witch hunt for communist sympathizers and fellow travelers holding positions in the federal government.

Accusing his enemies of anarchism, socialism, and communism, who were dedicated to wiping out American values of patriotism, free speech, freedom of religion, and free enterprise, McCarthy played on the fears of his conservative base in the white middle and blue-collar classes, to arouse their passions and to maintain his position of power.

Post-World War II Liberal Social Democracy

America emerged from the war victorious and entered the postwar era in an optimistic frame of mind. During the intense collective mobilization of the American people for the war effort, their pursuit of happiness had effectively been put on hold. But once the war was over and the wartime restrictions eased, the people were looking forward to, once again, resuming to their long-interrupted pursuit of happiness.

First, the Great Depression of the 1930s, then the war mobilization effort of the 1940s restricted, limited, and defined the people's notion of the pursuit of happiness. The Eutopia of their dreams rested first and primarily on the basics of life: the absence of want, of need, of hunger. Beyond that, they of the growing middle class aspired to enjoy the taste of affluence and share in the riches and wealth of the upper classes.

The postwar history of the U.S. economy can be divided into two distinct periods. The first, covering the late 1940s to the mid-1970s, will be discussed here. The second, spanning the 1970s until the present time, will be discussed in the next chapter. The first one was the period of the postwar liberal social democracy. The trend was to build on the social and economic policies of FDR and the Democratic Party to create, as President John F. Kennedy said, the wave "of a rising tide to lift all boats."

This effort included Republicans as well as Democrats. Eisenhower, for example, initiated and built the great interstate highway system, which was a fantastic boon to the economy, uniting all parts of the country, facilitating transportation for commerce and tourism. Johnson, with his war on poverty and Great Society programs, was also clearly in the tradition of Franklin Roosevelt. And even Nixon, despite his legacy of personal and political corruption and his extreme, right-wing, anti-communist policies, was, in his social policies, still clearly in the mold of the FDR tradition of government intervention to improve the lot of the people. Among the many social programs Nixon created were the EPA, the Clean Air and Water Acts, Earned Income Credit, the Equal Employment Opportunity Act, the Endangered Species Act, the Occupation Safety and Health Administration, among other progressive developments.

In this period, the dividend from a growing economy was shared evenly among all income groups. Those in the top 10% of earners grew richer at the same rate as those in the bottom 10% of earners. In the 1950s and 1960s, not only did the U.S. have the world's biggest economy with less inequality, it also grew faster. Investment was higher, and so were rates of growth of productivity. This was achieved with an income tax rate on the rich that peaked at 91% under Republican President Dwight Eisenhower.

As consumer capitalism increasingly took the place of wartime capitalism to keep the economy growing, it focused its enormous promotional machine on aggressively pushing competitive consumerism on the middle class. The message was always the same: the pursuit of happiness is defined by your ability to keep up with the Joneses, and your community status is there for all to see by your level of consumer ability, ostentatious and otherwise.

Along with equating happiness with consumerism, capitalism defined freedom as having the choice between an infinite variety of products in every conceivable category. Indeed, the pursuit of happiness became equated with the pursuit of excess! If owning one house is great, it's even greater to own a second one. And why not get a getaway cabin in the woods here and a condo share there? If one car served us well, two cars will surely serve us better. One for the missus, you know, maybe a third one for the kids when they grow into it. One TV in the living room is just so chintzy. Why not put one in the kitchen also, and one in the bedroom, and in the kids' rooms?

The material affluence offered to the people by consumer capitalism was touted as the sine qua non of the pursuit of happiness. The truth that material affluence is a precondition for happiness was inflated into the Big Lie that equated the consumption of material abundance with emotional and spiritual well-being and happiness. The culture of conspicuous consumption not only had the effect of diminishing traditional spiritual values and practices, it also had the temerity to offer itself as the new gospel, a substitute to fill the spiritual void created by the failure of traditional religion to speak to the needs of the people at the moment.

This increasing secularization of society, with the importance of wealth (or the appearance of wealth), led to a growing apart between the people and their religion. Religious practice became a matter of formality instead of the manifestation of an inner experiential life. And the religious anxiety created by the secularization of society would be the principal cause of the rise of evangelical Christianity and the search for "authentic" religious experience in the postwar decades.

So, in the postwar era, despite, or perhaps because of, the increase in material wealth and comforts enjoyed by the people, the culture was not producing happy people. Spiritually and emotionally speaking, the success of consumer capitalism in pushing the pursuit of happiness through material consumption was a dead end.

Contrary to appearance, all was not well in postwar consumer heaven, where reality turned out to be a mirage of happiness, rather than the real thing. As defined by consumer culture, the pursuit of happiness was resulting in its opposite. A thin veneer of pleasant surface smiles behind which smoldered the increasing unhappiness of a gradual loss of meaning in their lives.

To keep up with the Joneses was not cheap. Once you were hooked, the price of addiction was high. The social pressure to consume often resulted in reckless behavior and overspending, putting the individual and his family in financial distress that could sometimes lead to ruin.

To the men who had fought in the war, the nature of work in the postwar era was, on the whole, not challenging but stultifying. True, they had seen their comrades die, and often they were still suffering themselves from PTSD or nursing other hidden hurts, but at least it had been done in the name of a meaningful cause. The problem with most jobs was that they were essentially meaningless, leaving those who had to engage in them deeply unfulfilled.

The women, likewise, were not much more fulfilled or happier in their postwar lives. They who had been mobilized for the war effort were told after the war that they were no longer needed, so thank you very much, and now please go back to being home keepers. Not that they didn't want to raise kids, but they also missed being relevant in a wider context and being given opportunities to pursue interests, professional and otherwise.

So, there was a growing apart between men and women. Women were increasingly beginning to question the limited choices they had in the life they wanted to live beyond the domestic sphere.

And there was a growing apart between parents and children, creating a generational divide in which parents could no longer understand or relate to their kids, who were off to create their own culture in opposition to the parental model: the counterculture.

And there was a growing apart between the races, exacerbating a divide that was already centuries old. After generations of inflicting prejudice and violence on Black people, the white people had developed an unconscious, collective fear of possible violent revenge by Blacks.

After the war, the minorities of color led by the Black community and its leaders were ready to pick up the pace of the unfinished project of realizing and securing their full rights and place in society. White racist politicians, Democrats and Republicans alike, were quick to exploit these paranoid racist fears and began taking political advantage of them as a wedge issue, posing a threat to white middle-class affluence.

And so it was with other non-white races, with the white working-class fear of immigrants threatening their job security further aggravating racist tendencies and paranoid politics and feeding the right-wing politics of racial fear and grievance.

Loss of Faith in God and Government and the Rise of the Counterculture

The immediate postwar period was an optimistic time. People were joyful and euphoric. They had just vanquished a ruthless enemy of everyone's freedom and were beginning to taste the fruits of affluence promised by consumer capitalism. Feeling grateful and confident in the future, the people joined the churches of liberal humanistic Christianity in large numbers and fueled a religious revival of sorts.

At midcentury, Americans streamed back to church in unprecedented numbers. The baby boom (those born between 1946 and 1965) had begun, and parents of the first baby boomers moved into the suburbs and filled the pews, establishing church and family as the twin pillars of security and respectability. Religious membership, church funding, institutional building, and traditional faith and practice all increased in the 1950s. Things looked very good for Christian America.[37]

Unfortunately, the postwar feel-good period was not destined to last long. The 1960s, more than anything, was a decade of political turmoil and assassinations that added enormously to the national malaise. The American people were subjected to the trauma of the assassinations of three prominent democratic politicians and standard bearers in the 1960s. First was President John F. Kennedy who was gunned down in Dallas, Texas, on November 22, 1963. Second was his brother, Robert Kennedy, a candidate for president of the U.S., when he was gunned down in Los Angeles in 1968. Third was Martin Luther King, the esteemed leader of the civil rights movement and the Black community, who was shot and killed in Memphis, also in 1968.

Besides these acts of violence perpetrated on celebrated leaders, one more astounding development shook the mental and emotional confidence of the postwar generation. It was an event, or a series of events, really, that proved that the man who held the highest office in the land, President Nixon himself, supposedly a paragon of Republican virtue, was proven to be a deeply corrupt politician. Despite his protestations that "I am not a crook," the revelations of Watergate proved just that: Nixon was a criminally culpable politician who stopped at nothing, including illegal acts, to get and maintain power. With the irrefutable revelation of his corruption in Watergate, Nixon chose to resign rather than face impeachment by the House and be confirmed guilty by the Senate, leaving his own generation, which had trusted him with ultimate power, deeply confused and fearful, shaken in their belief in the integrity of their fellow men and their political institutions.

As the baby boomers grew up and matured in the 1950s and 1960s, conditions in society changed radically for the worst, with many new sources of stress that we have documented creating a rapid growth of anxiety throughout society but particularly in the lower middle and working classes. What followed were increased racial unrest and anti-war demonstrations, the woman's movement and abortion rights, recreational use of drugs, avant-garde artists, and revolutionaries of the counterculture.

All these currents and events resulted in a marked decrease in the people's trust in the government and their faith in their religious institutions. In 1964, 77% of people said they trusted the government always or most of the time. But as the Vietnam War continued and we continued losing it, by 1970, that majority had shrunk to 54%. By 1974, the percentage of Americans who had trust in their federal government shriveled further to 36%. Within the Protestant religious sphere, the pendulum swung back as membership and attendance in mainstream liberal humanist protestant churches declined precipitously. There were those who remained, and there were those who left the mainstream churches.

The 1960s counterculture was one such populist uprising against the status quo. Its targets were the three fundamental pillars of expansionist white male-centric authority: racism, war, and misogyny. The civil rights movement was particularly disruptive to the fabric of the status quo, especially in the American South, where school integration was seen as a threat to white families. Likewise, in the assessment of the powers that were, the anti-war movement against the Vietnam War and other imperialist ventures, all those hippies and men with long hair proclaiming "make love, not war," imperiled the nation's manhood, so to speak. Also the flowering of the feminist movement of the 1960s and 1970s attacked the inherent misogyny of mainstream American men and their institutions. Not surprisingly, the powers that be did not take kindly to being challenged in these fundamental ways and did everything conceivable, legally and illegally, to beat back the emerging progressive agenda.

As a result of the countercultural movement and its redefinition of traditional sexual roles and rules, several intertwined things occurred. For one, there was an exodus from organized religion and a drastic decline in both the numbers of religious affiliation and church attendance. This was especially severe in the Protestant churches, where a serious splintering occurred: people deserted the established Protestant churches to join the counterculture and begin their own idiosyncratic journeys to find their spiritual truth in the spectrum of spiritual practices of the anti-racism and anti-misogyny of the counterculture, the precursor of what, a half century later, would re-emerge as the Rainbow Coalition.

The Beats, the Baby Boom, and the Counterculture

The Beat Generation was the first expression of the fact that all was not well in American culture in the postwar era. The Beat Generation was primarily a literary movement started by a group of authors. Major trailblazers of the movement and their contributions were Allen Ginsberg with *Howl*, in 1956, Jack Kerouac with *On the Road*, in 1957, and William S. Burroughs with *Naked Lunch*, in 1959.

Their work explored and influenced American culture and politics in the postwar era. Beat culture championed a wholesale rejection of contemporary values of economic materialism and consumer society. Their literary endeavors chronicled spiritual quests that included the exploration of Eastern religions, experimentation with psychedelic drugs, and sexual liberation and exploration.

The Beats, who decried the shallowness of the life and values of their contemporaries, whom they considered to be trapped and lobotomized by the values of consumer society, found a more receptive welcome in the ears and hearts of their children.

The postwar baby boom was unique in that, for the first time in history, an entire middle-class generation grew up free of want, in relative abundance, unlike their parents, for whom hunger and deprivation had been constant companions, and who, for that reason, always reacted to events with caution, fear, and silence.

These kids were, therefore, of a different breed. Arrogant in their ignorance, when confronted with a reality of historical events that they disapproved of, they reacted with immediacy in righteous anger and intent to set things right. That is why the baby boomer generation erupted spontaneously and collectively. The counterculture emerged, indeed, as a rejection of and counter to the value system underlying the consumer culture pushed by consumer capitalism that emerged in the postwar era.

It started with (mostly) white college youth in the mid and late 1960s organizing teach-ins, seminars, and demonstrations on and off campus against the Establishment's War in Vietnam. The students fully realized that this war had begun on the basis of a lie and its maintenance was based on a continuing series of lies and false promises. The students' anti-war protests were also part and parcel of their more general protests against their parents' generation, who more often than not, supported the government in its war efforts.

The young people were not so much protesting their parents as protesting the unhappiness of their parents. Even if they could not articulate it, they sensed their parents' deep emotional unhappiness behind the surface veneer of cheer. And they were very certain they did not want that for themselves, which instinctually led them to a wholesale rejection of their parents' value system, parallel to the creation of an entire new paradigm of happiness they could substitute for it. That was the attitude, more or less, anyway.

Little by little, the civil rights movement joined forces with the anti-war youth movement. Then the women woke up again, and second-wave feminism started in the 1960s, taking off where the first wave had left off in the early part of century. The women's activism of the 1960s resulted in one important legislative victory. The Equal Rights Amendment finally garnered sufficient support to win approval by the House of Representatives in October 1971, followed by the Senate in March 1972. This cleared the way for submitting the Equal Rights Amendment to the state legislatures for ratification, as provided for in the Constitution.

This second wave of feminism also helped the emergence of new community activism and focus on LGBT issues. It also made common cause with the anti-war and civil rights movements in their critique of the patriarchal, male-dominated institutions and cultural practices throughout society.

Counterculture Politics and Spirituality

When you add it all up, the counterculture amounted to nothing less than a total rejection of the deepest essence and source of Western (White) Man's historical rise to global power, namely misogyny and racism, and the cosmic justification for them offered by Judeo-Christian monotheistic religion. The politics of the counterculture were, therefore, unabashedly left-wing and progressive and anti-right-wing, anti-Republican, anti-corruption, anti–big business, and antiestablishment.

Indeed, the counterculture had its own ideas about culture and religion. Just because it rejected the establishment churches of the Judeo-Christian monotheistic religions did not mean it rejected spirituality. On the contrary, and more precisely, the counterculture's rejection was a rejection prompted by the essential lack of genuine spirituality of the establishment religion. The counterculture, with its wide openness and receptivity to all manner and types of spiritual experience, announced and pronounced a new age of spirituality.

Many of its members went East, so to speak, and embraced one or more of the Oriental religions of Buddhism, Sufism, Hinduism, and Taoism. Many others turned back to re-examine the European roots of the pre-Christian polytheistic pagan religions of the Celts, Anglo-Saxons, Germanic, and other pre-Christian European tribal religious practices with their strong female-centric imprint, marking the return of the witches and their craft. Yet others were more anthropologically inclined and traveled the world, interested in studying the religious practices of other so-called "primitive tribes" for insight and enlightenment, often with the help of shamans and their psychedelic potions.

There was an increasing reliance on divinatory methods based on the synchronicity of events to consult the cosmos in making important decisions rather than obeying the orders of the male godhead at the top of the religious hierarchy and his earthly lieutenants.

Drugs, of course, especially the psychedelic ones, were an essential part of the countercultural spiritual quest. The essence of this quest was an expansion of consciousness that would transcend the limits of traditional understanding of interpersonal and spiritual values that establishment culture had to offer.

Any culture, and any religion, too, has its own music. As the glue that holds the culture together, its music both identifies it and expresses its essence. The music of the counterculture was, of course, rock and roll.

One aspect that was central to the countercultural identity was the rejection of traditional cultural sexual inhibitions and taboos and the exploration of sexuality in all its myriad forms. Along with that, the counterculture rejected the idea and reality of the nuclear family as the best method of organizing the biosocial aspects of mating and the rearing of the young. As a result, within the counterculture, extensive experimentation with different forms of collectives and cooperatives were engaged in during the 1960s and 1970s.

When you add it all up, all the aspects of the counterculture taken together amount to another manifestation, or resurgences, of the female-centric paradigm of the polytheistic pre-Christian and non-Christian world.

Endnotes

1 Pankaj Mishra, "The Religion of Whiteness Becomes a Suicidal Cult," New York Times, August 30, 2018, https://www.nytimes.com/2018/08/30/opinion/race -politics-whiteness.html.

2 Ibid.

3 Ibid.

4 Ibid.

5 Ibid.

6 Ibid.

7 Ibid.

8 Clay Risen, "The Rough Riders' Guide to World Domination," New York Times, May 31, 2019, https://www.nytimes.com/2019/05/31/opinion/sunday/spanish -american-war-power.html.

9 Ibid.

10 Ibid.

11 Ted Widmer, "Was the Treaty of Versailles a Victory for Democracy?" New York Times, June 28, 2019, https://www.nytimes.com/2019/06/28/opinion/versailles -treaty-woodrow-wilson.html.

12 Ibid.

13 Ibid.

14 Ibid.

15 Ibid.

16 Matthew Desmond, "American Capitalism Is Brutal," New York Times, August 14, 2019, https://www.nytimes.com/interactive/2019/08/14/magazine/slavery -capitalism.html?mtrref=www.google.com&gwh=260E221D8B1C37381A1 EF681A1796368&gwt=regi&assetType=REGIWALL.

17 Ibid.

18 Ibid.

19 Ibid.

20 Ibid.

21 Edward Shann, "Broad Facts of, U.S.A. Crisis," The Daily News, November 1, 1929: 6, https://trove.nla.gov.au/newspaper/article/85141129.

22 Wikipedia, "Wall Street Crash of 1929," June 13, 2023, https://en.wikipedia.org /wiki/Wall_Street_Crash_of_1929#cite_note-34.

23 Richard Lambert, "Crashes, Bangs & Wallops," Financial Times, July 19, 2008, https://web.archive.org/web/20081003034410/http://www.ft.com/cms/s/0/7173bb6a -552a-11dd-ae9c-000077b07658.html.

24 Galbraith, John Kenneth (1954). "In Goldman Sachs We Trust". The Great Crash, 1929. Boston: Houghton Mifflin. ISBN 0-395-85999-9., cited in Taibbi, Matt (April 5, 2010). "The great American bubble machine". Rolling Stone. Retrieved November 3, 2017.

25 "Market crash of 1929: Some facts of the economic downturn". Economic Times. Times Internet. October 22, 2017. Retrieved February 16, 2019

26 Wikipedia, "Presidency of Herbert Hoover," June 19, 2023, https://en.wikipedia.org /wiki/Presidency_of_Herbert_Hoover#:~:text=Hoover%20favored%20policies%20 in%20which,Agricultural%20Marketing%20Act%20of%201929.

27 Wikipedia, "1932 United States Presidential Election," June 19, 2023, https://en.wikipedia.org/wiki/1932_United_States_presidential_election.

28 Franklin D. Roosevelt Presidential Library and Museum, "FDR: From Budget Balancer to Keynesian: A President's Evolving Approach to Fiscal Policy in Times of Crisis," n.d., https://www.fdrlibrary.org/budget.

29 Ibid.

30 Ibid.

31 Ibid.

32 Tim Wu, "Be Afraid of Economic 'Bigness.' Be Very Afraid," New York Times, November 10, 2018, https://www.nytimes.com/2018/11/10/opinion/sunday/fascism-economy-monopoly.html.

33 Ibid.

34 Ibid.

35 Ibid.

36 Federal Trade Commission, "Federal Trade Commission Turns 100," November 18, 2010, https://web.archive.org/web/20110721040248/http:/ftc.gov/ftc/turns100/index.shtm.

37 Joanne Beckman, "Religion in Post-World War II America," TeacherServe: National Humanities Center, October 2000, http://nationalhumanitiescenter.org/tserve/twenty/tkeyinfo/trelww2.htm.

Part 4

The White Man's Global Descent into Dystopia

Chapter 12

The Engines Accelerating Time in the Global Descent into Dystopia

Excursus on Dystopia and Eutopia

The medieval mind conceived of the world as flat, with oceans surrounding the land, extending practically infinitely in all directions. This conception made people feel so inextricably tied to their place of birth that the idea of relocating and starting anew did not enter their consciousness as a way out of their suffering and misery. For medieval Western European humanity, as Hobbes wrote, "life was brutish, mean and short," a "war of all against all."[1] In all dimensions of life, geographically, economically, politically, religiously, educationally, common humanity was stuck in, and struck by, a condition of abject and profound powerlessness.

The biological imperative of creatures constrained in their behavior is to try and break free to regain their autonomy and power. The depth of the powerlessness experienced by feudal existence engendered in people the instinctual desire to conquer the causes and remedy the conditions of oppression. So when it was discovered that the world was round, and that there were other lands across the oceans fit for human habitation that promised freedom and wealth, the oppressed Western European masses happily redirected their Eutopian hopes and visions to the new promised land on the other side of the ocean, and the American dream was born.

Beyond escaping the reality of hunger and misery, and simply being able to make a living, putting food on the table, and living in the comfort of adequate shelter, the idea that drove the masses of people leaving Europe was the pursuit of happiness as a constellation of new rights, economic, political, and religious, that had been denied them in feudal Europe. What they wanted, why they decided to move away and risk life and limb, was nothing less than the Eutopia they had so far only dreamed of. They wanted the economic rights of having the opportunity to work for wages or start a business. They desired free speech and freedom of religion, to practice their religious beliefs free from persecution as well as asserting their political rights and being free from political persecution. Both in reality and in the imagination, it was the dawning of a new age that held the promise of leaving all the bad stuff behind and starting afresh with a new beginning.

Reflecting the spirit of the times, Thomas More published his *Utopia* in 1516. In it, he described an ideal culture on an ideal island located somewhere in or near the New World and populated by some 6,000 ideal households, each with some 10 to 16 ideal people. In naming his work *Utopia*, More was playing linguistic games with his knowledge of Ancient Greece. The etymology of the word is a straightforward combination of the Greek word *topos*, meaning place, and the suffix *-ia*, meaning region, so *-topia* can be rendered as a land or lands. The prefix *u-* is more ambiguous. It is a contraction of either the Greek prefix *ou-*, meaning something not real, i.e., fictional or in the imagination, or *eu-*, meaning "good" or "pleasant," as in eulogy, euphoric, euphemism, etc. *Outopia*, then, would refer to the lands conceived in the imagination, and *Eutopia* would be the "good lands" where good people can lead the good life. More cleverly combined the meaning of both terms. By dropping the first vowel of each prefix and keeping the *u-* common to both *outopia* and *eutopia*, he created a new word, *utopia*, to describe "the good lands which exist in the imagination." While, for More, the term *utopia* was cleverly ambiguous in the sense it could mean either the "good" lands or the "imagined" lands, in the popular mind, it was the latter meaning that sank into the collective unconscious. Over time, *utopia* came to mean a mere figment of the human imagination that was, by definition, impossible to realize on Earth.

When More was writing his opus, his utopia could only exist in the imagination (his and ours) because medieval reality was, in fact, quite the opposite—literally, a dystopia. The prefix *dys-* here is the same one as the word dysfunctional. It also comes directly from Greek, and its meaning is "bad, defective, difficult." So that the term *dystopia* can be rendered as "the bad land(s)." In their psychological reality, utopia and dystopia are, furthermore, abstractions derived from the realities of the class structure of society. Meaning that what the upper class has is the utopia of the lower class and what the lower class is lacking is the dystopia of the upper class. A good example of the former was the dream of medieval European peasantry about the imaginary land of Cockaigne as the land of milk and honey. In his book *Utopia for Realists*, historian Rutger Bregman describes Cockaigne in the following way: "To get there you first had to eat your way through three miles of rice pudding. But it was worth the effort, because on arriving in Cockaigne you found yourself in a land where the rivers ran with wine, roast geese flew overhead, pancakes grew on trees, and hot pies and pastries rained from the skies. Farmer, craftsman, cleric—all were equal and kicked back together in the sun."[2]

Now while Moore abolished private property in *Utopia*, he certainly did not do away with class structure, in as much as every family unit in *Utopia* was allotted two slaves. In this context, it's clear that life would hardly be a Eutopia for the slaves, for whom the everyday reality was dystopic. For the slaves, the possibility of life and existence as an owner would indeed be Eutopian, while for the owners to contemplate the life and existence as a slave would indeed be dystopian. At some later point, it seems, More came to regret his decision to entitle his work *Utopia*. In the addendum to his book, he indicated that he had come to favor the term *eutopia* over *utopia*: "Wherfore not Utopie, but rather rightely my name is Eutopie, a place of felicitie."[3] Why would More feel he made the wrong choice in this regard? I believe it was to emphasize that his utopia should be considered a real, physical place where people had real happiness rather than an imaginary place in a thought experiment.

In that spirit and for that reason, I will also use the term *eutopia* in this work to refer to that state of social organization that simply provides "a good place" for all of humanity to live in. A more precise description can be obtained by comparing *eutopia* ("the good lands") with its antithesis, *dystopia* ("the bad lands"), which constitutes our current collective reality. The White Man's dystopia is male-centric and inherently authoritarian. The foundations of his dystopian paradigm are misogyny, racism, class structure, disregard, and exploitation of nature. Being the antithesis of the dystopian paradigm, the values of the Eutopian paradigm are precisely its opposite. The universal "good place" of Eutopia is female-centric and inherently egalitarian. The foundations of the Eutopian paradigm are the absence of misogyny, racism, and class structure and a reverence toward nature as well as dedication to the true stewardship of it.

The Acceleration of Historical Time and the Shrinking of Global Space

The Western European White Man that conquered the world in less than half a millennium actually consisted of two competing subgroups. There was the White Man proper, of the Protestant faith, and inhabiting Northwestern Europe, and being of Anglo-Saxon ancestry. And there was the Not-So-White Man of the Catholic faith and of more Southern Mediterranean ancestry, mostly inhabiting the Iberian Peninsula. They were highly competitive and adversarial, but between them they carved up the world in few short centuries for the greater glory of the twin deities of God and Gold. The Spanish and Portuguese appropriated most of Central and South America, as well as vast holdings in Asia, and the real White Man from Northwestern Europe (the English, Dutch, Belgian, and French) claimed North America, Africa, South and East Asia and the rest of the world, and became the main actors in the drama of unfolding world history. And while the differences between the Northwestern and Southwestern European White Man were many, they shared the fundamental male-centric authoritarian values of misogyny and racism. In sum, the civilization of the White Man is made up of the Old World, where he came from—Europe—and the New World where he went to—America.

Of all the global colonization efforts by the European powers, none proved of greater import nor had farther reaching consequences than the colonization of the New World. Wave after wave they came. Millions of Europeans fleeing their home countries on account of religious and political persecution, famine, disease, and wars. Looking at a future that seemed to hold nothing but persecution, starvation and death for their own and their children's generations, they decided to make their way to the new continent, start over and not perpetuate the cruelties of their home countries. As such, the American dream that fueled the creation of the American nation had its origin in the centuries of misery suffered by millions of Western Europeans. It was a twofold reaction against the lack of freedom of their deeply male-centric authoritarian cultures. On the one hand, the American dream was about the pursuit of freedom and happiness for the many, and, on the other hand, it was about the pursuit of wealth and power by the few.

When the capitalist system was first evolving, infinite economic growth was not a problem, because geographical space, for all intents and purposes, appeared infinite. But then it turned out that the world was a globe, which in turn proved that geographical space was not infinite, but finite. And no sooner was the discovery made and the White Man filled that finite geographical space with his expanding presence, that in the blink of an eye, global space began to shrink. During a half millennium, the exponential global growth of power and profit was reflected in the simultaneous growth of the global population. As the global population grew, the space between people shrank to accommodate the increasing numbers. So paradoxically, the global expansion of the White Man's economy and empire from his European origins led to the shrinking of global space.

Two factors turned the White Man's economic and political expansion into a global problem. One is psychological and one is economic. Psychologically, the White Man personality structure suffers from a pathological addiction for profit and power that is never sated and remains unabated. Economically, the continued functioning of his capitalist system requires infinite growth and expansion of wealth and power. These two factors together will inevitably lead to the collapse and disintegration of the White Man's capitalist economic system.

The Dystopian Dynamics of the Global Engines Accelerating Time

This chapter will identify a number of trends I have dubbed "the global engines that are accelerating time," in the sense that their dynamics are to speed up and cause systemic collapse and global catastrophe sooner rather than later. As a most serious threat to the continued survival and growth of humanity's global civilization, these trends involve a number of critically interrelated national and global systems, including:

- global population explosion and the resultant migration pressures
- global warming, climate change, and the breakdown of global food systems
- global pandemic disease outbreaks, such as Covid-19
- global economic catastrophe and meltdown
- global dynamics of capitalism itself
- global dynamics of big business and organized crime
- global dynamics of the political catastrophe of illiberal democracy
- global dynamics of right-wing extremism
- global dynamics of apocalyptic religion

Each of these systems must be understood as an engine or dynamic that is accelerating civilization's crisis toward its dystopic resolution: implosion or explosion. Each of these systems is constantly and continuously increasing global stress and anxiety levels that, if unchecked, will hasten the collective explosive or implosive destruction of global human culture. A failure in any one of these systems is likely to cause failure in one or more of the other systems, and each system failure could act as the triggering event that could cause the collapse of global civilization. As these systems are all interacting and unfolding simultaneously, they are increasing the temperature inside our global pressure cooker.

The aggressive growth of the White Man's global expansion has peaked, and has begun reversing itself into a new global contraction. With the White Man's hegemony breaking up and down, his global influence has begun its decline. Having reached the limits of his global expansion, his economic and political systems are rushing toward the explosive or implosive crises of their self-destruction. Continuing to squeeze profit and power from a system requiring infinite expansion in a finite space accelerates the dynamic. Indeed, by their very nature, the power and money addicts cannot but hasten and exacerbate the dynamics of global economic and political disintegration.

A half century ago, the 1972 MIT study *The Limits to Growth*[4] predicted that society would collapse sometime in the 21st century. Using a system dynamics model, the scientists studied the risk of civilization collapse by identifying the "limits to growth" as predictors of the impending collapse of industrial civilization, due to over-exploitation of planetary resources. At the time of its publication, the MIT analysis generated heated controversy and debate and was widely derided at the time by the "experts" who misrepresented its findings and methods. But the analysis has recently received stunning vindication from a study written by a senior director at professional services giant KPMG, one of the Big Four accounting firms as measured by global revenue.[5] Its author, Gaya Herrington, a Dutch sustainability and dynamic system analyst at KPMG in the United States and adviser to the Club of Rome, analyzed data across ten key variables, namely population, fertility rates, mortality rates, industrial output, food production, services, nonrenewable resources, persistent pollution, human welfare, and ecological footprint. Her research, unfortunately but indisputably, shows that our species is right on schedule and that the current business-as-usual trajectory of global civilization is heading toward the terminal decline of economic growth within the coming decade—and at worst, could trigger societal collapse by around 2040.[6]

These interrelated global systems that are each operating in crisis time are caught in a contradiction that derives, ultimately, from their short-term function in the capitalist process: increasing profit, generating wealth, and consolidating power for the 1% while pushing human and natural resources to their limits, exponentially rushing to their depletion. Here are some examples of this process at work:

- The energy companies extracting oil and coal to burn for homes, factories, and automobiles and to produce electricity and, most of all, to make huge profits
- The mining companies extracting minerals, common and rare, for use in the production of machinery of all kinds and for all purposes but, mostly to make huge profits
- The agricultural companies on land and in the oceans producing and harvesting animals and fish, vegetables and fruits, trees for construction, and fertilizers to make it all grow (pollute everything in the process) and, of course, to make huge profits
- The development of global transportation and communication systems spanning and covering the globe

Global Population Pressures and Migrations Catastrophe

It is estimated that the world population reached 1 billion for the first time in 1804. It took 200,000 years of human history to get to that point. It took only 220 more years to reach the current 8 billion. It took 123 years before it reached 2 billion in 1927, but it took only 33 years to reach 3 billion in 1960. Thereafter, the global population reached 4 billion in 1974, 5 billion in 1987, 6 billion in 1999, 7 billion in 2011, and 8 billion in 2022.[7]

Beginning with when we emerged as a species in our African birthplace, humans have engaged in multiple migrations for a variety of reasons. But there can be no doubt that, along with natural catastrophes and infectious disease, the overcrowding of particular human habitats has motivated numerous human dispersals throughout history. For many eons, as our species evolved and grew in numbers, it seemed that geographical space was infinite, and as human numbers grew to intolerable levels, people could and did, just pack up and move to settle in new lands.

The title of Steinbeck's novel *Of Mice and Men* refers to a line from the poem by Robert Burns, "To a Mouse": "The best laid schemes of mice and men/often go awry." And indeed, the traits we have in common with rodents that have led to our greatest successes are precisely those that, in the end, threaten to do us in. Like rodents, we humans are prolific breeders with a high sex drive and proven procreative prowess. Like rodents, we humans are social beings; we love togetherness and, for the most part, prefer to live in groups. Human and rodents share not only the problem of overcrowding their habitat but also their response to it because humans share with rodents the fundamental mammalian hormonal system that deals with crisis and emergencies.

According to Edward S. Deevey, author of the prescient *The Hare and the Haruspex: A Cautionary Tale*, the lesson we can learn from the lemmings is that overcrowding leads to mass death and the destruction of society.[8] Based on extensive field and laboratory work and autopsies, according to Deevey, researchers have concluded with great certainty that the mass die-offs of rodents that terminate a growth cycle result from the exhaustion of the adeno-pituitary system on a mass level. In the years leading up to the lemmings' final mass death, and the simultaneous implosion or explosion of lemming society, there is a constant heightening of tension. This is expressed in, and leads to, great social discord and the complete disintegration of the social structure. There is increased fighting between the males, both over food and over females. On the part of the females, there is a decline in the nurturing function of the young that turns into its opposite, cannibalism, in the latter stages, when the food shortages become more and more acute.

The lemmings showed that overcrowding as a stressor in our own human society is a deep contributing factor to the widespread global increases of stress-related diseases: heart disease, cardio-vascular disease, high blood pressure, diabetes… Overcrowding inevitably led to such great stress on the lemmings that their systems became depleted and overloaded, and mass death from shock disease occurred.[9]

Overcrowding means constant and chronic stress, leading to the depletion of the adreno-pituitary systems (which handle stress) on a collective level, simultaneously. This pushes the entire rodent population to the breaking point.[10] A good percentage of the population just drops dead from hypoglycemic shock. The rest, also induced by hypoglycemic shock, take off running and jump off the rocks into the ocean and drown in a collective suicide. The dynamics humanity faces in its finite global environment are fundamentally the same as any rodent population when their environment is over utilized, maxed out, with no space to expand, no food to eat, and no resources to exploit. Will we, like the rodents, simply react to the forces acting upon us in a biologically instinctive way that is ultimately self-destructive? Or will we, as a species, be able to respond consciously and with intelligence to the global problems that face us and resolve them to reach a higher level of humanity and civilization?

Today, globally, hunger, famine, mass migrations, and war are in constant interplay, one causing the other and each aggravating the other. Today 10.8% of people around the world are undernourished, down only slightly from a decade earlier. The rate in sub-Saharan Africa (22.8%) is actually slightly higher than a decade ago, per the UN.[11] As food shortages affect poorer parts of the world far more than richer ones, the resulting increase in the flow of immigration is already redefining politics in North America, Europe, and other parts of the world. "People's lives will be affected by a massive pressure for migration," says Pete Smith, a professor of plant and soil science at the University of Aberdeen. "People don't stay and die where they are. People migrate."[12]

There are upward of 60 million refugees in the world today, the most since World War II. Syria, Afghanistan, South Sudan,

Myanmar, and Somalia are the biggest sources of refugees. Of these refugees, 85% are housed in the developing world, with massive burdens falling on countries like Colombia, Bangladesh, and Uganda.[13] Coinciding with a climate change–induced dry period that left many without enough food, the number of migrants from El Salvador, Guatemala, and Honduras showing up at the United States's border with Mexico increased fivefold between 2010 and 2015.[14] Today's deadliest conflicts are civil wars and insurgencies in Yemen, South Sudan, Venezuela, Sudan, and Zimbabwe.[15] Compared to the ones we will experience within 25 years, the present population displacements are minor.

Energy, Global Warming, and Climate Change Catastrophe

A three-year, UN-backed study from the Intergovernmental Science-Policy Platform on Biodiversity and Ecosystem Services has grim implications for the future of humanity. "The report, prepared by more than 100 experts from 52 countries, found that the window to address the threat is closing rapidly."[16] The report says that "human influence has been the dominant cause of global warming since the mid-20th century."[17] The largest human influence has been the emission of greenhouse gasses such as carbon dioxide, methane, and nitrous oxide. Fossil fuel burning is the dominant source of these gases, with agricultural emissions and deforestation also playing significant roles.[18] The effects of global warming include rising sea levels, regional changes in precipitation, more frequent extreme events, such as heatwaves, and the expansion of deserts. Increases in surface temperature have contributed to the retreat of glaciers, permafrost, and sea ice. Overall, higher temperatures bring more rain and snowfall, but in some regions, droughts and wildfires increase instead.

Environmental impacts include the extinction or relocation of many species as their ecosystems change, most immediately in coral reefs, mountains, and the Arctic. Climate change is diminishing crop yields and harming food security. Rising sea levels are beginning to flood coastal infrastructure and force the abandonment of many coastal cities. Some impacts, such as loss of snow cover, increased water vapor, and melting permafrost, cause feedback effects that further increase the rate of global warming. Ocean acidification caused by increased CO2 levels is commonly grouped with these effects, though it is not driven by temperature.

"Above two degrees of global warming, there could be an increase of 100 million or more of the population at risk of hunger," said Edouard Davin, a researcher at ETH Zurich and an author of the report. "We need to act quickly."[19] If we go further to the end of Lemming Road, "... global civilization will collapse within this century, with an estimated population loss exceeding six billion. And unfortunately, our extinction will take the rest of the biome down with us."[20]

On the road to dystopian perdition, humanity is at a crossroads. The historic and current degradation and destruction of nature undermines human well-being for countless future generations.[21] The ongoing human-caused deterioration of Earth's climate will render our "breadbasket" uninhabitable within forty years, and at that future time, none of our countries will possess the capability to deal with the crisis.[22]

Land degradation, biodiversity loss, and climate change are three different faces of the same central challenge: the increasingly dangerous impact of our choices on the health of our natural environment.[23] Nature is in freefall, and the planet's support systems are so stretched that we face widespread species extinctions and mass human migration unless urgent action is taken. Nature's ability to contribute food and fresh water to a growing human population is being compromised in every region on Earth.[24] Countries are using nature at a rate that far exceeds its ability to renew itself. The world's land and water resources are being exploited at unprecedented rates, and industrial farming, on land and in the water, is to blame for much of this loss.[25] Climate change will make those losses even worse, as floods, droughts, storms, and other types of extreme weather threaten to disrupt and, over time, shrink the global food supply.

A half-billion people already live in places turning into deserts, and soil is being lost between 10 and 100 times faster than it is forming.[26] Already, more than 10% of the world's population remains undernourished, and some authors of the UN-backed report warned in interviews that food shortages could lead to an increase in cross-border migration.[27] "A particular danger is that food crises could develop on several continents at once, says Cynthia Rosenzweig, a senior research scientist at the NASA Goddard Institute for Space Studies and one of the lead authors of the report... 'The potential risk of multi-breadbasket failure is increasing,' she said. 'All of these things are happening at the same time.'"[28] Activities such as draining wetlands, as has happened in Indonesia and Malaysia to create palm oil plantations, for example, are exceedingly damaging. Such peatlands "store between 530 and 694 billion tons of carbon dioxide globally" and, when drained, "release that carbon dioxide back into the atmosphere."[29] Carbon dioxide, of course, is a major greenhouse gas, trapping the sun's heat and warming the planet. "Every 2.5 acres of peatlands release the carbon dioxide equivalent of burning 6,000 gallons of gasoline."[30]

Of the five gigatons of greenhouse gas emissions that are released each year from deforestation and other land-use changes, "one gigaton comes from the ongoing degradation of peatlands that are already drained."[31] By comparison, the fossil fuel industry emitted about 37 gigatons of carbon dioxide last year, according to the report.[32] Since 1961, methane emissions from ruminant livestock, which includes cows as well as sheep, buffalo, and goats, have significantly increased, according to the report. And each year, the amount of forested land that is cleared—much of that propelled by demand for pastureland for cattle—releases the emissions equivalent of driving 600 million cars.[33]

As a warming atmosphere intensifies the world's droughts, flooding, heatwaves, wildfires, and other weather patterns, it is speeding up the rate of soil loss and land degradation.[34] Rising temperatures cut crop yields and harm livestock.[35] And higher concentrations of carbon dioxide in the atmosphere will reduce food's nutritional quality. These dynamics, at some point soon, will exceed the ability of the agricultural industry to adapt, the land itself—and its ability to grow food and sustain us—will reach the breaking point, and the industry will collapse.[36]

Pandemic Catastrophes

Humanity has been ravaged by pandemics throughout its history and impacted the growth and expansion of the population as it spread over the globe. The pandemic of 400 BCE in Athens, for example, most likely spreading typhoid fever, killed no less than 80,000 people, which was two-thirds of the entire Athenian population. This was the decisive factor in the end of the Peloponnesian War and the defeat of Athens by their enemy, Sparta. The cohesion of the Roman Empire was likewise threatened and weakened by successive pandemics. In 170 CE, the Antonine Plague of smallpox claimed the life of Roman Emperor Marcus Aurelius, among the 5 million people it killed. The even more serious Justinian bubonic plague of 541 CE killed an estimated 30 to 50 million people and seriously weakened the hegemony of the Roman Empire. In 1350, Western Europe was ravaged by the Black Death, the bubonic plague that killed an estimated 200 million people, fully one third of the world's population, leaving social institutions in a seriously sorry state of deterioration and collapse.[37]

The Columbian Exchange that started in 1492 caused a pandemic of momentous magnitude that the Western Europeans unleashed unintentionally on the newly discovered American continents. It was a combined pandemic of smallpox, measles, and bubonic plague that killed over 56 million of the native population of the Americas. The combined effects of this pandemic were so severe that they actually created a "small ice age" in Western Europe, as we have seen previously.

The 19th century saw three pandemics that followed the precedent set by the Columbian Exchange, becoming successful vectors for the global spreading of diseases. In 1917, the first cholera epidemic of Russian origin claimed one million dead and was subsequently spread by the British navy as far away as Spain, Africa, Indonesia, China, Japan, Italy, Germany, and America. In 1855, the third plague pandemic spread bubonic plague all over Asia, starting in China and spreading to India and beyond, claiming as many as 12 million dead. In 1889, the Russian Flu was also spread internationally, claiming another one million souls.[38]

In the 20th century, we had three pandemics, two of which severely impacted society. First, there was the Avian Flu of 1918, also often erroneously called the "Spanish flu," that infected half of the world's population and killed 50 million people worldwide.[39] The catastrophe focused society on the topic of public health and the need for consistent policies of prevention and treatment. Strict social distancing was practiced with good effect. Hygiene standards improved, and public health departments conducted campaigns of education and vaccination. The Spanish flu forever changed the role of women, as they left the farms and entered the mercantile and industrial workforce in unparalleled numbers. Women also began to assume leadership roles and became an economic force that demanded participation in making community decisions. This dynamic was a strong force behind women being given the right to vote by the Nineteenth Amendment in 1920.[40]

The second pandemic of the 20th century was, relatively speaking, minor. The 1957 Asian flu killed a total 1.1 million in China and the U.S. The third pandemic of the 20th century started in 1981. This was the HIV/AIDS pandemic that started in, and ravaged, the gay community and ultimately killed 35 million people globally. In the 21st century, so far, we have had four real scares: SARS in 2003 with 774 deaths, the swine flu in 2009 with 200,000 death, MERS in 2012 with 850 deaths, and Ebola in 2014 with some 11,000 deaths. But the most frightening of all was the Covid-19 pandemic that began in late 2019.

The Covid-19 pandemic is a stark reminder of how fragile our global society is. It is a system so highly interconnected that a breakdown in any one of its components can easily lead to breakdown of the entire economic, financial, and political system.

Mass deaths from pandemics have been a major factor in the decline and collapse of human culture and civilization in the Greek city-states, the Roman Empire, Western Europe, the America's indigenous populations. All were decimated by plagues that severely crippled their cultures. Two factors increase the probability that global pandemics will occur with greater frequency and intensity. First, the ever-expanding human population in a finite space is increasing the number and frequency of human contacts with many new animal species. This vastly increases the probability of new infectious pathogens being transmitted from animals that have (some) immunity to humans who do not. Second, obviously, the exponentially increasing global human population. As global population density increases, the communicable disease contagion vectors increase exponentially. Global society today is more vulnerable than ever before to attack by new contagious diseases that can swiftly lead to pandemic and mass fatalities.

Endnotes

1 Thomas Hobbes, Leviathan, (Germany: Macmillan, 1963).

2 Rutger Bregman, Utopia for Realists: How We Can Build the Ideal World, (Boston: Little, Brown and Company, Kindle Edition, 2017), 4.

3 Raphe Robynson, More's Utopia: The English Translation Thereof, second edition, (London: University press, 1556), 171.

4 Donella H. Meadows, Dennis L. Meadows, Jorgen Randers, and William W. Behrens III, The Limits to Growth: A Report for the Club of Rome's Project on the Predicament of Mankind, (New York: Universe Books, 1972).

5 Nafeez Ahmed, "MIT Predicted in 1972 That Society Will Collapse This Century. New Research Shows We're on Schedule," Vice, (July 14, 2021): https://www.vice.com/en/article/z3xw3x/new-research-vindicates-1972-mit-prediction-that-society-will-collapse-soon.

6 Ibid.

7 Vaclav Smil, "Global Population: Milestones, Hopes, and Concerns" Archived 3 February 2023 at the Wayback Machine, Medicine & Global Survival, October 1998; Vol. 5, No. 2, 105–108

8 Edward S. Deevey, "The Hare and the Haruspex: A Cautionary Tale," in Man Alone: Alienation in Modern Society, (New York: Dell Publishing Co., 1962), Eric and Mary Josephson eds.

9 Ibid.

10 Ibid.

11 Dave Lawler, "The World Is Less Free Thank a Decade Ago," Axios, December 30, 2019, https://www.axios.com/2019/12/30/freedom-house-freedom-around-the-world-map.

12 Christopher Flavelle, "Climate Change Threatens the World's Food Supply, United Nations Warns," New York Times, August 8, 2019, https://www.nytimes.com/2019/08/08/climate/climate-change-food-supply.html.

13 Dave Lawler, "The World Is Less Free Thank a Decade Ago," Axios, December 30, 2019, https://www.axios.com/2019/12/30/freedom-house-freedom-around-the-world-map.

14 Christopher Flavelle, "Climate Change Threatens the World's Food Supply, United Nations Warns," New York Times, August 8, 2019, https://www.nytimes.com/2019/08/08/climate/climate-change-food-supply.html.

15 Dave Lawler, "The World Is Less Free Thank a Decade Ago," Axios, December 30, 2019, https://www.axios.com/2019/12/30/freedom-house-freedom-around-the-world-map.

16 Christopher Flavelle, "Climate Change Threatens the World's Food Supply, United Nations Warns," New York Times, August 8, 2019, https://www.nytimes.com/2019/08/08/climate/climate-change-food-supply.html.

17 Union of Concerned Scientists, "How Do We Know That Humans Are the Major Cause of Global Warming?" July 14, 2009, https://www.ucsusa.org/resources/are-humans-major-cause-global-warming#:~:text=The%202018%20US%20National%20Climate,since%20the%20mid%2D20th%20century..

18 John Vidal, "The Rapid Decline of the Natural World Is A Crisis Even Bigger Than Climate Change," HuffPost, March 15, 2019. https://www.huffpost.com/entry/nature-destruction-climate-change-world-biodiversity_n_5c49e78ce4b06ba6d3bb2d44

19   Christopher Flavelle, "Climate Change Threatens the World's Food Supply, United
     Nations Warns," New York Times, August 8, 2019, https://www.nytimes.com
     /2019/08/08/climate/climate-change-food-supply.html.

20   John Vidal, "Global Catastrophe," HuffPost, March 15, 2019.

21   Ibid.

22   Ibid.

23   Ibid.

24   Ibid.

25   Ibid.

26   Christopher Flavelle, "Climate Change Threatens the World's Food Supply, United
     Nations Warns," New York Times, August 8, 2019, https://www.nytimes.com
     /2019/08/08/climate/climate-change-food-supply.html.

27   Ibid.

28   Ibid.

29   Ibid.

30   Ibid.

31   Ibid.

32   Ibid.

33   Ibid.

34   Ibid.

35   Ibid.

36   Ibid.

37   History.com Editors, "Pandemics That Changed History," History, December 21,
     2021, https://www.history.com/topics/middle-ages/pandemics-timeline\.

38   Nicholas LePan, "Visualizing the History of Pandemics," Visual Capitalist, March 14,
     2020, https://www.visualcapitalist.com/history-of-pandemics-deadliest/.

39   CDC (17 December 2019). "The Discovery and Reconstruction of the 1918 Pandemic
     Virus". Centers for Disease Control and Prevention. Retrieved 19 September 2022

40   Christine Crudo Blackburn, Gerald W. Parker and Morten Wendelbo, "How the
     1918 Flue Pandemic Helped Advance Women's Rights," Smithsonian Magazine,
     03/02/2018, https://www.smithsonianmag.com/history/how-1918-flu-pandemic
     -helped-advance-womens-rights-180968311/

Chapter 13
....

America's Institutional Descent into Dystopia

White Man's Dystopian Personality Disorder (W M D P D)

Let's begin by unpacking what I call the White Man's Dystopian Personality Disorder (WMDPD for short). I use the phrase "White Man" in two ways. First, in the narrow sense, I use it to describe the authoritarian male-centric white race of Western European Anglo-Saxon ancestry that has become the dominant culture in the world today. In the second, larger sense, I use the term "White Man" to refer to any and all male-centric cultures that exhibit the authoritarian, male-centric social structure. By "personality disorder," I am referring to the pathology of domination and authoritarianism that has misogyny, racism, and class structure as its foundational tripod. And I call it "dystopian" because it leads to and perpetuates class structures by intensifying the exploitation and upward transfer of money and power from the powerless to the powerful.

The psychological-emotional foundation for WMDPD is laid down in childhood through interference with the normal stages of child development. In the first stage, this interference is by sins of omission rather than sins of commission, for it is the absence of maternal love and nurture in the infant's earliest years that creates the fundamental insecurity complex underlying the WMDPD. In other words, the love of power that is the essence of the WMDPD pathology originates precisely in the perversion of the power of love that the adult addict never experienced as a child.

To a large extent more males than females become bullies on account of their different hormonal makeups. In the crisis polarity, the anger-aggression response manifests predominantly in males while the fear-submission response manifests predominantly in females. As a result, the majority of White Men who came to positions of power over the past four or five centuries and helped propel the growth of the White Man's civilization have been afflicted with WMDPD. Of course, each of them was a product of his age, embodying his own moment in history and personifying the particular configurations of events and the nature of his actions.

The Right-Wing, Male-Centric Power Paradigm Launches Its Counteroffensive

The Prophets of Profit, Milton Friedman and Lewis Powell, Redefine Ideology and Strategy

There was a flip side to post–World War II liberal triumphalism. Despite a soaring economy and record profits, the captains of industry capitalism and their fellow travelers in academia and culture were unhappy, experiencing a growing sense of alarm, dread, and panic. What was their concern? In one word: profit. Basically, their complaint was that there was not enough of it and that the growing "welfare state" was eating into what should be theirs. They wanted more and larger profits, which was to be accomplished principally by getting government out of the way of business, i.e., by lowering business taxes. In his book *Evil Geniuses: The Unmaking of America*, Kurt Anderson chronicles how, in the second half of the 20th century, a number of visionary "evil geniuses" exploited this deepening unease in the business community and channeled it into a collective revolutionary, or rather counterrevolutionary, mission of "deliberate reengineering of our economy and society."[1]

This "highly rational confederacy of the rich, the right, and big business"[2] hatched an open conspiracy that defined its mission as nothing less than to re-establish the pre–New Deal order: everybody for themselves; everything's for sale; greed is good; the rich get richer; buyer beware; unfairness can't be helped; nothing but thoughts and prayers for the losers.

The opening salvo in this new capitalist class war against the people, and against sharing any profits for the greater collective good, was fired by University of Chicago professor and Nobel Prize winner Milton Friedman in 1970. This prophet of profit published a piece in the *New York Times*[3] which was basically an updated rehash of his earlier book *Capitalism and Freedom*[4] but addressed more specifically the business class to set them straight on what their values should be and where their allegiances should lie.

Hammering home the basic tenet of his doctrine that "the social responsibility of business is to increase its profits"[5] and no more, Friedman viciously attacked the weak-kneed and squishy-minded business executives, owners and shareholders who had come to accept that they had a duty to decency and virtue in contributing to the collective good through taxation and other means. He demanded of business leaders to toughen up and recommit to the maximization of profits at all costs.

Within a few years of its first articulation, elite executives-in-training internalized and felt free to espouse the Friedman doctrine. Young Jeff Skilling, of later Enron fame, provides an apt example that highlights and illustrates the extent to which the Friedman doctrine struck a chord within the larger business community. Asked in the late 1970s at Harvard Business School about a hypothetical CEO who discovers his product could kill customers, young Jeff said he "would keep making and selling the product. My job as a business-man is to be a profit center and to maximize return to the sharehold-ers. It's the government's job to step in if a product is dangerous."[6]

If Milton Friedman was the theoretical, if not theological, mid-wife to this renewed movement against the people, Lewis Powell was its chief strategist and general. An establishment éminence grise, Powell was a former president of the American Bar Association, served on many corporate boards, and would eventually be nomi-nated to the Supreme Court by Richard Nixon. His law practice in Virginia was primarily in the area of corporate law related to mergers and acquisitions. He was a vocal ultraconservative and racist committed to the fight against any government regulation of big business whatsoever. Among his clients, for example, were Philip Morris, the largest cigarette maker, whose products had been labelled carcinogenic by the federal government and were banned from advertising. Also among his firm's clients was one of the defendant school districts who opposed desegregation in the Supreme Court decision *Brown v. Board of Education.*

Powell also despised the progressive beliefs and practices of the counterculture. In the summer of 1970, he delivered a keynote speech entitled "The Attack on American Institutions" at a big annual Southern business conference. In his speech, Powell warned that "revolution could engulf this country" because the U.S. political economy was "under broad and virulent attack [by] white and black radicals [whose] heroes are Fidel Castro, Che Guevara, Ho Chi-Minh and Mao Tse-Tung" and who behaved like "Hitler and his storm troopers."[7] One of his neighbors in Richmond, a retail-chain president and local politician who was also a national officer of the U.S. Chamber of Commerce, was so impressed by the speech that he urged Powell to rewrite it as a draft for a national counterrevolutionary strategy and plan of action, on the model of what he had done as a colonel in Air Force intelligence in planning for D-Day.

The result was an ultra-confidential 34-page memorandum that Powell's neighbor submitted to the Chamber's leadership and staff. So enthusiastic was the response of the U.S. Chamber of Commerce that in 1972, it leaked the Powell memo to its entire membership. The significance of this event was that "people in business and on the wealthy right, who'd regarded Friedman's *Times* essay as a kind of motivational St. Crispin's Day speech delivered by their Henry V, now had an actual battle plan from an experienced and distinguished general, their Duke of Richmond."[8] American big business entered an entirely new phase of operation. Never before had polite American businessmen been trained or equipped to conduct guerrilla warfare against the government and the people, but now, they were enlisted in a mobilization for a massive counterinsurgency. For this strategy to work, their movement needed two things: time and money. They needed to commit decades of effort to the project and millions, if not billions, of dollars to pay for it.

Powell envisioned waging this war on four fronts—in academia, in the media, in politics, and in the legal system—and doing so with unheard-of budgets and ferocity. For the first two fronts, they would need to find and fund scholars and other intellectuals "who do believe in the system... who will do the thinking, the analysis, the writing and the speaking [to effect] gradual change in public opinion." Next, political power needed to "be assiduously cultivated [and] used aggressively... without embarrassment and without the reluctance which has been so characteristic of American business."[9]

Finally, according to Powell, "the judiciary may be the most important instrument for social, economic and political change... and represents a vast area of opportunity."[10] Powell advocated a kind of "judicial activism in reverse." In order to tilt the game decisively in the direction of capital, he argued, the capitalist camp needed to copy the ACLU, "labor unions, civil rights groups and public interest law firms" and create similar institutions propagating the libertarian, free enterprise philosophy and way of life. The final line of the Powell memorandum expresses the urgency of its message and the need for decisive, even ruthless, action: "Business and the enterprise system are in trouble, and the hour is late." For Powell, the movement could no longer afford to be tolerant of the progressive left-wing deviances being perpetrated on the country. The line had to be be drawn, and it must be a hard line. No businessman could afford to be tolerant "of those who attack his corporation and the system." Rather, businessmen should "respond in kind," engage in "confrontation politics [and] attack the Naders... and others who openly seek destruction of the system." And they should "penalize politically" any and all opponents.[11]

And where would the tremendous sums of money required to finance these comprehensive and extreme visions of re-making society come from? Multibillionaire right-wing financiers like the Koch brothers (Charles and David), Joseph Coors, Richard Mellon Scaife,

John Olin, and many others were happy to step up to the plate and become the bankrollers of this vast capitalist counterrevolution.

Financing the Instruments of Political Insurgency:
Think Tanks, Lobbyists, PACS, and Media

The goal of Powell and his co-planners (or should we say, "co-conspirators"?) was to stimulate the growth of a powerful counter to the liberal establishment. What they accomplished in a decade was astonishing. It astounded even themselves, as even a brief summary of their efforts makes abundantly clear. High on the list of priorities was the adequate funding of existing conservative think tanks to bring them up to par with existing liberal institutions as well as, secondly, to go beyond that and establish a slate of new ones. For example, in 1970, the American Enterprise Institute (AEI), a conservative think tank in Washington, had a tenth of the funding of the big established liberal one, the Brookings Institution, a staff of ten, and only two resident scholars. By the end of the decade, the AEI's budget was equal to Brookings', and its staff had grown to 125. Likewise, by the end of the 1970s, the annual budget of the Hoover Institution, associated with Stanford University in California, had quintupled, and the endowment increased from $20 million to $300 million.

But the effort went far beyond reinforcing established right-wing institutions. In record time, a flood of new think tanks were financed and established. David Koch was quite explicit about this long-game strategy of donating large sums over many years to a large number of new right-wing nonprofits. As their goal was to minimize the role of government and to maximize the role of the private economy, the Koch brothers supported many different approaches to achieve those objectives, basically applying the well-known investment strategy of hedging your bets by achieving balance in diversity. Decades later, Richard Mellon Scaife's boast to Jane Mayer that he'd funded "133 of the conservative movement's 300 most important institutions"[12] aptly expressed the ambition and ultimate scale of the network of start-ups these billionaires began building in the 1970s.

Another area of priority was the cultivation and deployment of an army of lobbyists. In 1971, only about 175 big companies had full-time lobbyists, or "public affairs offices," in Washington. By 1978 the number had grown to 500, and just four years later, in the second Reagan term, the number of corporations employing Washington lobbyists had mushroomed to an astounding 2,500. This tremendous surge of lobbying also created a convenient and effective way for big business to infiltrate government and reward its supporters. While in the early '70s the hiring of a former member of Congress by big business was a rare event and never failed to raise eyebrows, within a decade the practice had become so established that it became known as the revolving door between big business and government.

After the Watergate scandal, Congress passed new campaign finance rules in 1975 to limit the size of donations and to disclose the identity of the benefactors. Those new rules were promptly subverted by the newly politicized corporations to legitimize the role of corporations in federal elections, allowing them to funnel unlimited funds to political candidates and civil initiatives through the so-called Political Action Committees (PACs).[13] By the fall of 1975, 300 corporations and business groups had set up one of these new species of donation pipelines. As soon as the Supreme Court removed limits from PAC donations, the number of these business PACs soared from 300 to 1,200, generating gushers of money to finance their far-right candidates and policy initiatives alike.[14]

So much business, so many opportunities, so many shenanigans. This was the period and atmosphere during which many young grifters and grafters, fixers and dirty tricksters first learned the tricks of their trade. Examples include Lee Atwater, Roy Cohn, Roger Stone, and Paul Manafort, who in the years that followed, would diligently work their way up the ladders of decision-making in right-wing politics and business to become stalwart Trump acolytes and actors in the 2021 attempted coup.

The Attack on Education and the Moronization of the Electorate

The relative economic abundance of the postwar era allowed the counterculture to spring up and flourish at its edges. Rejecting conventional wisdom and values, the counterculture embarked on its own little project of creating a Eutopia right then and there. In several ways, it approximated the Greek ideal of a participatory democratic society. One basic characteristic that the counterculture shared with the ruling elite of Athenian democratic society was that the participants had guaranteed economic abundance, had no need to work for a living, and were universally educated. They could, therefore, participate full-time and whole heartedly in collective democratic self-rule, fashioning lives of meaning by exploring their creativity. One truly great thing about the postwar era of the '50s and '60s was society's real commitment to higher learning. People were encouraged to go to college to get an education, not only to be able to get a decent-paying job but to become well-rounded human beings capable of thinking for themselves. Subsequently, the anti-Vietnam War movement, the Black protest movement and freedom riders, the free speech movement, the hippies and yippies, and the women's liberation movement re-emerged as a powerful voice for change.

Because of its deep societal impact, the emergence of the counterculture really scared and enraged the evil genius class. Here, the political and business worlds were faced with an educated proletariat that was armed with the capacity of critical thinking. This was very alarming and threatening to the 1% who came up with a long-range, two-pronged counterattack. First, the decision was made to dumb down education by presenting critical thinking, philosophy, and the humanities as not helping people get jobs and instead diverting and channeling people into business and technical schools. Second, the decision was made to stop giving education away for free as a kind of democratic right and to start charging for it, a lot and increasingly more. A key architect of this campaign was William J. Bennett, neo-con thinker and secretary of education under Ronald Reagan. He even wrote a book about it with the title *Is College Worth It?* in which he argued that, for most people, higher education is too expensive and not worth it. His argument was basically that a plumber doesn't need a Ph.D. in humanities, so just go to trade school and don't get a higher education. That may be true as far as the skill of plumbing goes, but it is not true as far as the skill of being a knowledgeable, educated participant in society's affairs goes. That's where even plumbers need sufficient higher education to distinguish between lies and truths.

There can be no doubt that the dumbing-down strategy of the Reagan administration was successful beyond the wildest dreams of its planners. The existing paradigm of a free liberal arts and humanities–based education was undermined and dismantled. It was replaced by a costly and strictly utilitarian educational paradigm that was geared to produce the necessary workers, technicians, clerks, capitalists, and technocrats necessary for the smooth functioning of the economy as a profit-making machine. It would also be one that failed, intentionally so, to produce citizens capable of critical thinking. The dumbing-down strategy produced several generations of highly specialized blue- and white-collar professionals who were incapable of grasping the larger historical currents unfolding around them because their capability for critical thinking was stunted and not developed in the education they received. What this really meant was that the educational system failed the American people deeply; it failed to raise their standards of thinking and reasoning to a level that is necessary to make informed decisions in a democracy.

The second part of the strategy, making education not free but expensive, is well illustrated by the example of the University of California. Created in 1868, the first public university in California was dedicated to high principles. Tuition was to be free for California residents, and when it soon became apparent that this was not enough, it was decided in 1897 that financial aid would be available for "needy and deserving students."[15] One hundred years later, in the 1960s, these lofty ideals were thrown to the wind. In 1968, the registration fee for all California resident students was set at $300 per year, while nonresident tuition was set at $1,200 per year. From then, starting slowly and almost imperceptibly, then at an ever-faster clip, student fee increases have been spiraling out of control, always increasing the student's total education costs, while steadily decreasing funding from the state and the university, as the following table illustrates.[16]

History of Annual Undergraduate Student Fees at the University of California		
Year	California Resident	Nonresident
1975–76	$ 630.00	$ 2,130.00
1985–86	$ 1,296.00	$ 5,112.00
1995–96	$ 4,354.00	$12,053.00
2005–06	$ 7,434.00	$25,254.00
2011–12	$14,460.00	$37,338.00

In the end, the reactionary education policies instituted by Reagan and his henchmen were deeply dystopian and severely impacted everybody financially, the educated and uneducated alike. Those who choose to forego higher education in favor of the more immediate payoff in wages, as time went on, got screwed. As the economic landscape changed, their jobs became obsolete. As new digital and technological industries arose that had no use for their limited skill sets, they were left behind, stewing in their discontent. Their education did not provide them with the critical intellectual skills to understand what happened to them, leaving them, in their existence, racked with stress and anxiety and constantly in dire financial straits.

Those who, despite the challenges posed by the unending increases in university tuition, carried through on their desire to get an education, also paid a dear price that would make them unhappy for years. Despite the economic advantages they gained through their education, they were saddled with huge debts running into hundreds of thousands of dollars at the time of their graduate or law school graduation. They became beholden to, and financial prisoners of, the system that produced them.

Today in the 2020s we are reaping the results of those decisions made and executed in the second half of the 20th century. In the relationship between education and democracy, the lessons from the counterculture and the counter-reaction that followed, both positive and negative, are most instructive for the future of our society. On the negative side, the lesson to be learned from the establishment response to the counterculture is about what happens when the educational system fails to produce an educated citizenry capable of critical thinking. If we do not educate all our people highly, the chances of sliding into dystopia and authoritarianism increase exponentially.

On the positive side, we must learn from and expand upon the absolute importance of education in creating an informed citizenry necessary for a well-functioning democracy. Indeed, the big lesson of the counterculture is that education will be the cornerstone of Eutopia and democracy. We cannot have democracy without education. Education teaches us, the citizenry, the ability of critical thinking based on facts. For reason to overcome passion (feeling), one must be educated, i.e., know the facts and how to reason with them. And here's the kicker. The segment of the population that most heavily bought into the Reagan administration's conservative arguments in the 1980s and chose to go to technical or trade school rather than university was the white male lower middle class. And those who decided to pursue higher education, despite its ever-increasing costs, were precisely those segments of the population that had historically and habitually been discriminated against: the colored, non-white minorities and women of all races.

The result is a truth that should not be ignored, because today, it is shaping the conflict between the dystopians and the Eutopians. Since the 1950s, minorities and women have continued to get educated and pursue the American dream while white men have become less educated and have been left behind living an American nightmare. Ever since, white men on the whole have not been doing well, and their quality of life has been steadily deteriorating. Socially, educationally, economically, mentally, and emotionally, men have suffered a steep decline in well-being over the past half century.

White men are getting married in fewer numbers. The last few decades have seen a big rise in single men, from about 29% in 1990 to 39% in 2019. As a group they have fallen behind their married counterparts in both earnings and education. Fewer men are seeking and completing higher education. Since the 1950s, white men in America have been falling behind girls in school. Today, nearly 60% of students in American colleges and universities are women. Fewer white men are working today, as unemployment has been steadily rising among white American men. As a result, more and more white men are suffering more anxiety and depression and are withdrawing into loneliness. Deaths of despair are more prevalent among men than among women.[17] Men are more likely to die of suicide and alcohol abuse than women. Likewise, white men are more likely than women to commit homicide (90%) as well as be the victims of it (77%). Aggravating the situation is that it has been well-established that if these white men identify with a traditional masculine ideology, they are less likely to seek psychological help, and on the contrary, they are more likely to descend into an ever-deepening spiral of violent, toxic masculinity.

Anxiety produces grievance and rage. It is part of human nature to want someone to blame for our suffering and on which to focus our anger and rage so we can make them suffer. Those young white men of yesteryear who were scared away by the rising costs of higher education and learned technical or mechanical skills instead are today's unemployed or underemployed adults who feel passed by history. They rejected the course of action that would be best for them in the long run and opted for the short-term advantage. Thus they were left behind, did not reap the economic benefits of society's progress, and relatively speaking, were thereby left disadvantaged. This is what fed the growing rage in this white male population in the last quarter of the 20th century. This rage increasingly found a natural expression in, and was directed at, those who they felt had passed them by in improving their lot in society: non-white minorities and women. In reaction they doubled down on these two traditional objects of white male authoritarianism, resulting in the intensification of the white male rage and blame-seeking in new far-right political movements.

Thus it was that in the last half century, a white male voting population came into being that had little-to-no education, low skills, no critical thinking, and were conspiracy-oriented, often religious, sometimes not, but always ready to buy into the trash peddled by the huckster preachers and politicians eliciting knee-jerk, right-wing, populist, racist, and misogynist reactions. And where there's loneliness, resentment, poverty, and fear, there's a fertile breeding ground for fascism. That's where politicians like Trump can successfully push their racist culture wars and channel the economic distress of their base into violence, both political and physical, against the perceived "uppity" non-white minorities and women.

Dystopian Dynamics of Electoral Democracy

The Stench of Corruption

American democracy has always been a work in progress, commenced by the Founders and continued by each generation, addressing the flaws in our system of government as they appear. Today, in the first quarter of the 21st century, a crack has appeared in the structure of our democracy that points to a fundamental shortcoming in the Founders' formulations and thinking about democracy. A fatal contradiction in our theory and practice of representative government has appeared that threatens the very destruction of our representative government.

That contradiction is that liberal electoral democracy inherently fosters the type of corruption that will inevitably lead to its own destruction and the establishment of its opposite: illiberal democracy. In illiberal democracy, the democratic forms are preserved, but the democratic spirit and essence is destroyed. In illiberal democracy the people get to vote, but there is no choice. People can vote only to rubberstamp the selections made by the powers that be. As recent world history is proving, power addicts will inevitably use the democratic electoral system to come into power and, once in power, will try to do everything to subvert liberal democracy into illiberal democracy in order to stay in power.

The numbers for the 2016 elections were the following. There were two federal elections: for president and vice president. In state contests, there were 100 elections for senators and 435 for the House of Representatives. For all state legislatures combined, there were over 7,000 elections. There were also 3,000 county elections and 19,000 municipal elections. No numbers are recorded for the numerous nationwide elections of judges, school boards, water boards, mosquito control boards, coroners, dog catchers, and other miscellaneous elections. But the grand total of elected officials in the 2016 elections came to 529,682. This averages to about one elected official out of every 1,000 people.[18]

First, consider the truly staggering monetary cost of elections. The total for the 2016 presidential election came to almost $2.5 billion. The combined costs of the 2016 congressional races (house and senate) were over $4 billion, for a total of $6.5 billion for the federal elections alone. Add to that the costs of all state and local elections, and the sums become truly astronomical. Compared with the spending for the same races in the year 2000, when the presidential and vice presidential races cost some $1.4 billion and the congressional elections cost $1.6 billion for a total of 3 billion, that is a 100% increase in 15 years.[19] Since, in the final analysis, it is "We the people" who pay for all this, not only monetarily but also in social costs, it's only fair to ask what we as a society get in return for shelling out all this money. The answer is that what "We the people" get for our money is a raw deal that leaves a bad taste.

As a society, we are knee-deep in the scum. For the vast majority of people, liberal democracy doesn't pass the smell test anymore. People hold their nose and distance themselves in quiet disgust and open rebellion. Everybody is unhappy. Indeed, our political system is very broken. A vast alienation has grown between the people as a whole and the ruling political and economic elites. People are fed up with their elected officials. They watch with disgust and disrespect as their elected representatives are mired in the morass of retributive power politics, proving incapable of governing meaningfully.

This billionaire ruling class, over the past century, has simply bought the electoral system by paying for its expenses of party and candidates, buying the politicians by financing their campaigns. In other words, the problem is that the electoral process has been hijacked by big business to the point where, today, we have a government of big business for big business and by big business. Elections themselves have become a multibillion-dollar industry where competing factions produce and market candidates for political office while propagandizing and influencing the electorate in their favor.

The politicians, in turn, pass the laws that favor and facilitate transferring the wealth from the 99% to the 1% through tax cuts in a never-ending, ever-intensifying cycle. Trump's 2017 tax cut dramatically illustrated the truth of this state of affairs. In an unprecedented rush and hurry, that tax bill took exactly seven weeks from introduction to passage without any substantive hearings held. Trump and the Republicans engineered an $11.5 trillion addition to the national debt, a transference of wealth from the people to the 1% to be financed by future cuts in entitlements—social security, Medicare, unemployment, etc.

The Electorate's Awareness of Corruption

The people are exactly aware of the shameful sham Trump's 2017 tax cut was. A new Gallup Poll in April 2018 showed that despite the propaganda, 52% of people disapproved of the bill, while only 39% supported it.[20] The kicker here was the Corker Kickback. After friendly insertions that guaranteed to net Senator Bob Corker millions of dollars with passage of the bill, that lion's share of fiscal responsibility suddenly found a new religion and changed his tune (and vote) in favor of the tax plan. According to a Chapman University poll, corruption of government officials ranks as the single most ubiquitous American fear, ahead of polluted drinking water, North Korea using weapons, and not having enough money for the future. According to Pew Research Center, public trust in the government has been mired "near historically low levels" for a decade.[21]

The sad truth is that our whole electoral democracy is deeply and widely corrupted. The system is rigged to benefit the billionaire class at the expense of "We the people." The increasing corruption through the buying of elections by the billionaire class is a symptom of the privatization of what should be a public electoral process.

The electoral paradigm turns the selection of decision makers into an expensive public gladiatorial contest. With millions invested and billions in possible payoffs, these contests have an inherently corrupting influence on the winners. The winners are beholden to, and will make decisions that will tend to favor, their financial supporters, and for that very reason, their objectivity is inherently tainted.

And this profoundly affects the sanctity and integrity of the electoral process, the attitudes of the electorate as a whole, and the types of individuals seeking political office. As far as the electorate is concerned, the vast majority hold their noses, keep their distance, refuse to get involved in the circus of running for office, and vote (if they even vote) for the least objectionable of the candidates running.

How did we get there and at what social costs? Nixon's Watergate scandal must be regarded, symbolically speaking, as the inflection point in time. Watergate crystalized the general public's mostly unconscious dis-ease with government and the electoral process into the public's consciousness: their president was, in fact, a crook. People came to realize, furthermore, that a significant part of our elected representatives are also crooks in as much as they do not serve the people but the special interests that finance them. What followed was the loss of faith in government, politics, and politicians and a rage against the decline in economic opportunity and social services and security, further proving the criminal paralysis and stagnation of government.

The Corruptors' Tool Kits

Paul Krugman identified the four main methods by which the financial resources of the 1% distort policy priorities and controls what issues the politicians will take up and decide:

1. "Raw corruption: We like to imagine that simple bribery of politicians isn't an important factor in America, but it's almost surely a much bigger deal than we like to think.
2. Soft corruption: The various ways short of direct bribery where politicians, government officials, and people with

policy influence of any kind stand to gain financially by promoting policies that serve the interests or prejudices of the wealthy. This includes the revolving door between public service and private-sector employment, think tank fellowships, fees on the lecture circuit, and so on.

3. Campaign contributions: Yes, these matter.
4. Defining the agenda: Through a variety of channels—media ownership, think tanks, and the simple tendency to assume that being rich also means being wise—the 1% has an extraordinary ability to set the agenda for policy discussion in ways that can be sharply at odds with both a reasonable assessment of priorities and public opinion more generally."[22]

In February 2018, a viral video of Representative Alexandria Ocasio-Cortez swept across the internet. It was shot during a hearing held by the House Oversight and Reform Committee on the subject of strengthening ethics rules for the executive branch. The video, put together by Now This News, shows the high-profile New York Congress member playing a lightning round game with witnesses. The purpose: to highlight how it's legal for congressional candidates to engage in a lot of corrupt and shady practices.[23]

AOC began the hearing by saying, "I'm going to be the bad guy, which, I'm sure, half the room would agree with anyway, and I want to get away with as much bad things as possible, ideally to enrich myself and advance my interests, even if that means putting my interests ahead of the American people [and] I have enlisted all of you as my co-conspirators, so you're going to help me legally get away with all of this."[24]

She then asked the witnesses a series of probing questions about the types of behavior candidates for Congress are legally allowed to engage in:

- Can she run a campaign entirely funded by corporate political action committees? Yes.
- Can she use that money to make hush payments and pay people off to get elected? Yes.

- Once in office, can she influence and write laws that might affect the groups from which she's taken special interest money? Yes.
- And can she hold stocks in companies that the legislation she's writing might boost? Yes.

AOC then drove the point home by pointing out that no matter how lax and permissive the restrictions are, candidates for the House are still held to a higher standard than the president, for whom, it appears, no ethics laws exist at all to limit his political behavior. "It's already super legal, as we've seen, for me [as a representative to Congress] to be a pretty bad guy [but] it's even easier for the president of the United States to be one," Ocasio-Cortez said.[25]

AOC then asked Walter Shaub, senior adviser to the watchdog group Citizens for Responsibility and Ethics in Washington and former head of the Office of Government Ethics, who resigned under President Donald Trump, whether the ethics limits placed on members of Congress and the president are comparable. Shaub replied that, "In terms of laws that apply to the president... there's almost no laws at all that apply to the president."[26]

Corruptors and Reformers

Within the class of elective office seekers, the essential corruption of the electoral process creates a divisive, even fatal, polarity between the power addicts and the power reformers. The power addicts run for elective office as a fast way to political power and the personal benefits that can be extracted from it. Drawn to the electoral process as flies to a carcass, they seek to feast on the festering body politic while hastening its demise. Opposed to them are the power reformers, those folks who see through the charade and shams and who seriously seek to right the wrongs of the abuses of power by the addicts. The reformers start out running for political office with honest ideals and a sincere desire to serve their fellow citizens. Often, though not always, as they manage to stay in positions of power, slowly, over time, almost imperceptibly, they get corrupted by power and become addicted to it. It usually starts small, often in times of great personal difficulty. It is justified by such reasonings as, "I already do so much for the people; surely I deserve the small personal benefit I accrue through this action." This process often coincides with the replacement of idealism with cynicism as the prevailing operant mood and mode of behavior.

The fact is that today, only rich people or candidates supported by and serving rich people have a chance to be elected for political office. The cost of running for office has grown so much over the past century, way beyond what any reasonable person would have at his disposal, affecting the numbers and quality of political office seekers. One the one hand, this reality of our present system of electoral democracy discourages those who truly seek to serve the greater good, thus further shrinking the pool of people possibly interested in running for office. On the other hand, this reality of our present system of electoral democracy encourages the least desirable people to run for office, namely power addicts, who seek office to gain and use power first and primarily for their own good and the good of the corporations that bankroll them, at the expense of the people they represent.

Both on the individual level and the collective, social level, the desire to acquire power is always rooted in the experience of powerlessness. Western man addicted to power, and having made a religion of the pursuit of it, must be considered as suffering from a pathology, an imbalance in his emotional makeup. Electoral democracy is failing us because an inherent contradiction leads to the chronic, endemic, and systematic corruption of its basic tenets. The failure of electoral democracy is that its rules of operation heavily favor power addicts gaining positions of great social and political power because it provides a ready method and means for the power sick, the power addicts, to rise to power. Like bees to honey, or flies to a pile of manure, electoral politics attract that minority of human beings that seek power over others. Once the power addicts come into positions of power through electoral victory, they will try to subvert the very rules and laws of democracy into an authoritarian structure to sustain their own power.

This situation is responsible for and aggravates the basic mistrust between the electorate and the office seekers because, basically, no one that is running for office can ever be fully trusted. All of the addicts, of course, act the part of the reformers. That makes it difficult, if not impossible, to discern accurately who is who. It often becomes a gamble really, to distinguish between power addicts and power reformers. And once they have tasted power, those reformers in the second group are also likely to be corrupted and become addicts.

A strong objection to electoral democracy is that it encourages a disproportionate number of would-be power addicts to give it a try while it discourages regular, non-power or status-driven people from seeking office. The very necessity of begging donors for campaign money makes a candidate beholden and makes running for office a demeaning experience for regular folk. But it doesn't bother the power addict candidate at all; (s)he understands pay to play. But the fatal flaw, the Achilles heel, of electoral democracy is that it allows itself to be used by people who are opposed to it (for whatever reason, religious, political, or personal) to come to power, then set about destroying it through the imposition of an authoritarian regime. For a society to invest in such a system is ultimately suicidal. Because it is possible, it will happen. Somebody will use the system to come to power, then get rid of the system to stay in power. It's only a matter of time and circumstance.

Comparing Democratic and Republican Stewardship of the Economy

Assessment of the stewardship of the economy by Republican and Democratic presidents and their administrations must be made on the basis of the effectiveness of their "greed management" policies. On this core, the fundamental differences between the two parties stand out in stark relief.

The Republican Party is the party of unrestrained capital and capitalism. It *is* the party of greed and represents the interests of the greediest of the greedy. For the Republican Party, governments exist to serve the interest of business, above all, with as little oversight of business and the economy as possible. It believes in unregulated greed and will do everything in its power to favor the unrestrained growth of business. "You guys want a tax cut? No problem! I'll give you three, and what else can I do for you?" is their consistent attitude.

The Democratic Party is more people oriented. It is the party of need and represents the interests of the neediest of the needy. The Democrats have a more consistent policy of restraining the greed of big business, managing the economy through government intervention in a more balanced way, and instituting social programs that actually improve the lot of the common men and women.

And how do these two different approaches to greed management and economic stewardship compare historically in maintaining the stability of the economy? The apparent paradox is that under Republican management, the economy consistently underperforms compared to its behavior under Democratic management. "'The U.S. economy has performed better when the President of the United States is a Democrat rather than a Republican, almost regardless of how one measures performance,' according to a report entitled 'Presidents and the Economy: A Forensic Investigation.'"[27]

"Every Republican president since Teddy Roosevelt in the early 1900s endured a recession in their first term... Four Republican presidents suffered through two recessions while in office and Republican President Dwight Eisenhower presided over three. Meanwhile, Democrats have largely skated past the recession quicksand. Four in five Democratic presidents saw no recessions during their terms since 1945."[28]

"Recessions aren't the only indicator of economic slowdown that appear during Republican presidencies." Another one is "real GDP growth... in the U.S... During the 64 years and 16 presidential terms going back to President Truman in the mid-1940s," the GDP "averaged 3.33%." "With a Republican in the White House, though, the economy's growth slowed to 2.54%, the economists found. With a Democrat in office, growth jumped to 4.35% on average."[29] Additionally, "a variety of other economic indicators, such as per capital GDP, stock market returns, real wages and the change in the unemployment rate, are also more robust with a Democratic president." For example, "unemployment fell by 0.8 percentage points with a Democratic president, on average, while it rose 1.1% with a Republican."[30]

All these facts still leave us with the question of why do bubbles and crashes occur generally under Republican management and have to be corrected by the Democrats, and why does the economy generally do better under Democratic than Republican management. Here's a theory:

The Republican Party, being more sympathetic and laissez-faire with respect to business, creates an atmosphere of arrogance, over confidence, overreach, and recklessness on the part of the greedy that is always part and parcel of creating an economic bubble of immense profit that at some point will burst into a crash of immense misery.

With a more consistent oversight and restraint under Democratic management, business atmosphere is less hyper and more cautious. And while this may result in a lesser rate of return or profit, it is steadier in its performance and will, therefore, eventually outperform the manic highs and subsequent crashes allowed to develop under Republican management.

The presidency of George W. Bush, Republican, from 2001 to 2009 was plagued by no fewer than three economic bubbles: the 2002 dot-com bubble, the 2004 housing bubble, and the 2008 subprime mortgage bubble, which exploded into a full-blown global financial crisis. "When it comes to sheer scale and size, few bubbles match the dot-com bubble. At that time, the increasing popularity of the internet triggered a massive wave of speculation in 'new economy' businesses. As a result, hundreds of dot-com companies achieved multibillion-dollar valuations as soon as they went public. The NASDAQ Composite Index, home to most of these technology/dot-com company stocks, soared from a level of about 750 at the beginning of 1990 to a peak of over 5,000 in March 2000. The index crashed shortly thereafter, plunging 78% by October 2002 and triggering a U.S. recession. The next time the Index reached a new high was in 2015, more than 15 years after its previous peak."[31]

"Some experts believe that the bursting of the NASDAQ dot-com bubble led U.S. investors to pile into real estate due to the mistaken belief that real estate was a safer asset class. While U.S. house prices nearly doubled from 1996 to 2006, two-thirds of that increase occurred from 2002 to 2006, according to a report from the U.S. Bureau of Labor Statistics. Even as house prices were increasing at a record pace, there were mounting signs of an unsustainable frenzy—rampant mortgage fraud, condo 'flipping,' houses being bought by sub-prime borrowers, etc. U.S. housing prices peaked in 2006, and then commenced a slide that resulted in the average U.S. house losing one-third of its value by 2009."[32]

On September 16, 2008, failures of massive financial institutions in the United States rapidly devolved into a global crisis. This resulted in a number of bank failures in Europe and sharp reductions in the value of stocks and commodities worldwide.

As always, investors across the country had been on the hunt to find new sources of income with high returns in a short time. In other words, they had been looking for the next bubble. They found it in the housing market. Investors looking to make a lot of profit would quickly purchase a large number of mortgages from banks and large financial institutions. Such bundling would theoretically allow the investor to make large sums of money because the rising home prices and their respectable interest rates promised a high return. In this way, investors and bankers poured billions of dollars into the United States housing market in the early 2000s. So the huge financial institutions began proactively buying up thousands of mortgages and bundling them up into what is known as "mortgage-backed securities." Shares of these would be sold to the investors; however, as the supply of mortgage-backed securities declined, lenders offered homes and mortgages to people of all backgrounds to access more mortgages, including people with drastically low incomes. These deals, known as subprime mortgages, seemed very promising to everyday citizens and especially investors.

And sure enough, after the bubble comes the crash, always. Mortgage payments for people with subprime mortgages soon ballooned, to the point where thousands of people started to default on their payments. This resulted in thousands of homes on the market with no one looking to buy them, leading to homes worth much less than what they were before, forcing many investors, big financial institutions, and banks to bankruptcy. These parties were the backbone of the United States economy, so as they plummeted, it started to affect everyone—from the auto industry to the citizens of the United States. Hundreds of billions of dollars were lost. The stock market crashed. There was widespread panic. Millions of workers were laid off. The economy contracted, and people had much less money in their pockets.

"The U.S. housing boom and bust, and the ripple effects it had on mortgage-backed securities, resulted in the biggest global economic contraction" since the Great Depression. "This period of the late 2000s thus came to be known as the Great Recession."[33]

Eight years in office, and what did Bush and company have to show for it? Three economic bubbles and busts doing widespread economic damage and dis-ease. The voters decided the Republicans had had their chance and had blown it. They elected Barack Obama and the Democrats to clean up the mess and restore the economy to vitality. Obama did not wait and did not disappoint. A scant two months after his election, President Obama signed the American Recovery and Reinvestment Act (ARRA), a $787-billion stimulus plan to jump-start the economy by providing relief to the widespread panic across the country. ARRA cut taxes by $288 billion, allocated $275 billion in federal grants and loans, and reserved $224 billion for unemployment benefits, education, and healthcare.

The recession ended only three months after the act was passed, and the Great Recession officially lasted a period of barely two years, from December 2007 to June 2009. With ARRA in place, the economic growth went from shrinking at a rate of 5.4% to growing by 1.3%. The government, instead of losing half a million jobs a month, added almost four million private sector and government jobs within two years. Soon, President Obama bailed out the auto industry, saving companies like General Motors and Ford from possibly going defunct and being sold off.

Dystopian Dynamics of Capitalism and Class Structure

The Confluence of Big Business and Organized Crime

Today, in the 21st century, the boundaries between "legitimate" and "illegitimate" business have blurred. For the average person, there is no essential difference between organized crime and big business. Both separate people from their money in any conceivable way, thereby causing and sustaining globally elevated levels of stress and anxiety. Organized crime has embraced and expanded into so-called legitimate big business, which in turn, has embraced the corrupt and criminal tactics and methods of organized crime to create the equivalency: organized crime is big business, and big business is organized crime.

After the collapse of communism in Soviet Russia in the late 1980s, Western liberal democracy reached the apex of its influence in global affairs, and the West, especially the USA, was unrivalled in its military, economic, and ideological power. As a result, many countries around the world in Asia, Africa, Latin America, including Russia and Eastern Europe, adopted Western liberal democracy's ideals and institutions. But the 21st century quickly saw a waning of Western influence in the world. The rise of China and the resurgence of Russia increased their sphere of influence at the cost of ours; the wars in Afghanistan and Iraq cost the West much international prestige and goodwill; troubles in the EU and the 2008 financial collapse further diminished and tarnished the appeal of the Western liberal democratic model. This situation provided the worldwide opportunity for a more authoritarian brand of leadership to rise to power.

The globalization of organized crime and big business is deeply and inextricably tied to the global decline of liberal democracy and the global rise of illiberal democracy in the 21st century. Organized crime and big business are partners in the corruption of Western liberal electoral democracy by buying the candidates who run for elective office. Of course, these candidates know to promise to fight for the people while pocketing the payoffs, legal or illegal, thereby creating distrust in the electorate against politicians and the liberal electoral democratic process.

The facts and figures of the global dynamics of the concentration of wealth and power presented below make clear that ever-greater power and wealth is accumulated by ever-fewer individuals and families. Consider: "Personal wealth around the globe reached $201.9 trillion in 2017, a 12 percent gain from 2016 and the strongest annual pace in the past five years."[34] "The growing ranks of millionaires and billionaires now hold almost half of this global personal wealth, up from slightly less than 45% in 2012."[35] According to *Forbes*, there are some 2,208 billionaires across 72 countries, sharing a combined total of $9.1 trillion.[36] These "billionaires have more wealth than 60% of the world's population," 4.6 billion people.[37]

Together, the top 25 families with the richest fortunes across the globe possess $1.1 trillion in wealth from retail industries, media conglomerates, agribusiness companies, tech giants, and more. These families and their fortunes are tied to each other in a highly interconnected global network that is not just covering but literally squeezing the Earth and its denizens of their resources for their own private benefit. In short, the greatest impediment to solving the multiple global crises threatening to destroy human civilization is the system of ongoing global kleptocracy run by worldwide oligarchs and plutocrats.

The Unequal Distribution of National Wealth

As far as the distribution of the nation's wealth is concerned, the facts are as follows:

- The top 0.00025% of Americans, "the 400 richest people in the nation... own more than the 150 million adults in the bottom 60%."[38]
- The top 0.1% of Americans own almost as much wealth as the bottom 90%.[39]
- The top 1% of Americans controls 40% of the nation's wealth, which is almost as much wealth as the middle and upper middle classes combined.[40]

- Over the last three decades, the top 1% of Americans saw their net worth grow by $21 trillion, while the wealth of the bottom 50% fell by $900 billion.[41]

Based on the rate of economic growth, the numbers are astounding and clearly delineate the process by which, in capitalism, the rich get richer and the poor get poorer.[42] The income of the top 0.1% in the last 30 years rose by an astounding 400%. The income of the 1% as a whole rose by 100%, a rise in income far exceeding the rate of economic growth. The income of 9% of the upper middle class has been growing at a rate almost identical to that of the economy. The income of the 90% of the lower classes has decreased as their incomes are increasingly trailing the rate of economic growth.[43]

What unites the wealthy against the poor is the myth of merit, a shared belief that they, the affluent, owe their success to their talent and intelligence, as opposed to the color of their skin, their sex, or the advantages they've inherited.[44] Under the spell of this conviction, the privileged 10%, segregating themselves in upscale neighborhoods, use their money and influence to get their children into elite colleges and, in general, engage in practices that entrench inequality even as they remain blithely unaware of their role in perpetuating it.[45]

What is important here is not just the facts and percentages of this disparity but that the problem will only get worse and not better. Because these trends are built into the very structural dynamics of capitalism, the elites will continue to get a proportionally larger and larger share of the national wealth pie while the rest of us will continue to get smaller and smaller share of that pie.[46]

But what exactly are those dynamics? How do the rich keep getting richer and the poor keep getting poorer? What is the nature of this reverse Robin Hood scam? How do the rich keep on engaging in class warfare and stealing from the poor?

The Huge Tax Cuts for the Superrich

Because the rich bankroll the politicians and, through them, control public policy, the federal government has handed huge tax cuts to the

290 : The Tao of the Species

small segment of Americans who need those tax cuts the least and gave the smallest, if any, tax cuts to the 99% who needed them most. "Since 2000… the top 1 percent of earners have received 22 percent of all tax cuts… the top 20 percent of earners… have received 65 percent of tax cuts."[47] Just so it's clear who's benefitting least: the working class and the poor! Indeed, "the top-earning 1 percent of households… will pay a combined $111 billion less this year in federal taxes than they would have if the laws had remained unchanged since 2000. That's an enormous windfall. It's more, in total dollars, than the tax cut received over the same period by the entire bottom 60 percent of earners."[48]

Trump's tax cuts for corporations and the rich accelerated inequality to the level where the 400 richest U.S. families are paying a lower tax rate now than the working class. These "400 families paid an average effective tax rate of 23%" in 2018 (the second year of President Donald Trump's new tax law) "while the bottom half of all American households paid an average rate of 24.2%."[49]

In 1950, the tax rate for America's wealthiest was 70%. In 1970, the "richest Americans paid, all taxes included, more than 50% of their income in taxes—twice as much as working-class individuals… In 2018, following the Trump tax reform, and for the first time in the last hundred years, billionaires have paid less than steel workers, schoolteachers and retirees… The wealthy have seen their taxes rolled back to rate last seen in the 1910s, [when] government was only a quarter of the size it is today."[50]

The result of this "inequality spiral" is that "the wealthiest have even more resources to further influence and skew the system to benefit them."[51] The richer the 1% becomes, the more opportunities they have. A large portion of their wealth comes from "huge returns in the stock market in the past decade, to the point that they now control more than half of the equity in the U.S. public and private companies."[52] Of course, while the rich are normally notorious for complaining loudly about the federal deficit, none of them issued any warnings that the tax cuts would inevitably inflate the government debt. Neither did they point out the contradiction that while during his campaign, Trump vowed to eliminate the federal deficit in eight years. Instead, propelled by his tax cuts, it soared 68% to $984 billion by the end of fiscal 2019.[53]

The High Disparity Between CEO and Worker Compensation

Between 1978 and 2017, CEO payouts rose about 1,000% (in 2017 dollars), while the typical worker's salary increased all of 11.2%. Put in slightly different terms, while in the 1950s, the average CEO made 20 times more than their employees, today some are earning more than 1000 times the median salaries of their employees. Three strategies devised by the ultrarich management class account for these outrageous disparities in compensation rates between corporate management and workers:[54]

1. Equity pay packages: The switch to equity pay package proved to be one of the main reasons behind those disproportionate benefits and started in the Clinton era. During their time in Washington, Bill Clinton and his administration passed serious legislation to limit the outrageous salaries CEOs were already receiving at that time. But in the George W. Bush era that followed, these new laws were circumvented by changing the compensation method for CEOs from cash in salaries to equity-based pay package in stock and stock options.

2. Interlocking boards of directors: Of course, a CEO's compensation is voted on by the board of directors of the company. And since the CEOs of many corporations also serve on the board of directors of many other corporations, this creates a reciprocally beneficial situation. By means of interlocking boards of directors, CEO pay gets ratcheted up by boards of directors stocked with other CEOs who can leverage the same reasoning to justify their own ballooning salaries.

3. Stock buybacks: In 2018, $806.4 billion in corporate stock buybacks propped up the market. Why so much in stock

buybacks? Because stock buybacks are a surer path to better pay than capital investments. Capital investments take a longer time to generate a return, but stock buybacks have a faster return because, by reducing the number of available shares, their value will rise, and that will translate into higher CEO pay. So while stock buybacks are not necessarily better for the company, they sure are better for the bosses.

Rubbing salt in the wound, the source of the buyback money was not, as you might think, increased profits created by superior management. Not by a long shot. The source of the money was Trump's corporate tax cut. In 2018, in fact, corporations spent more on buybacks than they did on capital expenditures. In 2019, buybacks were on another record pace. Thanks to the Trump tax cuts, the executives' earnings are being taxed at a lower rate, saving them hundreds of thousands of dollars. Employees, on the other hand, saved only hundreds of dollars, sometimes even less, or none.[55]

The inequality between the rich and poor not only occurs in the distribution of profits in the good times, but also applies in the distribution of pain during the hard times when the rich suffer less and the poor suffer more. The economic crash of 2007 hurt everybody, but it hurt the poor more than the rich. And in the recovery that followed, the same pattern prevailed: the rich recovered faster and the poor recovered slower, if at all. So while the ruling elites might be in a self-congratulatory mode because they figure they saved the system, that is a reality only true for them. Everyone else is still struggling just to get back to where they were before 2008, and they aren't particularly close.

According to the Federal Reserve, the top 10% of working-age households were the only ones who, adjusted for inflation, were richer on average in 2016 than they were in 2007. The other 90% was somewhere between 17 to 35% poorer than they'd been almost a decade before.[56] So if you were wondering why people remained angry so long after the crash, it's simply because they didn't get their fair share of the recovery. [57]

The Concentration of Wealth and Fascism

The rise of fascism in Nazi Germany taught us the truth of the lesson that the concentration of wealth and power is the critical, if not the main, ingredient in the rise of fascism and, therefore, poses an existential threat to liberal, constitutional democracy.[58] In the post–World War I era, the economic structure of Germany was dominated in a short few years by monopolies and cartels. This proved essential in Hitler's consolidation of power. Germany had built up a great series of industrial monopolies in steel, rubber, coal, and other materials. After the monopolies consolidated their power in Germany, they backed and promoted Hitler's rise to power and allowed him to instigate a new world war because it was "good for the economy," i.e., their bank accounts and pocketbooks. After they defeated Germany in that war, the Allies broke up the major Nazi monopolies specifically so that they could not, in the words of the law passed to compel it, be "used by Germany as instruments of political or economic aggression."

Domestically, the U.S realized it had to institute similar measures at home to ensure the U.S. would never be able to follow the German example. In 1950, Congress passed the Anti-Merger Act to politically and economically curb dangerous concentrations. It tasked the Justice Department and Federal Trade Commission to block or undo mergers when the effect was "substantially to lessen competition or to tend to create a monopoly." In recent years the anti-monopolistic measures the U.S. undertook post–World War II have been eliminated or diluted. The result, not surprisingly, has been not just to fail to stop the increasing concentration of wealth in the U.S., but to actually encourage it, creating a parallel situation between 1930s Germany and the USA today insofar as creating the opportunity for fascism to arise.

In the healthcare field, we have allowed the unhealthy consolidations of hospitals and the pharmaceutical industry. In the tech industry, we have failed to prevent firms like Facebook from buying up their competitors. We have allowed an extraordinarily concentrated banking industry to develop despite its repeated malfeasance.

AT&T, after a well-deserved breakup in the 1980s, has been allowed to reconsolidate. Over the last two decades, more than 75% of United States industries have experienced an increase in concentration, while United States public markets have lost almost 50% of their publicly traded firms.

The link between concentration of wealth and power and the distortion of democratic process can be very direct. For example, concentrated industries, like the pharmaceutical industry, find it easy to organize to take from the public for their own benefit. Take the law that prevents Medicare from negotiating for lower drug prices. Though that particular lobbying project cost the industry more than $100 million, the payoff was well worth it. As a direct result, the pharmaceutical industry receives some $15 billion a year in higher payments for its products.

The Obscenity of Too Much Money

So, what are the 1% superrich doing with all this money? In a fascinating article in Axios, Dion Rabouin describes the "truly bizarre" trend that is profoundly impacting the economy: "wealthy people and corporations have so much money they literally don't know what to do with it."[59] ICI chief economist Sean Collins points out that there are two things that money can do: (1) Money can "sit on a balance sheet unused... [as] earned income earning an interest rate of zero,"[60] or (2) it can be used to finance stock buybacks or dividends. Neil Shearing, chief economist at Capital Economics, identified a third thing money could do: increase wages for workers. But he rejected it as an unrealistic option because "that would be terrible for the stock market," leaving Collins's second option of financing stock buyback and dividends as the "rational" business decision.[61]

"Companies made a record $1.1 trillion in stock buybacks in 2018... but they still have record cash holdings of close to $3 trillion... and private equity has seen so much cash flow that firms have $2 trillion of unused capital. But even that hasn't been enough to account for all the new money. The top 1% of U.S. households are holding a record $303.9 billion in cash, a quantum leap from the under $15 billion they held just before the financial crisis"[62] of 2007. Federal Reserve Board policies and the globalization of the labor force were instrumental in allowing the process to get started. The first made the cost of borrowing money next to nothing for a decade while the second allowed companies to reduce labor costs. Both factors contributed to making huge amounts of money available for mergers and acquisitions, boosting revenue and stock prices. And combined with legislative policies that have consistently favored business owners over workers, these factors eroded unions and reduced employees' ability to demand higher wages.

The Trump tax cut only "exacerbated these issues, slashing the share of U.S. taxes that companies paid to its lowest level in at least half a century and provided companies even more capital for buybacks, dividends and executive compensation." As Mark Hackett, chief of investment research at Nationwide, told Axios, "the fallacy of the tax plan to begin with was companies were not starved for capital… They were starved for growth opportunities."[63] The shame and guilt of the 1% is that money that would previously have been split between businesses, workers, and the government for projects like education, healthcare, and infrastructure is, instead, sitting in corporate accounts, earning little to no return. And for decades, these superrich alleged masters of the universe—basking in the glow of their own self-confidence—celebrated their success at growing their fortunes, at the expense and detriment of the 99%, while attending the Davos World Economic Forum, an annual convening of the global 1%.

Forebodings of the Rich

At 2019's Davos conference of the ultrarich, the atmosphere was dark and pessimistic. Foreboding about the future was a prevailing theme, delivered often with a dash of dystopian prophecy. That year, the billionaires came off as perplexed and anxious about the future as the populist forces inveighed against them.

That year, it appeared that with all their money, entourages, and commanding views, both literal and metaphorical, many of the global movers and shakers were beginning to realize that they didn't have a clue as to what was really happening and were getting the feeling that they may be on a "toboggan ride to hell."[64]

This brooding was accompanied often, in speeches and interviews, by a rueful acknowledgment that government leaders are desperately improvising—often with bleak results—to meet the political crises of the moment, more so than the long-term technological and climatological challenges of the age. Listen to the one-percenters themselves ruminating on the impending implosion of the global political and economic system:

- United Nations Secretary-General António Guterres expressed "the general theme of people being buffeted by their circumstances rather than master of them": "Everybody agrees that there are dark clouds on the horizon, and there are risks," and added that on climate change, "I believe we are losing the race... And we have this paradox: The reality is proving to be worse than scientists had foreseen, and all the last indicators show that."[65]
- Tiger Tyagarajan, CEO of professional services firm Genpact, agreed, describing the "prevailing mood" as "more somber than last year... There's so many question marks [about political factors]... I don't think that any... [Davos attendees...] are masters of their destinies; I don't think they control their own situations."[66]
- Eric Weinstein, managing editor of Thiel Capital, summed the problem up succinctly:
    "The greatest danger is that the truly rich, I'm talking nine and 10 figures rich, are increasingly separated from the lives of the rest of us so that they become largely insensitive to the concerns of those who still earn by the hour. As such, they will probably not anticipate many of the changes, and we will see the beginning stirrings of revolution as the cost for this insensitivity."[67]

- Ray Dalio, founder of Bridgewater Associates, worth $16 billion, agrees and his assessment is that we've "seen capitalism evolve in a way that it is not working well for the majority of Americans because it's producing self-reinforcing spirals up for the haves and down for the have-nots." He elaborated that "disparity in wealth, especially when accompanied by disparity in values, leads to increasing conflict and, in the government, that manifests itself in the form of populism of the left and populism of the right and often in revolutions of one sort or another."[68]

Endnotes

1   Kurt Anderson, Evil Geniuses: The Unmaking of America: A Recent History, (New York: Random House, 2020).

2   Ibid.

3   Ibid.

4   Friedman, Milton, and Rose D. Friedman, Capitalism and Freedom, (Chicago: University of Chicago Press, 1962).

5   Ibid.

6   Kurt Anderson, Evil Geniuses: The Unmaking of America: A Recent History, (New York: Random House, 2020), 55.

7   Ibid.

8   Ibid., 59.

9   Ibid.

10   Ibid.

11   Ibid.

12   Jane Mayer, Dark Money: The Hidden History of the Billionaires Behind the Rise of the Radical Right, (New York: Anchor, 2017).

13   Kurt Anderson, Evil Geniuses: The Unmaking of America: A Recent History, (New York: Random House, 2020), 71.

14   Ibid.

15   Lilia Vega, "The History of UC Tuition Since 1868," Daily Californian, December 22, 2014, https://dailycal.org/2014/12/22/history-uc-tuition-since-1868.

16   Ibid.

17   J. A. Del Real, "The reinvention of a 'Real Man'," WaPo, 5/23/22

18   David Nir, "We Must Turn the Page on Kyrsten Sinema. Ruben Gallego's Just the Democrat to Do It," Daily Kos, June 15, 2023, https://www.dailykos.com/blog/David%20Nir.

19   Open Secrets, "Cost of Election," n.d., https://www.opensecrets.org/overview/cost.php.

20   Reuters and Bob Ryan, "The Most Vulnerable Republicans in the 2018 Midterms Are Talking Less and Less About Trump's Tax Bill," Business Insider, May 7, 2018, https://www.businessinsider.com/trump-gop-tax-law-republican-primary-ads-2018-5.

21   Zachary D. Carter, "Corruption Is Bad," HuffPost, May 2, 2018, https://www.huffpost.com/entry/government-anti-corruption-oversight_n_5ae8e4ebe4b06748dc8d4b43.

22   Paul Krugman, "Notes on Excessive Wealth Disorder," New York Times, June 22, 2019, https://www.nytimes.com/2019/06/22/opinion/notes-on-excessive-wealth-disorder.html.

23   NowThisNews, "Rep. Alexandria Ocasio-Cortez Calls Out Dark Money," Twitter, February 7, 2019, https://twitter.com/nowthisnews/status/1093680562424836096?ref%5Fsrc=twsrc%5Etfw%7Ctwcamp%5Etweetembed%7Ctwterm%5E1093680562424836096%26ref%5Furl=https%3A%2F%2Fwww.bustle.com%2Fp%2Falexandria-ocasio-cortezs-take-on-campaign-finance-laws-points-to-some-a.

24   Ibid.

25   Ibid.

26 Ibid.

27 Alan S. Blinder and Mark W. Watson "Presidents and the Economy: A Forensic Investigation" in "Trump's Turn? Republican Presidents Rule Recessions," Matt Kranz, USA Today, November 20, 2016, https://www.usatoday.com/story/money/markets/2016/11/20/trumps-turn-republican-presidents-rule-recessions/93976832/.

28 Ibid.

29 Ibid.

30 Ibid.

31 Elvis Picardo, "Asset Bubbles Through History: The 5 Biggest," Investopedia, April 19, 2022, https://www.investopedia.com/articles/personal-finance/062315/five-largest-asset-bubbles-history.asp.

32 Ibid.

33 Ibid.

34 Suzanne Woolley, "Millionaires Now Own Half of World's Personal Wealth," Bloomberg, June 15, 2018, https://www.bloomberg.com/news/articles/2018-06-14/millionaires-now-control-half-of-world-s-personal-wealth#xj4y7vzkg.

35 Bloomberg, "Rich Are Getting Richer Faster, Millionaires Now Own Half of World's Personal Wealth: Report," Hindustan Times, June 16, 2018, https://www.hindustantimes.com/world-news/rich-are-getting-richer-faster-millionaires-now-own-half-of-world-s-personal-wealth-report/story-4IFDCSjxEUpNHT8VNcyMJL.html.

36 Forbes Staff, "Forbes' 32nd Annual World's Billionaires Issue," Forbes, March 6, 2018, https://www.forbes.com/sites/forbespr/2018/03/06/forbes-32nd-annual-worlds-billionaires-issue/?sh=6982bfff10e0.

37 Josiah Bates, "Billionaires Have More Wealth Than 60% of the World's Population, Report Finds," Time, January 20, 2020, https://time.com/5768346/billionaires-wealth/.

38 Mary Papenfuss, "400 Richest Americans Own More Than 150 Million of the Nation's Poorest: Study," HuffPost, February 11, 2019, https://www.huffpost.com/entry/400-richest-own-more-than-150-million-poorest_n_5c60f627e4b0eec79b250c34.

39 Betsy Reed ed., "US Wealth Inequality – Top 0.1% Worth as Much as the Bottom 90%," The Guardian, November 13, 2014, https://www.theguardian.com/business/2014/nov/13/us-wealth-inequality-top-01-worth-as-much-as-the-bottom-90.

40 Mary Papenfuss, "400 Richest Americans Own More Than 150 Million of the Nation's Poorest: Study," HuffPost, February 11, 2019, https://www.huffpost.com/entry/400-richest-own-more-than-150-million-poorest_n_5c60f627e4b0eec79b250c34.

41 Matt Bruenig, "Top 1% Up $21 Trillion. Bottom 50% Down $900 Billion," People's Policy Project, June 14, 2019, https://www.peoplespolicyproject.org/2019/06/14/top-1-up-21-trillion-bottom-50-down-900-billion/.

42 David Leonhardt, "How the Upper Middle Class Is Really Doing," New York Times, February 24, 2019, https://www.nytimes.com/2019/02/24/opinion/income-inequality-upper-middle-class.html.

43 Ibid.

44 Eyal Press, "To Understand Inequality, Look at the 9.9 Percent," New York Times, November 18, 2021, book review of The 9.9 Percent: The New Aristocracy That Is Entrenching Inequality and Warping Our Culture by Matthew Stewart, (New York: Simon and Schuster, 2021), https://www.nytimes.com/2021/11/18/books/review/the-99-percent-matthew-stewart.html.

45 Ibid.

46 Megan McArdle, "The College Admissions Scam Reveals a Truth About Our Self-Perpetuation Elites," Washington Post, March 14, 2019, https://www.washingtonpost.com/opinions/the-college-admissions-scam-reveals-a-truth-about-our-self-perpetuating-elites/2019/03/14/a769b3a8-4684-11e9-90f0-0ccfeec87a61_story.html.

47 David Leonhardt, "$111 Billion in Tax Cuts for the 1 Percent," New York Times, July 11, 2018, https://www.nytimes.com/2018/07/11/opinion/trump-republicans-tax-cuts-inequality.html.

48 Ibid.

49 Mary Papenfuss, "400 Richest U.S. Families Paid Lower Tax Rate Than Working Class, Study Finds," HuffPost, October 11, 2019, https://www.huffpost.com/entry/richest-families-tax-rate-inequality_n_5d9fdd42e4b02c9da047ac23.

50 Ibid.

51 Ibid.

52 Matt Bruenig, "Top 1% Up $21 Trillion. Bottom 50% Down $900 Billion," People's Policy Project, June 14, 2019, https://www.peoplespolicyproject.org/2019/06/14/top-1-up-21-trillion-bottom-50-down-900-billion/.

53 Mary Papenfuss, op.cit.

54 Bill Saporito, "C.E.O. Pay, America's Economic 'Miracle,'" New York Times, May 17, 2019, https://www.nytimes.com/2019/05/17/opinion/ceo-pay-raises.html.

55 Ibid.

56 Ibid.

57 Mat O'Brian, "The Class Structure of the Economic Recovery," Washington Post, October 2, 2018.

58 Tim Wu, "Be Afraid of Economic 'Bigness.' Be Very Afraid," New York Times, November 10, 2018, https://www.nytimes.com/2018/11/10/opinion/sunday/fascism-economy-monopoly.html.

59 Dion Rabouin, "Too Much Money (and Too Few Places to Invest It)," Axios, June 6, 2019, https://www.axios.com/2019/06/06/money-companies-investors-assets-buybacks-dividends.

60 Ibid.

61 Ibid.

62 Ibid.

63 Ibid.

64 John F. Harris, "Davos Elites Fear They're on a Toboggan Ride to Hell," Politico Magazine, January 24, 2019, https://www.politico.com/magazine/story/2019/01/24/davos-economic-forum-2019-224216/.

65 Ibid.

66 Ibid.

67 Sean Illing, "I Interview Interesting People for Vox. Here Are the 5 Coolest Conversations I Had in 2017," Vox, December 22, 2017, https://www.vox.com/2017-in-review/2017/12/22/16769534/2017-year-in-review-vox-conversations.

68 Bess Levin, "Billionaire Hedge-Fund Manager Warns a 'Revolution' Is Coming," Vanity Fair, April 5, 2019, https://www.vanityfair.com/news/2019/04/ray-dalio-capitalism-revolution.

Chapter 14

The American People's Descent into Dystopia

The Stress of Life and the Yin-Yang of Unhappiness

The Pursuit of Happiness

The Declaration of Independence stated that people, i.e. "the People," have the "unalienable right" to "Life, Liberty and the pursuit of Happiness." But how is it that as a nation dedicated to the pursuit of happiness, we have wound up a nation caught in the vicious dynamic of the yin-yang of unhappiness? Why, as a society, do we burden our people with such widespread stress and anxiety as to lead to widespread depression and suicide when internalized and to widespread aggression and violence when externalized?

Unfortunately, the health and happiness of the people are not improving. In fact, on the whole, they are going in the wrong direction. The quality of life and the exercise of true liberty are sliding down a slippery slope of deterioration. Instead of being happy and well as a result of the pursuit of happiness, 99% of modern folk are drowning in an ocean of stress, swamped by distress and anxiety imposed on them by their exploitation in the 1% White Man's system. As stress and anxiety levels in society are increasing at exponential rates, health and happiness are decreasing proportionally.

"As U.S. performance on a range of health and social measures has been deteriorating," America's performance is not any better than most developing countries, many of which "score better than we do on a range of quality of life indices and markers of health and longevity." These include "life expectancy, working conditions, mothers' well-being, school performance, crime rates and violent death rates to mention a few. Could these factors explain our high stress levels and low levels of happiness?"[1]

The overwhelming majority of individuals in modern society suffer chronic stress and anxiety. Every dimension of an individual's identity has become a source for them. If you're a father, a mother, a son, or a daughter, you will be stressed and experience anxiety on that account. If you are white, Black, or in between, you will be stressed and experience anxiety on that account. If you are male, female, or in between, you will be stressed and experience anxiety on that account. If you're a student, a blue-collar worker, a white-collar worker, or a retired person, you will be stressed and experience anxiety on that account.

For the 99%, these stresses and anxieties have been part of our lives for so long that they have become chronic over time, always there, gnawing away at our well-being, threatening to overtake us, and never relenting in making us, the people, a bunch of really unhappy campers. And for all of us, it takes a continual effort to push these feelings down, to not give in to them and express them in order to remain functional and not lose it—our sanity, that is. But because these stresses and anxieties are cumulative. Many people cannot push down those fears and anxieties forever, and they reach the breaking point. On the one hand, chronically repressed fears and anxieties lead to mental depression, physical illness, and suicide. On the other hand, chronically repressed anger and rage leads to aggression and violence, both nonpolitical and political.

Family Life: An Institution in Crisis
Deeply troubling trends in America are stressing women's lives and posing increasing threats to their physical and emotional well-being. As a female, your access to abortion rights has become ever more restricted. Chances are that, as a female, you too may be affected

by declining fertility rates, rising mortality rate while giving birth, rising infant death rate, and rising infant poverty rates. According to the Centers for Disease Control and Prevention (CDC), the total U.S. fertility rate (i.e., the number of births that a woman is expected to have over her lifetime), is at an all-time low of 1.73. "This rate is well below the 2.10 births per woman needed for a generation to replace itself."[2]

As access to reproductive healthcare services has eroded, the well-being of our nation's mothers has been steadily deteriorating. Today America has the highest maternal mortality rate of all industrialized countries.[3] The mortality rate among American women between ages 15 and 45 has increased by 14% between 2010 and 2016.[4] And American women are 50% more likely to die in childbirth than their mothers. For Black women, the risks are three to four times higher than white women.[5] And for every death, hundreds of women experience childbirth complications that bring them to the brink and tens of thousands more suffer from preventable and undertreated chronic illnesses.

With respect to infant mortality, the United States is outpacing all other major developed countries. "An estimated 11,300 newborn babies die each year in the United States on the day they are born. This is 50 percent more first-day deaths than all other industrialized countries combined."[6] For example, the death rate in the United States was 5.7 per 1,000 births in 2017. That number is significantly higher than that of Canada (4.8 per 1,000 births), the United Kingdom (3.9 per 1,000 births), Australia (3.4 per 1,000 births), and Japan (2.1 per 1,000 births).[7]

If the newborn survives the odds against it, the environment that awaits it in infancy is as challenging to its survival as merely being born. The Organization for Economic Cooperation and Development (OECD), a group of 30 democratic countries, defined child poverty as "the ratio of 0 to 17-year-olds whose income falls below the country's poverty line."[8] According to that criteria, the U.S. has a higher child poverty rate than nearly all other OECD countries, with millions of American children suffering every day from abuse, neglect, malnourishment, poverty, and discrimination.

Every year, 13.1 million American households with children are considered "food-insecure," meaning they often go without enough food. In a given year, one in every 30 children in the United States experiences homelessness, which translates to about 2.5 million kids. Every year, an estimated 676,000 children are victims of child abuse or neglect, and a little fewer than 2,000 American kids die from it. This result is not surprising in view of the fact that the amount of money the U.S. spends yearly on family benefits (1.5% of GDP) is far less than what the OECD countries spend (2.43% of GDP).[9]

Based on in-depth interviews with working-class men, the economic, private, religious, and cultural dimensions of their life were found to be deeply scattered and disintegrated by the disruptive and dehumanizing aspects of capitalism.[10] Many men complained that the economy prevents them from attaining the same standard of living that their fathers achieved. To make up for this, they often bounce between three or four occupations or engage in side-hustles to make ends meet, causing their work lives to be fragmented and anxiety-ridden.

The private lives of these men are as loosely attached as their economic lives. The main finding in this area was that "Nearly all the men… viewed the father-child tie as central while the partner relationship was more peripheral."[11] They consistently expressed the desire to be better fathers to their kids than their fathers had been to them. But they expressed no similar commitment to the women who had given birth to their offspring and generally proved unwilling to remain in a family unit to try and work things out.

Regarding church life, these men are equally detached. Most say they are spiritual and pray, but their concept of faith is so individualized that there is no one else to share and practice it with. Generally they express contempt for organized religion and do not want to tie themselves down to any specific religious organization. "I treat church just like I treat my girlfriends," one man said. "I'll stick around for a while and then I'll go on to the next one." Another said he believed in God, but he rejected the idea of "a God with strings telling us how to live. That didn't work for me."[12]

"About 40% of adults said that, if faced with a $400 unexpected expense, they would either not be able to pay it or would do so by selling something or borrowing money, according to the Federal Reserve's Report on the Economic Well-Being of U.S. Households in 2017... Additionally, less than 40 percent of nonretired adults think they are on track in saving for their golden years and 25 percent have no retirement savings or pension at all, the report says."[13]

"We live in a fatherless nation," says John Kim, a therapist who has worked with hundreds of troubled teenagers and their parents. He recently pointed out in an article that "the common thread in over 95 percent of... troubled teens was an absent father. Dad was either physically or emotionally gone."[14] An absent father implies a dysfunctional family structure. And indeed, for the past half century, socio-economic trends have steadily eroded the traditional model of the stable family unit, where the dad was the head of the family, made up of a breadwinning father and a stay-at-home mom. These days, more often than not, the mom is the breadwinner of the family and the dad is nowhere to be seen or heard or felt.

As a result, "men everywhere [are] feeling lost or misunderstood, living without purpose and passion, and needing to inflate physical or superficial details to make up for what's lacking on the inside. Or giving up altogether."[15] If boys don't get from their dads what it takes to be a man, like true self-esteem, they get trapped in a vicious repeating cycle of also growing up to become fathers whose sons don't live with them.

Student Life: Habituating Anxiety
A 2018 study by the American College Health Association reported that more than 60% of college students said they had experienced "overwhelming anxiety" in the past year and over 40% said they felt so depressed they had difficulty functioning. Between the fall of

2009 and spring of 2015, the number of students who visited campus counseling centers increased by more than 30%.

Suicidal thinking, severe depression, and rates of self-injury among U.S. college students more than doubled over less than a decade, a nationwide study suggests. From 2007 to 2018:[16]

- "Rates of moderate to severe anxiety rose from 17.9% in 2013 to 34.4% in 2018."
- "The rate of moderate to severe depression rose from 23.2% in 2007 to 41.1% in 2018."
- "The proportion of students reporting severe depression rose from 9.4% in 2007 to 21.1% in 2018."
- "Student suicide attempts increased from 0.7% in 2013 to 1.8% in 2018."

It's not just the crises like the surge in school shootings and trauma from suicides and sexual assault that have shaken this generation. It's the everyday stresses, from social media pressures to relationship problems to increased academic expectations, that are grinding students down psychologically and emotionally. Money problems are exacerbating their worries. College students today experience financial burdens on a different scale than many of their predecessors. They grew up during the Great Recession and have seen family members lose jobs and homes.

Students are also part of a new class of growing numbers of single adults, who have experienced the breakdown of the family and the loss of neighborhood and community. These factors have all contributed to an immense sense of loneliness in many young people's lives. Indeed, nearly 50% of people surveyed admitted to feeling lonely or left out most of the time in their daily existence.[17] The potential effects of loneliness on health are, of course, well established. Loneliness causes elevated levels of stress hormones and inflammation, which in turn, can increase the risk of heart disease, dementia, Type 2 diabetes, and suicide attempts.[18]

Students today have great uncertainty about their career prospects and feel pressure to excel academically or risk losing job opportunities. It's like the student community today is infected by the feeling that you're either a winner or a loser. In the (peer) pressure cooker of today's dog-eat-dog student world, rank and performance count excessively and winning and self-interest are extolled as the supreme values. This climate in academia has put tremendous pressure on college students, is contributing a lot to the rising levels of anxiety we're seeing, and is turning our student population into a dysfunctional community of lonely perfectionists.[19]

The Religion of Work

When young adults finish their schooling, they enter the workforce only to meet new challenges there. The prevailing philosophy of work, rooted in Protestant ideology, all too often turns the dreams of happiness of those entering the workforce into the nightmare of stress and anxiety. The Protestant work ethic, as it arose in early capitalism, had a double function. The down-to-earth, secular reason, of course, was to provide cheap labor so that the capitalist owners could line their pockets with the profit. This base reality was sugarcoated by the religious dogma that believers needed to work in order to secure their access to heaven. Religious admonitions continually emphasized to the faithful that "God helps those who help themselves." You had to earn heaven and the afterlife by working your ass off in this life. Otherwise, it's the pits of hellfire and brimstone for you![20]

In the capitalism of the 19th century, in both Europe and America, with religion on the wane and the meaning of life without religion deteriorating, puritan Protestantism began to emphasize the value of work for its own sake. After the industrial revolution, these ideas were expressed emphatically by 19th-century philosopher Thomas Carlyle's theories in what he called the "Gospel of Work:" "All work, even cotton-spinning, is noble; work alone is noble, be that here said and asserted once more... Oh brother, if this is not 'worship,' then I say, the more the duty for worship; for this is the noblest thing yet discovered under God's sky. Who art thou that complaints of thy life of toil? Complain not."[21]

Under the barbaric 19th-century work conditions and relentless hours of early industrial capitalism, anything went. Owners felt free to squeeze their labor force for all they could get away with: child labor, 80-hour work weeks, what have you. They got away with almost everything because there were no laws against anything.

The greatest expression of the Carlyle ethos was expressed in the concentration camps of Nazi Germany, itself the result of the oligarchic consolidation of capitalist wealth. In Auschwitz, for example, the Germans who, in the Christian tradition, delighted in torturing the pagans "for their own good and salvation," erected a huge arc over its entrance gate that, in giant letters, proclaimed to all incoming inmates that "Arbeit Macht Frei" ("work makes [you] free" or "labor liberates").

In the U.S., it took untold lives, even more untold injuries, and a long and backbreaking struggle of labor to organize itself and fight back to establish less draconian working conditions. The 40-hour week was a hard-won concession, a victory for humanity over capitalism's unquenchable thirst for greater profits through greater exploitation. It was the leadership of FDR and his New Deal that put on the brakes on the exploitation of the working class by the captains of industry and big business. In the 1930s, that started a political tradition based on the strength of labor to moderate the excesses of capitalism that lasted into the '60s and '70s. It was during the Reagan years and the decades of the "greed is good" mentality, that a crew of evil geniuses began to reanimate Carlyle's "work as religion" movement.

In the 21st century, these efforts paid off with the emergence of a job phenomenon known variously as the as the TGIM (Thank God It's Monday) culture, the hustle culture, or the gig economy.[22] It evolved principally in the tech and financial sectors as a means of tapping into the labor pool of the millennial generation and put them to work. But whatever you want to call it, at its root, it's just the Protestant work ethic on steroids. The credo of this 21st century capitalism is "performative workaholism," and its devotees strive to be the best employees. They do so by showing unending loyalty to work, habitually putting in 18-hour workdays and staying late hours as well as being on call for bosses and clients anytime, all the time. At the coworking spaces WeWork, the throw pillows implore tenants to "do what you love." Neon signs demand they "hustle harder." The water coolers tell you, "don't stop when you're tired, stop when you're done."

It's the managers, financiers, and owners who are beating the drums of hustle-mania; the people buying into it and doing the actual work, increasingly less so. The difference, of course, is due to the gap in expected benefits. Elon Musk, for example, is an enthusiastic advocate of the "extreme work" credo, demanding and extolling the work by the many that will primarily benefit him. Press stories glowingly describe how, during very intensive production runs, Musk proves his solidarity with his workers by sleeping at the plant. But they fail to mention the real truth that if Tesla meets certain performance levels, Musk stands to reap stock compensation upward of $50 billion, of which no more than a minute amount trickles down to Joe Blow on the assembly line. Thus, overwork persists because it's used to create the extreme wealth for a small group of elite techies. But for the workers, it's grim and exploitative. And Musk does not deny it: "Nobody ever changed the world on 40 hours a week." The "correct" number of hours "varies per person," Musk explained, but it's "about 80 sustained, peaking above 100 at times. Pain level increases exponentially above 80."[23]

The millennials are a generation that was raised to expect that good grades and extracurricular achievement would reward them with fulfilling jobs that would feed their passions. How then, did they wind up becoming a new generation of alienated workers trapped in meaningless work and a mountain of student loan debt?[24] Usually, the process begins with the individual's economic necessity of having to make a living to make ends meet and pay off the accumulated debts. Aggravating the stress of financial burdens are preexisting conditions of psychic dis-ease, dissatisfaction with family relations, and the inability of traditional religion to deliver spiritual and social comforts. Under these conditions, work easily and often becomes an escape, offering millennials this new religion of work as a way to fill the inner void of a life emptied of spiritual meaning and empathy. As Roger Cohen put it, "emptiness is what people feel. At the end of all the myriad diversions offered up by technology-at-the-service-of-efficiency lies a great hollowness."[25] And what can fill this emptiness? Work, work, and more work! Everything and anything that optimizes their day and fits in even more work is desirable and good.

The spiritual and emotional toxicity of the "work as religion" culture is increasingly causing severe psychological distress in its workers. Half the time, workers are engaged in utterly meaningless or even counterproductive activities, usually under the orders of a person they dislike. Knowing that they have bullshit jobs that make no meaningful contribution to the world, and that the existence of their jobs is not really justified, workers are deeply dissatisfied with their lot. How can one even begin to speak of dignity in labor when one secretly feels one's job should not exist?

The 24/7 pressure of the attitude "to conform, comply, and compete" that exalts the ability to work as the highest human spiritual value is not only dehumanizing in its toxicity, but in the long run, it is also not sustainable. Its toxic mix of hatred, resentment, and suspicion has become the glue that holds the "work as religion" culture together. In the long run, Elon Musk, et al., cannot deliver spiritual fulfillment through participation in a visionary project indefinitely. The bubble will burst, and the deeply unhappy human being in this bubble will realize that (s)he was taken for a ride. The fury building up slowly inside the millennial psyche is already beginning to generate the "anything-but-this" anger that is asserting itself in the politics of developed societies.

The Yin of Unhappiness

The Mounting Toll of Stress Disease

The effects of prolonged chronic stress and anxiety from so many sources on the general health of the people are devastating in its consequences. People suffer from a number of debilitating physical ailments and diseases that are directly and indirectly caused by stress and anxiety.

The link between stress, anxiety, and eating disorders is a natural one that has been long recognized. Food is comforting; it is security. And many folks, when they are stressed and anxious, eat, often too much and often the wrong kinds of food that only make things worse. A dramatic increase in the prevalence of obesity appears to be one driver of the phenomenon. Altogether, more than 70% of Americans ages 20 and older are overweight.[26] Half of America will be obese within 10 years, a new NEJM study says. "One in four Americans will be 'severely obese' with a body mass index over 35, which means they will be more than 100 pounds overweight."[27]

Closely related to the obesity epidemic is the diabetes epidemic. "Diabetes is a chronic (long-lasting) health condition that affects how your body turns food into energy."[28] Over 37 million U.S. adults have diabetes, "and 1 in 5 of them don't know they have it." About 90 to 95% of people with diabetes have Type 2, which develops over many years and is usually diagnosed in adults, but more and more in children, teens, and young adults. Diabetes is the eighth leading cause of death in the United States, and the number one cause of kidney failure, lower-limb amputations, and adult blindness. Moreover, in the United States, more than one in three people have prediabetes, 80% of whom don't know they have it. Prediabetes significantly raises one's risk for Type 2 diabetes, heart disease, and stroke.[29]

Both obesity and diabetes are hugely important contributing factors to the nation's epidemic of cardio-vascular disease, the leading cause of death for men and women of all races. One fifth of all deaths in the U.S. each year, some 695,000 people, die from heart disease.

Each year the most common type of cardiovascular disease alone, coronary artery disease, kills some 375,476 people. Fully 5% of the population age 20 or over, have CAD (coronary artery disease). Every year, some 805,000 people suffer a heart attack, which amounts to someone in the U.S. having a heart attack every 40 seconds.[30]

In short, contributing factors of heart disease are many, including high blood pressure, high cholesterol, smoking, diabetes, being over-weight, obesity, unhealthy diet, physical inactivity, excessive alcohol use, and importantly, sleep deprivation.

Sleep deprivation is a profound stressor on the human system. Behaviorally, it causes memory issues and mood changes as well as dif-ficulty with thinking, coordination, and balance, leading to increased risks of accidents. Sleep-deprivation-induced fatigue and drowsiness, "the National Highway Traffic Safety Administration estimates... is a cause in 100,000 auto crashes and 1,550 crash-related deaths a year in the U.S."[31]

Multiple "studies show that sleep loss and poor-quality sleep lead to accidents and injuries on the job. In one study, workers who com-plained about excessive daytime sleepiness had significantly more work accidents, particularly repeated work accidents. They also had more sick days per accident."[32]

Indeed, "sleep deprivation was a factor in some of the biggest disasters in recent history: the 1979 nuclear accident at Three Mile Island, the massive Exxon Valdez oil spill, the 1986 nuclear melt-down at Chernobyl, and others." All this makes sleep loss "a big pub-lic safety hazard every day on the road."[33]

All these facts make one thing abundantly clear: though we may be the wealthiest nation in human history, we're certainly proving to be not the healthiest. On the contrary, it seems like we're giving all the other countries of the world a run for their money in becoming the unhealthiest nation. With midlife mortality rate on the rise, life expec-tancy in the U.S. declined for the third consecutive year in 2017.[34] At the other end, the nation's total fertility rate is now insufficient to maintain our existing population in the absence of immigration due to a steadily falling birthrate that, in 2018, hit a three-decade low.[35]

And while birth rates are falling, and our health is failing and our life expectancy is dropping, healthcare costs are rising. Health insurance "costs an annual average of almost $23,000 to cover a family… enough to buy a new Volkswagen every year."[36] "Altogether, the U.S. spent $3.6 trillion… on healthcare [in 2018]. We spend far more than any other wealthy country, and we are no healthier for it."[37]

Why on earth is it necessary that people must suffer so much illness and death from stress? The answer to that question is, as we've known all along, that there is no reason! Except, of course, the insatiable needs for more profit and power by the 1%.

Depression, Substance Abuse and Suicide

Today 40 million adults, 20% of the adult population, suffer from an anxiety disorder. "In 2017, more than 17 million Americans had at least one major depressive episode," and the number of adults "who described themselves as more anxious than the previous year was 36 percent."[38] And these are just the known cases of depression and anxiety. The actual numbers must be staggering. Given the statistics on depression, it is not surprising that suicide rates have also risen in a similar manner. "The annual death rate by suicide has steadily risen in the US since the turn of the millennium, according to a new report released by the Centers for Disease Control and Prevention."[39] Suicide rates in the U.S. have increased nearly 30% in less than 20 years, the CDC reported. From 1999 to 2016, the report found, the annual rate of suicide rose by nearly 30% among Americans over the age of 10. In 2016 (the latest year for which we have national data), nearly 45,000 Americans committed suicide, more than double the number of Americans known to have been murdered that same year. The sad truth is that suicide is the tenth leading cause of death among all Americans.[40]

More men die by suicide than women, and more white men than non-white men. And while white men as a group amount to only

30% of the population as a whole, fully 70% of the almost 46,000 who people died by suicide in the U.S. in 2020 were men. It is a rate that has climbed steadily over the past 20 years, making white men the highest-risk group for suicide in the country, especially in middle age, even as they are vastly over-represented in positions of power in the U.S. These facts are increasingly causing clinical researchers and suicide experts to ask whether there is "something particular about White American masculinity worth interrogating further."[41]

"The largest absolute increase in suicides was seen among people aged 45 to 64, though increases were seen across every age and racial/ethnic group, as well as in every urbanization level, from cities to rural areas. Firearms remained the most common cause of death overall, though rates of suicide by firearms were nearly double in rural areas compared to urban counties."[42] The CDC report noted "the mortality rate from drug poisoning, alcohol poisoning, and suicide increased by 52% between 2000 and 2014." In 2016, 42,249 people in the U.S. died from an opioid overdose, which is nearly as many as the number of people who died by suicide that year. The suicide rate in the U.S. is increasing steadily. Whereas from 2000 to 2006, it rose by an average of about 1% a year, from 2006 through 2016, it increased by 2% a year. There were 1.4 million suicide attempts in 2017 and 47,000 deaths.[43]

When people are stressed, they seek to escape their stress. One of the more readily available escape hatches is substance abuse. Almost 20 million American adults (aged 12 and older) suffered this disorder and engaged in substance abuse in 2017. "According to the National Survey on Drug Use and Health… in 2017 approximately 4% of the American adolescent population age 12 to 17 suffered from a substance use disorder." About 443,000 (1.8%) of them had an alcohol use problem, and an estimated 741,000 (3%) of them had an illicit drug use problem.[44]

In 2017, "about 5.1 million young adults age 18 to 25 battled a substance use disorder." This "equates to 14.8% of this population… about 1 in 7 people." About 3.4 million, or 10% of this population, had an alcohol use disorder, and "about 2.5 million… had an illicit drug use disorder... or about 7.3%." Heroin use, especially, rose sharply, more than doubling among this population in the past decade.[45]

"Approximately 13.6 million adults aged 26 or older [6.4% of this age group] struggled with a substance use disorder. About 10.6 million... had an alcohol use disorder... about 5% of this age group," and "about 4.3 million [2% of this age group]... had an illicit drug use disorder."[46] Moreover, "1 out of every 8 adults struggled with both alcohol and drug use disorders simultaneously... 8.5 million American adults suffered from both a mental health disorder and a substance use disorder, or co-occurring disorders."[47]

In individuals aged 65 or older, "more than 1 million *elderly* adults... had a substance abuse disorder." Some "978,000 of people in this age group had an alcohol use disorder and about 93,000 had an illicit drug use disorder." Significantly, "between 21% and 66% of elderly individuals battling a substance use disorder also suffer from a co-occurring mental health disorder."[48]

The Yang of Unhappiness

Violence: The Numbers
When we look at statistics on violence, the numbers are mind-numbingly high, tempting us to read faster and gloss over them, almost as if we were afraid to slow down and ponder their profound implications. The amount of gun violence in the USA is so far out of proportion with any other developed country as to be stupefying, leading us to cry out for the reforms that the right wing and their gun lobby have so long and stubbornly opposed and sabotaged. In 2017, the reported rates of violent crime for the U.S. population of 325.7 million people amounted to a total of 1,247,321 cases of violent crime, including 17,284 cases of homicide, 135,755 cases of rape, over 319,000 cases of robbery and aggravated assault, and almost 8 million property crimes.[49] All told, there were about 1.4 million U.S. deaths caused by firearms between 1968 and 2011, including suicides, homicides, and accidents.[50]

One study compared the U.S. with a bloc of 22 other highly developed nations with a combined population twice as large as that of the U.S., clearly showing that the U.S. is an outlier when it comes to gun violence. In this comparison, it was found that "the U.S. had 82 percent of all gun deaths, 90 percent of all women killed with guns," and over 90% of the children and young people between ages 14 and 24 "killed with guns." "Compared to these 22 other high-income nations, the U.S. gun-related homicide rate is 25 times higher."[51] Why does this continue to happen? Because pushed by right-wing populist fears, the profit motive of the arms industry, and the corrupt and racist politics of grievance of right-wing politicians, gun violence is steadily increasing in the United States.

Even comparing just two years, 2010 and 2017, shows a dramatic increase of 25% in seven years, amounting to thousands of deaths and injuries annually. In 2010, there were a total of 30,470 deaths from firearms, including 11,078 homicides and 19,392 suicides. In 2017, gun deaths reached their highest level since 1968, with a total of 39,773 deaths from firearms, of which 14,542 were homicides and 23,854 were by suicide.[52] Between 1999 and 2014, there were a total of 477,289 deaths from gun violence, with 185,718 homicides and 291,571 suicides. During that period, the rate of firearm deaths per 100,000 people rose from 10.3 in 1999 to 12 per 100,000 in 2017, with 109 people dying every day from gun violence.

As far as the insanity of mass killings go, a simple table will suffice to drive home the new normal of our dystopian social reality.[53]

1999: 42 dead, 47+ injured
2000: 7 dead
2001: 5 dead, 4+ injured
2003: 7 dead, 8+ injured
2004: 5 dead, 7+ injured
2005: 17 dead, 9+ injured
2006: 21 dead, 7+ injured
2007: 53 dead, 32+ injured
2008: 17 dead, 24+ injured
2009: 39 dead, 39+ injured

2010: 9 dead, 2+ injured
2011: 19 dead, 21+ injured
2012: 71 dead, 80+ injured
2013: 35 dead, 13+ injured
2014: 18 dead, 28+ injured
2015: 46 dead, 43+ injured
2016: 71 dead, 83+ injured
2017: 117 dead, 587+ injured
2018: 80 dead, 70+ injured
2019: 73 dead, 112+ injured
2020: 9 dead
2021: 31 dead, 7+ injured

Intimate Violence and Fake Masculinity

The white male global far right believes that today we are living in a time of a clash of civilizations of white versus non-white. To people in the white nationalist movement, the impending societal demographic change from white majority to non-white majority represents an existential threat that must be countered in every conceivable way. Discussions of Americans being "replaced" by immigrants, for instance, are a recurring feature on some programs on Fox News. Fox hosts Tucker Carlson and Laura Ingraham return to these themes frequently. Democrats, Ms. Ingraham told viewers last year, "want to replace you, the American voters, with newly amnestied citizens and an ever-increasing number of chain migrants."[54]

Indeed, even though the idea of that threat has been central to white power activism for decades,[55] the white nationalist movement of today is prominently pushing "replacement theory" as code for racial annihilation through intermarriage, immigration, and demographic change. That's why the white nationalists at Charlottesville in 2017 proudly chanted, "You will not replace us."[56] "You Will Not Replace Us" is also the slogan of the neo-Nazi group Identity Evropa.[57] The week before the New Zealand killer unleashed his atrocity, he released a document called "The Great Replacement." The first sentence of which was "It's the birth rates."[58] As racist Iowa congressman Steve King put it in a tweet in March 2017, "We can't restore our civilization with somebody else's babies."[59]

Within this context, they argue, the most pressing concern with plummeting white birth rates is that they will cause white people around the world to be replaced by non-white people. They feel strongly that "white men are in a weaker position because their women are not doing the work of reproducing [and they] are saying, 'Look, Muslims have got their women where they need to be, and we're not doing a good job at that.'"[60] Of course they blame the feminist movement for this and argue that women should not have the right to work and vote at all and should be limited to raising little soldiers to fight "the enemy." Indeed, their replacement theory is so deeply misogynistic and racist that it holds that the cause of the White Man may require the subjugation of white women in order to fight non-white races.

Clearly, the pathology of the extremist White Man's replacement theory is a classic campaign of "blaming the victim." Disregarding the clear evidence that he himself, the White Man, may be a factor in the declining sperm count and the white birth rate, his twisted logic projects all the blame for the White Man's fertility problems on "his" white woman for not bearing enough children.

Two issues that affect all of modern mankind are the decline in sperm count and testosterone levels. Naturally, biologically, testosterone levels decline as we age. But the scary thing is, today, that decline is accelerating. As this "negative trend seems to be getting worse," the decline happens "to men at much younger ages than ever before."[61] In the last 20 years, men's testosterone levels have dropped at least 20% with more and more younger men suffering the effects of low testosterone. For example, a Danish study found that "men born in the 1960s have on average 14% lower T levels than males from the 1920s."[62]

An international team of researchers, drawing on 185 studies conducted between 1973 and 2011 and involving almost 43,000 American, European, Australian, and New Zealand men found that sperm concentration fell from 99 million per ml in 1973 to 47.1

million per ml in 2011, a decline of 52.4% and an average of 1.4% a year.[63] "This means that, for example, a 65-year-old man in 2002 would have testosterone levels 15 percent lower than those of a 65-year-old in 1987."[64] It's likely, therefore, that a man's testosterone levels are half of those of his father and undoubtedly significantly lower than his grandfather.

Why is this so concerning? Because low testosterone negatively affects our sexual, physical, and emotional life, our quality of life, and even our very lifespans. First, low testosterone can lead to a host of sexual ailments, including reduced sex drive, erectile dysfunction, shrinking testicles, loss of armpit and pubic hair, hot flashes, and low or zero sperm count, i.e., infertility. Psychologically, low testosterone can lead to mood changes, including irritability and depression. Long-term testosterone deficiency also increases the likelihood of developing age-related diseases, including osteoporosis and heart disease.[65]

What is panicking white male extremists of the Anglosphere more than anything is that the worldwide decline in sperm and testosterone levels appears to be limited to white males. Though the causes of the decline remain unclear, the facts seem incontrovertible. Compared with non-white guys, the sperm counts of men from the Anglosphere, such as North America and Europe, Australia, New Zealand, and elsewhere, over the past 40 years, have decreased more than 50%. These are troubling trends, indeed, that must be seriously addressed by the medical and health communities through prioritized research into the causes and possible remedies. The results are "shocking," and "a classic under-the-radar, huge public health problem that is really neglected," says Hagai Levine from the Hebrew University of Jerusalem, an epidemiologist and lead author of the study that was published in the Human Reproduction Update.[66]

But it is an additional tragedy that the global right wing is experiencing this situation as an existential threat. It is having devastating effects on the mental and emotional stability of the white male leadership of the global far right fringe who have weaponized these sad and troubling trends in the global culture war they are engaged in against women and non-white people.

Intimate Violence and Incel Manhood

In 21st century America, toxic masculinity has led to an epidemic explosion of intimate violence, often culminating in murder. FBI statistics on nationwide homicides confirm that a vast proportion of women killed in the U.S. are killed by current or former intimate partners, "at a staggering rate of almost three women every day."[67] Of "all female homicides accounted for in 2018 where the relationship between perpetrator and victim could be identified, 92% of cases involved women or girls killed by a man they knew, 63% of whom were killed by current husbands, ex-husbands or current boyfriends."[68] When you add it all up, "according to the CDC, homicide is the fourth leading cause of death for girls and women one to 19 years old, and the fifth leading cause of death for women 20 to 44."[69]

The trend of toxic male-on-female violence is not race neutral. Non-white women suffer even more from it than white women. Case in point, "the homicide rate for Indigenous women and girls in the U.S. is six times higher than it is for white women and girls, and 94% of cases are attributable to former or current partners... while Black women and girls are being murdered by male offenders at a rate of almost three times more than white women."[70]

A "common thread that connects many of" today's right-wing mass killers "is a history of hating women, assaulting wives, girlfriends and female family members, or sharing misogynistic views online."[71] That what's "missing from the national conversation," says Governor Gavin Newsom of California. "Why does it have to be, why is it men, dominantly, always?"[72] The fact is that mass shootings are almost exclusively perpetrated by men and that a common trait among mass killers is a hatred toward women. "Most mass shootings are rooted in domestic violence... Most mass shooters have a history of domestic or family violence in their background. It's an important red flag."[73] In more than half of all mass shootings in the United

States from 2009 to 2017, an intimate partner or family member of the perpetrator was among the victims.

Many of these men have self-identified as so-called incels, short for involuntary celibates, an online subculture of men who express rage at women for denying them sex and who frequently fantasize about violence and celebrate mass shooters in their online discussion groups. Elliot O. Rodger killed six people in 2014 in Isla Vista, California, a day after posting a video titled "Elliot Rodger's Retribution." In it, he describes himself as being tortured by sexual deprivation and promises to punish women for rejecting him. Incel online communities are a kind of echo chamber of despair, where anyone who says anything remotely hopeful quickly gets ostracized. "You get a bunch of these guys who are just very angry and bitter, and feel helpless and in some cases suicidal, and that's just absolutely a combination that's going to produce more shooters in the future... What ties together many of the perpetrators is 'this entitlement, this envy of others, this feeling that they deserve something that the world is not giving them. And they are angry at others that they see are getting it.'"[74]

At least part of the solution to the White Man's low sperm count problem comes from the understanding of what is called, after the scientists who first described it, the Mossman-Pacey paradox.[75] From a purely evolutionary view, it involves the unique discovery by the human male of how to make himself more attractive to the opposite sex while damaging his ability to have children. They discovered that "taking steroids to get a buff physique or anti-baldness pills to keep a full head of hair can damage and kill their fertility."[76] Dr. James Mossman, now at Brown University in the United States, first made the connection between male infertility and steroid abuse, while studying for his doctorate in Sheffield, UK. He discovered that "anabolic steroids... are regularly used by bodybuilders" as "performance-enhancing drugs" because they "mimic the effect of the male hormone testosterone in the body" and "increase muscle growth."[77] Anabolic steroids work by fooling "the brain's pituitary gland into thinking the testes are going into overdrive. So the glands react by shutting down the production of two hormones—FSH and LH—which are the key hormones that drive the production of sperm."[78]

Dr. Mossman recalled noticing "some men coming in to have their fertility tested and these guys were huge... They are trying to look really big, to look like the pinnacles of evolution... But they are making themselves very unfit in an evolutionary sense, because without exception they had no sperm in their ejaculation at all."[79] Professor Allan Pacey from the University of Sheffield agreed, "Isn't it ironic that men go to the gym to look wonderful, for the most part to attract women, and inadvertently decrease their fertility?" "The researchers say there is a similar theme in men using medication to prevent male pattern baldness. The drug finasteride changes the way testosterone is metabolized in the body and can limit hair loss, but side effects can include erectile dysfunction and a hit to fertility." According to Professor Pacey, "Baldness is a bit more hit-and-miss, but sales are going through the roof and that makes it an increasingly common problem."[80]

Besides posing a plethora of health risks to the proper functioning of our body, including diminished testosterone production, psychiatric issues, and cardiovascular problems, anabolic steroids have been shown to cause the acceleration of "brain aging to the extent that your brain looks demonstrably older than your biological age on brain scans... High doses of certain common anabolic steroids appear to have toxic effects on brain cells and can even lead to their death." As a result, they have become "linked to psychiatric and cognitive issues, reduced connectivity in some parts of the brain, and changes in volume and density in certain regions."[81]

The White Man's apparent strength covers his underlying weakness, and his hyper-masculinity is a fake masculinity. The more widespread the taking of these vanity-based medications becomes, the greater the number of attractive dudes that are evolutionary duds. Professor Pacey told the BBC, "I would say more anabolic steroid users are likely to become sterile than you would think—90%, probably."[82]

One wonders if Harold Bornstein, Trump's doctor, explained to his client how the drug he prescribed him to treat his baldness actually works to diminish his masculinity indices and can possibly lead to birth defects in his offspring.

Populist Terrorist Violence

The White Man's fear and rage has fueled an exponential rise in gun ownership of all kinds that has turned the country into Fortress America. Several indicators show the extent of ever-growing arms sales. In 2016, 32% of American households owned guns. In 2021 that percentage has risen to 39. In 2020, some 17 million people bought guns. A fifth of all Americans who bought guns last year were first-time gun owners, and new owners were less likely than usual to be male and white. Half were women, a fifth were Black, and a fifth were Hispanic.[83]

As to the gender and racial makeup of gun owners overall in 2021, "63 percent were male, 73 percent were white, 10 percent were Black, and 12 percent were Hispanic... Estimates are that the total number of guns in circulation exceeds 400 million," which is more than the number of U.S. citizens. As Marqueece Harris-Dawson, who represents South Los Angeles, aptly put it, "Americans are in an arms race with themselves" as "there is a breakdown in trust and a breakdown in a shared, common reality."[84] In the final analysis, people buy and own guns because they feel threatened and unsafe. They operate from fear, fear of their safety in our violent society, fear of other cultures and races, fear of the government that it will not protect them, etc.

Extremists in the gun culture operate from the rage induced by those fears, and advocate the use of guns and armed force to prepare for Armageddon and race war. In 2017, hate crimes, generally defined as criminal acts motivated by the victim's race, ethnicity, religion, or gender, increased by about 17% nationally to 7,175 from 6,121. In some places, like Virginia for example, they were up by nearly 50%, from 137 to 202.[85]

Since September 11, 2001, *white supremacists and* other far-right extremists have killed far more people than any other category of domestic extremists. Between 2008 and 2017, domestic extremists killed 387 in the United States.[86] Out of those fatalities, 270 (71%) were committed by members of the far right or white-supremacist movements, whereas Muslim extremists killed 100 people (25%).[87, 88]

The number of terror-related incidents has more than tripled in the United States since 2013. In 2017, there were 65 incidents.[89] Forty-eight (60%) of these incidents were perpetrated by racist, anti-Muslim, anti-Semitic, anti-government, or other right-wing ideologies. Left-wing ideologies, like radical environmentalism, were responsible for 11 attacks (16%), and Muslim extremists committed just seven attacks (9%).[90] In 2018, "39 of the 50 killings committed by political extremists, according to the Anti-Defamation League, were carried out by white supremacists. Another eight were committed by killers with anti-government views. Over the past 10 years, right-wing extremists were responsible for more than 70 percent of extremist-related killings. 'Right-wing extremist violence is our biggest threat,' wrote Jonathan Greenblatt, the head of the A.D.L. 'The numbers don't lie.'"[91]

The Common Essence of Islamic and White Christian Extremism

To get a better fix on the nature of our white Christian nationalism and domestic terrorism problem, it helps to understand the extent to which it shares some very basic ideas and values with Islamic terrorism. To begin with, both Islamic extremism and white Christian extremism recruit their adherents from the class of young, marginalized and traumatized males in their societies. Both are severely "purist" in their religious and racist motivations and in their misogynistic attitudes and practices.

"In both, an apocalyptic ideology predicts—and promises to hasten—a civilizational conflict that will consume the world. In both, there is theatrical, indiscriminate violence that will supposedly bring about this final battle, but often does little more than grant the killer a brief flash of empowerment to win attention for the cause."[92]

In both, the message is one of "temporal acceleration"—the promise that an individual adherent could speed up time toward the inevitable endpoint by committing violence. And in both, the "apocalyptic narratives" exploit social media's tendency to amplify whatever content is most extreme. Both Islamic terrorism and white Christian nationalist terrorism promise their members a sense of purpose in a chaotic world by giving them the opportunity to participate in a cleansing fire. "They are called to take up the mantle of warriors for the cause. No longer are these men 'betas' (a common insult in alt-right circles)—they are would-be heroes."[93] Most importantly, both "these groups give their adherents, many of whom perceive themselves as socially isolated, a sense of community. Online message boards become disembodied Knights Templar."[94]

"The white nationalist terrorists of today echo," almost verbatim, those of "the ideological tracts, recruiting pitches and radicalization tales of the Islamic State during its rise." For the white nationalists, the world is "careening toward a global race war between whites and non-whites… So-called manifestoes left by the terrorist attackers at Christchurch, New Zealand, and El Paso, Texas, have warned of this coming war too. They also say their attacks were intended to provoke more racial violence, hastening the fight's arrival."[95]

"It is impossible to understand the resurgence of their reactionary political extremism without understanding it as a fundamentally religious phenomenon."[96] Both Islamic extremism and extreme domestic white terrorism share "a cosmic-level worldview that fetishizes violence as a kind of purifying fire: a destruction necessary to 'reset' the world from its current broken state. This atavistic worldview idealizes an imagined past, one that predates the afflictions of, say, feminism and multiculturalism."[97] And like Islamist jihadists, white Christian supremacists make claims on metaphysical truth, focus on God, and offer the promise of an afterlife or reward. Both Christian and Islamic terrorists believe in the cosmic battle between God and the Devil.

White Supremacy as a Religious Cult

Their brothers, the secular white supremacists, turn to conspiracy theories such as QAnon to explain the problem of evil. They find that "the world is secretly run by a network of Jews planning to wipe out the white race, with oppressive feminazis planning to make men obsolete"[98] a pedophilic cabal being run from a pizza shack by liberal perverts, etc. But in fact, for these secular believers, white supremacy as a concept assumes the functions of a religion. It gives "their members a meaningful account of why the world is the way it is." It "provide[s] them with a sense of purpose and the possibility of sainthood." It "offer[s] a sense of community." And it "establish[es] clear roles and rituals that allow adherents to feel and act as part of a whole."[99]

In other words, secular white supremacy isn't "just [a] subculture; [it is in fact a] church. And until we recognize the religious hunger alongside the destructive hatred, we have little chance of stopping these terrorists."[100] "This brotherhood has its own hierarchy and its own hagiography. Those who have committed mass murders are often venerated as martyrs for their causes: Elliot Rodger, the misogynist gunman behind the killings in Santa Barbara, is lauded across the incel internet as the 'Supreme Gentleman' within hours of the El Paso shooting, the gunman was deemed a 'saint' on white nationalist forums."[101]

The Aryan nation at the heart of white nationalism is not the United States. It is "imagined as a transnational white polity with interests fundamentally opposed to the United States and… bent on overthrowing the federal government."[102] White supremacy, whether Christian, secular, or a mixture of both, is a violent, interconnected, transnational ideology. Its adherents are gathering in anonymous online forums to spread their ideas, plotting attacks, and cheering on acts of terrorism. While its modern roots predate the Trump administration by many decades, white nationalism attained a new mainstream legitimacy during Trump's time in office.[103]

"The white supremacy movement imagines a race war, incited principally by mass violence. The core texts of this movement, like

'The Turner Diaries' or 'The Camp of the Saints,' aren't just quaint novels, but rather provide a road map to how such violence could succeed. To call them manuals is too simplistic: They provide the collective ideas and vision by which a fringe movement can attempt a violent confrontation that could lead to race war."[104] "These ideas run from the earlier period directly into today's manifestos. Dylan Roof's document discussed his desire to provoke a race war. The Christchurch manifesto used images and phrases from the earlier movement. In the El Paso manifesto, the anti-immigrant rhetoric is thoroughly ensconced in other white power ideas."[105] Much of these writings follow a strategy of first claiming a state of emergency that "gives a rationale for the act of violence," and "critically… also issues a call to action for others. The El Paso manifesto does so overtly, and offers tactical details about the attacker's weapons, meant to instruct others," and gives "specific advice about how to choose targets."[106]

In conclusion, this chapter has shown how the American promise to its people of a society dedicated to the "pursuit of happiness" has failed to deliver on that promise. For the people as a whole, the pursuit of happiness has become a nightmare of ever-intensifying misery and suffering. They, the American people, are clearly fundamentally unhappy, suffering widely and deeply in all dimensions of life: physically, emotionally, mentally, and spiritually.

The blame for all this dystopian misery of the American people must be assigned squarely to the racist and misogynistic system of white male-centric political economy that has dominated American society for the centuries of its development.

In the next section, we will describe the life and times of the one individual who, more than anyone, has come to personify the psychopathology of the White Man Dystopian Personality Disorder, namely, Donald Trump.

Endnotes

1 Monica Swahn, "Suicide Nation: What's Behind the Need to Numb and to Seek a Final Escape?" The Intelligencer, June 8, 2023, https://www.theintelligencer.com /news/article/suicide-nation-what-s-behind-the-need-to-numb-18142089.php.

2 Katie Kindelan, "US Fertility Rate Falls to a Record Low: What Women Should Know About Trend," GMA, n.d., https://www.goodmorningamerica.com/wellness /story/us-fertility-rate-falls-record-low-women-trend-68196854.

3 Annalisa Merelli, "Maternal Death Rates Are a Key Indicator of Why the State of Female Health in the US Is so Terrible," Quartz, August 28, 2018, https://qz.com /1363902/maternal-death-rates-are-a-key-indicator-of-why-the-state-of-female -health-in-the-us-is-so-terrible.

4 Ibid.

5 Ibid.

6 Maggie Fox, "More US Babies Die on Their First Day Than in 68 Other Countries, Report Shows," NBC News, April 30, 2013, https://www.nbcnews.com/healthmain /more-us-babies-die-their-first-day-68-other-countries-6c9700437.

7 Angela Morrow, "The 10 Leading Causes of Infant Death," VERYWELL Health, November 15, 2021, https://www.verywellhealth.com/leading-causes-of-infant-death -1132374.

8 OECD, "Poverty rate," 2023, doi: 10.1787/0fe1315d-en.

9 Annabelle Timsit, "From Survive to Thrive: The 70-year Battle to Change How Governments Support Families," Quartz, 6/30/2020; https://qz.com/1856334 /new-who-guidelines-could-change-how-governments-support-families

10 David Brooks, "The Rise of the Haphazard Self," New York Times, May 13, 2019, reviews Kathryn Edin, Timothy Nelson, Andrew Cherlin and Robert Francis, "The Tenuous Attachments of Working-Class Men," Journal of Economic Perspectives 33, No. 2, (Spring 2019): 211–28.

11 Ibid.

12 Ibid.

13 Sarah O'Brien, "Fed Survey Shows 40 Percent of Adults Still Can't Cover a $400 Emergency Expense," CNBC, May 22, 2018, https://www.cnbc.com/2018/05/22 /fed-survey-40-percent-of-adults-cant-cover-400-emergency-expense.html# :~:text=About%2040%20percent%20of%20adults%20said%20that%20if%20 faced%20with,in%202017%2C%20released%20on%20Tuesday.

14 John Kim, "So Many Men Are Miserable Jerks. I Should Know — I Used to Be One Too," Salon, February 2, 2019, https://www.salon.com/2019/02/02/so-many-men -are-miserable-jerks-i-should-know-i-used-to-be-one-too/.

15 Ibid.

16 Saumya Joseph, "Depression, Anxiety Rising Among U.S. College Students," Reuters, August 29, 2019, www.reuters.com/article/us-health-mental-undergrads/depression -anxiety-rising-among-us-college-students-idUSKCN1VJ25Z.

17 Rick McDaniel, Fox News, May 26, 2018, Cigna, "Cigna's U.S. Loneliness Index," May 1, 2018, https://www.multivu.com/players/English/8294451-cigna-us-loneliness -survey/.

18 Ibid.

19 Brad Wolverton, "As Students Struggle with Stress and Depression, Colleges Act as Counselors," New York Times, February 21, 2019, https://www.nytimes.com /2019/02/21/education/learning/mental-health-counseling-on-campus.html.

20 Olivia Goldhill, "One of History's Greatest Philosophers Thought Work Makes You a Worse Person," Quartz, June 30, 2018, https://qz.com/1316428/one-of-historys -greatest-philosophers-thought-work-makes-you-a-worse-person.

21 Ibid.

22 Erin Griffith, "Why Are Young People Pretending to Love Work?" New York Times, January 26, 2019, https://www.nytimes.com/2019/01/26/business/against-hustle -culture-rise-and-grind-tgim.html.

23 Kyle Kowalski, "Elon Musk's (Unbalanced) Workweek to Change the World," Sloww, n.d., https://www.sloww.co/elon-musk-workweek/.

24 Erin Griffith, "Why Are Young People Pretending to Love Work?" New York Times, January 26, 2019, https://www.nytimes.com/2019/01/26/business/against-hustle -culture-rise-and-grind-tgim.html.

25 Roger Cohen, "The Harm in Hustle Culture," New York Times, February 1, 2019, https://www.removepaywall.com/article/current.

26 Eric Levitz, "Americans Are Dying Younger, Having Fewer Babies, Studies Find," New York Magazine-Intelligencer, November 27, 2019. https://nymag.com /intelligencer/2019/11/americans-are-dying-younger-having-fewer-babies -studies.html

27 Sandee LaMotte, "Half of America Will Be Obese Within 10 Years, Study Says, Unless We Work Together," CNN, December 19, 2019, https://www.cnn.com/2019/12/18 /health/american-obesity-trends-wellness/index.html.

28 CDC, "What Is Diabetes?" April 24, 2023, https://www.cdc.gov/diabetes/basics /diabetes.html.

29 CDC, "Diabetes Fast Facts," April 4, 2023, https://www.cdc.gov/diabetes/basics /quick-facts.html.

30 CDC, "Heart Disease Facts," May 15, 2023, https://www.cdc.gov/heartdisease/facts .htm.

31 Camille Peri, "10 Things to Hate About Sleep Loss," WebMD, February 13, 2014, https://www.webmd.com/sleep-disorders/features/10-results-sleep-loss#1.

32 Ibid.

33 Ibid.

34 Eric Levitz, "Americans Are Dying Younger, Having Fewer Babies, Studies Find," New York Magazine-Intelligencer, November 27, 2019. https://nymag.com/intelligencer /2019/11/americans-are-dying-younger-having-fewer-babies-studies.html

35 Ibid.

36 Sam Baker, "Deep Dive: The Coming Health Care Collision," Axios, December 7, 2019, https://www.axios.com/2019/12/07/america-health-care-costs-life-expectancy.

37 Ibid.

38 Lee Siegel, "Why Is America So Depressed?" New York Times, January 2, 2020, https://www.nytimes.com/2020/01/02/opinion/depression-america-trump.html.

39 Ed Cara, "America's Suicide Rate Has Increased by Nearly 30 Percent Since 1999," Gizmodo, June 8, 2018, https://gizmodo.com/americas-suicide-rate-has-increased -by-nearly-30-percen-1826670729.

40 Monica H. Swahn, "Why Are Americans So Sad?" Quartz, June 17, 2018, https://qz.com/1306176/why-are-americans-so-sad; Deborah M. Stone, et al., "Vital Signs: Trends in State Suicide Rates — United States, 1999–2016 and Circumstances Contributing to Suicide — 27 States, 2015," MMWR 67, no. 22 (2018):617–624, DOI: http://dx.doi.org/10.15585/mmwr.mm6722a1.

41   Jose A. Del Real, "The reinvention of a 'Real Man,'" Washington Post, May 23, 2022, https://www.washingtonpost.com/nation/2022/05/23/real-man-wyoming-suicide -masculinity/.

42   Ed Cara, "America's Suicide Rate Has Increased by Nearly 30 Percent Since 1999," Gizmodo, June 8, 2018, https://gizmodo.com/americas-suicide-rate-has-increased -by-nearly-30-percen-1826670729.

43   Ibid.

44   Editorial Staff, "Alcohol and Drug Abuse Statistics (Facts About Addiction)," American Addiction Centers, May 4, 2023, https://americanaddictioncenters.org /rehab-guide/addiction-statistics#.

45   Ibid.

46   Ibid.

47   Ibid.

48   Ibid.

49   FBI: UCR, "Crime in the United States by Volume and Rate per 100,000 Inhabitants, 1998–2017)," n.d., Table 1, https://ucr.fbi.gov/crime-in-the-u.s/2017/crime-in-the -u.s.-2017/tables/table-1.

50   Wikipedia, "Gun Violence in the United States," June 19, 2023, https://en.wikipedia .org/wiki/Gun_violence_in_the_United_States.

51   Ibid.

52   Ibid.

53   Chris Canipe and Travis Hartman, "A timeline of Mass Shootings in the U.S.," Reuters, May 31, 2021, https://www.reuters.com/graphics/USA-GUNS/MASS -SHOOTING/nmovardgrpa/.

54   Jeremy W. Peters, et al., "How the El Paso Killer Echoed the Incendiary Words of Conservative Media Stars," New York Times, August 11, 2019, https://www.nytimes. com/interactive/2019/08/11/business/media/el-paso-killer-conservative-media.html.

55   Kathleen Belew, "The Right Way to Understand White Nationalist Terrorism," New York Times, August 4, 2019, https://www.nytimes.com/2019/08/04/opinion/el -paso-terrorism.html.

56   Jeremy W. Peters, et al., "How the El Paso Killer Echoed the Incendiary Words of Conservative Media Stars," New York Times, August 11, 2019, https://www.nytimes.com/interactive/2019/08/11/business/media/el-paso-killer -conservative-media.html.

57   Nellie Bowles, "'Replacement Theory,' a Racist, Sexist Doctrine, Spreads in Far-Right Circles," New York Times, March 18, 2019, https://www.nytimes.com/2019/03/18/ technology/replacement-theory.html.

58   Kathleen Belew, "The Right Way to Understand White Nationalist Terrorism," New York Times, August 4, 2019, https://www.nytimes.com/2019/08/04/opinion/el -paso-terrorism.html.

59   Charles M. Blow, "It's All Rooted in White Panic," New York Times, June 5, 2019, https://www.nytimes.com/2019/06/05/opinion/white-supremacy-trump.html.

60   Ibid.

61   Roberta Stringer, "Why Are Men's Testoterone Levels Decreasing?" Parla, June 17, 2021, https://myparla.com/decreasing-testosterone-levels/.

62   George Herrera, "Medical Study: Generational Decrease of Testosterone Levels in Men," BodyRX, October 15, 2020, https://www.bodyrxantiaging.com/medical -studies/medical-study-generational-decrease-testosterone-levels-men/.

63 Katie Kelland, "Sperm Count Dropping in Western World," Reuters, July 26, 2017, https://www.scientificamerican.com/article/sperm-count-dropping-in-western-world/.

64 Anne Harding, "Men's Testosterone Levels Declined in Last 20 Years," Reuters Health, January 19, 2007, https://www.reuters.com/article/health-testosterone-levels-dc/mens-testosterone-levels-declined-in-last-20-years-idUKKIM16976320061031.

65 Huanguang Jia, "Review of Health Risks of Low Testosterone and Testosterone Administration," World Journal of Clinical Cases 3, no. 4 (2015): 338–344, https://www.ncbi.nlm.nih.gov/pmc/articles/PMC4391003/.

66 Nicola Davis, "Sperm Counts Among Western Men Have Halved in Last 40 Years – Study," The Guardian, July 25, 2017, https://www.theguardian.com/lifeandstyle/2017/jul/25/sperm-counts-among-western-men-have-halved-in-last-40-years-study.

67 Rose Hackman, "Femicides in the US: The Silent Epidemic Few Dare to Name," The Guardian, July 25, 2021, https://www.theguardian.com/us-news/2021/sep/26/femicide-us-silent-epidemic.

68 Ibid.

69 Ibid.

70 Ibid.

71 Julie Bosman, Kate Taylor, and Tim Arango, "A Common Trait Among Mass Killers: Hatred Toward Women," New York Times, August 10, 2019, https://www.nytimes.com/2019/08/10/us/mass-shootings-misogyny-dayton.html.

72 Ibid.

73 Ibid.

74 Ibid.

75 James Gallagher, "Fertility Paradox in Male Beauty Quest," BBC News, May 28, 2019, https://www.bbc.com/news/health-48396071.

76 Ibid.

77 Ibid.

78 Ibid.

79 Ibid.

80 Ibid.

81 Sophie Putka, "Weight Lifters' Brains Reveal One Unexpected Side Effect of Steroids," Inverse, March 28, 2021, https://www.inverse.com/mind-body/weightlifters-brains-reveal-unexpected-side-effect-of-steroids.

82 James Gallagher, "Fertility Paradox in Male Beauty Quest," BBC News, May 28, 2019, https://www.bbc.com/news/health-48396071.

83 Kim Parker, Juliana Menasce Horowitz, Ruth Igielnik, J. Baxter Oliphant And Anna Brown, "America's Complex Relationship with Guns," Pew Research Center, June 22, 2017, https://www.pewresearch.org/social-trends/2017/06/22/the-demographics-of-gun-ownership/

84 Sabrina Tavernise, "An Arms Race in America: Gun Buying Spiked During the Pandemic. It's Still Up." New York Times, May 30, 2021, https://www.nytimes.com/2021/05/29/us/gun-purchases-ownership-pandemic.html.

85 FBI, "2017 Hate Crime Statistics Released," November 13, 2018, https://www.fbi.gov/news/stories/2017-hate-crime-statistics-released-111318.

86 Janet Reitman, "U.S. Law Enforcement Failed to See the Threat of White Nationalism. Now They Don't Know How to Stop It," Washington Post, November 3, 2018, https://www.nytimes.com/2018/11/03/magazine/FBI-charlottesville-white-nationalism-far-right.html.

87 Stimson, "Counterterrorism Spending: Protecting America While Promoting Efficiencies and Accountability," May 16, 2018, https://www.stimson.org/content /counterterrorism-spending-protecting-america-while-promoting-efficiencies -and-accountability.

88 ADL, "Murder and Extremism in the United States in 2017," January 12, 2018, https://www.adl.org/resources/reports/murder-and-extremism-in-the-united-states -in-2017.

89 Start, "American Deaths in Terrorist Attacks, 1995–2017," University of Maryland, September 2018, https://www.start.umd.edu/pubs/START_AmericanTerrorism Deaths_FactSheet_Sept2018.pdf.

90 Luiz Romero, "US Terror Attacks Are Increasingly Motivated by Right-Wing Views," Quartz, October 24, 2018, https://qz.com/1435885/data-shows-more-us-terror -attacks-by-right-wing-and-religious-extremists/.

91 David Leonhardt, "Conservatism Has a Violence Problem," New York Times, August 5, 2019, https://www.nytimes.com/2019/08/05/opinion/el-paso-shooting-republicans -trump.html.

92 Max Fisher, "White Terrorism Shows 'Stunning' Parallels to Islamic State's Rise," New York Times, August 5, 2019, https://www.nytimes.com/2019/08/05/world/americas /terrorism-white-nationalist-supremacy-isis.html.

93 Tara Isabella Burton, "The Religious Hunger of the Radical Right," New York Times, August 13, 2019, https://www.nytimes.com/2019/08/13/opinion/sunday/religion -extremism-white-supremacy.html.

94 Ibid.

95 Max Fisher, "White Terrorism Shows 'Stunning' Parallels to Islamic State's Rise," New York Times, August 5, 2019, https://www.nytimes.com/2019/08/05/world/americas /terrorism-white-nationalist-supremacy-isis.html.

96 Tara Isabella Burton, "The Religious Hunger of the Radical Right," New York Times, August 13, 2019, https://www.nytimes.com/2019/08/13/opinion/sunday/religion -extremism-white-supremacy.html.

97 Ibid.

98 Ibid.

99 Ibid.

100 Ibid.

101 Ibid.

102 Kathleen Belew, "The Right Way to Understand White Nationalist Terrorism," New York Times, August 4, 2019, https://www.nytimes.com/2019/08/04/opinion /el-paso-terrorism.html.

103 Jeremy W. Peters, et al., "How the El Paso Killer Echoed the Incendiary Words of Conservative Media Stars," New York Times, August 11, 2019, https://www.nytimes. com/interactive/2019/08/11/business/media/el-paso-killer-conservative-media.html.

104 Kathleen Belew, "The Right Way to Understand White Nationalist Terrorism," New York Times, August 4, 2019, https://www.nytimes.com/2019/08/04/opinion /el-paso-terrorism.html.

105 Ibid.

106 Ibid.

Chapter 15

Trump, Microcosm of the Macrocosm

Trump and the White Man's Dystopian Personality Disorder (WMDPD)

Trump's Addictions

As he ascended to the very pinnacle of wealth and power, Donald Trump came to personify and embody the White Man's Dystopian Personality Disorder (WMDPD) in its hour of crisis, namely, the beginning of the very breakdown of the White Man's culture of domination. Trump's fate, his defining time, his unique moment, would be that he, as the instigator, became the inflection point of the beginning of the Second U.S. Civil War, the conflict between the dystopian and the Eutopian streams of history. It will, therefore, be informative to probe Trump's childhood and trace the early origin and later development of his power addiction as he made his choices and charted his life. Understanding the pathology of power in this one man as the lack of true civility and empathy will help us not only to understand the pathology of his kind and class but also why their culture and civilization is crumbling under the weight of its own corruption. In rebirthing society as a Eutopia, out of the ashes of the White Man's Trumpian Dystopia, the Eutopian Coalition must learn the lesson from the past so they will not be condemned to repeat it in the future: A culture and society cannot succeed if it highest value is the love of power; it can only succeed if its highest value is the power of love.

Donald Trump never drinks alcohol and credits his abstemious behavior to his older brother, Fred, who died at age 41 from complications of his alcoholism. Fred was driven to his alcoholism by his father, Fred Sr. A licensed pilot, Fred Jr. had an avid interest in aviation, but his old man would not let him pursue his passion and forced him to work in the family real estate business by threatening disinheritance if he refused and went his own way. Boxed in and seeing no exit, Fred Jr. took to drinking to escape his problems and became a drunk. Donald did not share Fred Jr.'s negative sentiments about joining the family business. Quite the opposite! He gladly became his father's apprentice and acolyte in the art of selling substandard homes to Black people, relieving them of their hard-earned money, and adding to the family's burgeoning wealth, which Donald saw himself as the logical heir to.

However, just because Donald was dissuaded by his brother's example from engaging in substance abuse should not be interpreted to mean that Donald escaped the hells of addiction. It's just that the addictions Donald fell prey to were of a different, more insubstantial nature than alcohol, what in the recovery community is termed "process-based addiction." The main addiction that would rule and ruin Donald's life and psyche was power along with a complex of related secondary addictions involving fame, money, grievance, and cruelty. How it is both possible and common to become addicted to these non-substantial, more psychological values and pursuits becomes clear when we examine the dynamics of addiction and find that they are identical in all cases.

People engage in addictive behavior to escape feeling bad, to feel better than they have been and are feeling. Addictive behavior, whether it is substance abuse or the compulsive pursuit of food, sex, money, or power, intoxicates the individual and provides the experience of a temporary pleasure, a "high," thereby relieving an individual's current pain and suffering, whether emotional or physical. The downside is that once the substance has been depleted in the person's system or the activity has stopped, the original pain and suffering comes back ever so strongly and, each time, is intensified into a craving for the object of the addiction by the need for greater amounts of this object to achieve the same level of relief. This feature of the dynamics of addiction means that each time you need a higher dose of the fix to get the same rush. That threatens and wreaks havoc with social stability because it leads to criminality and the breaking of all social norms and laws, inevitably resulting in violence and death.

Mother Mary

Mary, Trump's mother, was a classic case of the absent mother, a stiffly repressed and coldhearted individual who interacted very little with her kids and delegated her maternal responsibilities as much as possible to the housekeepers she employed for that purpose. Mary's absence in Donald's life was not only psychological but also physical. Two years after Donald was born, in 1946, she gave birth to his brother Robert, her last child. It was a difficult pregnancy and an even more difficult delivery with severe complications that nearly cost Mary her life. It all adds up this way. His mother gets pregnant when he's only one and a half years old. Already, his new sibling is sucking energy and attention from his mother, energy that rightfully should be coming his way. Then, in the middle of the terrible twos, she forsakes him completely, almost dies, and during her long recovery, her mind and attention were more on the new arrival, Robert, than on him. So probably, for a period of several years, during this most formative of stages, young Donald was deprived in a serious way of maternal love and nurture that became the norm of their relationship for the rest of her life. His fate was not to experience the comforting love and embrace of the flow of maternal oxytocin, and as a result, his own neuroendocrinological pathways of empathy failed to develop.

Of course, the fact that he didn't receive the maternal love and attention that would have made him a loving child did not mean he did not need or want it. On the contrary, young Donald wanted and needed it very much and became adamant in demanding it through acting out in the most negative ways. The result was a bombastic and attention-demanding toddler whose need to be the center of attention became the basis for the development of his narcissistic personality. He would do anything, including pretending, cheating, and lying, to be the focus of attention. At the same time, and for the same reason, Donald, as a youngster, developed a bully personality and became so unmanageable by the time he was a teenager that his father had no recourse but to ship him off to the military academy for remedial behavior training that would enable him to function in larger society.

Father Fred

Unlike his mother, Mary, Donald's father, Fred, was more involved with Donald and his siblings during their formative stages. When young Donald started to have friends over after school or on weekends, Fred Sr. often showed his interest and joined the boys in play in the basement. And thus the pattern of Donnie's relationship to his parents was set. As a former close business associate and friend observed, "Donald was in awe of his father... and very detached from his mother."[1] Trump himself agreed with this assessment: "My father understood me more... He said, 'I want you to be successful.'"[2] One of Trump's classmates at the military academy also recalled the Gospel of Fred as told by his disciple Donald, "He did talk about his father... how he told him to be a 'king,' to be a 'killer.'"[3] In a rare moment of clarity, Trump conceded, "That's why I'm so screwed up, because I had a father that pushed me pretty hard."[4]

If we follow Trump's development through these early stages, we can see him emerge as a textbook case of the narcissistic bully characteristic of WMDPD pathology, laying down the fundamental patterns of abusive behavior in the first few years that have governed him throughout the rest of his life. In the yin stage, the basic fears and insecurities of character structure of the individual are created, including the narcissistic need to be the center of attention at all times. In the yang stage, as a cover up of and defense mechanism against these basic insecurities of character structure, the individual develops an antisocial, aggressive bully personality that tries to dominate others.

It is important to remember that bullies who lash out at their peers and inflict pain, including Trump, do so, first and foremost, because they themselves suffered deep hurts in childhood. Secondly, they lash out because, while lashing out, they experience a (temporary) release. The anger and rage they hurl at a target are an escape from, and mask for, their underlying loneliness and depression. The bully instinct, as a human psychological complex, derives from the biological predatory instinct. The predator has an innate, instinctual ability to read and evaluate his prey in terms of its weaknesses and how best to attack them. Trump's "genius," in other words, is not intellectual acumen or ability but the finely honed predatory instinct of how to belittle, overwhelm, and destroy people to make himself look bigger and better.

Looked at as a process, we have here the essential dynamics of the addiction to power. As the depression and loneliness grow and intensify with time, the bullies only escape from their fundamental emotional pains through more frequent and more intensive explosions of rage until it becomes fundamentally a steady state of being. Here, also, we find the source of the bully and power addict's need for enemies. Trump needs enemies and always needs more enemies to feed his need for the continuous adrenalin battle high of aggression in order to not fall into the depths of depression. This is the dynamic that governed the unfolding of all the major events in Trump's life, including his attempt at the ultimate power grab with the attempted coup d'état on January 6, 2021.

The Character Formation of an Autocrat

Sigmund Freud and Max Weber helped us understand why the character structure that emerged during the capitalist-protestant expansionist era was particularly suited to the needs of that historical era. Freud described and analyzed how the quest for power and control over others stems from interference with the natural development of the excretory and sexual functions in the second, yang stage of childhood development. Three traits, Freud discovered, are indicative of the anal character's larger complex of obsessional concern with issues of control and power, "They are especially orderly, parsimonious, and obstinate,"[5] tending toward, respectively, extreme cleanliness and punctuality, avarice and hoarding, and cruelty and aggression. All three sets of traits are abundantly evident in Trump and have been the core constituents of his bully character and the growth of his addiction to power.

Billionaire hedge fund manager David Tepper underscored how remarkably tightfisted his fellow billionaire Donald Trump is. He pointed out that despite having large business operations in New Jersey, Trump never contributed in the wake of the financial crisis or other disasters. "During Sandy, the big Sandy benefit, the big 9/11 benefit, not one dime. Not one dime!" Tepper said, his voice rising. "You can't tell me this is a charitable, generous person."[6] In fact, the Trump Foundation, his organ of charitable giving, was actually sued in federal court for "self-dealing," which bars nonprofit leaders from using their charity's money to help themselves, their businesses, or their families.[7] These were the types of "charitable" expenses the foundation engaged in: paying $20,000 for a portrait of Trump, making an illegal $25,000 campaign donation to Pam Bondi, Attorney General of Florida, as well as paying $258,000 to settle some of Trump's legal problems not connected to the foundation.[8]

Trump's extreme parsimoniousness is perhaps best illustrated by his business practices of not paying his bills, an art that he has perfected over the decades. Not paying, slow paying, employing exhaustive legal strategies of delaying, Trump is likely world champion and record holder in holding on to and not letting go of his money. In 2016, *USA Today* reviewed 60 lawsuits, 200 mechanics liens, and 24 violations of the Fair Labor Standards Act for an article documenting people who have accused Trump and his businesses of failing to pay them for their work.[9] The plaintiffs represented a true cross section of all services Trump contracted for, including a dishwasher in Florida, a glass company in New Jersey, a carpet company, a plumber, painters, waiters, bartenders, real estate brokers, and "law firms that once represented him in these suits."[10] "On just one project, Trump's Taj Mahal casino in Atlantic City, records released by the

New Jersey Casino Control Commission in 1990 show that at least 253 subcontractors weren't paid in full or on time, including workers who installed walls, chandeliers and plumbing."[11] The pattern of behavior was always the same: refusal to pay on the basis of some made up complaint and then frequently "tying them up in court and other negotiations for years. In some cases, the Trump teams financially overpower and outlast much smaller opponents, draining their resources. Some just give up the fight, or settle for less; some have ended up in bankruptcy or out of business altogether."[12]

While not synonymous, the pursuit of power is closely intertwined with the pursuit of money and wealth. Basically, power relates to the realm of politics, whereas wealth relates to the realm of economics. But the two realms certainly cross fertilize, and in as much as accumulating more wealth begets greater power and accumulating more power begets greater wealth, Trump also is a case study in how the addiction to power generally overlaps with the addiction to wealth.

Trump's Misogyny and Racism

One does not have to look very far or deep to document how misogyny and racism, as the twin pillars of WMDPD have dictated many of Trump's behaviors in life. The addiction to sex as a structural component of WMDPD is spectacularly evident in Trump's character structure. Because, for Trump, sex is not a reciprocal sharing of love and affection but only another way to exert power over people, an unconscious or subconscious act of revenge on the mother that failed him. In his adult life, Trump evolved into a full-fledged, self-admitted serial sexual predator. In the Access Hollywood video we all remember, Trump told his host Billy Bush, "You know I'm automatically attracted to beautiful [women]—I just start kissing them. It's like a magnet. Just kiss. I don't even wait. And when you're a star, they let you do it. You can do anything. Grab 'em by the pussy. You can do anything."[13]

Trump's use of language in talking about pursuing his victims is illustrative of his barely concealed contempt of women. Still talking to Billy Bush, Trump recounted how he failed to seduce Nancy

O'Dell, Bush's co-host at the time of the recording (circa 2005), "I moved on her, and I failed. I'll admit it. I did try and fuck her. She was married. And I moved on her very heavily. In fact, I took her out furniture shopping. She wanted to get some furniture... I moved on her like a bitch. But I couldn't get there. And she was married. Then all of a sudden, I see her, she's now got the big phony tits and everything. She's totally changed her look."[14] As of 2019, at least 26 women have come forward and accused President Donald Trump of sexual misconduct since the 1970s.[15] These included numerous instances where Trump initiated aggressive kissing, often without warning, and always acting without asking for consent.[16]

In truth, during his presidency, Trump consistently exhibited the mindset and upheld the values of a war criminal. In his opinion, waterboarding was good and should be reinstituted. He maintained that torture works and that he would go way beyond it. He advocated killing the families of suspected terrorists and threatened to destroy Iran's cultural heritage artifacts. He withheld congressionally mandated military aid to Ukraine because its president would not provide dirt on Trump's political opponent, Joe Biden. When the Black Lives Matter movement organized protests in the street of Washington, D.C., he wanted to unleash the military and "dominate the streets" by shooting at the protesters. And if anyone was ever convicted for doing any of these things, he promised to issue them pardons.

Thus the use of racism in his political campaigns to unify and excite his base was natural for Trump, and the result was his birtherism campaign against Obama. Trump's birtherism pushed the theory on his right-wing base that Obama was not a natural-born citizen but had been born in Kenya and was, therefore, ineligible to be U.S. president. His use of racism in his presidential campaigns was also greatly symbolized by his campaign proposals and presidential effort to build a wall on the U.S. southern border with Mexico to keep out the illegal immigrants from Mexico and other Latin American countries. Indeed, immigration and the wall are also the perfect messaging and politics that showcase the white, racist, right-wing, populist grievance dynamics between the demagogue and his base, with non-white immigrants as the proclaimed enemy.

By stoking the fear of foreign, non-white, immigration-based violence in his base, Trump is catering to, and actually inciting, the extreme right wing of that base to engage in the very violence he is accusing the immigrants of. It is no fluke that Trump's constant and insistent virulent rhetoric correlates with the extraordinary increases in domestic terrorism in recent years. So much so that by now, domestic right-wing terrorism incidents are far higher than the number of incidents of Islamic terrorism in the U.S. According to a new study reported by the *Washington Post*, counties that hosted political rallies with Donald Trump as the headliner in 2016 "saw a 226 percent increase in hate crimes over comparable counties that did not host such a rally" in subsequent months.[17]

Tony Schwartz, who co-authored *The Art of the Deal* with Trump, explained how, in the final analysis, Trump has no moral conscience because his need to win is so absolute and all encompassing. "I've always assumed like most people have," said Schwartz, "that the primary motivation is to be loved and admired and recognized and praised." While that may be true for normal people, for Trump "the deeper motivation is domination, is to win. And that is a function of the fact that he has no conscience."[18]

Trump's Base, Trump's Party, and Trump's Violence

Polarization in Post-World War II Mainstream Protestantism
Billy Graham, the famous American preacher of the 20th century, warned of the impending doom of apocalyptic destruction, "The greatest sin of America is our disregard of God... When I see a beautiful city like New York, I also have a vision of crumbling buildings and dust. I keep having the feeling that God will allow something to fall on us in a way I don't anticipate."[19] As proximate cause, Graham blamed the secular nonbelievers and fingered them as the agents of the Devil and the Antichrist. When these agents of destruction

completely controlled the globe and persecuted the Christians, God would unleash the Apocalypse.

It is true that in the 20th century, the post–World War II fissures in the liberal Protestant denominations led to an exodus from those churches in three different directions. One faction left to embrace the left-wing counterculture and sought a new spiritual home among other, non-Christian practices. A second faction left as they gravitated into the world of right-wing, Evangelical and nationalist movements. And the third, remaining faction stayed where they were, in the Protestant mainstream. In the early part of the 21st century, these trends continued and even intensified. The majority of the American people continued to move away from, and discard, traditional male-centric organized Christian religion in favor of exploring other religious and cultural traditions more responsive to their spiritual needs. But a large number of Christians doubled down and became Evangelical and Apocalyptic, clinging ever more tenaciously, or should we say ferociously, to the old faith in the superiority of the White Man and his God.

A recent Pew Research Center survey put numbers to these trends. The "survey found 29% of U.S. adults said they had no religious affiliation,"[20] a dramatic increase since the first decade of the 21st century. In 2007, Christians outnumbered those who identified themselves as not belonging to any organized religion by nearly five to one, and in 2021, less than 15 years later, this ratio decreased to little more than two to one. This exodus from organized, mainstream religion, led by the Millennial generation, represents an increase of 13 percentage points from 2007 in less than 15 years and an increase of 6 percentage points in the five years between 2016 and 2021. Not surprisingly, this decline in formal church membership has been accompanied by a marked decrease in personal religious habits and rituals, such as praying less often. Of those polled by the Pew Research, "about 32% said they seldom or never pray. That's up from 18% of those polled by the group in 2007."[21] And as Gregory Smith, associate director of research at Pew Research Center, noted, "The secularizing shifts evident in American society so far in the 21st century show no signs of slowing."[22]

The decline in the Christian population is largely centered among Protestants, a group broadly defined to include nondenominational Christians and people who describe themselves as "just Christian," along with Baptists, Methodists, and Lutherans. In the last decade, the Protestant population has dropped 10 points to the point where currently, only "40% of American adults are Protestants... In contrast, the Catholic share of the population, despite ticking downward between 2007 and 2014, has mostly remained steady in recent years. According to the survey, as of 2021, 21% of American adults identify as Catholic, identical to the Catholic share of the population in 2014."[23]

In a recent article in *Time Magazine*, this deepening fusion of "American identity with an ultraconservative strain of Christianity"[24] is described as a form of "Christian nationalism" that uses both violence and legislation, not in the service of democracy but instead for fundamentally antidemocratic goals. Their tactics of limiting access to voting and employing violence in order to disrupt the democratic process are not aberrations but simply the next chapter in the long, historical relationship between Christian Nationalism and antidemocratic attitudes in this country.

The Christian nationalist ideology is fundamentally a threat to a pluralistic, democratic society. They have their own version of the "elect," those chosen by God. They are "people like us," meaning white, natural-born conservative, Christian citizens. They believe that as "the elect," they should control the political process while others must be closely scrutinized, discouraged, or even denied access. The right-wing populist political-religious mass phenomenon we are witnessing today that culminated in the violence of the January 6, 2021, insurrection to prevent the duly elected government from taking office is in a direct historical and ideological line of descent from John Calvin's racist and misogynist theocratic Protestantism.

How strong and powerful is the Christian nationalist movement? The authors of the *Time* article, Andrew Whitehead and Samuel

Perry, put the number at 20% of the white population, or 30 million adults,[25] a number that merits profound consideration as a threat to national security and identity.

Modern Apocalyptic Evangelicalism

The source of Graham's unease and why he kept on having the feeling that "God will allow something to fall on us in a way I don't anticipate"[26] was that Graham did not fully understand the situation. Graham could not fathom the contradictions of his religious beliefs in the end of time and the progress and growth of America that he regarded as the crowning glory of Western Christian civilization. For how could he comprehend that the dynamics of the growth and expansion he so admired contained the seeds of its own destruction?

How could Graham fathom that many of his own Christian followers, the powerful politicians and super wealthy business leaders filling the pews at his shows, nodding piously to his exhortations during his sermons, and even subsidizing his evangelical efforts, were doing the work of the devil, as the real practitioners of the religion of greed? The White Man believed it was God's will and his own Manifest Destiny to spread His Glory and his dominion and conquer the Earth, economically where possible and militarily where necessary. In this, he has been successful beyond measure. His system of global capitalism, an economic system that requires infinite and exponential growth, has overrun and overpowered the globe, exceeding his wildest dreams. But this very fact made the Christian apocalyptic prophecy a self-fulfilling one. With greed, envy, hatred, aggression, abuse, exploitation increasingly defining the new normal in human interaction, the four horsemen of the Apocalypse are indeed running amuck in the world, bringing war, pestilence, famine, and death.

From the point of view of 21st-century Evangelical Christianity, the Apocalypse will be a good thing. The forces of evil will destroy the world, and the Christians will be high on rapture as they're being transported to heaven by Christ for an eternal existence of joy and happiness. So why not hurry things along a bit and help to make it happen sooner rather than later? Indeed, the apocalyptic Evangelicals moved far beyond their more orthodox brethren and crossed the line from passively waiting for the events prophesized by John to actively bringing them about. This evolution can only be understood as a response to the extraordinary stress experienced by the Christians in the post–World War II era.

Christians, when stressed, exhibit the same yin-yang response polarity as nonreligious people, only it is overlaid with their religious stance in the world. When Christians are stressed, the yin response of turning the violence inward against themselves expresses itself as Christian martyrdom. The yang response, turning the violence of the stress into external aggression, turns them into crusaders to battle and vanquish the cause of the distress, i.e., the non-Christian, secular world that they have no control over.

Recall how, in its infancy, Christians were persecuted by the Roman emperors, but as soon as the Roman ruling classes and Emperor Constantine adopted Christianity and made it the state religion, the Christians initiated a centuries-long orgy of destruction of classical Greco-Roman pagan civilization, persecuting and killing hundreds of thousands of non-Christians. We again saw this same dynamic play out in colonial times when Christianity ruthlessly imposed itself on native peoples all over the world. Moreover, history is rife with instances of Christians persecuting other Christians, as when the Catholics persecuted and killed the Protestants and vice versa.

In the contemporary era, we see this dynamic play out again. The shrinking social value and impact of traditional Christianity in American society in the post–World War II era caused a growing fear and abhorrence of secular, liberal society within the conservative Christian community. This secularization of society resulted in significant loss of Christian influence and power in government and setting social policy that, in turn, contributed to the breadth and depth of Christian despair. Kayleigh McEnany, Trump's press person, exemplified how people internalize the stress and attack themselves by exulting in their martyrdom for Christ. She quite eloquently expressed the yin response and summed up this attitude of defiant Christian martyrdom: "I am not going to apologize for speaking the Name of Jesus. I am not going to justify my faith to them, and I am not going to hide the light that God has put in me. If I have to sacrifice everything... I will."[27]

The rise of aggressive Evangelical Christianity in the second half of 20th and the first part of the 21st centuries speaks to the universality of the dynamic. Prolonged fear breeds anger and rage, and the persecuted become the persecutors. Christian martyrs, when the opportunity presents itself, tend to transform into cruel crusaders eager to mete out God's justice and take revenge on those damned unbelievers. The Evangelical crusaders of Christian Nationalism today are committed to the creation of a theocratic state and eager to tear every non-Christian pagan thing down. Being anti-science, anti-learning, these Christian nationalists recapture the zeal of the zealots who burned down the Library of Alexandria: "Onward Christian Soldiers, marching as to war, with the cross of Jesus, going on before!"

Trump as the Champion of Christian Nationalism

Many people were surprised by Trump's electoral victory because they had missed or underestimated the power of Evangelical Christianity as a template for Trump's campaigns. Trump's victory was the evolutionary offspring of the Moral Majority of the 1980s that Trump was able to galvanize and organize in 2016 into electoral victory in, hopefully, the first and last victory of Christian Nationalism. All the issues, tactics, and strategies utilized by Trump in 2016 had already been thoroughly explored and articulated in the 1970s and 1980s by Jerry Falwell and Paul Weyrich of the Moral Majority, with voter suppression topping their agenda from day one.

Of course, Trump's own Christianity had never progressed beyond learning from Norman Vincent Peale how "to worship himself,"[28] which, if anything, counted in his favor with the Evangelicals. So the mutual embrace of Trump and Evangelical Christianity into a political coalition made eminent sense from the very beginning to the parties themselves. The deal struck between Trump and the Evangelical leadership was simple: They would deliver the votes of their believers to Trump, and in return, Trump would appoint Evangelicals to important positions in the government.

The differences between Trump and the Evangelical leadership were superficial and easily discounted because, on a basic level, they shared the same value system. The preachers could easily minimize Trump's theological differences because who among them did not occasionally doubt themselves? Likewise, having engaged in many sexual peccadilloes themselves, they could easily commiserate with Trump on his womanizing problem. Trump also shared with the white Evangelicals their basic racist attitudes and outlook.

Indeed, Trump's less-than-Christian behavior, made him paradoxically a more appealing candidate to beleaguered, aggravated Christians. The growing fear of the future in the Christian community over the past half century had generated within it a desire for a strong leader that could unite the Christians and their churches in battle and protect them from what they perceived and felt as the approaching Apocalypse. And Trump fit the bill! Evangelical voters saw him as a president who acted like a bully but was fighting for them. A president who saw America like they did: a menacing place where white Christians feel mocked and threatened for their beliefs, and for whom Trump's very unholiness becomes an asset in the scourge-of-God role he is playing for them.

The pastor of the First Baptist Church of Dallas, Robert Jeffress, was typical in this respect. Jeffress had, for many years, been complaining about the ineffectiveness of such upstanding Republican presidents as Ronald Reagan and George W. Bush in smiting the foes of the faithful.[29] Jeffress spoke approvingly of Trump's practice of hitting back twice as hard whenever a critic took him on. Jeffress chuckled when he said approvingly that Trump's "favorite verse in the Bible… is, 'An eye for an eye and a tooth for a tooth.'" This is, of course, the very maxim Christ was rebutting when he taught believers to turn the other cheek and respond to offense with peace.[30] And so, yes, this sort of relish in the discomfort of the targets of Trump's frequent bouts of hate-rage is a bit out of line with the teachings of the Prince of Peace, but conservative Evangelicals have long been inclined to value Law over Gospel and righteousness over love. And when the Moral Majority turned, to their shock, into an embattled minority, the temptation to supplant the sweet Jesus with his angry Old Testament Father just became too strong to resist.

A Fox News poll found that 25% of all voters said that they believed God wanted Trump to be president, while a majority of 62% said no and 14% said they were unsure. More specifically, 55% of white Evangelical Christian respondents said they believed God wanted Trump to become president.[31] Ahead of the 2020 election, white Evangelicals stuck with Trump. "More than two-thirds of white Evangelicals continued to support President Trump, along with almost half of white Catholics and white mainline Protestants, according to a study released by Pew Research Center."[32]

It matters because white Evangelicals consistently have a disproportionate impact on elections and were key to Trump's 2016 victory. In 2018, "they only made up 15% of the population… but accounted for more than a quarter of midterm voters." And in 2020, Trump was "their favorite candidate."[33] "Throughout his tenure, Trump and his administration have pursued a number of key issues backed by Evangelicals, such as restricting abortion rights, eliminating a birth control mandate, and expanding school choice and voucher programs that would likely benefit private religious schools." In a 2019 tweet, Trump "endorsed a controversial campaign to introduce Bible literacy classes to public schools."[34]

During the years of the Trump administration, there was a significant change in the number of white Americans who identify as Evangelical Christians. The sobering fact is that during Donald Trump's presidency, the number of white Americans who started identifying as Evangelical actually grew. This increase is mostly attributable to the politization of the Evangelical movement and its ideological merger with the right wing of the Republican Party. "Instead of theological affinity for Jesus Christ, millions of Americans were being drawn to the Evangelical label because of its association with the GOP."[35] Those who embraced Trump swelled the ranks of the Evangelicals whereas as those who did not, did not. The result was the widespread self-acceptance of the believers of the identity equation that "to be a conservative Republican is to be an Evangelical Christian."[36]

A second factor bolstering evangelicalism during the Trump era is that many more people were embracing the Evangelical label who have no previous attachment to Protestant Christianity, such as Catholics, Muslims, and Mormons. A salient fact here is that these new Evangelicals are much more religiously devout than their predecessors. The rapid emergence of this new type of Evangelical has meant that the tradition did not fade but instead was radically remade. Whereas previously, Evangelicalism was thought of as fiery preachers imploring folks to accept Jesus, today "more and more Americans are conflating Evangelicalism with Republicanism—and melding two forces to create a movement that is not entirely about politics or religion but power."[37] The result is that "white Evangelicalism has never been more politically unified than it is right now. In the 1970s, only 40% of white, weekly churchgoing Evangelicals identified as Republicans; in more recent data, that number has risen to an all-time high of 70%."[38]

Trump's Evangelical Christian Foreign Policy

The deal between Trump and the Evangelical pastors was a perfect transactional one: the Evangelicals would deliver Trump the votes, and in return, Trump would push their policies and put "believers" in top decision-making positions in government, giving the Evangelicals more power and influence than they ever could have dreamed of previously. As a kind of insurance to close the deal, it was also helpful that Trump was able to leverage Jerry Falwell Jr.'s exploding sex scandal into Falwell officially backing him and thereby delivering the Evangelical vote to Trump, allowing him to win the 2016 election.[39] The result of Trump's political bargain with the Evangelical leaders for their support makes abundantly clear why having Evangelical Christians as foreign policymakers poses a serious danger to the stability of the global situation, particularly in the Middle East.

Secretary of State Mike Pompeo and Vice President Mike Pence are both Christian Zionists and typical of the growing influence of apocalyptic fundamentalism in the White House. Both Mike Pompeo and Mike Pence are also believers in Armageddon and that this final battle between good and evil which will end with the

Rapture.[40] And both of them have pushed Trump toward aggressive action toward Iran in the belief that this final battle will somehow involve Iran in a big way.[41] Also, one of the key beliefs of Evangelical Christianity was based on the biblical prophecy of the establishment of a "greater Israel" before the end of days. And today, fully 80% of Evangelicals believe that the creation of Israel in 1948 was a fulfillment of biblical prophecy that would bring about Christ's return and identify with Christian Zionism.[42] Evangelical leaders, including such luminaries as Pat Robertson and Jerry Falwell, have long woven Christian Zionism into conservatism. Falwell once said that, "to stand against Israel is to stand against God. We believe that history and scripture prove that God deals with nations in relation to how they deal with Israel."[43] Trump adroitly exploited the popularity of Christian Zionism when he recognized Jerusalem as Israel's capital, endlessly pleasing his right-wing allies in both Israel and the U.S.

Describing his work for Trump in an address to a Kansas church group, Pompeo has also emphasized the immense difficulties that will precede this end-times cleansing for the faithful: "It is a never-ending struggle... until the Rapture." Pompeo's hostility toward Iran is motivated by his extreme religious beliefs. Apparently, Pompeo has long had a fixation with a Bible passage about Queen Esther protecting Israel from Iran. Once, an interviewer asked him a question pertaining to the biblical tale about Queen Esther who saved Jews from slaughter by a Persian official. Did Mr. Pompeo think President Trump had been "raised for such a time as this, just like Queen Esther, to help save the Jewish people from the Iranian menace?"[44] Pompeo replied, "As a Christian, I certainly believe that's possible... The work that our administration has done [is] to make sure that this democracy in the Middle East, that this Jewish state, remains. I am confident that the Lord is at work here."[45] And the Lord was definitely working through his servant Mike Pompeo to strengthen and stabilize Israel. The Lord planted in Pompeo the seed idea that if Major General Qasem Soleimani, the feared mastermind of the Iranian military and intelligence establishments and Israel's archenemy, was eliminated in a preemptive strike, it would significantly enhance the chances of Israel's survival and improve its regional security. It was Mike Pompeo who pushed Trump into giving the final approval. The secretary spoke to President Trump multiple times every day during the week preceding the event. His efforts culminated in Trump's decision to approve the action to kill Soleimani.

The Devolution of the GOP into the Party of Violence

The polarization of white American religious life in the past half century was reflective of the political and social polarization that occurred simultaneously. The ensuing realignment of American politics has been more along "educational and cultural lines" and "less along class and income divisions that defined the two parties for much of the 20th century."[46] In 1952, only 5% of the voters were college graduates, while in 2020, 41% of people who cast votes were college graduates, making them a formidable voting bloc. As they grew in numbers, the college graduates instilled increasingly liberal cultural norms, nudging the Democratic Party to the left. In 2020, 60% of college-educated citizens voting for Biden secured his victory in that election.[47]

But in politics, as in physics, every action creates an opposite and equal reaction. Rising Democratic strength among college graduates and voters of color has been counteracted by a nearly equal and opposite reaction among white male voters without a degree, as evidenced by the fact that large portions of the party's traditional working-class base have defected to the Republicans.[48] As a result, in the 2020 election, while winning white college graduates, Biden lost white voters without a degree by a two-to-one margin. It also may help explain how Trump, while mobilizing racial animus for political gain, fared worse among white voters than expected and better among voters of color than previous Republicans.[49]

The net result is that the two political parties are polarizing ever more along educational lines. College graduates, increasingly women and people of color, and decreasingly white males, are flocking to and shaping the Democratic Party's future. In contrast, those increasingly without degrees, such as white males, have become the demographic base of the Republican Party.[50]

The very unfortunate truth is that this increasing difference in educational level has led to a divergence of opinion in the two party bases regarding the use of violence to promote and achieve political ends. First, note the increase: In the 1990s, more than 90% believed violence was never justified. But in 2022, that number fell to 62%.[51] That means today a third of Americans say violence against the government is justifiable.[52] This was indeed confirmed by a recent poll by *The Washington Post* and the University of Maryland that found "the percentage of Americans who say violent action against the government is justified at times stands at 34%."[53]

Often in the past, left-wing groups, such as BLM and other anti-fascists, espoused a readiness to take up arms in response to right-wing violence directed against progressive causes and events. But more recent events, including January 6, 2021, have amply proven that the right wing is ready and eager to engage in violence against our government and its democratic institutions. The new readiness to embrace violence as a tactic finds 40% of Republicans and 41% of independents but only 23% of Democrats who agree that violence is sometimes justified.[54] Many of the respondents identified issues of civil rights, gun policies, abortion rights, and labor policies as important enough that violence "might be justified, depending on the situation."[55] Not only does the no- to low-education level of the base of the Republican Party correlate with their penchant for violence, but it also explains the poverty of the intellectual constructs they use to explain the world around them. For their approach is not centered on ascertaining the facts to arrive at a conceptual understanding of their situation but is drawn from the simplistic explanations of Christian Nationalism, or sometimes fantastical conspiracy theories, such as QAnon, to justify their atavistic impulses.

The educational policies of the Reagan administration in the 1980s prepared the social soil to sprout the right-wing populist "know nothing" base of alienated white men that would become the shock troupes of the Trumpian politics of grievance, racism, and misogyny in the second decade of the 21st century. In the words of J. D. Vance before he flip-flopped from never-Trumper to staunch Trump loyalist, "We [the GOP] are, whether we like it or not, the party of lower-income, lower-education, white people, and I have been saying for a long time that we need to offer those people *something*... or a demagogue would. We are now at that point... I go back and forth... thinking Trump... is America's Hitler."[56]

The Violence of Trump and His Base

Understanding the relationship between Trump and his base begins with understanding the two grievances Trump shares with them. First, they share a deep distrust of the government and the upper-crust ruling class,[57] and second, they share the deep racism and misogyny that powered the White Man to world domination. Both Trump and his base felt they were the cause of their unhappiness in life and desirous of taking a "just" revenge upon them. Trump learned to hate New York's Manhattan business and political ruling class elites, not for their whiteness but for the "upper-crustiness" that made them disdainfully reject Trump's overtures to be accepted as an equal in their social circle. They found Trump's crass nouveau riche lifestyle disgusting and his bombastic over-the-top personality detestable. Also, Trump hated any and all "government" with a passion because it had the power to put the brakes on his insatiable appetite for wealth and power with their rules and regulations. Therefore, part of Trump's Big Lie was to paint and define the "deep state" inside the government, and the government itself, as the enemy.

So, in his campaigns, Trump could rage against the unfairness of the "deep state" and government officials in league with "aristocratic" upper classes with impunity, and his base would lap it up or chug it down like the poisonous Kool-Aid it was. Claiming that the "deep state" and the U.S. government itself was the enemy also allowed Trump to predict and maintain the fiction that if he lost the 2020 election, it was precisely because it was rigged by them. This is where and how Trump systematically roused the tempers of his base with his demagoguery, inciting them toward the violent mob of the January 6 "Stop the Steal" campaign against their own elected government.

Another characteristic Trump and his base share is the addiction to grievance politics. The question is, of course, why do both demagogues and their base of political "true believers" constantly engage in the politics of grievance and revenge? What's in it for Trump, and what's in it for his base? "It turns out that your brain on grievances looks a lot like your brain on drugs."[58] "Brain imaging studies show that harboring a grievance (a perceived wrong or injustice, real or imagined) activates the same neural reward circuitry as narcotics." Feeling wronged, people so afflicted experience "pleasure and relief through retaliation,"[59] or the anticipation of revenge and retaliation. To be clear, this retaliation doesn't need to be physically violent. In ordinary life, inflicting emotional pain through unkind words, or tweets, can also be very gratifying.

Occasionally, as it did on January 6, this retaliation spills over into physical force and use of violence. This points to why many people in Trump's base just can't let go of their grievances and why, in the end, some people resort to violence. Similar to the way people become addicted to drugs or gambling, in right-wing populist revenge, people become addicted to seeking retribution against their perceived enemies, real or imagined, needing more and more of it each time.

Typical of Trump's racist grievance against Black and other non-white people were his actions in 1989 after five young Black men were arrested on suspicion of the murder of a white female jogger in Central Park. Trump promptly paid a million dollars to take out a full-page ad in the *New York Times* demanding their execution. Trump wrote that, "I want to hate these muggers and murderers. They should be forced to suffer and, when they kill, they should be executed for their crimes. They must serve as examples so that others will think long and hard before committing a crime or an act of violence."[60] In a 1989 CNN interview about the ad, Trump doubled down and told Larry King that, "Maybe hate is what we need if we're gonna get something done." He concluded that "I am not looking to psychoanalyze or understand them, I am looking to punish them...

I no longer want to understand their anger. I want them to under-stand our anger. I want them to be afraid."[61] And predictably, Trump never apologized when it was later proven that the Central Park Five had been framed and manipulated into confessing, were conclusively proven innocent, and were released.

Underneath Trump's obsession with inciting violence is a deep fear of violence being used against him, as Trump testified to in a suit in response to a group of protesters suing him over their violent removal from a Trump campaign rally in 2015. Perhaps it was his being an extreme clean freak germophobic, the obsessive cleanliness of the anal-retentive character, that made him express his fear that his attire could be dirtied by all manner of fruit being hurled at him by protestors. He was urging his followers to especially keep an eye out for any protesters that might be getting ready to throw fruit at him, telling them from the podium, "If you see someone getting ready to throw a tomato, just knock the crap out of them, would you? It's very dangerous stuff. You can get killed with those things… I promise you I'll pay the legal fees."[62]

While president, even, Trump repeatedly alluded to extrajudicial physical force, including suggesting that his supporters might resort to violence if they didn't get their way.[63] "I actually think that the people on the right are tougher [than on the left], but they don't play it tougher." Was he already dreaming of January 6 when he said, in the 2016 campaign, that "I can tell you I have the support of the police, the support of the military, the support of the Bikers for Trump—I have the tough people, but they don't play it tough—until they go to a certain point, and then it would be very bad, very bad."[64]

In the final analysis, the feelings of his base toward Trump and Trump's feelings toward his base are not the same. Indeed, they are antithetical to each other. The emotions of Trump's base are genuine; they love him because he expresses and verbalizes their accumulated rage and continually encourages them to vent and act on it. Trump's feelings about his base are totally exploitative. He only caters to them because they are useful to him. Secretly he despises the workers and farmers of his base for allowing themselves to be manipulated by him, but he loves exploiting their hatreds and their resentments, as the following series of quotes by Howard Stern, the famous radio shock jock on SiriusXM, describe how Trump really feels about his base.[65] Trump was a frequent guest on Stern's shows over the years, and the host has said the two were once friends. "The oddity in all of this is the people Trump despises most love him the most… Trump loves celebrities, not the masses… He wouldn't even let them in a fucking hotel. He'd be disgusted by them." Stern then challenged Trump supporters to verify this for themselves by visiting the president's most famous property. "Go to Mar-a-Lago. See if there's any people who look like you." Stern said, specifying that "I'm talking to you in the audience… I don't hate Donald," Stern added, before unloading on the president's supporters, but "I hate you for voting for him, for not having intelligence."[66]

Trump's Coup

Pre-Election: Planning for Defeat

When Donald Trump ran for president against Hillary Clinton in 2016, a majority of Republicans as well as nearly all Democrats expected him to lose. Even Trump expected to, as was evident in the delighted surprise he showed when the reality sank in and he was proclaimed the winner. Knowing Trump's addiction to winning and his pathological fear of being a loser, it's a safe bet that, as his campaign progressed and he faced almost certain defeat, he spent a lot time thinking about how he would handle that dreaded situation. And since he could never own up to the fact that he and his own inadequacies could be the cause of his loss, there was only one thing that could explain his approaching humiliation. That was the electoral process itself: it had been rigged!

In other words, already in 2016, Trump was formulating and trying out the Big Lie on audiences in his campaign rallies. At an Ohio rally, for example, he announced that he might not be able to accept the election results if he lost because it would prove that the election had been rigged. And he then proceeded to mention it at other rallies and even in the debates against Hillary. No doubt he congratulated himself for devising a strategy where he couldn't lose. If he won the election, he won, for sure. But if he lost the election, he also won because he would claim and convince his followers that the election was fixed, and they, like him, would want revenge. In the end, it was probably a huge relief to him when he actually was elected because he did not have to try to sell the Big Lie to the people to convince them, and himself, that he had been a victim of foul play.

However, an important lesson had been learned. As he emerged victorious in 2016, Trump had already devised the strategy he would follow in dealing with any future defeat. Thus, when he ran again in 2020, and began sensing he might lose for real this time, Trump began to heat up his campaign with claims that if he were defeated, it would be because the election was rigged, preparing his base by haranguing them into constant irrational rage and readiness, if not eagerness, to engage in violent action to "stop the steal."

Strategies to Defeat Democracy

In the 2020 election, with the prospects of defeat looming ever stronger, Trump also began planning with those closest to him additional actions that he could engage in to maintain himself in the presidency if he lost the election. When it became apparent that Trump had been defeated by Biden, Trump and company went into a frenzy of planning and improvisation in an effort to nullify the election and remain in office. That led directly to the attempted coup and the insurrection of January 6, 2021.

At first, Trump's attempts at interference amounted to both indirect and direct corrupt solicitations. His team was in communication with "considered friendly" Republican secretaries of states and other officials responsible for the integrity of the elections in their states. Trump and his team published emails by John Eastman (a prominent lawyer in Trump's world) which showed that the idea of "recounting" and "recalibrating" the votes of certain states predates the idea of having Mike Pence choose alternate electors in schemes suspiciously similar to what main salesmen on this idea. As he told

Georgia Secretary of State Brad Raffensperger, "There's nothing wrong with saying, you know, um, that you've recalculated," Trump said, according to a recording of the call published by *The Washington Post*. "So look," he added. "All I want to do is this. I just want to find 11,780 votes… because we won the state." Biden won the election in Georgia by 11,779 votes.[67]

When this approach failed to convince officials like Raffensperger to commit fraud, perjury, and a host of other crimes, Trump and his team turned to plan B, the brainchild of John Eastman. Eastman's harebrained scheme was to disrupt the election ratification process through the Electoral College by messing with its voting procedures. Eastman's basic idea was to get Vice President Mike Pence to repudiate the electoral votes from specific states by vaguely citing allegations of fraud in those states and "returning their votes to the state legislatures." Never mind that this entailed exercising a hitherto unknown and unilateral power in the vice presidency! If by doing this, Pence could succeed in lowering Biden's electoral vote total to below 270, it would immediately trigger a new contingent election under the Twelfth Amendment. The house contingent election was the one place where Trump could still "win" the election.

Trump Inciting the Insurrection on January 6

Then came January 6, 2021, another day that will live in infamy, when the enemy within attacked the American constitutional order in an assault engineered and commanded by the president and his vice president against the people of the United States. The events of January 6, as Representative Jamie Raskin put it, amounted to "a self-coup [with] a president, fearful of defeat, overthrowing the constitutional process [in which] Trump was prepared to seize the presidency and likely to invoke the Insurrection Act and declare martial law."[68]

The planned rally was thought of as a tool to put pressure on Pence and other Republicans to act in accordance with the plot and repudiate the electoral votes of certain states as fraudulently obtained to swing the total in favor of Trump. At the rally, accordingly, Trump proceeded to whip up his adoring followers into a frenzy of righteous rage: "And we fight. We fight like hell. And if you don't fight like hell, you're not going to have a country anymore... Because you'll never take back our country with weakness. You have to show strength and you have to be strong... All of us here today do not want to see our election victory stolen by emboldened radical-left Democrats, which is what they're doing... We will never give up, we will never concede... You don't concede when there's theft involved... Our country has had enough. We will not take it anymore, and that's what this is all about... We will stop the steal."[69]

A few hours later, the insurrectionists, egged on and ordered by their commander in chief, Donald J. Trump, stormed the Capitol in order to "stop the steal" and delay the certification of President-Elect Biden's Electoral College victory.

What Trump Was Doing During the Insurrection

Contrary to his promises to his supporters that he would march with them, after delivering his incendiary call to engage in riotous violence, Trump retreated to safety. Once holed up in the White House, he made sure he wouldn't be denied the pleasure of watching the chaos he'd unleashed. According to Stephany Grisham, former chief of staff, "he was in the dining room, gleefully watching on his TV as he often did." The experience was a balm to his narcissism. Grisham added that Trump commented excitedly on the violent spectacle he was watching. "Look at all the people fighting for me." Then he would hit rewind and watch it again, repeatedly.[70]

Present with Trump was General Keith Kellogg, Pence's security advisor. Kellogg told Trump, "You really should do a tweet... You need to get a tweet out real quick, help control the crowd up there. This is out of control. They're not going to be able to control this. Sir, they're not prepared for it. Once a mob starts turning like that, you've lost it."[71] Trump replied with a bored, "Yeah," then just "blinked and kept watching television." Trump's eldest daughter, Ivanka, was equally unsuccessful in persuading her father to stop the mayhem.

Three times, she urged her father to intervene, telling him, "Let it go… Let this thing go," only to be completely rebuffed and ignored.

But Trump was not only enjoying himself; he was also working—the phones particularly. During the hours of the insurrection, he was in constant telephone contact with his closest advisors and co-conspirators and closely monitoring the ongoing proceedings at the Electoral College with them. Though the White House call logs for January 6 have mysteriously gone missing, we know that one of the calls Trump made was to Vice President Pence. Pence had not yet committed to joining the Electoral College vote conspiracy, and yet his participation was essential to its success.

So, in his call to Pence as the January 6 insurrection was unfolding, Trump put it to him in stark either-or terms, telling the vice president that, "You can either go down in history as a patriot, or you can go down in history as a pussy."[72] His choice of words here is telling and can be understood only in terms of the cultural values of the White Man's misogynist male-centric paradigm. For in the experiential world of Trump and company, women lie down for them because they are afraid to stand up to them. And the word "pussy," used in this context as a synonym for "woman," also becomes synonymous with being a "coward," regardless of sex.

Transfixed, watching TV for hours on end, Trump blithely ignored the advice of his closest circle of family and advisors who thought things had gone too far. For hours, he refused their repeated entreaties to speak publicly in an effort to stop the violence, all the while, plainly reveling in a supreme, narcissistic thrall, even gloating about the fact that all that violence was about him.

The Pathology of the Insurrection

The January 6 insurrection spectacle provided graphic proof of the merger and fusion of far-right religious groups and beliefs with factions promoting the wildest of wild conspiracy theories like QAnon. Christian flags, crosses on T-shirts, "Jesus Saves" signs, and prayers for victory in Jesus's name were famously conspicuous among the mob, along with signs supporting the secular insanity of QAnon and other conspiracy theories. This fusion of right-wing, religious, and secular extremism raised the question of why so many Americans who embrace Christian nationalism also have the propensity of believing in conspiracies theories. The QAnon conspiracy theory, for example, asserts that a democratic, liberal cabal of satanic, cannibalistic pedophiles runs a global child sex trafficking ring out of a pizza parlor in D.C. This cabal, QAnon teaches, worked first with Hillary Clinton, then with Joe Biden, against Donald Trump.

It sounds insane—because it is! But is it any more far-fetched to believe this conspiracy than it is to believe that a bearded old white guy is sitting somewhere up high, lording over humanity and choosing some for eternal life and sending others to eternal damnation? As pathologies, they are both the products of a highly stressed and fragmented consciousness that had no access to the relevant facts and knowledge, lacking the capacity for critical thinking.

Why would so many people support a violent insurrection in the name of Jesus or pass laws aimed at limiting minorities' access to the democratic process? The simple answer is because they trust Donald Trump implicitly and uncritically, above all other sources of information. And as their preachers have been telling them for years, and as Trump, their savior, also told them numerous times in no uncertain terms, in order to safeguard their values and save the country, they must support and be willing to participate in violence when necessary to keep the Immoral Minority of white Christian nationalist males in power.

The opposition of the Republican Party to establishing a 9/11-type commission to investigate the events of January 6 and its causes is a de facto admission of their complicity and guilt. Because the conclusions that would inevitably come to light became already obvious as the events unfolded live on TV: not only were the perpetrators the shock troops of the right-wing extremist movement, but also their activities, what they were able to do and how, had been planned and were being coordinated by the highest levels of officialdom in the Republican Party, including the president of the United States himself.

Trumpism Beyond Trump

The Trumpist Republican Party

While Trump as an individual will, in due time, inevitably disappear from the public square, Trumpism as a political force movement will continue to be an integral part of the national political landscape and struggle. Signs of Trump's diminishing appeal are all around. The attendance at his rallies has been abysmal. The major networks won't carry them live anymore. He's stuck on the past, refuses to admit he lost the election; it's a dead end. He's only been out of office a year, and every day, fewer and fewer people care about what he says or does anymore, especially because he sounds like such a broken record.[73] More and more Republicans, like Maryland Governor Larry Hogan, are ready move on and are willing to admit publicly that "With America on the wrong path, the stakes are too high to double down on failure."[74] We will not go into details about his well-known legal troubles that would only accentuate his political obsolescence.

Trump realized that in order to accomplish his larger goals of seizing and consolidating political power, he first had to gain complete control over his party. Consequently, even before January 6, he began to organize a concerted campaign to destroy the established institutional wing of the GOP and replace it with MAGA supporters. In this effort, Trump was largely successful by means of the adroit use of his base as a weapon. By successfully running his own more extreme right-wing MAGA candidates in the Republican primaries against the more moderate traditional Republicans, he infused the GOP with a new crop of the extremist radicals. By primarying his opponents into oblivion, he gained control over the local party chapters and their electoral institutional structures, all the while claiming that the January 6 events were just "normal political discourse."[75]

Having consolidated control over the Republican Party, Trumpism is now going full bore using it as a tool to gain wide control over local, state, and national governments, imposing a Trumpist vision on America. Numerous Trump clones like DeSantis, J.D. Vance, and others are already stepping out of his shadow, carrying Trumpism forward, often even Trumpier than Trump, while spewing their racism and misogyny.

The Trumpists do not consider the failure of January 6 as a moral failure that should never be attempted again but rather a failure of tactics and strategy that they must learn from and avoid in the future when other attempts are made. Having learned the big lesson that the Big Lie works, the MAGA crowd has come to see January 6 as a dress rehearsal for the next time.

Today, the Republican Party is split three ways between the traditional Republicans, who are in open opposition to Trump, the hard right-wingers that constitute his base and co-conspirators, and the undecided vacillators who are waiting to see which way the wind blows before casting their lots. The traditionalist faction is in retreat, and the Trumpist faction is ascendant and in control of the Republican Party. Under Trumpist control, "the Republican Party is no longer simply trying to compete with and defeat the Democratic Party on a level playing field. Today, rather than simply playing the game, the Republicans" are committed to "rig[ging] the rules" of the electoral process "so that they never lose."[76]

Trumpism on the Supreme Court

After 50 years seeking all-encompassing power, the conservative legal movement has reached its goal. It climbed the mountaintop after Donald Trump won the 2016 presidential election despite losing the popular vote by nearly three million ballots. Trump became the first president since Ronald Reagan to appoint three justices to the Supreme Court. The court's six-vote conservative super-majority then resolutely set about implementing the agenda that conservative presidents, going back to Ronald Reagan, could not do through legislation or executive action. Domestically, Trump's crowning achievement undoubtedly consisted of guaranteeing the ultraconservative bent of the Supreme Court for the long-term, foreseeable future. And its first target, not surprisingly, was *Roe v. Wade*.

Roe v. Wade, of course, was the decision handed down by the Supreme Court in 1973 that gave women the right to self-determination over their bodies by codifying their right to choose to have an abortion. No sooner had *Roe v. Wade* been decided than it became the all-consuming priority and battle of the Christian right to have the Supreme Court reverse that decision by declaring abortion illegal. It took half a century, but it was this new ultra-conservative court created by Trump that made the monumental decision to strike down and repeal *Roe v. Wade*. With that decision, the Supreme Court reversed its own evolutionary direction toward the universal expansion of personal rights and freedoms and restored the male-centric misogynistic mentality of the 16th and 17th centuries as the law of the land in the 21st century.

"I thought I was writing fiction," Margaret Atwood said about *The Handmaid's Tale*. "I invented Gilead [but] the Supreme Court is making it real,"[77] taking the U.S. back to a time when women's bodies were property for men to control. While the Alito opinion purports to be based on America's Constitution, it fundamentally relies on English jurisprudence from the 17th century, a time when women were considered men's property, and a belief in witchcraft caused the death of many innocent people. One of the people Alito cited frequently in his opinion was an English jurist by the name of Matthew Hale, who had at least two women executed for witchcraft.[78] Hale, as a male jurist and judge, was also fiercely defensive of his presumed prerogative as a husband and denied even the possible existence of marital rape. Hale once said, "For the husband cannot be guilty of a rape committed by himself upon his lawful wife for by their mutual matrimonial consent and contract the wife hath given up herself in this kind unto her husband which she cannot retract."[79]

The Supreme Court's infamous Dred Scott decision of 1857 and Justice Samuel Alito's majority opinion of 2022 share many parallel features, including junk history and a fierce desire to forestall the future.[80] What the first tried to roll back the progress of Black people and their emancipation, the second tried to roll back the progress of women emancipation and freedom, all for the purpose of maintaining the White Man's power.

Taney's *Dred Scott* opinion drips with contempt for anyone who could possibly think that Black people could be citizens of the United States or that any Founders would approve of such a belief. Taney argued that the United States, as a nation formed for the benefit of the White Man, is both originally and fundamentally racist toward Black people. This racism was inborn from English law, belief, and custom. And it was, therefore, ineradicable. For more than a century before the founding of America, Black people were "regarded as beings of an inferior order [who were] unfit to associate with the white race either in social or political relations," Taney wrote. "This opinion was at that time fixed and universal in the civilized portion of the white race," he added, therefore, "no one seems to have doubted the correctness of the prevailing opinion of the time."[81]

The *Dred Scott* decision was saying that the original sentiment of colonial and revolutionary era white Americans should apply to the law forever. This has a familiar ring to modern ears. Its sound can be heard in Alito's opinion. "The inescapable conclusion is that a right to abortion is not deeply rooted in the Nation's history and traditions," Alito writes. "On the contrary, an unbroken tradition of prohibiting abortion on pain of criminal punishment persisted from the earliest days of the common law until 1973."[82] And as Trump himself echoed, this should be restored. "'There has to be some form of punishment' for women who have abortions," insisted Donald Trump.[83]

A further parallel between the *Dred Scott* decision in 1857 and the reversal of *Roe v. Wade* in 2022 is the court's (and the Republicans') complete indifference of the opinion of the majority of the American people. In the *Dred Scott* case, it was the majority opinion of the people that slavery was unconstitutional and should be abolished. And in 2022, it was the opinion of the majority of people that only women have the inalienable right to make decisions about their own bodies, and no one else, least of all a bunch of bitter and angry, misogynistic, old white guys. Furthermore, the two cases parallel each other in that each one would be a precipitating cause of civil war, the First Civil War of 1861 to 1865, and the Second Civil War of the mid-21st century.

The GOP, Race and Misogyny: Two Turning Points

The tragedy of the Republican Party is that it was transformed from the noble ideals that inspired its birth into its antithesis, the ignoble clinging to power by old white men at the expense of everybody else, especially non-white minorities. The party founded on equality, the abolition of slavery, and the rights of the working man was captured by the anti-worker, racist, and misogynistic party of big (white) business, big (white) money, and big (white) profit.

The capture culminated, in a sense, with the election of Richard Nixon and the successful implementation of Nixon's Southern Strategy. Nixon and the GOP embraced the politics of white resentment tied to disenfranchisement. Since Richard Nixon's Southern Strategy, the GOP has pigeonholed itself in large part as an aggrieved white people's party. Nixon played on the fact that when a large segment of white people fears that democracy may benefit other ethnicities to their own detriment, they abandon their commitment to democracy in favor of autocracy and intolerance. For example, white people who did not want to have immigrants or people of different races living next door to them were more likely to be supportive of authoritarian rule, whether military rule or a strong-man type of leader who could ignore legislatures or secure election results.

Trump's racist campaigns in 2016 and 2020 took a page straight from Nixon's playbook. They were all about grievance and revenge, based wholly on exploiting and exacerbating the racist fears of his white base, constantly repeating that the woes of his suffering base were all caused by domestic and immigrant minorities.

As the multiculturalism of our country has been growing in size and influence, the response of white people has split into two opposing camps of affirmative, progressive responses and negative, regressive reactions. In the progressive camp, the white response has been to enthusiastically accept, support, and join the revival of the multicolored Rainbow Coalition of ethnicities, celebrating minorities coming into their power.

The term Rainbow Coalition was first coined and used in 1969 by the Black Panther Party's Fred Hampton to bring together a broad spectrum of all races and creeds for the purpose of education and voter mobilization for progressive causes. In 1983, the idea and theme was taken up again and expanded by Jesse Jackson. Running for the democratic presidential nomination, Jackson campaigned as the candidate of the Rainbow Coalition of diverse Americans—including Blacks, whites, Latinos, Native Americans, and Asian Americans, men and women, straight and LGBTQ. In the next few decades, we can expect the Rainbow Coalition to become an increasingly relevant idea and theme as the nation is about to reach a second major historical and symbolic milestone, namely, the transition from a white majority country to a white minority country. Around 2045, or the middle of the century, the moment will come when the number of non-white people will be greater than the number of white people. Crossing this inflection point will constitute a major and mighty challenge to the survival of our democracy because it's going to be impossible to win a national, democratic American election with a platform that alienates people of color.

Unsurprisingly, in the reactionary camp, a fierce, white, racist, right-wing reaction against it has also emerged to mobilize, reject, sabotage, fight this development tooth and nail. In 2016, this white male racist movement had its moment in history by electing one of its own, Donald Trump, as president. Trump's central promise as a politician has been the elevation, protection, and promotion of whiteness, particularly white men who fear demographic changes and loss of status and privilege. In the 2016 presidential election, white men were the only group in which a majority voted for Donald Trump—62%—though a plurality of white women did also—47%.[84]

Trump's victory represented the second turning point for the degeneration of the GOP. If the first was to turn from its anti-racist legacy and embrace racism, the second turning was its decision to

shed its commitment to democratic values and embrace Trump's autocratic and authoritarian values and tactics. The story of this second
GOP turning point cannot be told without discussing (1) the radical
changes that traditional Christianity was itself experiencing and (2)
the relationship of Trump and modern Evangelical Christianity.

David Brooks wrote about the shrinking ranks of Republican
voters by blaming the generation gap as what will destroy the Republican Party. He makes the point that young adults hate Republicans
and their appeal to white exclusivity and much prefer Democrats
and their agenda of ethnic and gender inclusivity.[85] Every single day,
millennials and Gen Z voters live with ethnic diversity and differences more than the Silent Generation and the boomers ever did.
In just over two decades, America will be a majority-minority country. Young voters approve of these trends. They have constructed an
ethos that is mostly about dealing with difference. Among millennials, 79% think immigration is good for America, and 61% think
racial diversity is good for America. Likewise, for gender politics.
They are much more sympathetic to those who identify as LGBT. On
the other hand, they are much less likely to say the U.S. is the best
country in the world.

Trump has had the effect of hastening this process of driving
out precious Republican voters, especially the female, non-white,
younger and more highly educated young. The voters Trump and
his party lost in 2016 and 2020 represent the future of American
politics. It underscores how the Republican Party has become the
party of the past, of aging white men with less education; that will
make winning elections increasingly difficult.[86] As the exodus drains
and shrinks the ranks of the GOP, it is left in the hands of the old
white guys.

As white people continue to decrease as a percentage of the U.S.
population, the growing concentration of intolerant white voters in
the GOP has created a party which grows less and less committed
to the democratic project. When faced with a choice between big-
otry and democracy, many Republicans today are embracing the first
while abandoning the second. As a January 2020 survey by YouGov

confirmed, the plain, sad truth is that, for the majority of members of the GOP, the issue of race trumps the issue of democracy,[87] and a majority of Republican voters today value "Making America White Again" more than they value the sanctity of the vote.

And if Trump decided to create a new political party and leave the GOP, these Republicans would be more than happy to follow him. Some 73 million Republicans voted for Trump in the 2020 election, and of these, as a recent joint survey by *USA Today* and Suffolk University found, almost half of them would support Trump if he started a new political party, while about a quarter of them would support the existing GOP as is, and another quarter of them remained undecided.[88]

As a result, most Republicans have come to the ironic conclusion that "the traditional American way of life is disappearing so fast that we may have to use force to save it."[89] More than 40% predicted that "a time will come when patriotic Americans have to take the law into their own hands." And more than 47% concurred with the premise that "strong leaders sometimes have to bend the rules in order to get things done." And on all of these questions, most of those who did not agree were merely unsure.[90]

GOP Strategy: Power by Any Means Necessary

It must not be thought that the transformation of the Republican Party from the party of the Moral Majority to the party of the Immoral Minority was driven by an intrinsic or ideological contempt for democracy on the part its leadership. No, the GOP leaders were driven, simply, by fear of losing what they've always been and always had: the majority ethnicity with all the power.

Half a century ago, white Protestant men occupied nearly all our country's high-status positions. They made up nearly all the elected officials, business leaders and media figures. Those days are over, but the loss of a group's social status can feel deeply threatening. Many rank-and-file Republicans believe that the country they grew up in is being taken away from them. Slogans like "take our country back" and "make America great again" reflect this sense of peril.[91]

The GOP's response has been to devise and evolve a collection of low-road strategies to find a way to maintain white supremacy and white-male dominance without the necessity of a white majority in the U.S. population. In their policies and politics, they are engaging in a flagrant display of a white-male exertion of power, authority, and privilege, in demonstrations meant to underscore that they will forcefully fight any momentum toward demographic displacement, no matter how inevitable the math.

Republican legislative strategy, in deference to its white male base, is fundamentally misogynist and racist. First, it's all about misogyny and controlling the bodies of women. Look no further than the reversal of *Roe v. Wade*. It's also about fighting the redefinition of gender as personified by the advances in liberty among people who are transgender. Second, it's about restricting the voting of non-white, less conservative groups, as well as controlling the flow of migrants into the country who do not bolster the white population. Especially in the South, Trump and the GOP keep their base animated and activated by weaponizing the fear of white-male displacement to keep white voters heated over the issue of immigration and an "invasion" or "infestation" of Latin Americans. Elsewhere in the Rust Belt, in the Coal Belt, and in the Farm Belt, Trump likewise keeps white voter support, even as they're waiting for the day that he will magically bring back the manufacturing industry, revitalize the coal industry, and re-energize the agricultural industry.

In the 2020 presidential election, when voters rejected the agenda of Republicans who think and behave this way in favor of the Democrats, Republicans went out of their way to use their power to subvert the democratic process. They did so in Georgia, Republicans trying to rig the voting process when it looked like Democrats would win. They did so in Wisconsin, when the Democrats finally ousted their nemesis, Governor Scott Walker, despite Republican attempts at election rigging. After he lost, Walker not only attempted to delay the elections for state seats that he believed Democrats would win but also signed a bill that seized key powers from Democratic Governor-Elect Tony Evers, who defeated Walker. They did so in North Carolina. After losing the governorship in North Carolina in 2016,

Republicans used lame-duck legislative sessions to push through a flurry of bills stripping power from incoming Democratic governors. Also in North Carolina, Republican legislators used a surprise vote to ram through an override of Governor Roy Cooper's budget veto, while most Democrats had been told no vote would be held.[92] They did so in Michigan: after a Democratic victory in the 2016 gubernatorial race, Michigan Republicans weighed a similar bill as North Carolina's to strip power from the newly elected governor.[93]

What we're seeing in America is an invasion of our institutions by right-wing partisans whose loyalty is to party not principle. This invasion is corroding the Republic, and this corrosion is already very far advanced.[94] Republicans have been stuffing the courts with such people for decades. And not just the courts. A growing number of positions in government agencies are being occupied by right-wing partisans who do not care about, or actively oppose, their agencies' missions. The Environmental Protection Agency is now run by people who don't want to protect the environment; Health and Human Services by people who want to deny Americans healthcare.

In the wake of the 2018 midterm election where the Republicans lost 40 House seats, Republicans were willing to call perfectly legitimate election results into question simply because they didn't like the outcome. President Trump, for example, "spread wild conspiracy theories about 'forged' ballots in the Florida Senate race, and of undocumented immigrants voting en masse for Democrats in California House contests. We heard similar sentiments from establishment figures like Lindsey Graham, Paul Ryan, and Marco Rubio."[95] The same takeover is taking place in politics. Under Republican control, the function of the Senate to "advise and consent" has been downgraded to simply "consent." Trump can do anything, including corruption and criminality, without the senators of his own party being courageous enough to exercise any oversight.

The strategy all along has been about controlling the courts by stacking them. "Trump's 231 appointments are a record among recent predecessors—as are his 54 circuit and 177 district court appointments."[96] One in every six seats on the nation's circuit courts is now filled by a Trump nominee. Out of Trump's circuit court nominees,

90% (and 92% of those confirmed) have been white. In a similar vein, 80% of his judicial nominees (and 74% of those confirmed) have been men. Another example of GOP constitutional hardball and their abandonment of fair play was showcased spectacularly in 2016, when the United States Senate refused to allow President Barack Obama to fill the Supreme Court vacancy created by Justice Antonin Scalia's death, in effect, stealing a court seat.[97] Adding insult to injury, when Trump was in the White House, McConnell no longer objected "to filling a vacancy during an election" like he did while Obama was president. Instead, he vowed to confirm any Trump nominee as soon as he was able.

The Electoral College came into being as a compromise workaround in the negotiations to achieve political balance between the slave-owning South and the anti-slavery North. Even though the white population of the North outnumbered that of the South, the Electoral College that was agreed upon functioned to give the South more electors and achieve parity with the North by allowing the South to count their slaves to get more (white) electors.[98] This situation is both obsolete and obscene. It has resulted in a situation where the U.S. Senate favors states with a small population over states with a large population. The result is that 70% of the people are represented by 30% of the senators, and 30% of the people are represented by 70% of the senators. That is why the Democratic Party must make Electoral College reform, along with public financing and ending gerrymandering an integral part of their election reform strategy.[99]

The Electoral College has, indeed, failed the test of time. The presidency went to the popular-vote loser in 1824, 1876, and 1888. In the 20th century, Americans had close calls in the elections of 1948, 1960, 1968, and 1976, with near splits in the popular and electoral vote. Despite winning the popular vote in six of the past seven presidential elections, Democrats have held the presidency for only four of those terms, under Bill Clinton and Barack Obama. It is also the reason why Donald Trump became president in 2016. A healthy plurality chose his opponent, but his supporters dominated key swing states. If in the election, all votes had counted equally, Trump would not have been made president. This showcases that the Electoral College is a subversion of democracy because it undermines the principle of "one person, one vote."[100]

It could happen again. America's future political demography offers four realistic scenarios in which Democrats win the national popular vote but lose the Electoral College because of the geography of the electorate.[101]

Over the last decade, there have been an increasing number of elections where Democrats won the most votes but nevertheless lost national elections for the presidency, the House, and the Senate. The reason is that Republicans have, for many years, been waging a successful House district gerrymandering campaign to secure a Republican monopoly that is fundamentally antidemocratic. The 2019 Supreme Court decision, which said federal courts can't bar partisan gerrymandering, not only preserves the unjust undemocratic status quo achieved by Republican manipulation but also threatens to put Democrats at an even greater long-term political and demographic disadvantage in the Senate and perhaps also the presidency. Thus the current situation continues to favor Republican efforts. In blue-leaning states, it is easy enough for Republican governments to draw heavily Democratic districts, anchored in cities, then divvy up the rest of a state to their advantage, as they did in Pennsylvania or Michigan. In red-leaning states, they can break up cities into multiple Republican-leaning districts, as they have in Utah or Ohio. Overall, gerrymandering probably gives the Republicans about ten more seats than they would have otherwise.

The Trump administration's effort to include a citizenship question in the census to facilitate gerrymandering schemes that would, in the words of one party strategist, be "advantageous to Republicans and non-Hispanic whites,"[102] fits the broader pattern. The underlying logic of these abuses are fearful, declining majorities' desperate attempt to maintain power while in effect turning into the minority population.[103] If a citizenship question is included in the census, it will result in a severe undercount of all minorities, but especially

Hispanics, with far-reaching effects on the distribution of political power and federal funding for the next decade and beyond. Wilbur Ross, Secretary of Commerce, lied and gave false and misleading testimony during the course of the litigation about why the Trump administration was so intent on including a citizenship query in the decennial count. Mr. Ross said in sworn testimony to Congress in March that he was responding "solely" to a Justice Department request for data to enforce the 1965 Voting Rights Act. He also said he knew of no talks with the White House about the matter.[104] This was unequivocally proved a lie when a trove of documents came to light. The documents belonged to Thomas Hofeller, a Republican specialist in gerrymandering who worked with Wilbur Ross on the question. The files came into the possession of Mr. Hofeller's daughter after Mr. Hofeller passed away from natural causes, and she made them public. According to one 2015 study written by Mr. Hofeller, adding a citizenship question would create "a structural electoral advantage" that would benefit Republicans and non-Hispanic whites.[105]

After Trump's 2020 election loss to Joe Biden, and the failed insurrection of January 6, the now Trumpified GOP increased its efforts on the legal, legislative, and judicial fronts to guarantee that future elections would be won by this white, right-wing Immoral Minority. By early April 2021, the Brennan Center for Justice reported that lawmakers in 47 states proposed over 350 bills that claim to address voter fraud by limiting mail, early in-person, and Election Day voting through stricter ID requirements, limiting eligibility to vote absentee and voting hours. The recent bills signed into law by Governors Brian Kemp in Georgia and Ron DeSantis in Florida are just two examples.

What Is Illiberal Democracy?

The current resurgence in the U.S. of Trump, Trumpism, and the white male supremacist movement is not an isolated American phenomenon but can only be understood within a wider context. This wider context involves several interrelated global developments that are occurring in response to the deepening global crises created by the engines that are accelerating time, as described in Chapter 12. The two interrelated phenomena that must be understood are the (1) increase in global anxiety and (2) the global increase in illiberal democracies. As described in Chapter 12, worldwide climatic catastrophes have already and will increasingly cause enormous population displacements and movements. At the same time, the increasing threats of impending war, famine, and disease are setting in motion powerful new global currents of balkanization, isolationism, and nationalism. When people move from the more affected to the less affected places and countries, many of the people already living in these better places will feel threatened by the "invasions." It is this fear that makes them easy prey for grievance and revenge politics of right-wing populism in illiberal democracies or outright fascism.

So, what is illiberal democracy? It is the authoritarian subversion, perversion if you wish, of electoral democracy. Illiberal democracy is fascism dressed up as democracy. It's a one-party state where the top autocrat writes, adjudicates, and executes, in short *is*, the Law but where sham elections are held so as to be able to claim they're democracies. Illiberal democracies maintain competitive elections, first, as the primary means of gaining power and, second, as the primary means of maintaining power once they've gained it. Illiberal democratic states are civilian authoritarian regimes that continue to hold elections once in power (1) because many autocrats lack the coercive and organizational capacity to consolidate hegemonic rule and (2) because, as the incumbents, they can rewrite the election rules to their benefit and facilitate staying in power and consolidating it.

Political leaders of this persuasion can always be identified through these two things. First, they pay lip service to democracy and use democratic institutions to get into position of power, but once in power, they work tirelessly to negate and subvert and undermine its institutions.[106] And second, they always find their base of support in the xenophobic politics of right-wing populism, and gin up that base by exploiting racial or ethnic hatred and grievances, blaming "foreigners" or "immigrants" for their troubles and fomenting hate against them to consolidate their power.

The Globalization of Illiberal Democracy

The astounding growth of the global right-wing populist movement and autocratic governments over the past two or three decades is no accident of history. Rather, it is the direct result of history and is caused by the increasingly dire crises the world is finding itself in as a result of global warming and global population and energy crisis and other dynamics that are accelerating time and generating anxiety. Wherever we look globally, fascism and its leaders are engaged in building up the threat of whomever they've defined as "the enemy" to redirect the discontent and rage of their people from its real cause: the policies of the government.

Putin in Russia was the first to undo the democratic gains made after the Soviet Union collapsed, and he blamed the West for it. In Western Europe, you have it with Marine Le Pen in France, in Italy with Giorgia Meloni, in Germany with Björn Höcke; you have it in the Scandinavian and the low countries. In Eastern Europe, you have it with Orban in Hungary, Duda in Poland, Yanukovych in Ukraine, and Lukashenko in Belarus. There's Erdogan in Turkey, who blames the Kurds. There is Modi in India, who blames the Muslims. In Asia, there's Duterte in the Philippines, who blames internal rebels. You have it Taiwan, Malaysia, and Cambodia. In China, you have it with Xi, who blames the Uyghurs. You have it in Central and South America, like Bolsonaro in Brazil, who blames the native tribes. In Africa, among others, you have it in Mozambique, Kenya, and Cameroon. In the final analysis, any and all male-centric authoritarian systems, no matter the skin color, are modeled on the example of the White Man and are, therefore, part of the White brotherhood of the International Right-Wing Populist Dictators and their misogynistic and racist value systems.

Trump did not initiate this movement, but he was part and parcel of its growth. And of course, because of the outside influence of the United States on world affairs, he was able to contribute significantly to its rapid spread. Make no mistake about it, Trumpists worldwide are now proven enemies of our democracy and have pledged to do everything conceivable to dismantle our own and others' democratic institutions and consolidate their White Man power on a permanent basis.

The Internet as the Womb of Right-Wing Violence

It's been astounding, really, how fast the internet and social media transformed themselves from Eutopian promise to dystopian peril. In their infancy, the internet and social media were touted as the ultimate universal panacea in communications and community building. Instant information and knowledge promised harmony and honesty, universal progress, and the expansion of consciousness. But as they grew and matured, the internet and social media revealed themselves as being the perfect vehicle for, and expression of, the dark side of humanity. For as they became a repository and outlet for accumulated human stress and anxieties, the internet and social media also became the favored way of individuals to intimidate, harass, exploit, gaslight, destroy people and their reputations with a deluge of misinformation and untruth, not only on an individual level but also collectively. Democratic regimes have proved vulnerable to sabotage and election interference by foreign powers, and there has been an enormous growth of cybercrimes, such as the extortion of public and private individuals and institutions. Indeed, politically, the global struggle between autocracy and democracy is forcing us to come to grips with the uncomfortable truth that social media has increasingly become the enemy of democracy. Racists and other authoritarians abuse the social media platforms to their own advantage and to the detriment of democratic values by spreading lies and falsehoods rather than the truth. Just consider these truths that on social media:

- It is easier to spread misinformation than to correct it.
- It is easier to inflame social divisions than to mend them.
- It is easier to stir up panics about minority groups than to improve their status.
- It's easier to abuse social media to demonize out-groups than it is to improve their images with the public.
- It is easier to undermine people's trust in the independent media than to reinforce it.[107]

The ease with which rumors and false information can be spread on social media, and the intrinsic difficulty in debunking these ideas once they're out there, makes them ideal platforms to spread demagogic messages. In the U.S., Trump pioneered the weaponization of the internet as a strategy to undermine democracy and create a womb for the incubation of right-wing violence. Not to be outdone, Russia, China, and other illiberal democracies have also become exceedingly skilled at manipulating these platforms to marginalize domestic dissidents and destabilize democracies abroad.

And even inside democratic states, the authoritarian factions of far-right politicians and parties actively use modern social media platforms to undermine democratic values and act to the detriment of the democratic functioning of their society.[108] Worse yet, attempts to quash rumors through direct refutation and efforts to correct falsehoods can ironically contribute to their further propagation and even acceptance.[109] The conclusion appears inescapable: Social media is increasingly serving the needs of far-right parties and authoritarians of all stripes, both in established authoritarian states and in authoritarian factions within democratic states.[110] Not only are social media platforms compatible with white racist supremacy, but they are fast becoming one of the main reasons why these attitudes are now spreading around the globe like wildfire.[111]

Endnotes

1   Michael Kruse, "The Mystery of Mary Trump," Politico, November/December 2017, https://www.politico.com/magazine/story/2017/11/03/mary-macleod-trump-donald -trump-mother-biography-mom-immigrant-scotland-215779/.

2   Ibid.

3   Ibid.

4   Ibid.

5   S. Freud, Character and Culture, (Ohio: Collier Books, 1963), 27.

6   William Watts, "Tepper Says Trump Is 'Father of Lies' When It Comes to Charitable Giving," Market Watch, November 7, 2016, https://www.marketwatch.com/story /billionaire-david-tepper-trump-is-father-of-lies-when-it-comes-to-charitable-giving -2016-11-07.

7   Conor Friedersdorf, "Donald Trump's False Bragging About His Charitable Giving," The Atlantic, December 28, 2016, https://www.theatlantic.com/politics/archive /2016/12/donald-trumps-mendacious-bragging-about-his-charitable-giving/511703/.

8   Ibid.

9   Steve Reilly, "Hundreds Allege Donald Trump Doesn't Pay His Bills," USA Today, April 25, 2018, https://www.usatoday.com/story/news/politics/elections/2016/06/09 /donald-trump-unpaid-bills-republican-president-laswuits/85297274/.

10 Ibid.

11 Ibid.

12 Ibid.

13 David A. Fahrenhold, "Trump Recorded Having Extremely Lewd Conversation About Women in 2005," Washington Post, October 8, 2016, https://www.washington post.com/politics/trump-recorded-having-extremely-lewd-conversation-about-women -in-2005/2016/10/07/3b9ce776-8cb4-11e6-bf8a-3d26847eeed4_story.html.

14 Ibid.

15 Eliza Relman and Azmi Haroun, "The 25 Women Who Have Accused Trump of Sexual Misconduct," Business Insider, May 9, 2023, https://www.businessinsider.com /women-accused-trump-sexual-misconduct-list-2017-12.

16 Ibid.

17 Ayal Feinberg, Regina Branton, and Valeria Martinez-Ebers, "Counties That Hosted a 2016 Trump Rally Saw a 226 Percent Increase in Hate Crimes," Washington Post, March 22, 2019, https://www.washingtonpost.com/politics/2019/03/22/trumps -rhetoric-does-inspire-more-hate-crimes/?noredirect=on%26utm%5Fterm=.aaafad 85f2fd%23click=https://t.co/bYXsN60xzH.

18 Lee Moran, "'Art of the Deal' Co-Author Spells Out Why Coronavirus Deaths 'Don't Matter' to Trump," HuffPost, May 16, 2020, https://www.huffpost.com/entry/tony -schwartz-donald-trump-coronavirus_n_5ebf85dfc5b64d3dbf40ee28.

19 Article on Billy Graham in Time Magazine, LXIV, 38; 1954, quoted by W. Sargant in Battle for the Mind, (New York: Perennial Library, Harper & Row, 1957), 217.

20 Seema Mody, "Millennials Lead Shift Away from Organized Religion as Pandemic Tests Americans' Faith" CNBC, December 29, 2021, https://www.cnbc.com/2021/12/29 /millennials-lead-shift-away-from-organized-religion-as-pandemic-tests-faith.html.

21 Ibid.

22 Ibid.; Maya Yang, "More Americans Are Shifting Away from Religious Affiliation," The Guardian, December 15, 2021, https://www.theguardian.com/us-news/2021 /dec/15/us-religious-affiliation-study-results.

23 Maya Yang, "More Americans Are Shifting Away from Religious Affiliation," The Guardian, December 15, 2021, https://www.theguardian.com/us-news/2021/dec/15/us-religious-affiliation-study-results.

24 Andrew Whitehead, "The Growing Anti-Democratic Threat of Christian Nationalism in the U.S.," Time, May 27, 2021, https://time.com/6052051/anti-democratic-threat-christian-nationalism/.

25 Andrew Whitehead and Samuel Perry, "The Growing Anti-Democratic Threat of Christian Nationalism in the U.S.," Time Magazine, May 27, 2021, https://time.com/6052051/anti-democratic-threat-christian-nationalism/.

26 Article on Billy Graham in Time Magazine, LXIV, 38; 1954, quoted by W. Sargant in Battle for the Mind, (New York: Perennial Library, Harper & Row, 1957), 217.

27 Jeff Sharlet, "'He's the Chosen One to Run America': Inside the Cult of Trump, His Rallies Are Church and He Is the Gospel," Vanity Fair, June 18, 2020, https://www.vanityfair.com/news/2020/06/inside-the-cult-of-trump-his-rallies-are-church-and-he-is-the-gospel.

28 Gwenda Blair, "How Norman Vincent Peale Taught Donald Trump to Worship Himself," Politico, October 6, 2015, https://www.politico.com/magazine/story/2015/10/donald-trump-2016-norman-vincent-peale-213220/.

29 Ed Kilgore, "Do Conservative Evangelicals Like Trump Not Despite But For His Hatefulness, New York Magazine, August 18, 2019. https://nymag.com/intelligencer/2019/08/do-conservative-evangelicals-like-trump-for-his-hatefulness.html.

30 Ibid.

31 Dana Blanton, "Fox News Poll: Did God Favor Trump in 2016?" Fox News, February 13, 2019, https://www.foxnews.com/politics/fox-news-poll-did-god-favor-donald-trump-in-2016.

32 Stef W. Kight, "Ahead of 2020, Why Evangelicals Are Sticking with Trump," Axios, March 18, 2019, https://www.axios.com/2019/03/18/white-evangelicals-support-trump-2020-voters-demography.

33 Ibid.

34 Rebecca Morin, "Sarah Sanders: God Wanted Trump to Become President," Politico, January 30, 2019, https://www.politico.com/story/2019/01/30/sarah-huckabee-sanders-trump-god-1137547.

35 Ryan Burge, "Why 'Evangelical' is becoming another word for 'Republican,'" New York Times, October 26, 2021, https://www.nytimes.com/2021/10/26/opinion/evangelical-republican.html?searchResultPosition=1.

36 Ibid.

37 Ibid.

38 Ibid.

39 Meet the Press, "Jerry Falwell 'Paved the Way' for Donald Trump's Presidency Says 'God Forbid' Director," NBC News, October 28, 2022, https://www.nbcnews.com/video/jerry-falwell-jr-paved-the-way-for-donald-trump-s-presidency-says-god-forbid-director-151825477843.

40 Edward Wong, "The Rapture and the Real World: Mike Pompeo Blends Beliefs and Policy," New York Times, March 30, 2019, https://www.nytimes.com/2019/03/30/us/politics/pompeo-christian-policy.html.

41 Ibid.

42 Ibid.

43 Ibid.

44 Ibid.

45 Ibid.

46 Nate Cohn, "How Educational Differences Are Widening America's Political Rift," New York Times, September 8, 2021, https://www.nytimes.com/2021/09/08/us /politics/how-college-graduates-vote.html.

47 Ibid.

48 Ibid.

49 Ibid.

50 Ibid.

51 Ivana Saric, "Poll: Americans Increasingly Justifying Political Violence," Axios, January 2, 2022, https://www.axios.com/2022/01/02/poll-america-violence-against -government.

52 Ibid.

53 Martin Pengelly, "One in Three Americans Say Violence Against Government Justi- fied – Poll," The Guardian, January 2, 2022, https://www.theguardian.com /us-news/2022/jan/02/one-three-americans-violence-government-justified-poll.

54 Ivana Saric, "Poll: Americans Increasingly Justifying Political Violence," Axios, January 2, 2022, https://www.axios.com/2022/01/02/poll-america-violence-against -government.

55 Ibid.

56 Cameron Joseph, "Trump-Endorsed Candidate JD Vance Once Said Trump Might Be 'America's Hitler," Vice, 4/18/2022, https://www.vice.com/en/article/bvn4b8/jd -vance-trump-messages.

57 McKay Coppins, "The Outer-Borough President," The Atlantic, January 30, 2017, https://www.theatlantic.com/politics/archive/2017/01/the-outer-borough-president /514673/.

58 James Kimmel, Jr., "What the Science of Addiction Tells Us About Trump," Politico, December 12, 2020, https://www.politico.com/news/magazine/2020/12/12/trump -grievance-addiction-444570.

59 Ibid.

60 Gretchen Smail, "Donald Trump Reportedly Spent $85K to Call for the Deaths of the Central Park 5 Teens," Bustle, May 31, 2019, https://www.bustle.com/p/the-when -they-see-us-donald-trumps-ads-from-when-they-see-us-are-entirely-real-he-stands -by-them-17934733.

61 Ibid.

62 Adrian Horton and Richard Luscombe, "Trump Mocked for Fearing Protestors Would Throw 'Dangerous' Fruit at Him," The Guardian, April 29, 2022, https://www .theguardian.com/us-news/2022/apr/29/trump-dangerous-fruit-tomato-jokes.

63 David Leonhardt, "Conservatism Has a Violence Problem," New York Times, August 5, 2019, https://www.nytimes.com/2019/08/05/opinion/el-paso-shooting-republicans -trump.html.

64

65 Ed Mazza, "Howard Stern Tells Trump Voters What the President Really Thinks of Them," HuffPost, March 12, 2020, https://www.huffpost.com/entry/howard-stern -donald-trump-voters_n_5ebb4b43c5b6ae915a8bd391.

66 Ibid.

67   Ben Hoyle, "Donald Trump's Hour-Long Call with Brad Raffensperger Begging to Swing Georgia Election," The Times-The Sunday Times, April 1, 2021, https://www.thetimes.co.uk/article/pense-backs-american-senators-last-ditch-effort-to-defy-biden-gtx79djk3.

68   Ankita Rao, "January 6 'Was a Coup Organized by the President,' Says Jamie Raskin," The Guardian, April 20, 2022, https://www.theguardian.com/us-news/2022/apr/19/donald-trump-jamie-raskin-january-6-committee-capitol-attack.

69   Ben Hoyle, "Donald Trump's Hour-Long Call with Brad Raffensperger Begging to Swing Georgia Election," The Times-The Sunday Times, April 1, 2021, https://www.thetimes.co.uk/article/pense-backs-american-senators-last-ditch-effort-to-defy-biden-gtx79djk3.

70   Aaron Parsley, "Trump 'Gleefully' Viewed Jan. 6 Insurrection on TV, 'Hitting Rewind' to Watch Again, Former Aide Says," People, January 6, 2022, https://apple.news/AIqFcrMxwS5Kg3ArGf-uQSg.

71   Tom Porter, "Trump Ignored Pleas to Intervene During Capitol Riot and Kept Watching the Violence Unfold on TV Instead, Book Says," Business Insider, September 15, 2021, https://apple.news/AioSOPvc0RP2gP2u2RbYGNg.

72   Megan Garber, "The 'Pussy' Presidency," The Atlantic, January 17, 2021, https://www.theatlantic.com/culture/archive/2021/01/donald-trump-pussy-presidency/617699/.

73   Bill Press, "Trump Is Running Out of Gas," The Hill, February 1, 2022, https://thehill.com/opinion/campaign/592205-press-trump-is-running-out-of-gas/.

74   Ibid.

75   Michael Tomaskey, ""The Republican Party Can't be Saved," TNR, 2/7/2022, https://newrepublic.com/article/165301/republicans-violence-normal-political-discourse

76   Michael Tomasky, "Do the Republicans Even Believe in Democracy Anymore?" New York Times, July 1, 2019, https://www.nytimes.com/2019/07/01/opinion/republicans-trump-democracy.html.

77   Margaret Atwood, "I Invented Gilead. The Supreme Court Is Making It Real," The Atlantic, May 13, 2022, https://www.theatlantic.com/ideas/archive/2022/05/supreme-court-roe-handmaids-tale-abortion-margaret-atwood/629833/.

78   Bess Levin, "Samuel Alito's Antiabortion Inspiration: A 17th-Century Jurist Who Supported Marital Rape and Had Women Executed," Vanity Fair, May 3, 2022, https://www.vanityfair.com/news/2022/05/samuel-alito-roe-v-wade-abortion-draft.

79   Ibid.

80   Paul Blumenthal, "Yet Again, a Judicial Counterrevolution Looks to Chain the Country to an Imagined Past," HuffPost, May 5, 2022, https://www.huffpost.com/entry/scott-alito-roe-v-wade_n_6274013be4b046ad0d7964f4.

81   Ibid.

82   Ibid.

83   Alex Thomas, "Donald Trump's Gaff About Roe Has Become America's Worrisome Future," The New Republic, May 16, 2022, https://apple.news/A_Jntm78kT9OLM13KkvvYkQ.

84   Charles M. Blow, "White Supremacy Beyond a White Majority," New York Times, May 15, 2019, https://www.nytimes.com/2019/05/15/opinion/race-government-politics.html.

85   David Brooks, "The Coming G.O.P. Apocalypse," New York Times, June 3, 2019, https://www.nytimes.com/2019/06/03/opinion/republicans-generation-gap.html.

86   Sean McElwee, Brian F. Schaffner, Jesse H. Rhodes, and Bernard L. Fraga, New York Times, February 16, 2019. https://www.nytimes.com/2019/02/16/opinion/sunday/trump-youth-vote.html?searchResultPosition=1

87 Eric Levitz, "Many GOP Voters Value America's Whiteness More Than Democracy," New York Magazine, September 2, 2020, https://nymag.com/intelligencer/2020/09/many-gop-voters-value-whiteness-more-than-democracy-study.html.

88 Susan Page and Sarah Elbeshbishi, "Defeated and Impeached, Trump Still Commands the Loyalty of the GOP Voters," USA Today, February 21, 202, https://www.usatoday.com/story/news/politics/2021/02/21/exclusive-trump-party-he-still-holds-loyalty-gop-voters/6765406002/.

89 Eric Levitz, "Many GOP Voters Value America's Whiteness More Than Democracy," New York Magazine, September 2, 2020, https://nymag.com/intelligencer/2020/09/many-gop-voters-value-whiteness-more-than-democracy-study.html.

90 Ibid.

91 Steven Levitsky and Daniel Ziblatt, "Why Republicans Play Dirty," New York Times, September 20, 2019, https://www.nytimes.com/2019/09/20/opinion/republicans-democracy-play-dirty.html.

92 Steven Levitsky and Daniel Ziblatt, "Why Republicans Play Dirty," New York Times, September 20, 2019, https://www.nytimes.com/2019/09/20/opinion/republicans-democracy-play-dirty.html.

93 Eliza Relman, Business Insider, December 3, 2018.

94 Paul Krugman, "Hard-Money Men Suddenly Going Soft," New York Times, December 20, 2018, https://www.nytimes.com/2018/12/20/opinion/conservative-economics-trump.html.

95 Zack Beauchamp, "The Republican Party Versus Democracy," Vox, December 17, 2018, https://www.vox.com/policy-and-politics/2018/12/17/18092210/republican-gop-trump-2020-democracy-threat.

96 Russel Wheeler, "Based on Biden's Two Years of Judicial Appointments, Trump's Four-Year Record Seems Secure," Brookings, January 30, 2023, https://www.brookings.edu/blog/fixgov/2023/01/30/based-on-bidens-two-years-of-judicial-appointments-trumps-four-year-record-seems-secure/.

97 Steven Levitsky and Daniel Ziblatt, "Why Republicans Play Dirty," New York Times, September 20, 2019, https://www.nytimes.com/2019/09/20/opinion/republicans-democracy-play-dirty.html.

98 Jamelle Bouie, "The Electoral College Is Our Greatest Threat to Democracy," New York Times, February 28, 2019, https://www.nytimes.com/2019/02/28/opinion/the-electoral-college.html.

99 Ibid.

100 Jamelle Bouie, "The Electoral College Is Our Greatest Threat to Democracy," New York Times, February 28, 2019, https://www.nytimes.com/2019/02/28/opinion/the-electoral-college.html.

101 Rob Griffin, Ruy Teixeira, and William H. Frey, "America's Electoral Future: Demographic Shifts and the Future of the Trump Coalition," Brookings, April 19, 2018, https://www.brookings.edu/research/americas-electoral-future_2018/.

102 Steven Levitsky and Daniel Ziblatt, "Why Republicans Play Dirty," New York Times, September 20, 2019, https://www.nytimes.com/2019/09/20/opinion/republicans-democracy-play-dirty.html.

103 Ibid.

104 Michael Wines and Danny Hakim, "Four Fights Over Voting Rights," New York Times, November 3, 2018, https://www.nytimes.com/2018/11/03/us/politics/voting-rights-lawsuits.html.

105 The Editorial Board, New York Times, May 30, 2019, https://www.nytimes.com/2019/05/30/opinion/census-citizenship-supreme-court.html.

106 Steven Levitsky and Lucan Way, "The New Competitive Authoritarianism," John Hopkins University Press Journal of Democracy 31, No. 1 (2020), https://www.journalofdemocracy.org/articles/the-new-competitive-authoritarianism/.

107 Ibid.

108 Zack Beauchamp, "Social Media Is Rotting Democracy from Within," Vox, January 22, 2019, https://www.vox.com/policy-and-politics/2019/1/22/18177076/social-media-facebook-far-right-authoritarian-populism.

109 Ibid.

110 Ibid.

111 Ibid.

Part 5

The Global Paradigm Shift to Eutopia

Chapter 16

Turning the Wheel of Time: Paradigm Shift from Dystopia to Eutopia (2000-2050)

The Sleeping Giant of Female-Centric Progressive Populism Awakens

Four Waves of Feminism

We have traced the process of the White Man embarking on the creation and development of the American nation and how racism and misogyny were the twin pillars of his psychology of superiority of his White Male–centric paradigm of power. The racist cruelties suffered by Black and other people of color were a glaringly obvious and accepted fact of life from day one. Whether you approved or disapproved, slavery and racism were facts of life recognized by oppressor and oppressed alike. It was different for the experience of misogyny by the white women. Their exploitation was not always so obvious to them. For one thing, sharing the White Man's whiteness, they could also consider themselves superior. Moreover, white women also shared in the material wealth created by the White Man by his divinely mandated mastery of the "lower races."

Of course, as women began to experience more and more the fundamental inequality inherent in their status, they began objecting to it, at first inwardly and privately, then, increasingly, outwardly and publicly. The first collective expression of women's dissent became known as the first wave of feminism, centered around the women's suffrage movement at the turn of the 20th century, which resulted in women acquiring the right to vote in the early 1900s. The second wave of feminism was the widespread mass movement in the West in the 1960s and 1970s, both against many of the cultural structures of the nuclear family and most especially in the continuing battle for women's reproductive rights. Their big victory occurred when the Supreme Court struck down many U.S. state and federal abortion laws in *Roe v. Wade* (1973) and ruled that the Constitution of the United States protects a pregnant woman's right to choose to have an abortion.

The third wave of feminism emerged in the 1990s from riot grrrl feminist punk subculture[1] and the televised testimony by Anita Hill before the Senate Judiciary Committee accusing Supreme Court appointee Judge Clarence Thomas of sexual harassment. Rebecca Walker coined the term "third wave" to marshal "women power" to finish their unfinished agenda:

"Let Thomas's confirmation serve to remind you, as it did me, that the fight is far from over. Let this dismissal of a woman's experience move you to anger. Turn that outrage into political power. Do not vote for them unless they work for us. Do not have sex with them, do not break bread with them, do not nurture them, if they don't prioritize our freedom to control our bodies and our lives. I am not a post-feminism feminist. I am the Third Wave."[2]

One outgrowth of the third wave of feminism was the "Me Too" movement started by Tarana Burke, a Black woman, in 2006. The "Me Too" movement started as a response to violence against women to help them heal, reaching out to female survivors of sexual assault, particularly women of color in low-income communities. But the "Me Too" movement touched a very raw nerve across all races and mushroomed globally into an ongoing, multiethnic effort of outing high profile sexual abusers such as Donald Trump, Harvey Weinstein, Jeffrey Epstein, and other sick luminaries.

The fourth wave of feminism started in the 2010s and grew enormously, both in numbers and scope of concerns. One focus of the fourth wave has been on the empowerment of women and its expression online on social media and the internet. Part and parcel of the fourth wave's fight against the White Man's discrimination based on one's sex or gender has been the fight to redefine the very categories of male and female. The fourth wave seeks to replace this raging imbalance of power with the infinitely richer, female-centric, Taoist-inspired concept of the interpenetration of the opposites of male and female. Long advocated by the LGBTQ+ and Rainbow Coalition people, the fourth wave argues we all must come to accept sexuality and gender as a non-binary spectrum between the extremes of male and female polarities.

The Intersectionality of Female-Centrism

What has been different and hopeful about these populist uprisings is their spontaneous practice of the "E Pluribus Unum" principle: "out of many, one." For, as the many signs that are carried in the protests attest to, no matter what the announced main purpose or cause, these protests are multipronged. Thus, one has been able to see many different signs for many different causes with such demands as: "defund the police," "cancel rent," "pass the Green New Deal."[3] All these are different social movements that are in conversation with each other and cross-endorse each other's agendas. They demand more than just reforms; their demands are revolutionary in nature because their implementation requires upending the status quo and redistributing power from the elites to the working class.

Each of these various demands demonstrates the new attitude among progressive social movements against isolated, partial reforms in favor of a systemic re-evaluation. They don't want to reduce police violence; they want a break from prisons and the police, and they want counselors in place of cops. They don't want to sidestep our environmentally unsustainable global supply chain; they want to break the hold of carbon. They don't want grace periods for late rent;

they want housing for all and a job guarantee. Polls, participation in protests, and growing membership in social movement organizations show these demands are drawing larger and larger parts of the public toward a fundamental, revolutionary critique of the status quo and a radical, integrative vision for the future.[4]

The progressive Eutopian populism of today's Rainbow Coalition sees all our crises as intersectional. "Police violence, global warming and unaffordable housing are not disconnected, discrete problems; instead, they emerge from colonialism and capitalism. Organizers recall these histories, and tell stories of freedom struggles. In July 2020, for example, racial, climate and economic justice organizations have joined in hosting "a four-day crash course on defunding the police."[5] And while it is important to remember that these many groups do not want exactly the same things, their power is drawn from the commonality of their overlapping concerns.

As we have seen, Trump, as polarizer, was both the product of and responsible for the rise of an extreme right-wing populist movement based on exploiting long-standing racist and misogynist resentments. As described and analyzed in previous chapters, Trump used every page in the book in his 2016 campaign, pushing all available racist and misogynist buttons to rouse his base to a fever pitch in his quest for the presidency. But in stoking the fires of his own right-wing, regressive, dystopian populism, Trump also counter-stimulated and energized his opposition.

Repulsed by Trump's antics, tactics, and policies, a tremendous outpouring of left-wing populist mass protests and demonstrations occurred against the dystopian violence of Trump and his MAGA crowd. Led by the women and people of color, this Rainbow Coalition of anti-misogynists and anti-racists that arose to stop Trump and his movement organized literally millions of people nationwide, in big towns and small, participating in the 2017 and 2018 Women's Marches protesting systemic endemic violence against women.

A like number of protesters joined in the demonstrations organized by students nationwide against the dystopian violence of mass killings. Further millions demonstrated against those responsible for the violence of climate change and political corruption. These protests are setting in motion a period of significant, sustained, and widespread sociopolitical change. "We appear to be experiencing a social change tipping point—that is as rare in society as it is potentially consequential."[6]

Black Women and the Black Lives Matter Movement

It is, therefore, no accident that the populist revolt and revulsion against the Trumpist pathology of the dystopian authoritarian complex of racism and misogyny has found its leadership cadres emerging from the ranks of non-white women, especially Black women. Take the Black Lives Matter movement, for example. Black Lives Matter was co-founded in July 2013 by Alicia Garza from Oakland, California, and two other women. Incensed by George Zimmerman's acquittal of the murder of Trayvon Martin, they posted a notice on the internet, and a movement was born[7] to address a broad array of causes: stopping police violence, advocating for domestic workers, mobilizing women, and building Black political power. And its slogan, Black Lives Matter, is both beautifully simple and complex because it states the problem and offers the solution.

Asked once by an interviewer, "Do you think there's any significance to the fact that Black Lives Matter was founded by three women?" Garza answered, "Absolutely! I think that fact lends itself to a deep understanding of who has been left out and who's been left behind. We already knew in this [2020 election] cycle that women were going to be the linchpin in deciding which direction this country goes. And we know that has been true throughout history. Even though we're told different stories, we know the facts. And the facts are that women have always weaved community in places where it was missing because our survival depended on it. I think the same is true today."[8]

Ms. Garza explained how the surging mass movement for police reform is giving her hope. In the seven years that followed her interview, this movement has exploded worldwide with each new case of the police killing a Black person. "Remember," she said, "this is the second time around. The first time we were fighting people to even say Black Lives Matter. Now everybody's saying Black Lives Matter… The fact is that Black Lives Matter is such a major part of our global conversation right now. And it's forcing people across all walks of life, all sectors in our economy, and every corner of the planet really, to assess whether we are where we need to be—and what we need to do to get to where we're trying to go. That makes me feel hopeful."[9]

The fourth wave reinvigorated the movement for racial and ethnic parity and justice. The growth of the Black Lives Matter movement, both in numbers and in geographical spread, has been unprecedented in scope and scale. Since the first protests began, on May 26, 2020, there have been more than 4,700 demonstrations, an average of 140 a day. These happened in more than 2,500 small towns and large cities.[10] Between 15 and 26 million people participated in them, mostly spontaneously. On June 6, there was a peak, of sorts, in the demonstrations over the death of George Floyd[11] when more than half a million people demonstrated in 550 different places across the U.S.[12] The sustained duration of these protests has also been another remarkable feature. One of the most encouraging things about the BLM movement has been the great increase of white participation under Black leadership in their demonstrations, as compared to, for example, the Black organized demonstrations of the 1960s. There were BLM demonstrations in at least 1,360 counties, which is 40% of all counties in the U.S. Moreover, 95% of these counties are majority white, and more than 75% are more than 75% white.[13]

What is also new and significant about these spontaneous mass populist demonstrations and protests is that, this time around, they have produced not only immediate positive results but also a framework for ongoing mutual support and cooperation between different factions of the movement. First, "the amount of change that the protests have been able to produce in such a short period of time has been very significant. In Minneapolis, the city council pledged to dismantle its police department. In New York, lawmakers repealed a law that kept police disciplinary records secret. Cities and states across the country passed new laws banning chokeholds. Mississippi lawmakers voted to retire their state flag, which prominently includes a Confederate battle emblem."[14]

White Woman and the Paradigm Change
in the White Man's Masculinity

Not only did the feminist movement reinvigorate the movement for race and ethnic equality, but it also stimulated, within the white-male community as a whole, a paradigm shift from toxic to healthy expressions of masculinity.

The obvious continuity between Obama and Biden stands in stark contrast with, and opposition to, Trump, who represented an interruption in that continuity. Obama-Biden and Trump represent the two polar-opposite conceptions and traditions of manhood that are engaged today in a defining struggle for dominance in American politics and life. Comparing the Obama-Biden attitudes toward women and race, misogyny and racism, with Trump's, the contrast stands out in sharp relief. Trump's male-centric hyper-masculinity is quite properly described as toxic and dystopian, whereas the female-centric Obama-Biden masculinity is the balanced Eutopian model to be aspired to by individuals and society alike.

Obama and Biden represent progressive continuity of the Eutopian paradigm. Obama, the first non-white, Black president, and Kamala Harris, the first female vice president and also a woman of color, both represent that part of the American people who want to extend democracy and are dedicated to overcoming the misogynist and racist influences on our collective national character structure and history. Obama-Biden embody the yin, female-centric paradigm and conception of manhood and masculinity, characterized by a balanced, interpenetrating masculinity. That is to say, the male testosterone-adrenalin axis for power-competition is moderated in its actions by the actively functioning oxytocin-empathy axis.

The toxic masculinity exhibited by Trump points to the exclusive action of the male hormones of power and competition: extremely high testosterone and adrenalin levels that fuel a constant need for violence and aggression, distrust and intolerance. Moreover, the behavioral skill set exhibits the complete absence of empathy as the result of the nurturing hormonal action of oxytocin because they were never developed in infancy. Trump embodies the hyper-masculinity of the yang, male-centric paradigm and conception of manhood, where the natural empathy channels and pathways of oxytocin release are dysfunctional and exert no restraining influence on their masculine hormonal axis of testosterone and adrenalin. This is why and how the misogynist and racist influences have come to define our collective national character structure and history, defining the pathology of the White Male Dystopian Personality Disorder (WMDPD) that is the lowest common denominator of the White Man.

Trump's base shares his embracement of the hyper-masculine ideal and, like him, suffers from the same WMDPD that holds white male racist and misogynistic power as the highest possible value. Trump's is a cult of warriors, where economic and emotional grievances are channeled into racist and misogynistic hatred of women and non-white peoples. This made them a real threat to democracy. Besides the insurrection on January 6, his supporters sent death threats to fellow Republican election officials to pressure them into corruption and falsely changing the vote counts of their counties. Trump, as the personification and embodiment of Western White Man, led his base into the insurrection of January 6. Powered by his WMDPD and the addiction to power, Trump took the entire human species and the planet to the brink of destructive collapse.

Historically situated between Obama and Biden, Trump represents the worst America has to offer sandwiched between the best America has to offer. It is as if the American people chose to follow their better instincts with Obama, then got scared by the difficulties encountered and flipped back into their worst instincts with

Trump, then realized what utter chaos that approach resulted in and veered back to choose the path of the heart and progress, despite the hardships.

For the eight years of his presidency, Obama's progressive legislative policies, except ultimately Obamacare, were successfully sabotaged by the increasingly right-wing Republican Party under the leadership of Mitch McConnell. During the same time, many of the Obama voters who had voted for "change you can believe in" became disillusioned with the lack of change. The next time around, these voters fell for the empty promises of revenge for grievances suffered and voted for Trump. The boisterous thug who, with his MAGA campaign, promised to make America White again also vowed to change the direction of national political climate, though in the exact opposite direction of Obama's vision.[15] Thus it was that some 7 to 9 million people who voted for Obama in 2012 voted for Trump in 2016.[16] And thus it was that Trump, who received some 3 million fewer votes than Clinton (63 million versus 66 million), was elected president because, under the arcane and undemocratic rules of the Electoral College, he got 304 electoral votes while Hillary only received 227.

In the 2016 election, these voters continued their support for Trump and did not return to the Democratic fold to help Biden.[17] Nevertheless, during Trump's presidency, American people, on the whole, came to realize what a completely incompetent psychopath they had given the reins of power to and how his completely disastrous handling of the Covid-19 pandemic had cost many Americans their lives. They chose, in the 2020 election, that Biden and the Democratic Party presented a rational alternative of proactive government that worked for the total, all-around well-being of the many, not just the financial well-being and political power of the few.

In the final analysis, as President Obama said, most of the problems in the world come from old people, mostly men, holding onto positions of power. He said that if women ran every country in the world, there would be a general improvement in living standards and outcomes.[18] "Women aren't perfect," he said, but are "indisputably better" than men. "I'm absolutely confident that for two years if every nation on earth was run by women, you would see a significant improvement across the board on just about everything… living standards and outcomes."[19]

Biden's appointments to his cabinet and other senior positions in the government leave no doubt that he shares Obama's fundamental view on the desirability and superiority of women in all three branches of government—legislative, executive, and judicial. To begin with, he chose Kamala Harris, first female and colored person as his vice presidential partner, and Biden's senior appointments have been almost 60% women, giving rise to the most diverse cabinet in history. Twelve of Biden's cabinet positions are held by women (the previous record was nine under Bill Clinton), including eight women of color. Biden also appointed an all-female communications team of seven, led by Jen Psaki.

With Obama's and Biden's assessment and vision, I believe we are witnessing the initial stages of the rebirth of a global, female-centric, multiethnic global civilization. It is a tentative indication that (some of) the White Men are learning to step back and let the women and non-white people step up to the plate of governing and steering global affairs from the state of imbalance his WMDPD induced to a female-centric and multiethnic balance.

But since we are not now in a position to affect such a far-reaching global change, we must focus our first effort more modestly on a target that we can affect and restructure: the Democratic Party. Second, the party must govern the country accordingly. Third, our example will inspire neighboring countries, leading to global changes. The platform of the Democratic Party should explicitly rest on and be supported by these five pillars of economic and social justice: (1) female centrism, (2) ethnic and racial equality, (3) equal compensation of all work, (4) universal, life-long healthcare, education, and reeducation, and (5) global warming and climate change.

The Paradigm Shift in History

A Return to Balance: The Paradigm Shift from Male-Centrism to Female-Centrism

One major thesis of this book is that in the human species, like many if not most other mammals, the polarity of the female and male human hormonal axes gives rise to correspondingly polarized female-centric and male-centric social paradigms that express their biological drives as social functions. Female humans, on account of their hormonal progesterone-oxytocin axis, are constitutionally predisposed to peace and not war. This makes the female-centric social paradigm inherently Eutopian: empathy, egalitarianism, and voluntary cooperation characterize the functioning of the female-centric social, religious, economic, and political structures of society. Male humans, on account of their hormonal testosterone-adrenalin axis, are constitutionally predisposed to war, not peace. This makes the male-centric social paradigm inherently dystopian as its foundational pillars—authoritarianism, misogyny, racism, and tribalism—enforce the involuntary subjugation of women and "outsider enemies" that characterize the functioning of the male-centric social, religious, economic, and political structures of society.

We also had occasion to see how the Taoist yin-yang symbol can visually express the balance of the female-centric paradigm and the imbalance of the male-centric paradigm, respectively, as in Fig. A and Fig. B.

FIG. A   FIG. B

The female-centric paradigm (Fig. A) expresses balance in the sense that: (1) the yin and yang fishes are of equal size, (2) the interpenetrations of yin and yang, represented by the white and black dots, are also equal, and (3) the black fish (yin) is properly positioned in the superior position over the white fish (yang).

The male-centric paradigm (Fig. B) expresses imbalance in the sense that: (1) the white fish (yang) is inordinately larger than the black fish (yin), expressing the oppression through compression of the female principle by the male, (2) the white dot in the black fish and black dot in the white fish are missing, meaning they are strictly in binary opposition and with no interpenetration between the yin and yang, (3) imbalance of the black fish being in the inferior position below and not in the superior position above.

Tables A and B below feature a number of intersecting polarities that we have had opportunity to become familiar with throughout this book—biological, hormonal, sexual, psychological, cultural, economic, political, etc.

In the representation of pairs of polar opposites, time and space impose their own constraints and force us to consider one of each pair as primary in meaning and the other as secondary. For example, because thinking or talking or writing about these polar dyads are processes that occur in time, one of the terms of the dyad must necessarily be mentioned first and the other mentioned last.

In Table A, the balance of the female-centric paradigm is expressed by the fact that all the yin terms are placed in the primary position on the left, and all the yang terms are placed in the secondary position on the right. It represents the balance of the female-centric paradigm, where the yin is placed superior to the yang.

In Table B, the imbalance of the male-centric paradigm is expressed by the fact that all the yang terms are placed in the primary position on the left, and all the yin terms are placed in the secondary position on the right. It represents the imbalance of the male-centric paradigm, where the yang is placed superior to the yin.

Table A: The balance of the female-centric paradigm (see Fig. A)		Table B: The imbalance of the male-centric paradigm (see Fig. B)	
Primary	Secondary	Primary	Secondary
female	male	male	female
yin	yang	yang	yin
black	white	white	black
progesterone	testosterone	testosterone	progesterone
oxytocin	adrenalin	adrenalin	oxytocin
empathy	antipathy	antipathy	empathy
non-white	white	white	non-white
socialism	capitalism	capitalism	socialism
cooperation	competition	competition	cooperation
service	profit	profit	service
workers	owners	owners	workers
abundance	scarcity	scarcity	abundance
democracy	autocracy	autocracy	democracy
egalitarianism	authoritarianism	authoritarianism	egalitarianism
paganism	Christianity	Christianity	paganism
Eutopia	Dystopia	Dystopia	Eutopia

Female Emancipation as the Key to Ending Racism and Ethnic Strife

On account of its essential female-centrism, the Eutopian coalition's inextricably linked twin political goals are (1) equality between the sexes and genders and (2) equality between the different races and ethnicities. Of these two equal goals, the first guarantees, leads to, and promotes the second. In other words, in any male-centric culture, the relationship between the sexes must be resolved before the relationship between the races can be remediated. Equality between the sexes and genders will result in and guarantee equality between the different races and ethnicities. Why? Because it is precisely the female-centric hormonal axis of progesterone and oxytocin that, as the biological basis for our capacity for empathy and cooperation, will create and guarantee the truly multiethnic nature of the Eutopian coalition. Peace and harmony between races and tribes will occur first between those ethnicities whose women convinced their men to see the wisdom of abandoning their misogynistic ways.

This way of looking at things opens up the possibility for a global but decentralized strategy to bring about the female-centric, Eutopian paradigm change. Today, all human cultures on earth have been infected, to a lesser or greater degree, by the virus of the male-centric love of power. From the most primitive, out-of-the-way villages to the most sophisticated metropolises, misogyny rules the roost, and globally, it is the defining standard in the relationship between the male and female sexes. The only force on Earth powerful enough to change the narcissism and authoritarianism inherent in any and all male-centric cultural paradigms is the empathy inherent in the female-centric paradigm. The only antidote to the love of power is the power of love. And oxytocin is the only known inhibitor of testosterone-adrenalin-induced behavior.

But where to start? How can we mobilize that force? Let us do a thought experiment. Imagine a campaign of female-centric self-expression that starts at the most local of local levels and irradiates outward in ever expanding concentric circles to create interference levels with lower and higher levels of organizations. Imagine a "women of the world unite" campaign of education and awareness, in which a simple thought experiment to be carried out at every level of society all over the world, would make a powerful statement of self-definition by the female half of the human species.

The question that would be posed to every woman in the world: If things could be different in your village, tribe, province, state, country, or region, how would you like them to be different? What would make your life easier? What would make life in the village, tribe, province, state, country, or region easier? Then listen and record. Collect, collate, and disseminate the results for global discussion. This would be a way for the women of the world to let the men of the world know in clear and unequivocal terms what it is they, the women, want and what behavioral and structural changes they would like to see in their village, tribe, province, region, nation, and continent.

Thus, women of all the cultures of the world would get the opportunity to define themselves. From the most local to the greatest collective levels, they will be able to map out the ways in which their cultures could be improved. Most, but not all, changes that are considered desirable would certainly include major changes in the male-centric behavior pattern to become more egalitarian and female-centric.

This would be an excellent project for the United Nations to take on. They already have much of the necessary global infrastructure to conduct such research projects. This global effort will also present white women in particular with a great opportunity for service to the cause, with their privileged position, their relatively greater emancipation, their greater resources to help initiate these "sisters of the world unite" projects on the grassroots level in the less-developed global regions. As the women in all cultures put a stop to male-centric features of their cultures, particularly misogyny, those cultures will become more female-centric and egalitarian, creating the necessary conditions to resolve remaining issues of racism and tribalism.

It is the fate of the species' female to civilize their males out of their misogyny and keep them civilized and committed to a course of conscious evolution, guided not by the love of power but by the power of love. In practical terms, this means that the women of all the human races and ethnicities are committed to take on the responsibility to help their men shed their misogynistic ways and find new ways of equality to define the partnership with the opposite sex in which they can earn the love and respect of their women. It's the evolutionary calling of white, Black, brown, yellow, and pink women to civilize the white, Black, brown, yellow, and pink men. In short, it's the evolutionary calling of women to civilize men.

The assertion of their autonomy—physical, psychological, biological, spiritual—by the women of the world, marking the end of their submission and the beginning of their freedom will cause a great commotion and split in the male body politic into factions: (1) Eutopian males favorable to and supporting the women's rights movement, (2) the unsure and wavering, the fence-sitters and equivocators, and (3) the dystopian males of the lower, middle, and upper classes enjoying the power and the privilege of misogynistic economic, political, and religious institutions.

In the past half century, the continued evolution of the women's rights movement has resulted in the concomitated growth of the first of these men's factions, increasingly winning over to the Eutopian cause members from the second. Increasingly, white males from the second faction are accepting the reality of the supremacy of the female-centric paradigm and, as a result, have been evolving in their relationship with the White Man, going from toxic to healthy, from pathological to natural, from fake to real. In the third faction, unfortunately, there is increasing resistance borne of fear. The MAGA world is regrouping for civil war and combat in solidarity with and dedication to the misogynistic and racist white male power structures.

The Paradigm Shift in Religiosity

Decline of Male-Centric Monotheism

The post–World War II period was marked both by the rise of consumer culture and the secularization of society. As the baby boomers grew up and matured in the 1950s and 1960s, conditions in society changed radically for the worst, with many new sources of stress creating a rapid growth of anxiety throughout society, but particularly in the lower middle and working classes. What followed was an increase in racial unrest and anti-war demonstrations, the women's movement and abortion rights, recreational use of drugs, avant-garde artists and revolutionaries of the counterculture.

The cumulative effect of these social changes was to precipitate a growing decline in attendance and membership of the mainstream, liberal, humanist, Protestant churches. As we saw in Chapter 15, this exodus divided Protestantism into three different groups: those who remained mainstream Protestants, those who fled toward Evangelical Christianity, and those who became areligious, non-Christian, or pagan.

This religiously unaffiliated demographic is less likely to attend a house of worship, and is suspicious of institutions, authorities, and creeds, because they feel, see, and understand the complicity of the traditional churches in the historical exploitation of race and gender. But tellingly, few among this demographic identify as atheists or agnostics. A full 72% of "nones" say they believe in God, or at least some kind of nebulously defined Higher Power. So even with America's churches in decline and the failure of traditional Christian religion, the religious impulse has hardly disappeared. In the early 2000s, over 40% of Americans answered with an emphatic "yes" when Gallup asked them if a profound religious experience or awakening had redirected their lives.

In fact, as traditional institutional religions were declining, the number of people reporting deep religious experiences in the 21st century has doubled since the 1960s. Even in the most secular parts of society today, young people identify as spiritual creatures who have a great and unfulfilled yearning for transcendent experiences. The spiritual search of these young people consists of finding a way to be spiritual that works for them. What has become increasingly obvious is that patriarchal, male-centric, Judeo-Christian monotheism, as the religious paradigm for the organization of society in an inherently hierarchical, authoritarian, misogynistic, and racist manner is obsolete. People are no longer buying into an angry God Almighty providing cosmic justification for the aggression of the WMDPD paradigm. No more cosmic justification for misogyny. No more cosmic justification for racism. No more cosmic justification for worker exploitation. No more mission of spreading Christianity and converting everybody, with heaven and hell as the cosmic carrot and stick.

Female-Centric Paganism Revisited

What is emerging to replace male-centric monotheism in the 21st century culture war is, in fact, its polar opposite, namely the rebirth of the pagan religious conception, which was always only half-buried by the rise of Christianity. Being female-centric, pre-Christian paganism offers a viable replacement to the patriarchal, male-centric form of civil religion that stamped American history from its beginnings to well into the 1950s. Providing a religious umbrella covering a multitude of different disciplines and currents, the rebirth of pre-Christian, female-centric paganism as the new civic religion of immanence provides a new, genuinely post-Christian religious paradigm for America.

A key characteristic of the emerging neo-pagan spirituality is its synthetic and syncretic nature. Its practitioners show a willingness to effectively mix and match spiritual, ritualistic, and religious practices from a range of traditions, divorced from their original institutional context, to suit their particular needs. Each person borrows practices from, say, Native American, Buddhist, Christian, Jewish, and Soul Cycle traditions and blends them in a way he or she finds moving.[20] A member of this "remixed" generation, for example, might attend yoga classes, practice Buddhist meditation, read tarot cards, cleanse their apartment with sage, and also attend Christmas carol concerts or Shabbat dinners.[21]

While the New Age counterculture of the 1960s was predominantly based on the experience of white women, the new millennial pagan witch culture frames itself as proudly, committedly intersectional: an umbrella community for all those pushed to the side by the dominant (white, straight, male, Christian) culture.[22] There is no doubt that in pre-patriarchal, monotheistic times of the pagan era, life was female-centric. Core to paganism is the idea and the reality that the intuitional, usually female self can access deeper truths than patriarchal religions like Christianity. It was considered axiomatic that "power comes from within, not outside."[23]

In the late 1960s, we had a foretaste of pre-Christian, female-centric paganism making a comeback as a candidate for a genuinely post-Christian religious paradigm for America. The counterculture of the 1960s combined a variety of anti-authoritarian spiritual practices that stressed the primacy of the self, the power of intuition, the untrustworthiness of orthodox institutions, and the spiritual potential of the "forgotten"—often women.[24] Like the civic paganism of old, the new paganism makes religious and political duties identical. Treating the city of man as the city of God (or the gods), paganism defines it as the place where we make heaven (Eutopia) ourselves instead of waiting for the next life or the Apocalypse. Most of the impetus and energy powering this neo-pagan syncretic religious movement is being provided by the women's movement, to the great distress of conventional Christianity. Back in 1992, already, Christian broadcaster Pat Robertson warned of the dangers of feminism, predicting that it would induce "women to leave their husbands… practice witchcraft, destroy capitalism and become lesbians." Many of today's witches would happily agree.[25]

Today neopaganism is on the rise again, more seriously and more powerfully, and the outlines for a new Eutopian religion are emerging. "Progressive millennials have appropriated the rhetoric, imagery, and rituals of what was once called the New Age—from astrology to witchcraft—as both a political and spiritual statement of identity."[26] For the young generation of progressive activists, traditional organized religions are implicated in the existing power structures. They demand a robust, cosmic-level, anti-Christian, or at least anti-conservative and anti-Evangelical, metaphysical and rhetorical grounding.[27]

Young people of the 21st century are looking for, and desirous to live within, a coherent creed and community that does not impinge on their individual autonomy. And they are finding it in the resurrection of the ancient pagan religious conception. What is this pagan religious conception? For paganism, divinity is fundamentally inside the world rather than outside it. The gods are ultimately part and parcel of nature rather than nature being the creation of an external being. That means that for paganism, "meaning and morality and metaphysical experience are to be sought in a fuller communion with the immanent world rather than a leap toward the transcendent."[28]

This paganism is not materialist or atheistic; it allows for belief in spiritual and supernatural realities. It even accepts the possibility of an afterlife. But it is deliberately nondogmatic about what awaits beyond the shores of this world, and it is skeptical of the idea that there exists some ascetic, world-denying moral standard to which we should aspire.[29] Instead, paganism sees the purpose of religion and spirituality as more therapeutic, a means of seeking harmony with nature and happiness in everyday things and activities. Many strands of paganism insist that every day, and every moment of every day, is divinely endowed and shaped, meaningful, and not random, a place where we can truly be at home.[30]

The Eutopian Intersection of Politics and Religion: The Example of the Green New Deal

The generational trends in the U.S. population in the first quarter of the 21st century strongly favor the Democrats over the Republicans. In fact each recent generation has been and is moving to the left of the one preceding it.[31] Generation Z is the most ethnically diverse and progressive generation ever and counts over 68 million people born in 1996 and after. In political attitudes and orientation, Generation Z mirrors its predecessor, the millennial generation consisting of the over 80 million people born between 1981 and 1996.

Being more diverse ethnically than any previous generation, they are characterized by being very open to, and demanding of, social change; they have a very low approval rating for Trump; they believe humans cause climate change; and they want more government action to solve society's problems. Even Generation Z Republicans are moving way left of Trump and GOP orthodoxy, as evidenced in their being far more accepting of LGBTQ+, largely less supportive of Trumpism and gun control, and believing Black people are treated less fairly than whites.

Millennials and Gen Z add up to a powerful voting bloc that is deeply at odds with Republican orthodoxy and evolving in the opposite direction from the GOP. While Trump and GOP are shifting right, the Gen Z Republicans are shifting left, spelling disaster for the GOP's future. These generations will be the implementors of the New Social Contract and usher in the United States of Eutopia.

The natural religious focus of the female-centric Eutopian movement is on Mother Nature and Mother Earth. The project of healing Mother Earth and restoring the ecological balances the White Man has destroyed is an urgent one because it is an existential threat to the very future of humanity. Here, also, increasingly women are emerging as the most eloquent of climate activists and are rising to positions of leadership in the movement that has formed to address and redress the wrongs and injuries inflicted by the White Man on Mother Earth in his quest for profit and power.

Take for example, the Green New Deal, as proposed by Alexandria Ocasio-Cortez and Ed Markey. The Green New Deal is the most comprehensive national proposal to transform our energy system. It is a progressive, realistic, integrated, 21st century approach to solving our climate and environment problems based on the premise that "environmental policy is economic policy."[32] The Democratic Party should make it the cornerstone of its economic platform and policies.

The Green New Deal proposes a ten-year plan, the goal of which is "meeting 100% of the power demand in the United States through clean, renewable, and zero-emission energy sources, including, (1) by dramatically expanding and upgrading renewable power sources; and (2) by deploying new capacity." Mark Z. Jacobson, a Stanford University civil and environmental engineering professor, concludes, based on his extensive studies on the topic, that a transition to 100% clean, renewable energy is "technically and economically possible... by 2030... But for social and political reasons, it will probably take longer, maybe up to 2050."[33] Jacobson's findings are among 37 recent studies that have found that all (or nearly all) power needs could be met by renewables by 2050. These studies include findings from 11 independent research groups, including scientists in Denmark, Colombia, Japan, and Australia. "Of the people who actually analyze 100 renewable systems," says Jacobson, "they're virtually unanimous that it's possible."[34]

As Jedediah Britten-Purdy pointed out in the *New York Times*, the Green New Deal aims to fix the problem of the environment with a comprehensive and integrative strategy of progressive populist ideas. As part and parcel of fixing the problems of economic inequality, poverty, and even corporate concentration, these ideas include universal healthcare, stronger labor rights, and a job guarantee.[35] The beauty of the Green New Deal is the way it integrates the issues plaguing infrastructure, jobs, and agriculture into a comprehensive strategy for climate and environmental action.

The Green New Deal is based on the insight that the pollution of human carbon emissions is not just about the price of gasoline or electricity. It is fundamentally about infrastructure. Why? For every human being, there are over 1,000 tons of built environment: roads, office buildings, power plants, cars and trains, and long-haul trucks. It is a technological exoskeleton for the species. Everything most of us do relies on this exoskeleton: calling our parents, getting to work, moving for a job, taking the family on vacation, finding food for the evening, or staying warm in a polar vortex. Just being human in this artificial world implies a definite carbon footprint—and for that matter, a trail of footprints in water use, soil compaction, habitat degradation, and pesticide use. You cannot change the climate impact of Americans without changing the built American landscape.

You might say that producing the disaster of global climate change has taken a lot of economic policy and produced a lot of job programs. Reversing this direction will take the same: policymakers creating jobs. So the Green New Deal proposals to retrofit buildings, retool transportation, and build a clean-energy system. These are simply ways of tackling the problem where it starts. They are public works projects because large capital projects—especially ones that, like highways, involve widespread public benefit—have always required public money. They are job programs and expressions of the fact that *any* economic policy is a job policy. Take, for example, the energy sector. Oil and gas provides at least 1.4 million American jobs—more if you believe industry estimates—and depends on public subsidies and infrastructure. Since environmental policy can happen only through economic policy, there is no avoiding decisions about what sorts of work there will be and in which industries. It's unsettling but maybe a little less so when you consider that we've been doing it all along, usually without owning up to it.

Also consider the Green New Deal's proposal to work with family farmers and ranchers to reduce the carbon footprint of agriculture. Food is our everyday metabolism with the natural world, which is why agriculture emits 9% of U.S. carbon, according to the Environmental Protection Agency. (Other estimates are considerably higher.) Forty percent of our land is farmed or ranched, which is to say, the soil is basically conscripted as a food factory. The food system is already pervasively shaped by the Farm Bill, which spends nearly $15 billion per year on subsidies and $10 billion on conservation measures, deeply shaping what farmers grow and where and tending to benefit large, industrially oriented operations. Food production can be much less carbon-intensive with changed practices in cropping, fertilizing, irrigation, and waste management, many of them well suited to small farming. Moving in that direction, though, would require rattling the cage of big American agriculture.

The Green New Deal is very cost effective. Professor Jacobson estimates that the total cost of a nationwide energy transition would be $15 trillion. But, he adds, that is "much cheaper than the current system—it's like one-eighth the social cost and one-half the direct energy cost, so it's really foolish not to do so."[36] By "social costs," Jacobson includes healthcare costs—such as the 62,000 annual deaths from air pollution—and the costs of climate change–related damages, both of which would be cut if we got rid of our fossil fuel emissions.

The costs of energy will decrease because electric power is more efficient than combustion. In a gas-burning car, only about 20% of the energy from fuel goes to turning the tires—the rest is lost as heat. In an electric car, around 80% of energy is used in moving. "So if you electrify transportation, you have one-fourth the energy required," says Jacobson.[37] That reduction—along with switching out gas-heating for more efficient heat pumps, cutting out the energy needed to refine and transport fossil fuels, and other efficiency upgrades—would reduce energy costs by about one-half in coming years.

Moreover, it is important to keep in mind that the government wouldn't spend those trillions all at one time. Instead, the money would likely be spent over a couple of decades, and "you'll get it back over 30 years," says Jacobson. He adds, "When I say it costs 15 trillion, this is not what the government's going to outlay. It's going to put out a small fraction of that, to incentivize, because these things make money on their own."[38]

The Paradigm Shift in Economics: From Scarcity to Abundance

Greek Democracy and the Economic Paradigm Based on Abundance

For Aristotle and his Athenian democrats, true democracy and equality required an economy of abundance. Working like a merchant or a farmer was anathema to the Greeks and considered "ignoble." Indeed, it was considered noble and a necessity for all citizens to have the freedom of leisure to really make democracy work. For Aristotle, "leisure is needed both for the development of virtue and for active participation in politics."[39]

Aristotle's use of the word "citizen" here of course refers to the 1% upper class of the Athenian population. It did not include, and indeed specifically excluded, the noncitizens of Athens that constituted the 99% of the population, who were by definition, inferior, unequal, and unfree. Like all other class societies, Aristotle and his fellow Athenian democratic citizens naturally equated the ruling 1% as 100% of the citizens, not 100% of the denizens, and took it as their gods-given, natural-born right to exploit the other 99% to create that reality of abundance for the 1% they considered the 100%.

And so it has remained through the ages up until the present moment in human history. The basis of the Roman Empire, European feudalism and imperialism, and American and European capitalism has been the class structure of the society that arose from the economics of scarcity and the competition for resources.

The thing that Aristotle and his democrats got right was the idea that, for society to secure true equality and freedom, it must solve the problem of economic scarcity and create conditions of economic abundance. The thing that Aristotle and his democrats got wrong, through omission rather than commission, was that the nature of class society is such that the true freedom it promises to the 1% upper class is really a false freedom, for if the oppressor needs the oppressed in order to be free, how free is he, really? He is bound in an exploitative relationship that demeans the humanity of both exploited and exploiter.

The Achievement of Abundance as Eutopian Inflection Point

What is different today from all previous times in history is that our evolutionary development has reached the point where the notion of scarcity as the fundamental tenet of economic theory and practice has become obsolete. The generations of the 21st century have been given the opportunity and the challenge to carry out the transition from a competitive, scarcity-based economy to a post-scarcity economy of abundance based on the cooperative principle.

As a species, our economic capacity to produce is now sufficient to provide the basic needs and necessities of life for every human being on the planet. The means to accomplish this are provided by developments of automation and robotization, artificial intelligence and 3D printing, which have given humanity the capacity to produce and satisfy the basic necessities and needs of life.

With the realization of the economy of abundance, scarcity, by definition, will no longer be an issue. And in as much as scarcity is the fundamental economic reason for the existence of society's class structure of exploiters and exploited, its absence makes obsolete the very idea of a class structure that is based on economic worth and political power. Humanity as a whole, the peoples of the world, have the means to abolish class structure globally and bring the blessings and responsibilities of true freedom and equality to every individual and group on the planet.

It is an extraordinary coincidence that at the very same time the global limits to economic growth are being reached, and breached, AI and related technology is giving birth to the economics of abundance. Reaching the global limits of economic growth tells us that, in order to re-establish a global balance between economic production and consumption, we must stop the exponential, ceaseless growth required by capitalism and its competitive, for-profit economic system.

The development of AI, 3D printing, and related technologies tells us that yes, indeed, we can do so and still feed, clothe, house, educate, and provide medical care for the entire global population as we scale back our economies to achieve a new balance. You would think that such a momentous historical inflection point would be celebrated worldwide by the peoples of all nations. But it is not. It is seldom mentioned, let alone celebrated. Why not? Because we must resolve a contradiction and win a war before we can celebrate.

The Struggle for AI and the Fate of the World

The question remains: if the human species now has the potential and promise of economic abundance, does it have the will to transition to global economics of abundance based on the cooperative principle? Do we have the courage and vision to replace the White Man's crumbling paradigm of crisis with its very antithesis, the female-centric global paradigm of harmony and balance?

Consider the twofold effect automation and AI will have on society. On the one hand, it will create unprecedented material wealth, and on the other hand, it will cause an unprecedented loss of jobs. This situation will resolve either in a dystopian or a Eutopian manner. It will prove to be either a recipe for complete social disaster and disintegration or an unprecedented opportunity to free the human spirit from economic bondage. Which of the two possible results will materialize will depend on how the gains from automation and AI are distributed. If all of this extra money that companies are going to make with these robots is given to the people, Eutopia is within reach. If the companies hoard all of this extra money for themselves and their shareholders, dystopia is inevitable.

The choices are clear; the opposing camps are assembling; the battle is joined. On the one side, there are the purveyors of dystopia and class structure, the profit seekers, the power hungry, the big business elite, the right-wing politicians of the Republican Party, and the Trumpist base. All these various dystopian types will work together to allow companies to keep *all* the profits from automation and AI. These companies, in turn, will fire or layoff all their workers and pocket the money, creating a huge unemployment and poverty problem, vastly increasing suffering and resentment among the people. The dystopian coalition will sabotage and resist with all their awesome might and power any and all efforts to realize the Eutopian potential of abundance for all. The dystopians seek to maintain scarcity and class structure and not let these realities wither on the vine, because it gives them, the ruling classes, the levers of control. With this control, they can exploit and wield power over the people for their own private interest at the expense of the common good.

Opposing the dystopian forces in the struggle for survival of the future is the Eutopian coalition dedicated to designing a system that embraces this technological future for the benefit of all: feminists, people of color, progressive anti-racists, anti-authoritarians of all stripes, the Rainbow Coalition, the minority of businesses that realize their ultimate goal is not profit or power but humanity, all the progressive thinkers who want to distribute this new wealth generated by automation and AI fairly to improve the standard of living for people more than ever before, all those committed to the idea that class structure will become obsolete through economic abundance replacing scarcity, all those committed to a civilizational paradigm shift from yang to yin, from male-centric to female-centric.

This civic struggle about who gets to control and benefit from the advances of AI is most clearly reflected in the personalities of the leaders of the dystopian and Eutopian movements: Trump, as the embodiment of the toxic masculinity and power pathology of the White Man, and Biden, as the woke feminist and anti-racist, the de facto leader of the Eutopian coalition. Each is so clearly reflective of the fundamental biological polarity of crisis and harmony animating their respective dystopian and Eutopian movements.

Trump and his base thrive on a steady diet of enmity. They feast on the biology of fear and despair, rage and retribution, and the bedrock of their dystopian politics are resentment, grievance, and violence. It is the quality of enmity that made Trump the undisputed master of polarization that has been tearing our nation and culture apart.

Balancing Human and Artificial Intelligence in Eutopia

In so far as this technological revolution contains a recursive loop of innovation, it appears unstoppable. The smarter the machines get, the more they will help us make even smarter machines, accelerating the pace of progress. It is Moore's law, on steroids, for everything. First formulated by Moore in the field of semiconductors, Moore's law articulates a link of inverse proportion between the rate of progress in design and production and the cost of production. Every two years, the same amount of money would buy chips that were twice as powerful as the last iteration. In other words, as technology improves, prices, relatively speaking, fall.

Now, in our economy, one's wealth is one's buying power, and if prices fall, everyone collectively becomes wealthier. The conclusion, obviously, is that the best way to increase societal wealth is to decrease the cost of goods. And it is precisely the technology of robotics and AI that will be the determinative factor in the falling of prices, rapidly driving that decline in many categories, from food to video games. For example, if robots can build a house on land you already own from natural resources mined and refined on-site, using solar power, the cost of building that house is close to the cost of renting the robots. And if those robots are made by other robots, the cost to rent them will be much less than it was when humans made them. Similarly, we can imagine a day in the near future where AI doctors may be able to diagnose health problems better than any human and AI teachers may know exactly what a student doesn't understand.[40]

Since, to a large extent, it is human labor that drives up the cost of goods and services, once sufficiently powerful AIs "join the workforce," the price of human labor will fall toward zero for the simple reason that human labor will be obsolete and no longer necessary. Thus, by lowering the cost of goods and services, the AI revolution will create phenomenal wealth in the process of liberating people from alienating labor. "Moore's law for everything" should be the rallying cry for the post-scarcity generation. In the words of Sam Altman, "It sounds utopian, but it's something technology can deliver (and in some cases already has). Imagine a world where, for decades, everything—housing, education, food, clothing, etc.—became half as expensive every two years."[41]

The consulting firm McKinsey has predicted that, by the year 2030, automation and artificial intelligence will have basically taken over the workplace and displaced 45 million U.S. workers.[42] Even if the predictions only come true partially, we will still be faced with an unprecedented situation, and the enormity of this change must be fully explored and debated in public discussion. Only through such a process can workable strategies be devised as to how to cope productively with the consequences of this technological revolution. Only through such a process will we find answers to the many pressing questions that jump out at us immediately once we start considering this transformative event. Questions like: What are all these millions of people going to do with their newly acquired time? What are their options? And how are these millions of people going to get the money necessary to live in today's society?

If the world is going to be shared between human intelligence and artificial intelligence, it will be important to establish a balance between them. This concept of balance requires the relationship to be Eutopian, i.e., human-centric, in the sense that AI and robots must serve human purpose and not the other way around. If the relationship is reversed and machine-centric, and the human serves the needs of the AI, the relationship would be, from the human point of view, out of balance and dystopian.

Accordingly, the two laws of robotics that define the balanced human-centric division of labor between humans and AI and robots can be stated as follows: (1) no task that can be done by robots should be done by humans (unless they choose to do them); (2) no task that can only, or better, be done by humans should be done by robots.

When defining the balance between human intelligence and AI, we must consider their two fundamentally different natures and the strengths and weaknesses associated with each. Doing this will also illuminate the three areas where the workforce, liberated from alienating labor and given the freedom to choose all over again, can redirect their lives in newly meaningful ways. These are the areas of (1) creativity jobs, (2) jobs in crisis management, and (3) jobs requiring emotional intelligence.

Computers are good at repetitive jobs, but they are not good at improvising and creating new things. Humans are the other way around, not good at repetitive jobs but good at improvising and creating new things. With their economic existence guaranteed by a universal basic income, many of those sidelined by the progress of AI and automation will have the opportunity to liberate their undeveloped or underdeveloped creative abilities and develop the necessary skills to express themselves. Whether working by themselves or within the context of a larger human organization, artists and craftspeople of all stripes and persuasions will be able to proliferate and be part of a global cultural renaissance unparalleled in human history.

Computers are not good at dealing with the unexpected, and humans are. Humans are good at dealing with surprises, especially crisis jobs that involve responding to danger. No one wants to call 911 and speak to a robot, so jobs that involve high stakes situations are pretty safe from automation. Therefore, another portion of the new army of unemployed displaced by AI could choose to recommit their life and purpose by joining with crisis management teams of all kinds to help save human lives and property. EMS, police, fire, flood, earthquake, and other disaster response could finally actually be properly staffed and equipped for their respective areas of responsibility.

AI and computers, which operate on the linear logic of sequence and categorization, are no good in dealing with emotions and feelings. Emotional intelligence is powered by the logic of feelings and emotions that are generated biologically through hormonal influence on neural activity. Therefore, human intelligence is, first and foremost, emotional intelligence, capable of precisely the kinds of skills involved in empathy-sympathy-based labor that will be a defining characteristic of the female-centric Eutopian society of the future. These include the physical, psychological, and spiritual healing arts, the service industry in all it manifold branches, domestic work, and service work, all of which provide tremendous opportunities where those displaced by AI and automation can redirect and recommit their life and purpose.

The Second U.S. Civil War

The White Man's Split Personality Prepares to Fight Its Selves

We are witnessing today a major political convulsion in the American political experiment that will determine whether that experiment will fail or succeed, whether democracy will continue and thrive or be disbanded in favor of a white racist autocracy. To understand the frightening drift into religiously motivated right-wing conspiratorial extremism a large proportion of the Republican electorate is falling prey to today, we must understand both the deep underlying historical causes and the more recent trigger events and mechanisms.

Among the Founders, as we have seen, there existed a spectrum of Protestant religious belief. There was, basically, a left wing and a right wing to the Protestantism of the Founders. On the one hand, there were the humanist democratic Protestants who, grounded in the philosophies of the Enlightenment, believed in the separation of church and state. And on the other hand, there were the theocratic hierarchical protestants who, based mostly on the teaching of John Calvin, believed in the integration and unification of church and state.

The humanistic Protestants were truly democrats. They believed everyone was created equal, economically, socially, and politically. In the religious sphere, too, they wanted to create an open society where everyone could practice whatever they believed. Women and men, non-white and white races were all born with the equal rights of access to all dimensions of life. Even, and especially, if those beliefs had not yet been realized in society, they were held out as goals of inclusivity for our society to strive for.

Theocratic Protestants believed that people were inherently created unequal; a few were chosen by God to share an eternal life of joy with him, while most others were condemned to eternal hell and suffering at the hands of the Devil. On Earth, John Calvin and his followers preached a form of Protestantism that provided cosmic justification for the suppression of all women and non-white races. They proposed a civic hierarchy, supposedly modeled on the cosmic hierarchy in heaven that was both misogynistic and racist: men were divinely ordained to have power over women, and white people were divinely ordained to have power over non-white people.

The history of our country must be evaluated in terms of how these progressive and regressive Protestant paradigms have coexisted and struggled with each other for the soul of the American people and for dominance and control in and over the public sphere. American history is precisely the account of how the realization of the progressive agenda of the humanist Protestant paradigm—true liberation of minorities and their equality—has been hampered, sabotaged, and held back by the regressive theocratic paradigm of racist white male power and privilege. For example, after the Civil War and throughout the Jim Crow era, theocratic Christian leaders routinely provided the theological arguments needed to rationalize limiting Black Americans' access to participation in the democratic process. They explicitly tied these efforts to their desire to protect the purity of a "Christian" nation.

With Trump and the constitutional, cultural, and political crisis he instigated, the White Man has come to the final fork in the road. It is as if history is suddenly holding up a mirror in front of the White Man that is forcing him to confront himself with the reality that he has a split personality that is at war with itself. Indeed, the psychic dynamic of the White Man's collective internal conflict today is that of the good Dr. Jekyll confronting the reality of his alter ego and evil twin, Mr. Hyde. The stakes in this battle are enormous and will shape the global landscape of humanity for centuries to come. Either the White Man's Dr. Jekyll persona emerges victorious over

Mr. Hyde and learns to transcend his darker impulses, or Mr. Hyde prevails and wipes out good Dr. Jekyll.

This is the essence of the conflict that is roiling our culture and our country today. The Second U.S. Civil War is the conflict between the egalitarian Eutopians and the authoritarian dystopians. Either the White Man is able to transcend his dark side and make the world a better place, a Eutopia, or in the end, he will kill himself and make the planet a worse place, a dystopia. The White Man is confronted with an existential choice. He must choose to either become enlightened and committed to Eutopian egalitarianism, or pursue his addiction to the infinite growth of power—a pursuit that has become quite clearly dystopian, a quest leading nowhere but a dead end, literally speaking.

The Eutopian part of the White Man is ready and eager to let go of his male-centric conquest and ownership-oriented masculinity. That part of him is ready to embrace a female-centric masculinity that will help heal society. These are the white men committed to progressive Eutopian policies of the Rainbow Coalition.

In stark contrast, the Dystopian Coalition of White Men seeks to hold onto those male-centric values for dear life because power and violence define his identity. The white males that inhabit this male-centric universe of authoritarian, misogynistic, and racist values are a mix of Evangelical Christians, the blue-collar lower class, the right-wing ultrarich, the grifter-enabler class, and the GOP machinery.

Red Against Blue America

The Second U.S. Civil War is already occurring. One America is regressive and dystopian in outlook and nature, largely rural or exurban, white, and older. The other America is progressive and Eutopian in outlook and nature, largely urban, racially and ethnically diverse, and young. As red zip codes are getting redder and blue zip codes bluer, this split is accelerating, both physically and psychically. This is reflected in the number of super landslide counties—where a presidential candidate won at least 80% of the vote—which almost quadrupled in less than 20 years.[43] This trend is accelerated as Americans find it increasingly important to live around people who share their political values. A corollary to this is that increasingly, Americans are less tolerant of and have more animosity toward those who do not share their political values.

Increasingly, red and blue America are running under different laws. The red states are becoming increasingly dystopian and draconian, centered on the white male–centric values of misogyny and racism, more autocratic than democratic. They want to control women's bodies by banning abortions and forcing LGBTQ+ students to use bathrooms and join sports teams that reflect their gender at birth. They are banning the teaching of America's history of racism and making it more difficult for minorities to vote. They want to put limits on the First Amendment and the expression of free speech and protest while elevating the Second Amendment to encourage buying of ever more powerful guns. They are making it more and more difficult to qualify for unemployment benefits or other forms of public assistance and making it almost impossible to form labor unions. They oppose the expansion of health programs to provide medical care to *all* citizens.

Blue states are moving in the opposite direction. They are on the path of becoming more Eutopian, their policies based on the Rainbow Coalition's egalitarian and democratic values of anti-misogyny and codifying the right to abortion, teaching critical race theory to students, supporting LGBTQ+ rights, valuing the First Amendment over the Second Amendment by supporting free speech and protests while passing common guns laws to prevent the spread of the weapons of war in the civilian population. They want to make it easier to qualify for unemployment benefits or other forms of public assistance and favor the creation of more labor unions as well as universal health insurance for all.

Where will all this end? Robert Reich does not believe it will end with two separate nations. He thinks it is "a kind of benign separation analogous to unhappily married people who don't want to go through the trauma of a formal divorce." He also sees it as a process analogous to Brexit, "a lumbering, mutual decision to go separate ways on most things but remain connected on a few big things (such as national defense, monetary policy, and civil and political rights)." In the end, Reich feels "America will still be America. But it is fast becoming two versions of America. The open question is like the one faced by every couple that separates: how will the two find ways to be civil toward each other?"[44]

That, indeed, is the question. Others are not so sanguine, and they believe the potential is there for the polarization to erupt in armed conflict. Political scientist Barbara F. Walter of UC San Diego, author of *How Civil Wars Start*, describes the current American civil and political climate as "a state of 'anocracy,' suspended between democracy and autocracy."[45] She likens it to the period of social and political unrest and uncertainty that preceded the first Civil War. "On the eve of the first Civil War, the most intelligent, the most informed, the most dedicated people in the United States could not see it coming... The United States today is, once again, headed for civil war, and, once again, it cannot bear to face it. The political problems are both structural and immediate, the crisis both longstanding and accelerating. The American political system has become so overwhelmed by anger that even the most basic tasks of government are increasingly impossible."[46]

With the Second American Civil War that is taking shape these days, Stephen Marche says, "Nobody wants what's coming, so nobody wants to see what's coming."[47] But as evidenced by the January 6 insurrection and attempted coup, the polarization of American society has radically heightened the likelihood of episodic bloodletting in America, and even the risk of civil war. And as it was in the first Civil War, the second one will be fought between the forces of democracy and the forces of autocracy, the forces of dystopia against the forces of Eutopia. Now, as then, the white supremacists cannot be considered a marginal force because they are inside the institutions. Now, as then, the right is preparing for a breakdown of law and order while they are also overtaking the forces of law and order. Now, as then, hard right organizations have infiltrated hundreds of police forces, so many that they have become unreliable allies in the struggle against domestic terrorism.

The military brass is acutely aware of this reality. In a chilling *Washington Post* column, three retired U.S. generals warned that another coup attempt in America in 2024 could divide the military and plunge an unprepared nation into civil war.[48] Former Army Major General Paul Eaton, former Brigadier General Steven Anderson, and former Army Major General Antonio Taguba wrote that, "With the country is still as divided as ever, we must take steps to prepare for the worst. As we approach the first anniversary of the deadly insurrection at the U.S. Capitol, we are increasingly concerned about the aftermath of the 2024 presidential election and the potential for lethal chaos inside our military, which would put all Americans at severe risk."[49]

They continued, "We are chilled to our bones at the thought of a coup succeeding next time, because there were a large number of veterans and active-duty members of the military who participated in the January 6 attack on the Capitol." The generals expressed the fear that the next insurrection could be assisted by breakaway factions within the military, and urged immediate action to prevent the "potential for a total breakdown of the chain of command along partisan lines… from happening." The generals warned that in a "contested election, with loyalties split, [some might] follow orders from the rightful commander in chief, [while other] rogue units [might] follow the Trumpian loser… It is not outlandish to say a military breakdown could lead to civil war."[50]

Eutopian Strategy in the Second U.S. Civil War

In contemplating the nature of this Second U.S. Civil War, one fact stands out. The Eutopians can never hope to emerge victorious by means of armed struggle. Apart from the moral question, we simply don't have the guns to wage a war with. No, the threat of violence is entirely from the enemy, the right-wing dystopian coalition who have about 95 to 99% of the guns. They are the Second Amendment people who believe in gun rights and might-makes-right authoritarianism and will engage in multiple types of violence.

Following the precedents of recent years, these are the kinds of violence we may continue to expect from the dystopian coalition: continued mass shootings by individual right-wing "bad apples," continued domestic misogynistic violence against women, continued racial violence against Blacks and other minorities, continued violent interference with the rights of free speech at demonstrations, continued election terrorism through intimidation at the polls, increased strategic violence against infrastructure such as power station bombings, etc.

The pathology of the dystopian politics of projection is to accuse "the enemy" of the crimes and lies you are committing yourself. An example is Trump's Big Lie that the election was stolen from him, while he was doing everything in his power—legal and illegal—to steal the election from Biden. The dystopian coalition will do everything and anything to maintain power. They will steal, lie, rig elections by controlling the machinery, limit voting rights to allow more white than non-white votes. As a logical corollary to this pathology, there is nothing more fearful to the Republican dystopians than enlarging the number of voters. Their entire strategy of acquiring and maintaining power is based on restricting the number of non-white voters. As Donald Trump correctly commented on the Voting Rights Bill the Republicans boycotted, "We have a bigger problem, because they have a so-called voting rights bill, which is a voting rights for Democrats, because Republicans will never be elected again if that happens…"[51]

So the Eutopians have no choice but to make the Second U.S. Civil War a war of hearts and minds. We must count on our greater numbers, our bigger hearts, and our deeper collective wisdom, to achieve our aims. We must safeguard democracy and prevent the right-wingers from turning it into an autocracy of some kind, most likely theocracy. And our main weapon in this fight is the vote. Our arena of battle is the ballot box. The real arena of the Second U.S. Civil War will be the "deep state": between the Eutopians and the dystopians, who will control the fundamental institutions of government on all levels and branches (local, state, federal, civil, military, legislative, judicial, executive, and the electoral process)?

Ask yourself why Steve Bannon, Trump's theorist and "intellectual," never missed an opportunity to express how much he despised the "deep state," that layer of civil servants that actually makes the institutions of government work. The simple and true answer to that question is that Bannon wanted to replace them all with his own team of MAGA grifters and enthusiasts who cared about these institutions not for their sacred purposes but as a means to carry out the will of a would-be dictator and his team.

American Resistance by David Rothkopf documents precisely how the "deep state," Bannon's targeted enemy, was the institutional barrier that held against the onslaught of the dystopian coalition during and after the 2020 presidential election and saved the nation.

In this Second U.S. Civil War, the strategy of the Eutopian coalition to deal with the violence of the dystopian coalition must be a two-pronged and coordinated exercise of our constitutional rights of free speech and the exercise of our democratic voting rights. It is only through educating and informing the people, then using the electoral process, that we Eutopians can strengthen the deep state so that it will be able to withstand the next dystopian attack on our institutions.

Eutopianism is based on truth and facts, egalitarianism, democracy, female-centricity, and is rainbow colored. Time and math are on our side. We Eutopians are and will be the majority, and will not be denied. Our right to vote will not be abrogated. We will vote and we will win. We will populate the deep state and control the machinery of our institutions, and when the dystopians will attempt to unleash their violence on us, the institutions will respond and decisively win this Second U.S. Civil War.

The Yin-Yang of Capitalism and Socialism
Along the spectrum of economic systems, capitalism and socialism are at opposite ends and represent a yin-yang polarity that is expressive,

respectively, of the male-centric and female-centric biopsychological paradigms embodied in the yin-yang of competition and cooperation. Capitalism, the yang pole, taken as a whole, embodies, is based on, and extolls as its highest values competition and antipathy, if not enmity. Socialism, the yin pole, taken as a whole, embodies, is based on, and extolls as its highest values cooperation and empathy.

In the formation of the American mind and culture, these systems have generally been presented as mutually exclusive and antagonistic. Sad to say, the attitude still prevails today among the white, male, right-wing business class and the Trumpist base of blue-collar Christian nationalists. In their identification of socialism with the boogeyman, these population groups are still constantly spewing the stream of antisocialist vitriolic propaganda.

In Europe, the Scandinavian and other European countries came to the realization early on that unfettered capitalism would destroy civil democratic society and turn into autocracy and fascism and that a balance was needed between them. In other words, in their debate of capitalism versus socialism, it became not a question of either capitalism or socialism, competition or cooperation, but a question of the mix, of how much of each is necessary to have a properly balanced economy between socialism and capitalism.

In the early 20th century, faced domestically with the disintegration of the capitalist system on account of its excesses, FDR followed suit to start the American tradition of balancing the excesses of capitalism with vast and extensive public programs that directly benefitted the people and the quality of their lives. Call them social democracy or democratic socialism or put whatever label on them that you prefer, but for the next half century, this paradigm was dominant in U.S. politics and, in a way, culminated with LBJ's Great Society, his War of Poverty, and the Civil Rights legislation.

As we have documented in previous chapters, in the late 20th century, this tradition was sabotaged and nullified wherever possible by Reagan's throwback philosophy of extreme conservative and social policies that dominated American society in the next half century. The express purposes of Reagan's policies were (1) increasing the revenue of business and capital, and (2) (re)creating the Christian-right political base of the GOP. In both, they succeeded beyond their own expectations to create the dystopian dynamics that now threaten to destroy the global climate and, with it, the global economy.

When Biden and the Democrats came to power, they inherited a situation that Joseph E. Stiglitz, Nobel Prize winner in Economics, World Bank chief economist, and chairman of President Clinton's Council of Economic Advisers, described as follows: "It is not just economics that has been failing but also our politics. Our economic divide has led to a political divide, and the political divide has reinforced the economic divide." In late capitalism, the vicious cycle whereby the rich get richer and the poor get poorer is as simple as it is old. As the rich get richer, they use their economic wealth to acquire more political power, which they then use to further rewrite the rules to strengthen their position at the top of the pyramid. As the 1% not only controls the economy but also the politics of the nation, the rich get richer and the rest get poorer.[52]

Stiglitz's solution to this problem lies in the strengthening of the state. He tells us that from the view of big business and the right wing "government is the problem, not the solution, is simply wrong. To the contrary, many if not most of our society's problems, from the excesses of pollution to financial instability and economic inequality, have been created by markets." To that end, what will be required, according to Stiglitz, is a whole host of concrete government and political reforms, including significant investments in public goods like basic research, more stringent regulation of firms, and measures to preserve and protect the voting franchise. For the time being, then, until we have had the national discussion and agree upon the system of economic democracy that should replace it, the Democrats running the government will have to save capitalism, once again!

To get this redistribution of wealth right, Eutopians see the necessity for implementing drastic change in socio-economic policy by increasingly taxes on the assets that make up most of the value in the world, i.e., companies and land. Many researchers are engaged in serious research to mitigate the immediate socio-economic effects of large-scale unemployment caused by automation and AI. Recognizing that these problems present a unique opportunity to envision a radical new egalitarian restructuring of society, Eutopian thinkers are making it the very cornerstone in the formulation of a New Social Contract between the individual and society.

In the 21st century, in order to avoid global catastrophe, we have no choice but to act boldly and thoroughly to re-establish the lost balance. With the fate of the world at stake, it has become obvious that the world and humanity cannot afford the imbalance of unfettered capitalism; the competitive spirit must be bound by, channeled, and expressed in the service of empathy and cooperation. To restore the balance we need more yin and less yang, more cooperation and less competition, more socialism and less capitalism. Instead of cooperation in the service of competition that we have under capitalism, we must embrace a socialism that incorporates competition in the service of cooperation. Then we will "know the yang, but keep to the yin."

The Evolution of Joe Biden

From Conservative Rank and File to Eutopian Midwife

Forty years ago, newly elected President Reagan stood before a joint session of Congress and delivered a simple message: "Our government is too big, and it spends too much." With that statement, he announced his intention to implement revolutionary changes in the economic system. Reagan vowed to repeal and undo many of the liberal policies and programs initiated by FDR and developed by subsequent Democrats and Republican administrations alike, that had been addressing the direst of social and economic needs of the people. Reagan's new economic paradigm would become known as the "trickle down" theory and would dominate U.S. politics for the next 40 years. Trickle down meant basically reducing the tax burden on business and corporations by all available means and hoping that the surging corporate profits would "trickle down" to the people.

The culmination of decades of Reaganomics was Donald Trump's obscene 2018 tax cut. By pushing through a $2 trillion tax cut that did little for middle-class families, Trump drove the national debt to its highest level since World War II.

Among those sitting in the audience in 1980, listening attentively to Reagan's speech, was a junior senator from Delaware, young Joseph R. Biden, Jr. For the decades that followed, Mr. Biden, along with most officials and operatives of the Democratic Party, would operate in Reagan's shadow. Fearful that an outright embrace of big government would be politically detrimental to their career, Biden, like so many Democrats, joined efforts to curb deficits, fretted about government spending, jumped on the law-and-order bandwagon and endorsed draconian legal policies like "three strikes and you're out," and generally supported the more incremental kinds of social policies that could attract bipartisan support. In truth, Biden and many of his fellow Democrats, starting out as moderate, slightly left of center, were pushed by Reagan's right-wing populist movement to become slightly right-of-center Democrats who often joined the Republicans to vote for and implement regressive legislation. Joe Biden started out as the personification of the traditional moderate, centrist Democrat, staunchly pro-market and pro-business while at the same providing basic social safety nets for the disadvantaged.

Today, four decades later, President Biden is singing a different tune and dancing to the beat of a different drummer. The approach Biden has articulated is one that harks back to FDR and is one that historians, political scientists, and strategists in both parties believe could signal the end of fiscal conservative dominance in our politics. Indeed, Biden has become the self-proclaimed heir to FDR, and FDR's picture is prominently displayed in Biden's Oval Office. In the final analysis, Biden's evolution from right-wing trickle down and fiscal restraint to left-wing populism and government spending was the result of a combination of factors. The most important among these was Biden's sensitivity to the changing needs of people in general, and his deeply held commitment to improving their lives accordingly. The sociocultural changes affecting the lives, feelings, and opinions of the people were, of course, also reflected in the Democratic base. This, in turn, generated new political pressures that engendered new leadership within the Democratic Party. This new leadership was much farther left than Biden's traditional moderate inclinations, ranging from social democrats to democratic socialists.

Biden Claiming the Mantle of FDR

The 2020 Democratic primaries had an unusually large field of more than 20 candidates competing and reaching for the ultimate brass ring, spanning the entire spectrum of progressive democratic thinking and aspirations. As the race progressed and the number of contestants dwindled in the last phase, only three candidates were left standing. These three candidates represented the spectrum of the Democratic Party, from left to center: Sanders (democratic socialist), Warren (progressive), and Biden (moderate). Then Warren fizzled, Sanders flopped, and Biden emerged as the strong choice of the Democrats to be their unity candidate. Hardly any money, no campaign staff, only a skeleton of a campaign platform, and few if any real concrete plans, only name recognition, a friendly demeanor of a unifier and pleaser, with a legacy of a more civil age, and a team player with the very popular President Obama, Joe Biden became the standard bearer of the Democratic Party for 2020 and defeated the dystopian megalomaniac and his MAGA fascists, thereby becoming the first de facto hero of the Eutopian Democratic Party.

In his first address to a joint session of Congress, Biden put on the mantle of FDR. He called on the U.S.'s top 1% to pay for his $1.8-trillion American families plan, boosting higher spending in areas such as education, childcare, and infrastructure. It's about the government taxing the wealthy to pay for the betterment of the not wealthy. "Trickle down has never worked," Biden declared, adding that the task ahead is to build the country from the middle and the bottom outwards, not from the top down. "It's time we remembered that 'We the People' are the government. You and I," he said. "Not some force in a distant capital."[53] "We have to prove democracy still works, that our government still works and can deliver for the people."[54]

To its great credit, the Democratic Party has come to strongly support the healing and integrative journeys of individuals searching for and defining the unique mix of the yin within the yang and the yang within the yin that constitute their psychological and physical reality. They have also come to support their healing integration with an acceptance by the rest of society still burdened by the White Man's limiting paradigm.

Joe Biden, in all respects, is proving to be the complete antithesis of his predecessor. Biden's most effective, and not-so-secret, political weapon is his obviously deep capacity for empathy. Rooted in the manifold traumas he experienced in his personal life, Biden's strength is knowing how to enter a human being's grief and suffering and sharing the load of carrying it. He personifies the biology and politics of hope, empathy, and cooperation. It is these qualities that make Biden the totally logical and appropriate person to assume the role of the political healer in an age of extreme political polarization and to be midwife to the age of balance and harmony.

Biden the Unifier

Actually, despite the intense competition and differences underneath the surface, there was a high degree of unity among Democratic voters. Among Biden voters, the second choice for president was Sanders. Among Sanders voters, the second pick was Biden. Kamala Harris supporters picked Biden second. Warren supporters picked Sanders second, and Beto O'Rourke supporters picked Sanders too.

Additionally, Biden smartly enlisted Bernie and his people to create six task forces—on climate, healthcare, immigration, education, economy, and criminal justice reform—to iron differences and come up with a unified campaign proposal.[55] Biden also hired Bernie's former press secretary, Symone Sanders (no relation), "the uncompromising outsider whose progressive crusade galvanized the American left" as a senior adviser and cable TV surrogate.[56]

In a similar vein, Biden had adopted and adapted critical ideas from Elizabeth Warren in his $700 billion "Buy American" campaign, which he acknowledged in an email to members of the Progressive Change Campaign Committee, a Warren-allied progressive group: "I am grateful to so many—including my friend Elizabeth Warren, labor unions, and other progressive partners—for their help in putting together this bold new set of ideas aimed at healing our economy and ensuring good, dignified jobs for American workers."[57] In return, Warren is helping Biden with her fundraising expertise and bringing millions into Biden's war chest.

The involvement of Sanders, Warren and their people helped unite Democrats behind the moderate nominee while pushing Biden leftward, ideologically and policy wise,[58] coming up with a unified approach. The term "progressive" has come to express this unity since all the varieties of Democrats left of "conservative (Southern) democrats," including moderate democrats, social democrats, and democratic socialists, like to call themselves "Progressive Democrats."

Most Democratic progressives favor a private sector–driven economy, but with a stronger social safety net, enhanced bargaining power for workers, and tighter regulation of corporate malfeasance. They want America to be more like Denmark, not more like Venezuela.[59] The Democratic Party has clearly moved left in recent years, but the "progressives" among the Democrats, including Sanders, are "social democrats" in the European sense, and not, by any stretch of the imagination, socialist in the classical sense of advocating government ownership of the means of production.

Biden and the Democrats Against the Wealthy

In recent years, starting with the 2018 elections and again in the 2020 elections, the Democratic Party, its candidates, and their campaigns have successfully weaponized voters' anger into a renewed national conversation around income and wealth inequality. There is clear evidence that economic populism has taken root across the political spectrum, largely thanks to prominent left-wing voices in the Democratic Party pushing tax hikes on the wealthy and demanding that billionaires and corporations stay out of politics.[60]

Polling has long shown that a majority of Americans believe corporations and the wealthy don't pay enough in taxes. Recent polls have found that nearly 60% of voters—and 45% of Republicans—are in favor of Ocasio-Cortez's 70% marginal rate on the ultrarich. Democrats believe the conversation will continue to gain momentum as long as Americans are hurting and the wealthiest grow disproportionately richer. Indeed, the left argues that high top tax rates are designed to keep American society democratic. "They aim at preventing an oligarchic drift that, if left unaddressed, will continue undermining the social compact and risk killing democracy." As Ocasio-Cortez put it, her marginal tax hike is "one answer to the question of: at what level are we really just living in excess and what kind of society do we want to live in?"[61]

Progressive Democratic politicians responded to the sentiments of their base with a number of far-reaching proposals for reform. Representative Alexandria Ocasio-Cortez's proposal to raise marginal tax rates on those who make over $10 million has sparked a growing debate over tax policy. And the young Democrat then rattled the political establishment by arguing that it's "immoral" for billionaires to exist in a society with widespread poverty.[62] Senator Elizabeth Warren built her political career fighting a system she says is "rigged" for the wealthy. She reports that she will propose to levy a 2% wealth tax on Americans with assets above $50 million as well as a 3% wealth tax on those who have more than $1 billion.[63] Senator Bernie Sanders's 2016 presidential bid had one central theme: "standing up to the billionaire class." He rolled out his proposition, "For the 99.8% Act," which would expand the federal estate tax and include a 77% tax on billionaires' estates. [64]

In 2009, when the Democratic Obama government launched its stimulus plan in response to the Great Recession, Republican conservatives and their fringe allies helped ignite the right-wing populist Tea Party movement. In 2020, after Congress passed Biden's $1.9 trillion relief bill, there was no such backlash against the big spenders in Washington. Even many Republican voters were supportive of the legislation, and no Republicans in Washington mounted a cohesive line of attack against the policy. And some who voted against the bill were only too glad to laud its benefits after it had been passed, an implicit acknowledgment of public support.

In fact, a shift of mood and perception among the people at large occurred since the start of the pandemic, with Americans expressing more and more positive sentiments about their government over all. In the 2020s, there was an 8% increase, from 47 to 55%, in the general approval rating of the government. Nearly two-thirds of Americans supported Mr. Biden's relief bill, with similar numbers backing his infrastructure plans. In a policy that dovetails with the "75 percent of Americans who favor higher taxes for the ultrawealthy," Biden has proposed raising federal income tax to just under 40% for Americans earning more than $400,000 a year.

"The idea of a federal law that would guarantee paid maternity leave has attracted 67 percent support. Eighty-three percent favor strong net neutrality rules for broadband, and more than 60 percent want stronger privacy laws. Seventy-one percent think we should be able to buy drugs imported from Canada, and 92 percent want Medicare to negotiate for lower drug prices. The list goes on and on."[65] Having self-consciously cloaked himself in the legacy of FDR, Biden sees government as the solution for a more abstract kind of problem: a deeply polarized country that might be unified around a national response to a series of crises involving climate change, racial justice, public health, and the economy.

The 2020 election of Biden to the presidency and the Democrats gaining control over both the House and the Senate is yet another chapter in the history of the Democrats coming to the rescue of capitalism. As we have recounted in previous chapters, economic recessions and depressions in American history have largely been caused by the irresponsibly greedy behavior of big business and their GOP political henchmen. That's why FDR followed Hoover, Obama followed Bush, and Biden followed Trump.

Endnotes

1　Steve Feliciano, "The Riot Grrrl Movement," New York Public Library, June 19, 2013, https://www.nypl.org/blog/2013/06/19/riot-grrrl-movement.

2　Rebecca Walker, "Becoming the Third Wave," Ms. More Than a Magazine Movement, January 1992: 39–41, https://web.archive.org/web/20170115202333 /http:/www.msmagazine.com/spring2002/BecomingThirdWaveRebeccaWalker.pdf.

3　Amna A. Akbar, "The Left Is Remaking the World," New York Times, July 11, 2020, https://www.nytimes.com/2020/07/11/opinion/sunday/defund-police-cancel-rent .html.

4　Ibid.

5　Ibid.

6　Larry Buchanan, Quoctrung Bui, and Jugal K. Patel, "Black Lives Matter May Be the Largest Movement in U.S. History," New York Times, July 3, 2020, https://www .nytimes.com/interactive/2020/07/03/us/george-floyd-protests-crowd-size.html.

7　Rachel Hartigan, "She Co-founded Black Lives Matter. Here's Why She's so Hopeful for the Future," National Geographic, July 8, 2020, https://www.nationalgeographic .com/history/article/alicia-garza-co-founded-black-lives-matter-why-future-hopeful.

8　Ibid.

9　Ibid.

10　Larry Buchanan, Quoctrung Bui, and Jugal K. Patel, "Black Lives Matter May Be the Largest Movement in U.S. History," New York Times, July 3, 2020, https://www .nytimes.com/interactive/2020/07/03/us/george-floyd-protests-crowd-size.html.

11　Ibid.

12　Ibid.

13　Ibid.

14　Ibid.

15　Yamiche Alcindor, "Some Who Saw Change in Obama Find It Now in Donald Trump," New York Times, November 2, 2016, https://www.nytimes.com /2016/11/03/us/politics/obama-donald-trump-voting.html.

16　Kenneth T. Walsh, "Clinton Wins Popular Vote by Nearly 3 Million Ballots," U.S. News & World Report, December 21, 2016, https://www.usnews.com/news/ken -walshs-washington/articles/2016-12-21/hillary-clinton-wins-popular-vote-by -nearly-3-million-ballots.

17　Stephanie Muravchik and Jon A. Shields, "Trump's Democrats," Brookings, September 29, 2020, https://www.brookings.edu/book/trumps-democrats/.

18　Saira Asher, "Barack Obama Says Women Better Pass Men Well-Well," BBC News Singapore, December 16, 2019, https://www.bbc.com/pidgin/tori-50805724.

19　Ibid.

20　David Brooks, "The Age of Aquarius, All Over Again!" New York Times, June 10, 2019, https://www.nytimes.com/2019/06/10/opinion/astrology-occult-millennials .html.

21　Tara Isabella Burton, "The Great Awakening: The Rise of Progressive Occultism," The American Interest, June 7, 2019, https://www.the-american-interest.com/2019/06/07 /the-rise-of-progressive-occultism/.

22　Ibid.

23　Ibid.

24　David Brooks, "The Age of Aquarius, All Over Again!" New York Times, June 10, 2019, https://www.nytimes.com/2019/06/10/opinion/astrology-occult-millennials.html.

25   Tara Isabella Burton, "The Great Awakening: The Rise of Progressive Occultism," The American Interest, June 7, 2019, https://www.the-american-interest.com/2019/06/07/the-rise-of-progressive-occultism/.

26   Ibid.

27   David Brooks, "The Age of Aquarius, All Over Again!" New York Times, June 10, 2019, https://www.nytimes.com/2019/06/10/opinion/astrology-occult-millennials.html.

28   Ross Douthat, "The Return of Paganism," New York Times, December 12, 2018, https://www.nytimes.com/2018/12/12/opinion/christianity-paganism-america.html

29   Ibid.

30   Ibid.

31   Dan Levin, "Young Voters Keep Moving to the Left on Social Issues, Republicans Included," New York Times, January 23, 2019, https://www.nytimes.com/2019/01/23/us/gop-liberal-america-millennials.html.

32   Ula Chrobak, "Everything you need to know about the Green New Deal ", Popular Science, Feb. 12, 2019, https://www.popsci.com/green-new-deal-explained/.

33   Ibid.

34   Ibid.

35   Jedediah Britton-Purdy, "The Green New Deal Is What Realistic Environmental Policy Looks Like," New York Times, February 14, 2019, https://www.nytimes.com/2019/02/14/opinion/green-new-deal-ocasio-cortez-.html.

36   Ibid.

37   Ibid.

38   Ibid.

39   Olivia Goldhill, " One of History's Greatest Philosophers Thought Work Makes You a Worse Person," Quartz, June 30, 2018, https://qz.com/1316428/one-of-historys-greatest-philosophers-thought-work-makes-you-a-worse-person.

40   Sam Altman, "Moore's Law for Everything," March 16, 2021, https://moores.samaltman.com/.

41   634 Ibid.

42   CNBC, "NYT's Kevin Roose: Robots and AI Have Potential to Replace White-Collar Jobs," March 23, 2021, https://www.cnbc.com/video/2021/03/23/nyts-kevin-roose-robots-and-ai-have-potential-to-replace-white-collar-jobs.html.

43   Robert Reich, "The Second American Civil War Is Already Happening," The Guardian, May 11, 2021, https://www.theguardian.com/commentisfree/2022/may/11/second-american-civil-war-robert-reich.

44   Ibid.

45   David Remnick, "Is There a Civil War Ahead?" New Yorker, January 5, 2022, https://www.newyorker.com/news/daily-comment/is-a-civil-war-ahead; book review of How Civil Wars Start by Barbara F. Walter, (New York: Random House, 2022).

46   Ibid.

47   Stephen Marche, "The Next Civil War Is Already Here—We Just Refuse to See It," The Guardian, January 4, 2022, https://www.theguardian.com/world/2022/jan/04/next-us-civil-war-already-here-we-refuse-to-see-it?CMP=Share_iOSApp_Other.

48   Mary Papenfuss, "Generals Warn of Divided Military and Possible Civil War in Next U.S. Coup Attempt," HuffPost, December 18, 2021, https://www.huffpost.com/entry/2024-election-coup-military-participants_n_61bd52f2e4b0bcd2193f3d72; Michael Smolens, "The Risk to U.S. Democracy and the Threat of Civil War," San Diego Union, December 24, 2021, https://www.sandiegouniontribune.com/columnists/story/2021-12-24/the-failing-of-u-s-democracy-and-threat-of-civil-war.

49 Ibid.

50 Ibid.

51 Steve Benen, MSNBC, December 22, 2021. https://www.msnbc.com/rachel-maddow-show/maddowblog/trump-says-more-he-intended-while-slamming-voting-rights-bill-n1286450

52 Joseph E. Stiglitz *People, Power, and Profits: Progressive Capitalism for an Age of Discontent, (New York: W.W. Norton & Co, 2019).*

53 Larry Elliott "Biden Attempts to Consign Trickle-Down Economics to the Dustbin of History," The Guardian, April 29, 2021, https://www.theguardian.com/business/2021/apr/29/biden-trickle-down-economics-us-president.

54 Lisa Lerer, "Joe Biden, the Reverse Ronald Reagan," New York Times, May 1, 2021, https://www.nytimes.com/2021/05/01/us/politics/joe-biden-the-reverse-ronald-reagan.html.

55 Charlotte Alter, " How Joe Biden Is Defusing Tensions with the Left," Time, July 10, 2020, https://time.com/5864952/joe-biden-bernie-sanders-task-forces/.

56 Ibid.

57 Kevin Robillard, "Joe Biden Credits Elizabeth Warren with Helping Craft His New Economic Plan," HuffPost, July 10, 2020, https://www.huffpost.com/entry/joe-biden-credits-elizabeth-warren-with-helping-craft-his-new-economic-plan_n_5f089e66c5b63a72c3414f28.

58 Giovanni Russonello, "Biden and Bernie, United (at Least Briefly)," New York Times, July 9, 2020, https://www.nytimes.com/2020/07/09/us/politics/biden-bernie-sanders-policy.html.

59 Paul Krugman, "The S Word, the F Word, and the Election," New York Times, June 27, 2019, https://www.nytimes.com/2019/06/27/opinion/socialism-2020.html.

60 Eliza Reiman, Business Insider, February 2, 2019, https://www.businessinsider.com/alexandria-ocasio-cortez-the-left-fight-with-billionaires-tax-rich-2019-1

61 Ibid.

62 Ibid

63 Ibid

64 Ibid

65 Tim Wu, "The Oppression of the Supermajority," New York Times, March 5, 2019, https://www.nytimes.com/2019/03/05/opinion/oppression-majority.html.

Chapter 17

The American Dream and the Birthing of Eutopia (2050-2100)

Restoring Economic Balance to Achieve Eutopia

Class Therapies for the White Man

The therapies for the White Man's collective sociopolitical-economic system as a whole, as well as the individual White Man of the various classes, will consist of replacing the male-centric paradigm of power with the female-centric paradigm of balance.

On the individual level, all three classes of the dystopian coalition, the upper, middle, and lower classes are in the grip of the rage and violence of the male-centric "warrior" paradigm. All three classes share the addiction to aggression and violence, and for all three classes of the dystopian coalition, the goal of reeducation and therapy will be recovery from the addiction to aggression and violence. Such a recovery will entail letting go of the dystopian, male-centric "superior warrior masculinity" paradigm and embracing the empathy and cooperation characteristic of the female-centric paradigm of balance. Each recovering toxic-masculinity addict will find new meaning in their lives in the balance of the female-centric paradigm, by living life in service to others rather than the narcissistic satisfaction of personal greed, profit, and power.

Yet, given the differences between the upper, middle, and lower classes, different educational and therapeutic strategies will need to be formulated for each class of White Man. For each class, it will be an education-driven therapy. In the great Eutopian restructuring of society driven by the economics of abundance and obsolescence of conventional work categories and jobs, everybody, including the White Man of all three classes, will be going "back to school" as they're working through their therapeutic process. The choices of educational goals and curriculum will be made in close consultation with the professional therapy team the individual becomes a patient of.

Each White Man who makes the commitment to enter into this therapeutic process will complete, in some form or other, a two-step process. First, as the result of his enlightenment and transformation, he will take one step forward, issue a declaration of mea culpa, and acknowledge publicly and take responsibility for the sins of the fathers and the male-centric paradigm. Second, as the next logical step due to his enlightenment and transformation, he will take two steps backwards to allow and promote the individual and collective healing of body, mind, and emotions into the harmony of the female-centric paradigm. To take this therapeutic process out of the realm of abstraction and into concreteness, I am framing the description of this therapeutic process in terms of my own personal realizations.

Truth-and-Hope Therapy for the 90% Lower-Class White Guys

The explosion of right-wing violence from the White Man lower class in the early 2020s saw their general frustration and anger, pent-up over decades and brought to the boiling point by Trump and company. The White Man lower classes are now at the point where they explode like mini-volcanoes and feel justified to go after their perceived liberal enemies with violence and threats of violence. The extent of this violence might lead one to despair that any rehabilitation attempts will fail.

Yet of the three classes of the White Man's dystopian coalition, I believe that all things considered, it will be easiest by far to convince the lower class to change their hearts and minds and mend their ways than it will be to convince the upper and middle classes. In as much as the lower class have been conned into their belief system of grievance and retribution by the upper class, they first and foremost need education and therapy to make them conscious of that fact. Consciousness of the con will provide them ample justification for rejecting the old values of rage and violence and embracing new values that will restore their capacity for love and empathy.

In this transformative experience, the experience of life as a series of dead ends and no-exits will turn into a life of unlimited opportunities, despair turning into hope, absurdity into meaning, and hate into love. With their new and heightened critical awareness, the base will realize that they have nothing to lose and everything to gain—materially, economically, psychologically, and spiritually—from joining the Rainbow Coalition march to Eutopia. The truth will set them free and enable them to transition from right-wing populism to left-wing populism.

Addiction Therapy for the 9% Middle-Class White Guys

It is important to understand that the disease of power, in its etiology and progression, is, in all respects, a disease of addiction. The quest for power over people and use of violence against them are symptoms of the addiction to the testosterone-adrenalin high. It is a need that must constantly be satisfied lest the individual suffer its opposite and sinks into the doldrums of depression, despair, and self-loathing. In the final analysis, more than craving the high, the addict is an addict because he is always desperate to prevent his ever-threatening depression from overwhelming and paralyzing him.

As a result of AI, automation, and associated other factors, millions of blue- and white-collar substantive or bullshit jobs will disappear. For example, there will be thousands of stock traders, on and off the floor of the exchange, who made their living buying and selling stocks, their own and their customers', who will become unemployed. These marketeers will face a deep existential crisis as they confront the end of their lifestyle. Hopelessly addicted to the frenzy of the market, whether panic or manic, where the accumulation of profit was the only yardstick of measurement, they will have to look and ask themselves what gives their life meaning.

In this situation, the middle-class White Man will also have a more difficult time with completing successful therapy than the lower-class White Man because he actively bought into the upper-class White Man's paradigm of amassing wealth and power. The central question in the lives of the newly deposed crisis-and-power addicts becomes how to find meaning in a life without pursuing wealth or power. From the societal point of view, this particular subset of humanity represents a tremendous pool of human energy, consciousness, and creativity, which if understood and channeled properly, will be a tremendous boon to social evolution and, if not, can represent a tremendous danger to the cohesion of the new Eutopia.

So it's important to get this right. Any proposed therapy must have a clear exit strategy from the warrior paradigm. The essence of the warrior paradigm consists of the testosterone-adrenalin axis that had become the invariant feature of Western man's behavioral paradigm in general, and has been observable for centuries in a particularly rampant and virulent form operating in the stock market and infecting its players.

These guys are addicts, and like addicts, they need their fix, or they will act out irrationally and irresponsibly. So the therapy will need to include a strategy for the withdrawal signs and symptoms from dependency. But whatever the approach, they will need help, a lot of help, to rebalance their lives along different values and parameters. It will take an army of "special teams" of health professionals, addiction experts, psychotherapists, sociologists, ethicists, etc., to help them enter into the paradigm of balance.

Disentitlement Therapy for the 1% Ruling Class White Guys

The 1% and the Eutopian Revolution

Profound changes in the socio-economic landscape will occur as a result of the implementation of the Great Eutopian Reorganization of Society. While for the 99%, these will be profoundly positive and liberating, for the 1%, it will be a time of profound disorientation and readjustment to their diminished social stature. The Great Eutopian Transformation of Society will also be a time of profound disorientation for the upper-class white men as they adjust, or fail to adjust, to their removal from the top of the power pyramid. Indeed, it will be the upper-class White Man who will be the most intransigent and difficult to convince to engage in and commit to and complete successful therapy. Predictably so, for various reasons.

Since the upper-class White Man stands to lose the most wealth and power, he may decide that, since there will be no profit in it for him, he won't want to be part of a collective national enterprise to transform society. Many will close up shop or declare bankruptcy. Being the instigators and perpetrators of the con, the upper class will be less amenable to reeducation and therapy because it will mean accepting guilt, blame, and remorse for their actions. The easier strategy will be to go into denial and double down.

Moreover, their therapeutic needs must be weighed within the context of judicial investigations that will assess their possible criminal culpability in their uses of the capitalist system to exploit their workers and the planet.

The obstacles in this therapeutic effort will be many, and most likely, success will only be partial. I mean, can you imagine the amount of therapy it would take to restore Trump to his humanity? So we may not succeed fully in our efforts, in this lifetime. But we will help some get to the point of living a life of meaning. That's why we must make the effort, knowing full well that, in the end, only time and attrition can fully finish the job of ridding humanity of its most aggressive and poisonous elements.

The Mental Health of the 1%

Clay Cockrell, a mental health therapist to the 1%, writes that the reality of the superrich is that they "struggle with the toxicity of excess, isolation and deep mistrust." [1] According to Cockrell, the mental health of billionaires is negatively affected and unbalanced by three fundamental, interrelated issues of trust, purpose, and money.

First, being filthy rich is an almost unsurmountable barrier to developing a relationship of trust and closeness with anyone; they are fundamentally deeply suspicious that everyone is out to exploit them in some way for their money and not for their personal qualities.

Second, Cockrell points out that, contrary to popular imagination, immense riches do not create satisfaction and fulfillment but foster boredom and depression. With all necessities covered for the rest of their lives, and their companies so successful that they run themselves and no longer need them, the life of the superrich is rife with the afflictions of boredom, purposelessness, and lack of meaning, often leading to addictive and abusive behavior.

Third, Cockrell comes to the crux of the pathologies of the 1%, which is, of course, the money. He writes that most of the 1% that he counsels are "much more willing to talk about their sex lives or substance-misuse problems than their bank accounts. Money is seen as dirty and secret. Money is awkward to talk about. Money is wrapped up in guilt, shame, and fear." Cockrell concludes by emphasizing that, contrary to popular belief, money and wealth, far from immunizing people against mental health problems, makes "you—and the people closest to you—much more susceptible to them."[2]

Those poor, troubled one-percenters! By aiming to eliminate the root of their misery, which is their wealth and power, their therapy must be both compassionate and radical. For in the end, only the systematic disentitlement of the 1% White Man and the imposition of relative austerities on them will restore their humanity: Limits must be placed on their conspicuous and competitive consumption. The obscenities of executive compensation must be revisited and equalized with other creative work. Inheritance must be eliminated. Economic enterprises, large and small, should be publicly owned and collectively managed. The private profit motive in economic enterprises should be abolished, and the stock market should be allowed to wither away. And fear not, we will examine all these points in more detail in the sections to come!

Limits on Conspicuous and Competitive Consumption
The affluence of the superrich is literally killing the planet. At the very top, just over 0.5% of the world's wealthiest, "about 40 million

people, are responsible for 14% of lifestyle-related greenhouse gas emission." Next, "the world's top 10% of income earners are responsible for at least 25% and up to 43%" of our species' destructive impact on our environment. In sharp contrast, "the bottom 50% of income earners, almost 4 billion people, only emit around 10%" of total greenhouse gas emissions. "To put it bluntly: the rich do more harm than good."[3] The "affluence" of the 1% "trashes our planetary life support systems" because, "by driving up power relations and consumption norms," "it obstructs the necessary transformation towards sustainability."[4] For the planet and the species' health, therefore, it is imperative for the affluent to drastically reduce their consumption levels by adapting a sufficiency lifestyle of "better but less."[5]

Unfortunately, this is easier said than done. The main stumbling block to reducing consumption by the superrich as much as necessary in a socially sustainable way, while still safeguarding human needs and social security, is the economic imperative to grow the economy. Affluent, powerful people and their governments have a vested interest in discouraging sufficiency-oriented lifestyles and deliberately promoting high-consumption lifestyles for the rich and famous. In reality, the affluent create a growth spiral that is driven by competitive "positional consumption," where everyone is always striving to outdo and "stay superior" relative to their peers, even as the overall consumption level continues to rise.[6]

Social movements will play a crucial role in pushing the superrich to reform themselves. They can challenge the notion that riches and economic growth are inherently good and push toward "social tipping points." Post-development thinkers, degrowth advocates, eco-feminists, eco-socialists, and many other like-minded grassroots initiatives such as transition initiatives and eco-villages are examples of this, leading to cultural and consciousness change. What all these approaches have in common is that they focus on positive environmental and social outcomes and not on economic growth. Interestingly, there seems to be some strategic overlap between them, at least in the short term.[7]

Eventually, however, far-reaching policy reforms are needed, including maximum and minimum incomes, eco-taxes, collective firm ownership, and more. Examples of policies that start to incorporate some of these mechanisms are the Green New Deals in the U.S., UK, and Europe, or the New Zealand Wellbeing Budget of 2019. In the final analysis, the rich will have to take their medicine and join in the goal to establish economies and societies that protect the climate and ecosystems and enrich people with more well-being, health, and happiness instead of more money.

The Obscenity of Executive Compensation

In Chapter 12, we presented the facts of the dystopian process of the ever-increasing concentration of wealth and power into fewer and fewer individuals at the expense of those inevitably left behind. We pointed out that nowhere is this process more glaring than in the disparity between compensation of the lower and middle-class workers, compared to executive compensation.

The explosion of pay for top corporate executives over the last four decades is a particularly salient feature of the obscene rise in American income inequality. In the 1960s and 1970s, the ratio of CEO pay to typical worker pay was 20 or 30 to 1. In recent years, it has blown up to 200 or 300 to 1. "The average CEO at a Fortune 500 firm now makes close to $20 million per year, and it is not uncommon for a CEO to make $30 or $40 million if their company has an especially good year or if they have a favorable contract."[8]

But now we must pose the question of executive compensation within the larger social context of Eutopian reconstruction. And this must begin with a consideration of the question of what should be the rewards for creativity in any field—financial, economic, psychological, social, material, and spiritual.

In capitalist culture, typically, the highest compensation for creative effort is always expressed in terms of money, especially in the fields related to the management of corporate entities. As a consequence of the fact that creativity in economic, financial, and business professions is far more rewarded than creativity in other fields, these fields draw a disproportionate number of talented "creatives" who choose to exercise and hone their talents in the pursuit of making more money to the detriment of other sectors of society.

The Eutopian conception of the relationship of the rewards for creativity is the complete antithesis of this reality. It is based on the inherent equality of all creative effort and the idea that all creative effort should be its own reward; creativity should be engaged in for the love of creating, not the promise of wealth or power. This is also in line with the Eutopian framework that since, in Eutopia, everyone will have economic security of guaranteed income, medical care, housing, etc., there is no need to reward creativity with wealth or power.

Moreover, in the Eutopian conception, all businesses will be considered and treated as various types of social utilities. Accordingly, businessmen and CEOs will be considered civil servants whose social responsibility is to run that enterprise for the benefit of society, not to increase profits for private interests. Again, there should be no special material or monetary rewards for creativity in the management of corporate entities, but such rewards for creativity should be limited to social recognition.

Proponents of the capitalist for-profit culture have argued continually and perpetually that de-elevating the money-and-profit motive would mean fewer people would be motivated to take on these challenges of institutional management simply for the love of creative problem-solving. We agree with them that eliminating the private profit motive in business will result in a decrease in people attracted to the field of institutional management. But we disagree with them that this would be a bad thing. Quite the opposite: we need to eliminate the rewarding of people who live to accumulate money; there are far too many of them already. It is, after all, a sickness, a psychological affliction that needs therapy and healing. There is no reason that the Sackler family and other pharma billionaires should make more money than Dr. Fauci.

Elimination of Inheritance

Politically, financially, and economically, the U.S. is a functional plutocracy if not an oligarchy. In this system, the dynastic wealth of the 1% is passed on through the institution of inheritance, from each generation to the next, to generations of people that did not earn that wealth. Indicative of the basic unfairness of the institution of inheritance, the inheritance tax rate in many countries is way higher than income from other sources, such as salary or profits. Japan has the highest rate in this respect with 55%, France has 45%, and the UK and U.S. both have 40% inheritance tax rate.

The reason that, in most countries, income from inheritance is taxed at a higher rate than income from other sources is straightforward and simple: High incomes serve a social purpose when they reward hard work and innovation. High incomes from being born rich serve no such purpose. Therefore, taxing inherited wealth at a higher rate than earned wealth makes sense from both the standpoint of economic efficiency and the standpoint of social fairness. And it must be realized and admitted that along with inheritance comes the undemocratic inheritance of advantage.

So, if we are really serious about economic democracy, the institution of dynastic inheritance of plutocratic wealth must be addressed frontally with a complete abolition of the institution of inheritance. It must be cut off at the roots because the practice of inheritance is, in principle, wholly contradictory and opposite to the ideal of equality and a level playing field, and it undermines the meritocratic ideals we claim to espouse.

As all individuals will be endowed equally with the Five Prosperities of the New Social Contract (as we will see later), none need to enjoy the benefit of additional inherited money. At the death of an individual, therefore, their private property would be auctioned off and the proceeds accrued to society, i.e., the government. Of course, some exemptions to this law, such as transfers to spouses and dependent lineal descendants, will undoubtedly be factored in. Legislation will also be needed to prevent the use of gifts as a way of circumventing the abolition of inheritance.

As inheritances in the United States account for two-fifths of all wealth, systemically, the transfer of wealth across generations is not a minor economic or social activity. It is beginning to dawn on Democrats that a tax on massive inherited fortunes should be an integral part of financing their domestic programs such as the New Social Contract. Moreover, such a strategy would help them make their broader thematic case against the Republican Big Business and Organized Crime Party of Trump, his oligarchs, and their army of grifters and grafters.

Small Business and Big Business

Profit is the engine of capitalism. Without the prospect of financial gain, the theory goes, nobody would take risks on new businesses, new products, or new ideas. Sales of products are maximized by offering them on the market at lower prices than the competition. To increase both their total revenue and their profit margin, private-sector companies must optimize efficiency and cut costs wherever possible, continually improving their offerings and luring new customers. Generally, it is agreed that the role of government in a capitalist system is to set the rules and enforce them to assure nobody cheats.

But there is wide debate about the extent of government interference in the dynamics of capitalism. Capitalism ultimately wants to privatize everything, that is, all collective, governmental, and social institutions, such as prisons, post office, social security, armies, police, education, health, transportation, communication, tech, you name it. The superrich want to own them privately and operate these institutions for their private profit.

Socialism wants to go in the opposite direction and aims to "socialize," or collectivize, private industry, making them publicly owned and collectively managed to make certain that their primary aim is to serve the people and not make profit for the 1%. Why? Because private, for-profit enterprise ownership has an inherent conflict: its purpose is to make profit, not to serve the people, and many such essential services, if they are run for profit, inevitably wind up screwing the people they are supposed to serve.

Take for example, the healthcare industry. We should have no talk of profit when it comes to helping people who are sick. It is easy to demonstrate why the profit motive should be nowhere involved in this because, as private companies, insurance companies have a fiduciary responsibility to their shareholders to maximize their profits. So, as Michael Moore points out, "the way they make more money is to deny claims or to kick people off the rolls or to not even let people on the rolls because they have a pre-existing condition. You know, all of that is wrong."[9] That's what happens when profits supersede the needs of people, in healthcare as well as in every other area of human need.

There is growing awareness of this contradiction in the hall of Congress. Bernie Sanders, always leading the charge, insisted that, "Healthcare is a human right, not something to make huge profits off of."[10] Senator Cory Booker of New Jersey adds, "from pharmaceutical companies to insurers… there are too many people profiteering off of the pain of people in America."[11]

It is a very hopeful sign indeed that Democratic lawmakers are increasingly calling for the removal of the profit motive from lawmakers' decisions and the nationalization of the nation's healthcare system.[12] In the words of Alexandria Ocasio-Cortez, "We have to start demanding… that we strip the profit motive out of our decisions and reprioritize the public good, and the health of everyday people."[13] Republican Ilhan Omar says, "It is important for us to nationalize the supply chain. It's important for us to take action in nationalizing our healthcare system."[14] As Senator Elizabeth Warren of Massachusetts argued persuasively, "The insurance companies [in 2019] alone sucked $23 billion in profits out of the health care system."[15] Moving to a single-payer healthcare system will make these kinds of profits available to run the system, pay for itself, and more.

The progressive, socialist wing of the Democratic Party now insists we should extend the same logic not only to healthcare but also in all the other industries, including prescription drugs, prison management, and higher education. Senator Kirsten Gillibrand of New York, for example, argued that, "I would not be spending money in for-profit prisons to lock up children and asylum-seekers."[16] The needs of the people must always supersede the needs of profit. That is why capitalism must only be allowed to operate in the service of socialism. So along with the healthcare industry, prisons, the post office, social security, armies, and law enforcement, most of what are currently private enterprises in education, health, transportation, communication, tech, production, construction, all of these must be considered social services that provide for the common good rather than private business that make money for the 1%.

Does that mean that socialism wants to kill small business as the privateer-profiteer enthusiasts will claim? Of course not. It is one of the 1%'s favorite lies and diversionary tactics. Eutopian socialism embraces small business; especially the sole-owner variety, and those who choose it as their life's occupation will be aided in every possible way. Of course, questions remain that will have to be answered in due time, such as: How big is small? How big can a sole-owner business become?

And what about medium businesses under Eutopian democratic socialism? Medium-size businesses with more than one owner would be allowed with collective ownership as well as collective management, inclusive of any employees. The same questions will need to be answered here. How big is medium? How big can collective ownership and management become? Of course, the answers to all these critical questions will only come after extensive public debate.

No, the target of the great Eutopian socialist restructuring of our socio-economic system must be the big business–organized crime axis, owned and operated by the 1%. Here, private ownership and its private management with its for-profit motive must be replaced with public ownership and collective management with the motive of serving the people. Of course, as a society, we will have to go through a transition period during which the change from private ownership and private management to public ownership and collective management is implemented.

In the transition, private corporations will be given a choice between cooperation and noncooperation. The transitional process from private to public may take several generations to complete, depending on the level of cooperation of the private owners. The strategy must be to get big business to cooperate in this transition process. Key in this will be the formulation of the policies regarding the expropriation of personal wealth and the inheritance laws.

Those of the 1% who are cooperative will naturally be treated more leniently than those who continue to resist it. There must be carrots, and there must be sticks. For example, as an incentive for their cooperation, private companies owned by the 1% could initially be exempted from the expropriation laws making ownership public. As a further incentive for their cooperation, it is possible their personal wealth will remain inheritable and may be transmitted to the second and third generations with decreasing amounts for each generation.

After ownership of a business has been transferred from the private to the public sector, the new owners can enter into a lease agreement with the new management collective made up of (1) current owners (stockholders), (2) current management, and (3) employee representatives. As the worker collective increasingly takes on the management responsibilities over time, the ownership and management components can be progressively eliminated so, ultimately, it will become a lease for that particular means of production and management agreement between the worker collective and society.

If the choice of the private corporation is noncooperation, they will receive exactly what they put on the table: nothing. They will get what they ask for. They will be increasingly isolated socially, given pariah status, and boycotted economically. Their personal as well as their private corporate properties will be collectivized expeditiously, and their personal properties will be drastically downsized and not eligible for any down-the-line inheritance.

The transformation from private to public ownership and from private to collective management will lead to the obsolescence of private monetary profit. This profit will become social gain, and as such, will be collected and redirected toward paying the costs for the New Social Contract and its programs. That is how private profit can be eliminated through redirection into a service economy that is based on and dedicated to the service of human needs.

The Elimination of Private Profit and the Withering Away of the Stock Market

The public ownership and collective management of economic resources, coupled with demise of the profit motive, will have the further collateral effect of functionally eliminating the stock market. Let's start with the question of what the economic purpose and psychological function of the stock market are.

The answer is quite simple. The stock market is the place where a person can buy and sell stocks as private ownership stakes in corporations for the purpose of making more and more profit. The psychological function of the stock market is a bit more complex. The stock market imitates, or re-creates, a Hobbesian reality of the "war of all against all," where everybody is duking it out to see who will be the last man standing, so to speak.

Thought of this way, the stock market is an arena and stage, a kind of colosseum of the collective mind, where its self-proclaimed cultural warriors come to do battle in their dominance games based on the violence of profit and greed. On this stage, the hyped-up, competitive conflict that is powered hormonally by the yang testosterone-adrenalin axis is on permanent display, acted out daily by the warrior marketeers in the all-out, unrestrained pursuit of infinite greed laser focused obsessively on the profit motive.

The kicker is that, in the end, once our socialist program is implemented and the ownership of all productive resources is public, its management collective, and the profit motive in economic transactions eliminated, the stock market really will have no functioning role to play in the economics of service and cooperation under conditions of sufficiency, if not abundance. In Eutopia, the stock market, not the state, will wither away and become a shriveled anachronistic holdover from a previous, more primitive stage of human development.

The New Social Contract

The New Social Contract and Its Quid Pro Quo

Social contract theory came down to us from the age of Enlightenment. Jean-Jacques Rousseau, among others, wrote a book on the subject with the same title. The gist is that citizens, implicitly or explicitly, enter into a social contract with each other, in which they all gain security in return for subjecting themselves to the state or other supreme authority to maintain peace in civil society.

These days, some three centuries later, we are entering an entirely new chapter in human history. The obsolescence of the economics of scarcity and its coming replacement by the economics of sufficiency, if not abundance, will require an expanded conceptual framework and a redefinition of the relationship between collective society, embodied by the state and the individual.

The economic system of abundance must articulate a new paradigm of values to replace class structures and the Puritan work ethic. At the center of that new paradigm of value will be a New Social Contract between the collective and the individual. This New Social Contract, or NSC for short, will articulate and define the exchange of value and services between society and its citizens, based on true universal freedom and equality, expressed in human creativity, and powered by lifelong education and learning.

The NSC is a quid pro quo between the individual and society. It is a contract for an exchange of entitlements for services or, more basically, an exchange of society's resources for the individual's time. This is the *quid*: in as much as each individual human is born with the innate right to the fundamental entitlements of (1) food, (2) shelter, (3) income, (4) medical care, and (5) education, society pledges to provide and fulfill these entitlements for each individual. And this is the *quo*: in return, the individual agrees to serve his fellow humans, i.e., society, in the service sectors of his or her choice, when called upon, for specific periods of time.

The incredibly liberating consequences of this approach will be noted and emphasized as the discussion moves along. As the individual grows up, they will, at certain points in their life, be asked to fulfill their part of the bargain and serve their fellow human beings and society with their time and skills. Except for these periods of social service, an individual is free to pursue his or her own individual interests. These are the individual's freedom years to do with as they please.

Education, knowledge, and insight are the alpha and the omega, the source and beginning of the journey as well as its end goal. The individual's first service, or "job," at least for the first 15 to 20 years of their life, will be to be a student and acquire the manual, intellectual, and social skills necessary to become a productive and contributing citizen. Most likely, a citizen's last "job" will also be in the education sector, a continuation of the pattern of lifelong learning habit the education sector is tasked with teaching.

Moving toward economic democracy under socialism entails these two things: prosperity for the 99%, the poor and powerless, and (relative) austerity for the 1%, the rich and powerful. We must start with the equalization at the bottom. So, in the first stage, the poor and dispossessed must be elevated to a level where each individual is guaranteed equality and dignity of basic economic needs in the coming age of abundance.

In the second stage, we will equalize things at the top through the imposition of austerity programs for the 1% rich and powerful, consisting, basically, of the transformation into public ownership and collective management of their private companies. While these programs are being instituted, the 1% will be designated as the stewards of the collective wealth they've amassed, and will be held responsible, and liable, for their stewardship.

The Quid of the New Social Contract: Prosperity for the Poor and Powerless

Basic Universal Income
In this chapter, we seek to solve all the basic problems that are causing stress and anxiety in the 99% in one fell swoop, with one coherent strategy, all parts of which support and strengthen each other while achieving the intended goal.

In 2018, 38.1 million people lived in poverty in the USA, meaning the poverty rate for 2018 was 11.8%. The poverty threshold for a family of four is about $25,700. The following are some figures illustrating the distribution of poverty: 12.9% of women, 10.6% of men,

16.2% of children, 9.7% of seniors, 25.4% of Native Americans, 20.8% of African Americans, 17.6% of Hispanics, 10.1% of whites, and 10.1% of Asians live in poverty.[17]

The inhumanity of this situation is underscored by the fact that low-income Americans have proportionally higher rates of physical limitations—heart disease, diabetes, stroke, and other chronic conditions—compared to higher-income Americans. Americans living in families that earn less than $35,000 a year are four times as likely to report being nervous and five times as likely to report being sad all or most of the time compared to those living in families earning more than $100,000 a year.[18]

Currently, it seems the time for Basic Universal Income has come. Many experiments in universal basic income are being conducted all over the world. In Stockton, California, for example, one of the first major Basic Universal Income programs in U.S. history was undertaken. Stockton Mayor Michael D. Tubbs, in partnership with some UC Berkeley alumni, created the Stockton Economic Empowerment Demonstration (SEED), that has been paying $500 a month to a group of 130 residents making below the city's median income since early 2019, no strings attached.

The Covid-19 Pandemic has pushed the notion of Basic Universal Income to the forefront of global discussions. Take Spain, for example, one of the hardest-hit countries in the early days of the pandemic. The nationwide lockdown curbed the spread of the virus but came at a staggering financial price. Millions of people lost their jobs as the economy shrank rapidly, putting many of the most vulnerable citizens at risk.

In response, Spain's government launched a website offering monthly payments of up to $1,145 USD to the nation's poorest families.[19] The program supports 850,000 households and is the largest test yet of the idea of a Basic Universal Income. Economists around the world are watching closely to see what the impact of the scheme on livelihoods will be.

These experiments in Basic Universal Income come at a time of unprecedented economic turmoil brought on by the pandemic.

Even the U.S. federal government's payments to those who lost their jobs on account of the pandemic prove the point of the arguments for Basic Universal Income. If people don't have money, they can't spend. And what keeps the economy going is the money circulating through spending. Ergo, if they don't have jobs and they don't have money, we should give them money so they can spend and keep the economy going. The Basic Universal Income has the potential to solve both the employment and the unemployment problems, the job-versus-no-job dilemma of changing economic realities.

The stimulus checks sent to the people during the pandemic are best understood as a de facto experiment in Universal Basic Income that proved highly successful. The pandemic experience proved, beyond the shadow of a doubt, that government payments to workers kept them from falling into the deepest poverty and maintained the health of the economy because the consumers, despite being unemployed, were still able to spend. In other words, the pandemic affirmed and proved that the health of the economy is based no longer on the need of the citizen to work but on the citizen's ability to consume so, in the absence of work, citizens must continue to get paid by the government so the economy will not stall.

Basic Shelter for Life

According to the National Alliance to End Homelessness, 582,462 people are experiencing homelessness on any given night in the U.S..[20] Of these 161,0780 are people in families, 33,129 are veterans, and 127,768 are disabled and unable to work.[21] Ethnically, the numbers break down to: white 291,395; Black 217,366; Latinx 140,230; Asian and Pacific Islanders 18,722; and Native American, 19,681.[22] This lack of affordable housing is one of the main consequences of endemic poverty and exacerbates all its other contributing factors, such as joblessness, lack of healthcare, mental illness, substance abuse, domestic violence, etc.

Therefore, it is perfectly natural that the demands of BLM and other movements increasingly include the right to shelter and lodging as a basic human entitlement. This is the message of signs demanding to "Cancel Rent" or "Abolish Rent" that were carried by demonstrators during the George Floyd protests and other demonstrations against police brutality. These signs and the movement are questioning the basic validity of the concept of rent as the product of a private contract about private property. They are demanding that the primary allegiance of the government and society is to the needs of the people, rather than the needs for profit of the private property owners. By considering housing as an entitlement rather than a commodity, the people are saying it is society and the government's responsibility to take over the tenants' obligations to pay their landlords each month.

Basic Food and Sustenance for Life

Predictably, households with incomes near or below the federal poverty line had rates of hunger and malnutrition substantially higher than the national average. Poverty and hunger are inextricably linked. More than 38 million people are living in poverty in America, and an almost equal number, more than 37 million, people struggle with hunger, including 11 million children.[23]

"One in 8 families in America are hungry. That's 12.3% of all U.S. households, including what economists call 'the working poor' who earn about $25,000 a year for a family of four. Out of that estimated $2,017 a month, families need to pay for housing, utilities, child care, transportation, health care—and groceries."[24]

Food insecurity occurs in all social strata and age groups. *"Some 48% of college students in America are food insecure."*[25] Not surprisingly, it is "more prevalent among college students of color, up to 57 percent."[26] Rural areas are not immune: *"15% of people in rural areas are hungry.* Often, they don't have access to grocery stores or transportation."[27] And *"60% of households led by older Americans must choose between buying groceries or paying utility bills."*[28]

All these figures are found to increase when society undergoes periods of intense stress, as was underscored by the pandemic.

It is difficult, if not impossible, to call a society civilized if it fails to produce enough quantity and quality of nourishment to all its citizens. It is a shameful situation, and we must resolve to end it once and for all.

Free Lifelong Medical Care

One of the things that keeps people poor is the lack of adequate healthcare and the inability to afford medical insurance. Consequently, they don't engage in preventive healthcare, and they wait to seek medical care until it's almost too late. And even if the medical problem is corrected, they are stuck with the enormous medical bills that bury them ever deeper in the pit of debt. Obamacare was a huge accomplishment and step in the right direction. Now, we must take the next steps and guarantee and implement full, universal healthcare as a human entitlement to all.

As Basic Universal Income, basic shelter, basic food sustenance, and universal healthcare are implemented to guarantee the physical, emotional, mental, and psychological well-being and welfare of all citizens, we will witness profoundly beneficial changes in society, including mass lowering of stress and anxiety, less crime, less illness, new hope, and new pathways to human fulfillment and renewal.

Free Lifelong Education

Each citizen is entitled to free lifelong education as a means of service to oneself and society. With Basic Universal Income and other entitlements of shelter, food, and medical care in place, all citizens are enabled and encouraged to enjoy lifelong journeys of learning in pursuit of meaning and renewal. For reasons that will become clear in the next section, we will first propose a reframing of the student's task of learning as work. And secondly, we will propose a reframing of all work as a service to society and one's fellow human beings.

As we have mentioned earlier, the individual's first service to society and himself, at least for the first 15 to 20 years of their life, will be to be a student and acquire the manual, intellectual, and social skills necessary to become a productively contributing citizen and service provider. Most likely, as I mentioned before, a citizen's last service to society and himself will also be in the education sector as a continuation of the pattern of lifelong learning habit taught by the education sector.

The Pro Quo of the New Social Contract: Citizens as Service Providers

Within the context of the New Social Contract, we conceive of society as consisting of a manifold number of service sectors that intersect both horizontally and vertically, from the lowest grunt work to the highest decision-making levels. In this context, also, we conceive of government as society's facilitator and coordinator of all individual contributions of time and effort to the collective and cooperative management of society's service sectors. To name only a few, we have governmental service sectors at the local, state, and federal levels. We have governmental service sectors in the legislative, judicial, and executive branches. We have military service sectors of the Army, Navy, Air Force, Marines, National Guard, Space Force, etc. We have the educational service sectors from kindergarten through university. We have the healing arts service sector, the caring arts service sector. We have the service sectors of large- and small-scale economic production, management, promotion, and distribution. We have the transportation, communication, and entertainment service sectors. We have the service sectors of arts and crafts and of small business. We have the service sectors of science, technology, IT, and so on... We must learn to recalibrate and consider all and any human work activity as a possible service sector, as a caring industry for the 99% rather than a profit-making engine for the 1%.

Work as Service and Service as Work

Historically, a major division in capitalist economics has existed between the economy of mass production and consumption, and the economy of caring for and service to other humans. Human labor in the production sector was first and always more greatly valued and financially rewarded than the human labor involved in the caring and service sectors.

As the human species has evolved technologically more sophisticated and socially more complex, it is generating increasingly profound changes in society. The same technological capabilities that are giving us the economics of sufficiency and abundance are also redefining the nature of work and the workplace. With automation, robotization, AI, etc., taking over and becoming more and more prevalent and proficient, economic production can increasingly be relegated to the machines.

The sector of economic production that used to employ the great majority of all human beings as wage workers is now getting ready to shed them because they are no longer as efficient or productive as machines. And we should rejoice in the opportunity that this presents. Having machines, rather than human beings, do the work of economic production frees all those millions of human beings from the onerous tasks of alienating labor, freeing up people's energy and potential and giving them the opportunity to redefine their lives and move on to meaningful new directions of service to humanity, artistic creativity, life-long learning, etc.

And as the human involvement in the economic sector of the physical production of "things" decreases, human involvement in the economic sector of caring, service, and growth has been and will continue to explode exponentially. This once-neglected and undervalued economic sector is booming and becoming preeminent as a result of the explosive demand for well-being and meaningful-being in the age of Eutopia.

And what about work? To be human is to enjoy meaningful work and to despise meaningless work. So the essence of work for humans is to provide meaning. Fortunately, as a species, we are now at the point where we have machines that can do all the meaningless work, freeing humans to do that work which is meaningful to them. This makes the rules regarding the division of labor between human work and machine work straightforward and simple: (1) any work that can be done by a machine must not be done by a human being, and (2) a human being should only do work that cannot be done by machine.

The New Social Contract articulated here will codify the exchange of the five entitlements provided by society to the individual and the time in service provided by the individual to society. And in the new Eutopian economy of abundance, the work in all service sectors, whether manual, intellectual, or social, is redefined as and becomes the expression of service.

Life as a Citizen Service Provider

With the New Social Contract, the life of a citizen in the Unites States of Eutopia will most likely be marked by an alternating rhythm of other-directed years of service to society and self-directed years devoted to one's personal growth and development.

The individual's first service to himself, at least for the first 15 to 20 years of their life, will be to be a student and acquire the manual, intellectual, and social skills necessary to become a productively contributing citizen service provider. Actually, of course, his early educational efforts are also a service to society, which will benefit from it to the extent that he maximizes and fulfills his potential.

After the first period of self-directed years in basic educational training, at age 18 to 20, the student is due for a break and will enter into his first other-directed service project for the next three to four years that should be, in most cases, a physically oriented type of service, as in military, civilian Ameri-corps, police, medical trauma, etc.

Individual service contributions would be one of two types. The first, basic service (grunt work) consisting of a minimum number of years an individual may be called upon, by means of individual preference indications and sortition democracy, to serve in any one of the service sectors. Let's say the basic service period is a four-year time commitment. It would make sense to split it in half, a period of educational and academic training about the structure and function of that particular service sector followed by a hands-on practical stint in the service sector function.

At the end of the four-year stint, the individual would be faced with a decision between these options: (1) continue in the same service sector with a tour of advanced specialized service, (2) switch laterally to a different service sector for a new service experience, (3) opt out and defer making any decisions about career choices; just continue one's life of general education and development as part of the individual's freedom years period. The advanced specialized service would be an option for those who liked their chosen "grunt service" sector and decided to make a career out of service work in that sector. As their careers advanced, these individuals would become eligible for membership in higher and higher management pools of peers from which the different levels of managers would be chosen through sortition democracy.

Much study and experimentation will have to go into answering the question of what would be the optimal, i.e., the most satisfying and most productive, ratio of service years to freedom years. One to one? One to two? Two to one? Time will show society's needs in this respect that will have to go into that determination.

As indicated, a citizen has the option of skipping, or foregoing, a scheduled freedom-years period in favor of continuing their career in their chosen service sector and reaching higher decision-making levels. Any service sector will have multiple levels or departments of production and administration that will provide opportunity for individual advancement. Those who put in a greater effort and excel at higher levels of responsibility should be rewarded in their lifetimes for their service achievements as they achieve them.

As one grows older and gains more expertise, the competition between equals will be to gain inclusion into the next higher pools of peers, from which leadership positions will be filled through sortition democracy, as I will discuss in detail later in this chapter. Each successful step up the professional ladder by a professional service provider should be rewarded in some fashion, both with modest economic rewards as well as public social recognition of their achievement.

Now, what about the lazy ones, the parasites who think it's beneath them to contribute productively to the running of society? (1) If the educational sector is doing its job properly, there will be very few of these. So let them be, and let social stigma be the punishment. As a society, we are wealthy and tolerant enough to afford a few misfits and miscreants. (2) If there are many, it indicates a failure in the educational system that we must fix first, rather than punish the antisocial elements it produced. As a last disciplinary resort, one possible punishment for unacceptably below-par service work is to increase their number of service years, meaning a decrease in their number of freedom years.

The Freedom Years of Lifelong Learning

The New Social Contract recalibrates the balance between the individual and society so an individual's life is balanced between his service to society and his efforts to maximize his own creative potential.

In the transitional period of the near future, we will see a tremendous exodus of millions of blue-collar workers from the workplace as a result of technological innovation of automation, AI, etc. These numbers will be augmented even more as the programs to transfer ownership of private companies into the public domain, making their management collective, are implemented. Much waste and duplication can be rectified in this process, liberating additional millions of people from drudgery and other "bullshit jobs."

All these millions of "jobless" people should be encouraged to go back to school and take the time to figure out what they want to do next in their lives, if anything. They should be financially incentivized to seek the necessary, fully funded education and training to take this next step. Universal basic income and lifelong free higher education combined with the concept of alternating freedom and service years will give all these individuals the freedom of choice to discover their passions and how they want to pursue them.

They can opt out of the production sector workforce altogether and take early retirement. They can become caregivers and partner more fully in running the family and household. They can become community organizers or party activists. They can decide to obtain more education and retrain for service in a different service sector. Or they can choose to walk the path of the creative, artistic self and seek to manifest in external reality their inner visions or concepts.

For, as an entitlement under the New Social Contract, the education system exists to guide and help the individual to find their passions and fulfill—and potentially exceed—their expectations and potential. The Eutopian conception of entitlement to universal continuing education is, minimally, threefold:

- To provide the individual with whatever concrete, technical training they need for the project at hand
- To nurture the individual's development of the ability for critical thinking on the social level
- To facilitate the individual's access to the inner sources of their creative self, in which the supreme satisfaction of the creative act is always sufficient reward in and of itself

The Key to Democratic Eutopia: Education

The most dangerous, limiting factor of the transitional period that we are now entering is the discrepancies in the levels of education among our citizenry—not so much in the participatory-operational aspect of sortition democracy, but in the final selection result. Under these less-than-ideal conditions, it may be necessary to attach certain conditions of eligibility in order to qualify for the various pools of peers. Simply put, it is not desirable to have people with little or no education selected to positions of the highest authority. And unfortunately, we have a lot of people with little or no education.

Under ideal Eutopian conditions—a situation toward which we must move with all haste—for (sortition) democracy to work as intended, the entire citizenry must be equally educated. Only universal education can provide the equality needed for a true pool of peers, in which it does not matter who is selected because all are equally qualified.

As we are reordering and restructuring society into our Eutopia based on the economics of abundance, guaranteed universal income, no need or pressure to have a job, it becomes one of our highest social priorities to send everyone back to school and get a higher education.

Funding for such a universal, continuing higher education program should be swift and generous. Educating an entire citizenry to the level of humanity, knowledge, and skills necessary to become a competent president, governor, senator, representative, district

official, county government official, utility district official, or municipal councilor is no mean task.

The fundamental prerequisite of democracy is extended universal
education. To prepare any individual for roles as diverse as president
and garbage man and at the same time, to nurture the process of his
self-realization, the educational system will be required to develop the
entire yin-yang spectrum of his human nature. It will need to produce
a populace skilled simultaneously in the arts and meditation and in
practical, technical and nontechnical skills and theoretical knowledge.

Paradigm Shift in the Practice of Democracy: The Case for Sortition Democracy

The Yin-Yang of Democracy

The Yin-Yang of Sequence and Simultaneity

Both in assigning meaning to events and in their respective decision-
making processes, the perceptual-experiential paradigms of the modern Western world and those of the non-Western cultures, whether
ancient or contemporary, exhibit a yin-yang polarity between diachrony and synchrony, between sequence and simultaneity.

Our Western, scientific paradigm is one that takes diachrony and
the principle of causality as axiomatic. The conception that sets our
Western paradigm apart from all cultures that preceded it, and that
still surround and coexist with us worldwide, is that causality assigns
meaning to events by discerning cause and effect over time, continually transforming the past into the future.

In sharp contrast, the prescientific (or nonscientific if you prefer) mindset of the ancient and contemporary non-Western peoples
is almost exclusively occupied with the chance aspects of events,
the synchronicity or simultaneity of events in the present moment.
As Jung so aptly observed, just as causality describes the sequence
of events, so synchronicity deals with the coincidence of events:
"Synchronicity takes the coincidence of events in space and time
as meaning something more than mere chance." He adds that that

"something more" refers to "a peculiar interdependence of objective events among themselves as well as the subjective (psychic) states of the observer or observers."[29]

Even a short glance at the historical and geographical world reveals the worldwide ubiquity of oracular and divinatory practices after the human species emerged from the mists of prehistory into the Bronze Age. In Africa, indigenous America (both North and South), in the ancient Babylonians, Hittites, and Egyptians, in the Mosaic Jews, pre-Christian Celtic and Germanic tribes, in the Far East of China, Tibet, and Japan, and in the classical worlds of Greece and Rome, people everywhere engaged in the practice of utilizing supernatural or magical procedures to ascertain future events, discover hidden phenomena, or determine the actions the Gods required.

These procedures have frequently included unusual natural phenomena, such as meteorological, solar, and lunar behavior, the peculiar behaviors of animals (especially birds and horses), unusual births, and so on. Among phenomena induced by humans we may mention roasting animal bones and turtle shells to induce cracks that can be read, analyzing the behavior of the smoke of fire, and haruspicy, the examination of the entrails of sacrificial animals, especially the liver. Also widespread is the human manipulation of arrows, yarrow stalks, or rosaries and the throwing of the dice to obtain decisions, procedures often involving human psychological states of second sight, visions and dreams, and trance revelations.

One example here is the ancient Chinese oracular tradition of consulting the *I Ching* or the *Book of Changes* for advice on how to proceed in a particular situation. It is a fortuitous accident of history that the *I Ching*, a highly complex and complete oracular ritual that, like the *Tao Teh Ching*, has come down to us from ancient, more female-centric times in such a complete form. In their exposition of the *I Ching* and the elucidation of the principle of synchronicity, Carl Jung and Richard Wilhelm made a profound contribution to a greater understanding how the human psyche has been functioning since time immemorial. Their description and analysis of how to consult the *I Ching*, as an oracle articulating the grounds for action or nonaction based on the synchronicity of events, provides us with a window of understanding into the mindset, customs, and institutions of the ancient female-centric cultures and civilizations we are discussing.

For questioners of any oracle, including the *I Ching*, human events are always a mix of objective situations to be assessed or questions answered and the subjective factors of mindset, timing, etc., The casting of the stalks or coins produce the form and pattern characteristic of that moment. The latter includes, of course, the ability to accurately interpret the meaning of the passages selected by means of casting the sticks or coins. This is why, in ancient times, of course, the oracular interpreter and their reading of synchronistic meaning were primarily functions of the educated and priestly class.

None of these practices, however, has been more widespread than the lottery itself; it is in the lottery that the utter impartiality of the laws of chance has been recognized, since antiquity, as the ultimate source of both democratic and divine justice. For, unlike consulting oracles and similar methodologies that require subjective interpretations from human beings, lotteries are a way of asking the universe to unambiguously manifest its cosmic designs and choices. The ancestor of the die, the astragalus (or ankle bone) of any cloven-footed animal, has been found inscribed with names at many prehistoric sites, providing evidence of the role of the lottery in the earliest religious and quasi-judicial procedures.

Among the ancient Babylonians, from early times, lots were cast to distribute shares of inheritance, temple income, and elected offices. In ancient Greece and Crete, the use of lottery was widespread. In some ancient cities, even the determination of tariffs for public and private divinatory consultations were determined by lot. The pre-monotheistic Semites, Arabs and Jews alike, were no different. Divinatory practices, including the widespread use of lotteries as oracles of the gods, were widespread in such practices as the Kahina, Fagnut, and Istiquuam, the latter being a settling by lot through the manipulation of arrows.[30] The chief official procedure among ancient Jews for consulting the oracle was the casting of lots; this was the purpose of the priest manipulation of the Urim and Thummin. Likewise, the pre-Christian Celts and Germans set great store by lotteries. According to Tacitus, the Germans practiced the drawing of lots whenever they needed to make decisions, decisions pertaining to matters of war and hostilities; they settled by lot such questions as what battle should be waged, what action should be taken, whether a town should be burned down, or how many captives should be killed.

Sortition in Greek Democracy

In creating our own democratic institutions, we usually credit the Ancient Greeks for inspiring us with their ideas about democracy. But if Aristotle and the Ancient Greeks were able to take a look at how our system works, they would criticize it as being undemocratic and oligarchic in nature. How so? First, the Greeks would point that our current democratic concepts of majority rule, one vote per person and elected representation, were not original features of Greek democracy but features of oligarchic Roman Republicanism.

Second, for the Greeks, the word "democracy" had quite a different, even opposite, meaning than it had for the Romans. In Ancient Greece, especially, Athens sortition was the traditional and primary method for appointing political officials, and its use was regarded as a principal characteristic of democracy. In sortition democracy, choosing the decision makers is not done by popular elections but by the process of selecting officers as a random sample from a larger pool of candidates. In other words, a lottery.

The rationale used by the ancient Athenians for using sortition as opposed to electoral democracy was that it is actually more democratic than electoral democracy because it is free from any human influence. They predicted that any civilization chosen by electoral methods will be brought down from internal corruption and the ownership of the political class by the economic powerhouses. Sortition democracy, the Greeks argued, prevents the inevitable corruption of electoral democracy that would lead to the collapse of the government and civilization. Roman civilization proved that point, a neglect for which their society and culture paid the price. And now, as we have detailed ad nauseam, with Emperor Trump, Western man's global civilization is proving it for the second time, on an unimaginable scale.

Sortition in American Democracy

Our American government is actually a mixture of the two types of democracy: electoral democracy and sortition democracy. But it is not an even or equal mix. Electoral democracy is widely and exclusively used in the elections of candidates to positions of power in the legislative and executive branches of government. Historically, until 1975, sortition democracy successfully operated the Selective Service lottery that determined who of the eligible pool would be chosen to serve in the military. This use was discontinued along with the draft, and the military became purely voluntary. Currently, there are only two uses of sortition democracy. The judicial branch uses sortition democracy to select potential members of the jury of peers that will determine the guilt or innocence of those accused of serious crimes. Sortition democracy is also used to solve situations where electoral democracy inevitably fails, namely, in the case of tie votes.

In December 2017, when a three-judge panel certified the vote in District 94 as tied at 11,608, Virginia Board of Elections Chairman James Alcorn, citing state election law, said, "the Board would have to pick a winner at random, likely picking a name from a bowl..."[31] In November 2015, Blaine Eaton II "drew the long green straw and won" the race for House District 79, where each candidate had received exactly 4,589 votes in a tie.[32] In December 2014 in Mt. Dora, Florida, a tied city council race was broken after choosing names from a felt top hat on a red-velvet-covered table.[33] In November 2014 in Minnesota, a commission seat was decided by whoever picked the "Z" first from a bag of wooden Scrabble tiles.[34]

As our electoral democratic system of government has been captured by the interests of big business and organized crime and is failing us. We the people must start taking to heart the Greek insight that electoral democracy will inevitably be corrupted by the powers that be for their own purposes. Perhaps the fact that we are already familiar with the successful functioning of sortition democracy on a limited scale will make it easier for us as a society to accept this hard truth of our collective decline, prompting us to move toward implementing the sortition democratic way of choosing our representatives by lottery as the only way to rid ourselves of the corruption that is eating us from the inside—and of preventing this corruption in the future.

Sortition democracy is far older than electoral democracy, dating back beyond the Greeks to the female-centric cultures of the Mediterranean basin that preceded male-centric civilizations. Athenian sortition democracy, in fact, can only be understood as a last remnant of the previous female-centric age that, in its basic outlook on life, was the polar opposite of what replaced it.

Perhaps also, as the cosmic wheel is turning again and, in this new age of global humanity, a new female-centric paradigm is emerging to guide our species on the path to global peace and harmony, sortition democracy will evolve to become one of its main pillars guaranteeing impartiality, fairness, and equality.

Discarding the Competitive Electoral System
The conclusion is inescapable: both the current governmental paralysis and the polarization of the electorate are the result of the fact that it is the money of the 1% that buys political elections and power and which has subordinated the activity of governing to winning the electoral process at any cost.

As citizens of a democracy, we must act on this realization and demand that the competitive pursuit of power be removed from the way that we choose our leaders and governmental authorities. Deciding who will serve as our representatives and decision makers cannot be left to the vagaries of those who happen to have the money to buy or otherwise influence our elections.

How can we hope to deinstitutionalize the quest for power in politics and restore the art of governing? To solve the problem of corruption in government, we will have to engage in an out-of-the-box rethinking of democracy and representative government. The box we're talking about here is the assumption that representative government is best achieved through electoral democracy.

Historically, electoral democracy represented the institutionalization of the competitive principle in politics and government in the process of determining how the positions of power in society should be chosen. As Aristotle and the Athenian democrats argued millennia ago, to do so is a mistake, which would only lead to inevitable corruption of the process and the government.

And here we are today, with Trump, at the apex of corruption, the personification of the larger social trends of the subversion of the interests of the American people. Those subversions being, of course, the appropriation of the wealth of society that rightfully belongs to the people, the 99%, by the machination and corruptions of the few, the 1%.

As a society, we must do everything in our power to assure that representatives are chosen in a way that does not facilitate power addicts like Trump coming into office. We must choose a design that, by its very nature, minimizes the chances of that occurring. The way forward is to go back first. We must really take to heart the insights of Aristotle and the Athenian democrats and revert to the ancient universal form of democracy through lottery.

This process of reversion to sortition democracy is the road to the deinstitutionalization of the competitive principle in politics and government. It is also the road toward the institutionalization of impartiality, equality, and cooperation in the process of determination as to how the positions of power in society should be chosen.

We pride ourselves in being a nation of laws that, as citizens and leaders, our behavior in society is governed by laws and not human caprice. This principle is enshrined in the tripartite division of governmental powers. The legislative or deliberative bodies write or craft the laws. The executive branch administers, enforces, and applies the laws. And the judiciary branch determines if laws have been violated and the consequences thereof.

The smooth functioning of all three branches of government, each operating on the local, state, and federal levels, literally requires an army of functionaries, involving hundreds of thousands, if not millions, of people in the enormous collective effort that makes our culture and civilization.

These positions are filled at present through a mixture of election or appointment to governmental agencies. Though enormous, the number of positions of power that must be filled competently in our socio-economic-political fabric for society to function smoothly is finite.

As a society, we must start slowly, from the bottom up, to replace the paradigm of electoral democracy with the paradigm of sortition democracy.

There can be no doubt that sortition selection produces results of unimpeachable integrity and fairness, if the pool of eligible participants is constructed fairly. In the experience of our own country with the Selective Service and the judiciary uses of sortition, there was never any question about the intrinsic fairness of the procedure. And because it was so noncontroversial, both agencies carried out their processes of running their lotteries with minimal fanfare, away from the public eye.

The rationale for service in legislative and executive governmental service is no different from that for military service or jury duty: society maximizes the chances for the individual to realize his potential, and in exchange, the individual owes society a debt of service, payable by periodic service in its various branches, legislative and executive, on local, state, and federal levels.

The corruption of liberal electoral democracies worldwide demand we abandon the political rat race as a mechanism for selecting decision makers. We should instead adopt the principle of sortitional selection to decide who shall serve in the government. By letting fate decide who decides our fate, the people as a whole can rid itself, in one fell swoop, of the entire class of parasitic politicians and pathological power seekers.

When collective humanity adopts the concept of a democratic lottery, it will no longer be deflected from the purpose of confronting and solving its real problems. Governments chosen by sortition will be far less belligerent and bellicose in their outlook and attitudes toward each other and will be willing to find the middle win-win way. It can then begin the systematic deinstitutionalization of the pathologies of the competitive spirit and the disease of power addiction.

The CCORE Values of Sortition Democracy

As experiments in sortition democracy at the local level are undertaken and prove successful, a collection of rules will emerge to govern the makeup of the various eligibility pools and the algorithms that will run the actual computer operations on Selection Day. I have designated this collection of rules and algorithms as the Collective Consensual Oracle Response Engine (the CCORE) of our sortition democracy. The CCORE, when consulted by all citizens, speaks true and will express the determinations of our collective unconscious.

The CCORE's basic values are twofold, both in its operation and in its result. Its operation is democratic in that it is participatory, and the result is democratic in the possibility that each or any citizen may be chosen. (1) Democracy resides in each citizen having the right and duty to participate physically in the operation of the CCORE selection process. Each citizen is guaranteed that, by so participating, they have the power to change the final outcome of the random selection process in all local, state, and federal levels of the selection. (2) Democracy resides in each citizen being ready to serve when selected by the CCORE. Accordingly, each citizen is assigned to various selectoral pools on the local, state, and national levels according to established rules of inclusion and eligibility.

In sharp contrast to the electoral paradigm, the sortitional paradigm would:

1 Make the determination inexpensively. And because it does not cost much money, it is incorruptible because the process cannot be bought.
2 Be conflict free, having only winners and no losers in a fair fashion without creating antagonism and conflict.

3 Guarantee results of unimpeachable democratic integrity and complete impartiality of the result, and that the person(s) selected will be truly representative of the citizens.

To the detriment of society, narcissists and power addicts are drawn to our electoral process as bees are to pollen or bears to honey. Perhaps flies to excrement would be the best analogy. The percentage of narcissistic power addicts among office seekers is way higher than 1% of the population. As our thought experiment showed, sortition democracy would immediately reduce the concentration percentage of narcissists and power addicts that make it into office or positions of power and more accurately reflect their percentage among the general population.

Thought Experiment: A Small-Town Council

Let's do a simple thought experiment and compare electoral and sortition democracy in action. Say we have your basic small town of 10,000 adults of voting age that needs a city council of 10. The psychological makeup of the citizens is such that 0.1 to 1.0%, i.e.,10 to 100 of the 10,000 citizens really want the power and status the job confers. The rest, over 99% of the people, would rather not be bothered to serve and prefer to just live the lives they're living.

In electoral democracy, the process would start by the "hungry ones" declaring themselves candidates. Since the electoral process makes political power a prize to be fought for, individual candidates are thought of as, and behave like, combatants who enter an arena to duke it out.

This makes campaigning for the job at once highly personal and competitive. For that reason, elections campaigns inevitably deteriorate into battle strategies that consist of tooting the candidate's horn while denigrating the opponent's character and achievements, all to sway the court of public opinion in their favor. Small surprise, then, that electoral campaigns inevitably produce a lot of bad feelings. Disputes frequently arise that will eventually be settled in a court of law by further lengthy and costly proceedings.

And election campaigns are expensive! To start raising money to mount a campaign, candidates hit the fundraising trail the day they announce their candidacy, and often way before that. This consists of making nice with the people with the big wallets, the donors who will gladly open those wallets if they make the judgment that, once in office, the candidate will look out for their interests, business and otherwise.

At election time, regrettably, only a small portion of those who would rather not be bothered (generally no more than 10 to 20% of the 10,000 eligible voters, i.e., 1,000 to 2,000 people) actually bothers to show up and cast their vote. The rest of those who don't want to be bothered, don't. If the election ends in a tie, the electoral system would fall to sortition democracy as a last resort. So, why not bypass the whole competitive expensive electoral process of choosing our representatives and go directly to the lottery system? Why not indeed?

Still continuing with the thought experiment, let's use sortition democracy to select our town council of 10 for our town of 10,000. How would that work? There are two ways to make it work. The first and simplest relies on a computer algorithm to cast the die and randomly select the 10 people. It's fair and impartial and relatively inexpensive. The second way would be to add a participatory aspect and actually draw lots. Let's say there are 10,000 slips of paper in the hat, and every citizen would be required to draw out one slip. Of the slips, 9,990 would be blank and 10 would be marked with "council member," or something equivalent printed on them. Those who drew those 10 marked slips would constitute the new city council.

If the community, or pool of peers, is small enough, citizens could actually draw real slips from a real hat. In larger communities, this would have to be solved by any number of means, but most likely electronically. For example, the drawings of the slip could easily be simulated online, and each citizen would have the privilege and duty to check in online to see if they were selected.

The laws of probability tell us that 95% of those selected will belong to the 95% of the "don't bother me" class, and only 5% of the lots drawn will go to the 5% "I want it" class of narcissistic power addicts. This is good and a powerful argument for sortition democracy. Five percent of 10 is 0.5, so when 10 out of 10,000 people are selected, the chance that one of the 10 selected belongs to the 5% addict class is 50%. Compare this with the results of the 10 councilpersons elected by electoral democracy in which certainly almost half or more belong to the narcissistic power addict class.

For sortition democracy, political power is not a prize to be fought for but a burden to be shared and endured and a citizen's duty and responsibility to carry out if called upon to do so. So if you're chosen, you serve. As jury selections prove, day after day and year after year, once selected by sortition democracy, those who don't want to be bothered initially, consistently rise to the occasion, take the job very seriously, and succeed with outstanding results.

It would be proper, and best for society, if the impetus for the implementation of such a huge paradigmatic shift grew from the bottom up, starting with small experiments in various localities. Anyone who is attracted by or interested in the idea of sortition should start by discussing it with their fellow neighbors and or co-workers. Moreover, at the grassroots level, sortition is not only applicable to selecting decision makers in politics and government but also in any area where decision-making positions need to be filled, as in labor unions, company management, etc.

The cost of sortition selection being way cheaper than having elections, local community leaders might be initially attracted by the low cost to select town councils. And these leaders would soon find out they made a wise decision. Because it guarantees fairness, equality, and impartiality, the lottery system is more democratic than the electoral system. Sortition democracy is, at once, highly impersonal and noncompetitive, even cooperative. This can be achieved without generating any animosity. Eliminating the artificial strife present in electoral democracy would significantly lower the temperature of social discourse and political life, an achievement for humanity and a beginning step on the path to collective wisdom.

Training for and Expansion of Sortition Democracy

At a minimum, once an individual is selected to fill a position of authority, there will be a period of specialized, on-the-job training. An additional way of guaranteeing that those sortitionally selected to higher state and federal office have the proper training would be to delimit the pool of peers to those who had already served in lower levels of local government.

As a further hedge against corruption and to insure greater transparency and continuity of function, it might be wise to stagger CCORE selections for office in such a way that, once selected, the individual will become the apprentice of the current holder of the job for a couple of years before assuming the mantle of authority.

This would result in overlapping tenures for two CCORE selected officials, a junior and senior member, for any given position. The junior member, in effect, would be getting two to three years of training. For example, someone selected by the CCORE to be a senator for, say, a term of six years, will serve the first three years as the apprentice and junior senator to the current senior senator, before serving three more years as the senior senator preparing his own junior senator and successor.

But as the idea of sortitional democracy expands into other realms of decision-making, other criteria will become relevant. For example, for labor union representation, the pool of peers would be the members of the labor union. For political parties, the pool of peers would be the members of that political party. Likewise, in professional organizations of all kinds, the pool of peers from which the leadership position will be filled by sortition are the members of that organization. In short, each position of power that needs to be filled has its own pool of peers from which the representative will be selected.

For some selections, other criteria may also be appropriate in establishing pool eligibility, such as age, experience, education, training, merit. In education, for example, the more education and the greater the professional achievement, the more a person may qualify to be included in higher-level decision-making pools of peers. In this way, an individual's drive for competitive achievement can be channeled into the effort to meet the qualifications necessary for higher pools of peer eligibility. Finally, depending on their place of residence, professional achievements, and other defining factors, an individual may belong to several pools of peers, each different in their composition and purpose.

It would seem that our three-tiered government structure of local, state, and federal government might lend itself to a gradual, piece-meal, and peaceful, replacement of the electoral system of democracy with the sortition system of democracy. All citizens of a local community are in the pool of selectables for that community to be chosen democratically by the local pools of selectors. As we have seen in our thought experiment, at the municipal level, the pool of eligibles is identical to the participating citizen selectors.

Now consider the next level of government, the state level. The governor is chosen by citizens of the state. State senators are chosen by the people in the senatorial districts, and state assembly members are chosen by the people in their congressional districts. The federal government's structure parallels that of the states, and the pool-of-peer criteria for representation to government chief executive and legislative bodies are primarily geographic. Federally, the president is chosen by citizens of the entire nation, which is the largest possible pool of participating peers. The two senators from each state are chosen by all the citizens of that state, and congressional representatives are chosen by the people living in those congressional districts.

The Participatory Aspect

The sortitional process is democratic and participatory in that each member in the pool of eligibles is part of the process of activating and questioning the oracle and equally responsible for, and invested in, the outcome. By giving each participant the right and responsibility to spin the wheel of chance, a truly collective determination of fate is possible where the wheel would stop with the arrow pointing at this and that person. For maximal accuracy and psychological effect, participation in this cooperative effort of collective selection should be made obligatory.

By participating in a sortitional process, whether by pressing a button, pulling a lever, or some other means, a person completely changes the outcome of who gets selected by the sortition process. Realizing this makes the action enormously significant for each individual. It has a vastly greater psychological effect than the weight of casting one vote in a choice between two or several individuals that electoral democracy offers.

For that reason, it is important that each person takes sufficient time to cultivate the proper state of mind in which to approach the moment and time for the collective determination effort. Each individual may determine their own ritual to activate their private CCORE process. When they know with the utmost certainty that the time has come to do it, they must push the button, pull the lever, throw the dice, or count the yarrow stalks. They will accept that those selected as a result of his participation were those destined to be his representatives for the next period.

Every citizen could be issued a simple selection device keyed to the individual's fingerprint or eyeball. It could also be a software simulating the rolling of a dice, the spinning of the wheel of fortune, the drawing of cards, or any game of chance, according to the user's preference. At a predetermined time on Selection Day, all devices would be pre-activated simultaneously by the CCORE. After logging in on their individual devices, people could take their turn at spinning the wheel of chance for the collective selection process by pushing the button on their devices. As all devices would be connected to the central cloud computer via the internet, the result would be the unquestionable expression of the collective unconscious will of the people revealed in the moment of collective synchronicity.

For the consultation with the oracle, altered states of consciousness are appropriate for all participants. Depending on individual preference, meditation, prayer, drugs, alcohol, abstinence, or indulgence, are encouraged to induce the proper trance, one which will enable the individual to tune into and express the collective unconscious during his participation.

Since, on Selection Day by the CCORE, there are no losers and only winners, the prevailing spirit on Selection Day would be bacchanalian, bound to exhibit a mix of carnival celebration, casino gambling high, and religious ceremony exultation. During and after the selection process, the country as a whole would have reason to indulge in prolonged revelry and debauchery, in the best Mardi Gras spirit.

The participatory lottery in selectoral democracy is the way of both gambler and priest and represents a marriage of the secular and the sacred, levity and gravitas. In surrender to the serendipity of synchronicity, both priest and gambler try to divine and influence a universe where meaning is determined by the simultaneity of a diversity of incongruent events. From the sacred viewpoint, the participatory lottery of selectoral democracy is a collective throwing of the yarrow stalks of the *I Ching* to let fate, or the gods, decide the representatives who will decide our fate. The process executed in such a way unquestionably expresses the will of the gods, if you will, but more importantly, the will of the people.

Endnotes

1 Clay Cockrell, "I'm a Therapist to the Super-Rich: They Are as Miserable as Succession Makes Out," The Guardian, November 22, 2021, https://www.theguardian.com/commentisfree/2021/nov/22/therapist-super-rich-succession-billionaires.

2 Ibid.

3 Thomas Wiedmann, Julia K. Steinberger, and Manfred Lenzen, "Affluence Is Killing the Planet, War Scientists," Phys.org, June 24, 2020, https://phys.org/news/2020-06-affluence-planet-scientists.html .

4 Ibid.

5 Ibid.

6 Ibid.

7 Ibid.

8 Dean Baker, Josh Bivens, and Jessica Schieder, "Reining in CEO Compensation and Curbing the Rise of Inequality," Economic Policy Institute, June 4, 2019, https://www.epi.org/publication/reining-in-ceo-compensation-and-curbing-the-rise-of-inequality/.

9 Michael Moore, "Profit Motive," Wikipedia, June 7, 2023, https://en.wikipedia.org/wiki/Profit_motive.

10 Rick Newman, "Democrats Are Fighting a Dangerous Battle Against the Profit Motive," Yahoo Finance, July 3, 2019, https://finance.yahoo.com/news/democrats-versus-profit-motive-160617400.html.

11 Ibid.

12 Dom Calicchio, "AOC Omar Call for Removing 'Profit Motive' from US Coronavirus Decisions, 'Nationalizing' Health Care," Fox News, April 10, 2020, https://www.foxnews.com/politics/aoc-omar-call-for-removing-profit-motive-from-us-coronavirus-decisions-nationalizing-health-care.

13 Ibid.

14 Ibid.

15 Rick Newman, "Democrats Are Fighting a Dangerous Battle Against the Profit Motive," Yahoo Finance, July 3, 2019, https://finance.yahoo.com/news/democrats-versus-profit-motive-160617400.html.

16 Ibid.

17 Poverty USA, "The Population of Poverty USA," n.d., https://www.povertyusa.org/facts.

18 Druv Khullar and Dave A. Chokshi, "Health, Income, & Poverty: Where We Are and What Could Help," HealthAffairs, October 4, 2018, https://www.healthaffairs.org/do/10.1377/hpb20180817.901935/full/.

19 674 Carrie Arnold, "Pandemic Speeds Largest Test Yet of Universal Basic Income," Nature, July 10, 2020, https://www.nature.com/articles/d41586-020-01993-3.

20 https://endhomelessness.org/homelessness-in-america/homelessness-statistics/state-of-homelessness/#key-facts

21 Ibid.

22 Ibid.

23 Feeding America, "Hunger and Poverty in America," n.d., https://www.feedingamerica.org/hunger-in-america/facts.

24 Rachel Perry, "5 Surprising Facts About Hunger in America," Untied Way, October 15, 2019, https://www.unitedway.org/blog/5-surprising-facts-about-hunger-in-america.

25 Ibid.

26 Ibid.

27 Ibid.

28 Ibid.

29 R. Wilhelm and C. Jung, The Secret of the Golden Flower, (Princeton University Press, 1962), Bollingen Series XIX, xxiv.

30 M. Loewe and C. Blacker, Oracles and Divination, (Colorado: Shambala, 1981), 218.

31 Ben Finley and Alan Suderman, "Virginia Legislative Race Tied, Court Rules," Associated Press, December 21, 2017, https://www.arkansasonline.com/news/2017/dec/21/virginia-legislative-race-tied-court-ru/.

32 Richard Fausset, "Democrat Wins Mississippi House Race After Drawing Straws," New York Times, November 20, 2015, https://www.nytimes.com/2015/11/21/us/mississippi-house-race-comes-down-to-one-deciding-straw.html.

33 Elyssa Cherney, "Judge Allows Mount Dora to Draw Lots for Tied City Council Seat," Orlando Sentinel, November 20, 2014, https://www.orlandosentinel.com/2014/11/20/judge-allows-mount-dora-to-draw-lots-for-tied-city-council-seat/.

34 Jennifer Brooks, "Luck of the Draw Breaks Tie Vote in Cook County," Star Tribune, November 11, 2014, https://www.startribune.com/luck-of-the-draw-breaks-tie-vote-in-cook-county/282206491/.